Why Is Public Expenditure on Education in Japan Low?

Re-examining the Public Function of Education

Wataru Nakazawa

Osaka University Press

Osaka University Press

Osaka University West Front, 2-7
Yamadaoka, Suita-shi, Osaka, Japan
565-0871

Published in Japan
by Osaka University Press
First published 2016

Why Is Public Expenditure on Education in Japan Low?
Re-examining the Public Function of Education
by Wataru Nakazawa

Copyright © Wataru Nakazawa, 2014
Original Japanese edition published by Keiso Shobo
English translation copyright © Osaka University Press

All rights reserved. No part of this publication may be
translated, reproduced or transmitted in any form or by any means,
electronic or mechanical, including photocopy, recording,
or information storage and retrieval systems,
without permission in writing from the publisher.

ISBN 978-4-87259-547-5

Acknowledgements

This book was originally published in Japanese by Keiso-shobo in 2014, and won one of the most prestigious awards for humanities and social sciences for works in Japanese, the 36th Suntory Prize for Social Sciences and Humanities. First, I would like to thank Keiso-shobo for permitting this translation in English, and the editor of this book, Nahoko Matsuno, for supporting my work.

I believe that the average standard of social sciences and humanities in Japan is high. However, most works have been written in Japanese and are not well known outside Japan. Because of the financial crisis in Japan, the pressure on researchers in social sciences and humanities to produce clear, beneficial, and useful knowledge became stronger. Sometimes they were seen as symbolizing an insular Japanese society because they had not published their works in English. For their own sakes, Japanese researchers in social sciences and humanities need to ensure that their works have internationally appeal. Fortunately, Osaka University started a new program of financial help for translating and publishing books in the social sciences and humanities in 2015, and The publication of this book is supported by Management Expenses Grants of Osaka University. I would like to express my appreciation three colleagues: Masayuki Nakamichi, Dean of the Graduate School of Human Sciences, and Eisei Kurimoto, Vice-President of the Graduate School of Human Sciences, who supported the adoption of my work, and Hiroyuki Kondo, a professor of the sociology of education, who stimulated my ideas through our daily conversations. In addition, Nobuyo Kawakami and Shiori Bando, editors with Osaka University Press, also supported the publication of this book in English.

The research for this book was also supported by the Grant-in-Aid for Scientific Research (C) (Number 15K04359) and (B) (Number 15H03490) from the Japan Society for the Promotion of Science. I was permitted access to the data of the International Social Survey Programme (ISSP) from the Data Archive for the Social Sciences in the German Social Science Infrastructure Services (GESIS), a data entitled "Japanese General Social Surveys <JGSS-2010>, the JGSS Research Center at Osaka University of Commerce" was provided by the Social Science Japan Data Archive, Center for Social Research and Data Archives, Institute of Social Science, the University of Tokyo.

I started writing this book when I was working in Toyo University in Tokyo. I would like to thank my colleagues at the Department of Sociology in Toyo University, whose cooperation and professionalism ensure a tranquil and harmonious working atmosphere. In 2007, when I was a research associate at the Institute of Social Sciences at the University of Tokyo, the longitudinal survey project (Japanese Life Course Panel Survey: JLPS) started. I was a member of this project, and the project committee permitted me to use the data in this book.

Hiroshi Ishida, a professor at the Institute of Social Sciences and the leader of this survey, always supported my study and gave me helpful suggestions.

Although this book mainly focused on the Japanese situation, I broadened my attention to include comparative perspectives. Therefore, I believe that this book will be of interest to readers outside Japan. According to the survey of the Organization for Economic Co-operation and Development (OECD), there is similar low public expenditure on education in South Korea, and many other developing Asian countries also face declining fertility rates and aging societies. Since comparative studies on social policies, including education, have been mainly focused on western societies, it would be interesting to compare the situations of Asian societies with those of western countries. In addition, the experiences of an unprecedented declining fertility rate and aging society in Japan would give useful information to other similar societies.

Finally, I would like to dedicate this translation my wife, Akiko, and my son, Hironao. Hironao was born in February, 2015, an event that has made me even more conscious of how serious an issue education in Japan is for the future of our society. Her devoted help and his carefree smile encouraged me in my work.

Wataru Nakazawa

Contents

Acknowledgements	iii
Abbreviations	ix

INTRODUCTION Where the Problem Lies	1
1. Issues Surrounding Obstructed Education Spending	1
(1) Risks and Social Security in a Society with an Aging Population and a Declining Birth Rate	1
(2) Unequal Education Opportunity in a Society with a Widening Educational Disparity	3
(3) Small Public Spending on Education and People's Attitude Reflecting this Fact	6
(4) Issue of National Burden	10
2. Can We Increase Public Spending on Education?	13

PART I
PEOPLE'S ATTITUDE AND THE STATE OF POLICY REGARDING EDUCATION SPENDING   19

CHAPTER 1 Reconsidering the Social Role of Education	21
1. Society where Education Takes Root	21
2. Modernization and Education: A Sociological Look at School Education	24
(1) Function of School Education in a Modern Society	24
(2) School Education in the Emerging Society in America	26
(3) American-Style Liberalism and the Education Philosophy	29
(4) School Systems and the Societal Role of Education	32
3. Reconsidering the Social Function of Education	34
(1) Equalization and Human Resource Allocation	34
(2) Japanese People's Sense of Injustice as regards Educational Attainment	35
(3) Equality Debates and Public Education that Accounts for Individual Potential	37
(4) The Meaning of the Government's Involvement in Education	40
CHAPTER 2 The State/Government and Education	47
1. Education from the Perspective of the Government	47
(1) The Role of the Government in Education from the Perspective of Economics	47
(2) Introduction of Quasi-Market Reform	50
2. Establishment of Modern States and Development of Education Systems	53
(1) State and Bureaucracy	53
(2) Bureaucratization of the Education System	55
(3) Introduction of the Modern Education System in Japan	58
3. Development of the State Mechanism and Its Spread in the World	61
(1) Spread of Institutional Isomorphism and the Modern Education System	61
(2) State and Tax	63
(3) Under Neoliberalization	64

CHAPTER 3 Relationship between Education and Social Security/Welfare	69
1. Education as Social Policy	69
(1) The Difference in the Scope of Social Policy	69
(2) Who Receives More Benefit from Education?	71
(3) The Ways of Positioning Public Education Expenditure and their Problems	73
2. Education Policy in Japan and the Welfare System behind It	75
(1) Establishment of a Japanese-Style Welfare System	75
(2) Welfare Systems that Rely on the Private Sector	79
(3) Beneficiaries of Social Security	81
3. Globalized World and Social Policies	82
(1) Economy that Goes beyond the Framework of the State	82
(2) Social Exclusion and Inclusion	83
4. The Relationship between Education System and Social Security/Welfare System from the Perspective of International Comparison	85
(1) Complementarity of the Systems	85
(2) Education under Social Policies	86
(3) Position of Education Policy in the Overall Public Expenditure	88
(4) Distance between Education and Each Policy Area and the Classification of Country Based on Distance	92
CHAPTER 4 The Structure of Japanese People's Attitude toward Education and Social Policies from the Perspective of International Comparison	97
1. Attitude toward Welfare Policy and Social Security	97
(1) Rationale for Focusing on the Attitude	97
(2) Competing Interests for Public Spending on Education	99
(3) The Low Level of Trust in the Government among the Japanese	100
2. Determinants of Social Policy	103
(1) Relationship between the Welfare Regime and Attitude	103
(2) Relationship between Personal Attributes and Attitude	106
3. International Comparative Analysis	107
(1) The Data Used and Angle of Analysis	107
(2) Relationship between the Attitude that Government Expenditure Should Be Cut and the Attitude that the Government Should Cover the Cost More	108
(3) Basic Tendency with Attitude Responses	111
(4) Logistic Regression Analysis to Predict the Attitude toward Government Expenditure	117
(5) Logistic Regression Analysis to Predict the Attitude toward Government Responsibilities	120
(6) Public Education to Increase Support for Public Spending on Education	121

Contents vii

PART II
WHY HAS THE PUBLIC BURDEN OF EDUCATION NOT INCREASED?   127

CHAPTER 5 Public Finance and Education in Japan	129
1. Causes of Government Deficit Financing	129
(1) Sociology of Fiscal Crisis	129
(2) Causes of Fiscal Deficit	131
2. Public Finance and Budgets	133
(1) Idiosyncrasies of Public-Finance Activities in Japan	133
(2) Mechanism of Budget Compilation	135
(3) Composition of Education-Related and Science and Technology Promotion Expenditure and Child Learning Costs	138
3. Balance between Burden and Benefit	144
(1) Sociology of Public Finance	144
(2) Public Works that Utilize Fiscal Investment and Loans	146
(3) Considering the Balance between Tax Burden and Received Benefit	149
CHAPTER 6 Post-War History of Rising Education Costs	153
1. Foundation of Post-war Democratic Education System and Burden of Education Costs	153
(1) The Gap between the Center and the Local Areas	153
(2) Tuition Fee Rises Directly after the War	158
2. Education Costs from the High Economic Growth Period to the Stable Economic Growth Period	161
(1) Student Movements and the Rise in School Costs	161
(2) Introduction of Beneficiary-Pays Principle and Increase of National University Tuition Fees	162
3. Institutionalization of the Heavy Share of Education Cost Burden	168
(1) Soaring Education Costs Before and After the Introduction of Subsidies for Private Schools	168
(2) Increase of Education Cost Burden on Families during a Restructuring of Public Finance	171
(3) Trend of Education Cost Burden from 1990s Onward	174
CHAPTER 7 Battleground Issues on Education Costs	185
1. Shifting of Education Cost Burden to Self-Responsibility	185
(1) Formation of Mistrust toward the Government	185
(2) Discontent toward Welfare Recipients	187
(3) Expectations of Individual Burdens by Parents	191
2. Campaign Pledges and Manifestos	193
(1) The Start of the Manifesto Election	193
(2) Historical Transitions of Battleground Issues in Elections	194
(3) Election Results and Popular Will in Post-war Japan	200
3. The People's Verdict on the Education Policies Put Forward by the DPJ	204
(1) Data and Variables Used	204
(2) Balance between Public Service and the Public Burden	205
(3) Concerning Support for the DPJ Policies	209

CHAPTER 8 Realization of Policies and Stance toward Political Parties 215
   1. The Critical Gaze on "Bureaucracy" 215
      (1) Parliamentary Cabinet System and Enforcement of Policy 215
      (2) Dysfunctions of Bureaucracy and Criticism Directed at Public Servants 218
      (3) Affinity between Criticisms toward Bureaucracy and Neoliberalism 221
   2. Reflection of Popular Will in Indirect Democracy 223
      (1) Toward a Political Power Assertive on Burden Increase 223
      (2) Political Party Support and Voting Behavior 225
   3. Relationship between Political Party Support and Attitudes on Policies 226
      (1) Changes in Voting Behavior among Individuals 226
      (2) Political Party Favorability Rating and Political Attitude 229
      (3) Analysis of Panel Data 232
      (4) What Should Be Done to Reflect the Popular Will? 236

EPILOGUE The Responsibility to Publicly Support Education **243**
   1. Tolerating "Failure" 243
      (1) Legacy of the DPJ Government 243
      (2) Filling in the Gaps in Society 245
      (3) Reconsidering the Structures of Democracy 247
   2. Education and Publicness: the Public Burden of Education 249

References 253

Index 269

Abbreviations

CIE	The Civil Information and Education Section
DPJ	The Democratic Party of Japan
DSP	The Democratic Socialist Party
FY	Fiscal Year
GHQ	The General Headquarters
ISS	The Institute of Social Sciences, at the University of Tokyo
ISSP	International Social Survey Programme
JASSO	The Japan Student Services Organization
JCP	The Japan Communist Party
JGSS	The Japanese General Social Survey
JLPS	The Japanese Life Course Panel Survey
JNP	The Japan New Party (Nihon Shin-to)
JRP	The Japan Renewal Party (Shinseito)
JRP	The Japan Restoration Party (Nihon Ishin-no-kai)
JSP	The Japan Socialist Party
LDP	The Liberal Democratic Party
MAFF	The Ministry of Agriculture, Forestry and Fisheries
METI	The Ministry of Economy, Trade and Industry
MEXT	The Ministry of Education, Culture, Sports, Science and Technology
MHLW	The Ministry of Health, Labour, and Health
MOF	The Ministry of Finance
NFP	The New Frontier Party of Japan (Shinshin-to)
NK	New Komeito
NPS	The New Party Sakigake
ODA	Official Development Assistance
OECD	Organisation for Economic Co-operation and Development
PCA	Principal Component Analysis
PISA	The Programme for International Student Assessment
RMI	The Revenu minimum d'insertion
SOCX	Social Expenditure Database
SPJ	The Social Democratic Party of Japan
SSM	The Social Stratification and Social Mobility (Survey)
YP	Your Party (Minna-no-to)

INTRODUCTION
Where the Problem Lies

1. Issues Surrounding Obstructed Education Spending

(1) Risks and Social Security in a Society with an Aging Population and a Declining Birth Rate

According to *Vital Statistics* published by the Ministry of Health, Labour, and Welfare, the number of live births in Japan in 2012 dropped to 1,037,231, the lowest since the end of World War II. Meanwhile, the number of deaths exceeded 1.2 million, indicative of the country's aging population. The difference between the number of live births and deaths in 2012 indicated a decline of more than 200,000 people in the population. The required birth rate to maintain the current population level is called "replacement level fertility." In Japan, the live birth rate has remained below the replacement level fertility since the late 1970s, a state referred to as sub-replacement fertility (Wada, 2006). The persistent state of sub-replacement fertility has been attributed to employment instability, inadequate provision of the environment for raising children, and huge education expenses; employment instability includes increased non-regular employment among young people and the widened gap between regular and non-regular employment, whereas the inadequate provision of the environment for raising children includes childcare-facility shortage as well as lack of or inadequate childcare support policies at companies and public institutions (Higuchi and Zaimushō Zaimu Sōgō Seisaku Kenkyū-jo, ed., 2006; Yamaguchi, 2009; Matsuda, 2013).

The declining birth rate will reduce the working-age population in the long run. At the same time, the number of elderly citizens will increase as the average life expectancy rises partly owing to improvement in medical and health environments. Hence, the expansion of the elder population will lead to increased social security government spending that relies mainly on taxes. The government's heavy reliance on direct taxes, such as income tax, will inevitably impose an undue burden on the working-age population, particularly the workers. In addition, tax avoidance by corporations and high-income earners increases as globalization and borderlessness of the economy advances; for instance, corporations relocate their headquarters to locations with less taxation and high-income earners move to "tax haven" countries where there are almost no taxes (Shiga, 2013). According to Shigeki Morinobu, corporate tax in Japan is considered high and seems remarkably higher compared with that in other developed countries. Corporate burden includes taxes and social insurance premiums for employees. This burden is lesser in countries in continental Europe, such as Germany and France, and greater in the United Kingdom and United States when all factors are taken into consideration. As such, the situation presents difficulties given that the worldwide competition for lower corporate tax makes corporate tax a less than promising candidate for government funding source (Morinobu, 2010: 203–237). Such circumstances cause indirect taxes, such as consumption tax, to attract more attention.

Nevertheless, satisfying people's lives only through social security policies on the assumption of simple lifecycle has become increasingly difficult as the economic center shifts from manufacturing to service industries and lifestyles diversify. Moreover, women's social advancement in the workplace has made it particularly urgent to arrange childcare facilities for infants. The increasingly borderless economy of Japan indicates that the nation's economic condition has become more susceptible to foreign economic influence, rendering economic forecasting difficult. In Japan, even large companies can no longer afford employee benefits, which they have conventionally been able to provide. This situation has exposed workers to the risk of unemployment even with the slightest change in the economic environment. Although it is the government's responsibility to react to changes in the economic environment, it has not been able to cope adequately because the changes have been abrupt. This has been seen as the government's failure and resulted in people having extreme distrust with government policies (Taylor-Gooby et al., 1999).

A strong distrust of pensions has been created particularly among young people partly owing to extensive news coverage of the Japanese public pension systems (that mostly leave out key aspects of the system); this has roused people to question whether such system is sustainable (Kenjo, 2004: 106–110).[1] Although opinions are divided whether the media coverage is correct, people with limited knowledge will lose confidence in the public system. The loss in confidence will drive people to take a defensive stance, such as saving money for the future; people's saving behavior, in turn, will promote an economic downturn. This behavior causes people to be concerned about their post-retirement years (especially as the cultural expectation that "children have to look after their aged parents" has been changing, even after the parents have covered their children's huge education expenses), and consequently, their motivation to bear and raise children declines. Of course, people consider raising and caring for a child not only as future investment; these are also viewed as sources of invaluable happiness and fulfillment. In fact, many couples want to bear and raise children but they are unable to do so; women struggle to get pregnant. Such efforts are done not only because of the potential future returns that the parents will gain from their child. However, apart from the numerous factors inhibiting childbirth and childcare in Japan, the problem is that the choice of bearing and raising a child has generally become one based on financial burden and significant risk as the period of paying education expenses has become longer owing to the popularization of higher education. As described above, the issues arising from having an aging population and a declining birth rate are closely related. Japan is seemingly caught in a vicious cycle where a failing social security system causes more people to take a defensive stance, increases the number of people who do not consider childrearing because of an uncertain future, and results in a declining birth rate.

(2) Unequal Education Opportunity in a Society with a Widening Educational Disparity

Here, I wish to review briefly the educational situation in Japan.

Figure Intro-1 shows the changes in the percentages of students continuing their education and high school graduates securing employment in Japan since WWII. The high school enrollment rate, which was only about 50% immediately after the war, rapidly increased during the high economic growth period. Subsequently, it exceeded 90% and reached the state of saturation in 1974. The enrollment rates in universities and higher education institutions include graduates in the previous fiscal year (so-called *ronin* or students who failed their school entrance exam and tried again). Higher education institutions include technical colleges, a system launched in 1962, technical high school teacher training schools (1961 to 1966), national school nurse training schools (1967 to 1977), and specialized training college's upper secondary courses (1977 and later). The figures show that the higher education enrollment rate continued to stagnate through the 1980s after hitting 50% for the first time in 1978. The figures likewise show a stagnation trend as well as a slight decrease in university (undergraduate) enrollment rate, despite an uptrend for a certain period until it settled at nearly 30% in 1975. This uptrend in the university enrollment rate through the 1970s is mainly attributed to the private school sector. The establishment of universities was aggressively sought during

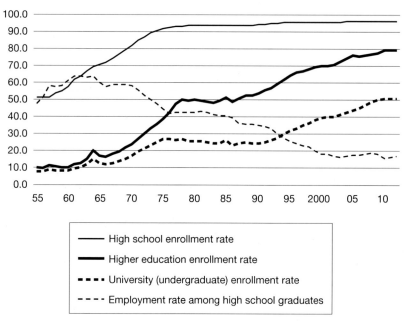

Figure Intro-1 Higher Education Enrollment Rates and
the High School Graduates Employment Rates, 1955–2012

Source: FY 2013 *Statistical Abstract (Education, Culture, Sports, Science and Technology)*

the 1960s to address the growing number of baby boomers and industry concerns on technical labor shortage. Other ministries and agencies would have been careful with the expansion measure given the concerns on budget cuts in existing allotments, considering that the measure required a large budget. The higher education sector expanded, nonetheless, without establishing a financial foundation, with the government (particularly the Ministry of Education) relying on private universities, which in turn relied on tuition to expand. Low public spending on higher education in Japan is not new. Such a government policy exacerbated the educational conditions at universities and increased the barriers for low-income people to advance to higher education; moreover, poor educational conditions gave rise to violent student movements (Pempel, 1978, trans. 2004).

The establishment of new universities dwindled eventually as the government adopted a decentralization policy to avoid the concentration of universities in urban areas. The university enrollment rate was also suppressed during the 1980s owing to the adoption of the private school subsidy program, which tightened the management of university enrollment quota. The program was partly in anticipation of the declining birth rate. In fact, the university enrollment rate began to increase after the 1990s when the second wave of baby boomers started to take college entrance exams. The higher education enrollment rate increased proportionally. Consequently, the number of high school graduates who immediately obtained employment, which was large at the time, suddenly dropped. Although the percentage of students who became employed immediately after high school graduation was already below 50% by the 1970s, it fell below 30% by the early 1990s and then dropped to below 20% at the beginning of the 2000s. These figures show that those who become employed right after high school graduation were a minority among current high school students; the vast majority, in contrast, advanced to another school level. The percentage of those who advanced to university (undergraduate) began to stabilize at around 50%. Toru Kikkawa presented the rate of "college graduates vs. non-graduates" as among the leading indicators that divide Japanese society; this finding suggests the advent of a society divided by educational attainment (Kikkawa, 2006; 2009).

However, the number of households paying the cost for higher education has not changed significantly. Kazuhisa Furuta looked into the *Student Life Survey*[2] data and found that the number of individuals advancing to university rapidly increased among the low-income segment; these students were even attending expensive private universities. The increasing number of low-income university students had been possible via the "scholarship[3]" expansion policy implemented by the Japan Scholarship Foundation (currently Japan Student Services Organization, or JASSO) in 1999. Furuta examined the cause of this increased enrollment rate in the low-income segment by carefully taking into consideration all possibilities other than the JASSO "scholarships"; he concluded that the increased JASSO "scholarships" significantly reduced the gap in university enrollment by income class. However, the definition of "scholarship" in Japan as a loan (debt) that imposes repayment obligation is an important consideration. Moreover, the amount of repayment is fixed, which is different from the student loans in the United Kingdom where repayment is based on income level after obtaining employment. Furuta comprehensively considered the abovementioned points and warned that this "scholarship" system could result in imposing the burden of tuition only on students from the low-income segment (Furuta, 2006).[4]

Problems such as disparity and inequality in educational advancement opportunities are also main subjects in sociology, such as in educational sociology and social stratification theory. Many studies have been conducted in these streams, but it is impossible to list them all. Previously, international comparative studies held the predominant view that the disparity (inequality) in opportunities based on social class remained constant despite the increase in educational opportunities (i.e., an increase in school enrollment rate) (e.g., Shavit and Blossfeld, eds., 1993). However, in recent years, a number of scholars have questioned this finding and stated that the expansion of education has helped reduce inequality in opportunities in the long run (Breen et al., 2009). It has been noted that the sample size of the survey data used in past studies was relatively too small to obtain reliable results (i.e., a sufficient statistical power had not been obtained in the past). Results similar to the ones Breen and others obtained from their analyses on European countries have been confirmed in Japan (Kondo and Furuta, 2009; 2011). These results might seem contradictory to the recent trends in the active debate on a society with a widening educational disparity. However, these data analyses are typically studies on a wide range of age groups, whereas the scope and interest in the said debates seem to be found in more recent and short-term changes. Dividing the existing data into cohorts and analyzing them to compare trends and identify such recent and short-term changes would make the sample size of each cohort small, thus potentially increasing the estimated error. In other words, the current survey data cannot detect the type of trends mentioned in the said debates owing to the nature of the samples in the surveys conducted. Therefore, the results do not possibly contradict the issues raised in the debates depending on the survey design; continuing careful long-term observations (surveys) in the future is thus necessary. Another reason is that significant changes, such as an increase in the number of unstable non-regular employment workers among younger people, can be observed using the same data that Kondo and Furuta used (the Social Stratification and Social Mobility Survey in 2005, or the so-called "2005 SSM Survey"), as in the work of Sato and Ojima, eds. (2011).

Japan's image of a prosperous society with increased equality in educational opportunities has made people overlook the issues of inequality, disparity, and poverty. In Japan, educational expenses are largely covered by households in a scenario where the percentage of private schools increases as the school level goes up. Further, there is no sign that this trend will suddenly change in the future. It is no longer possible to expect a considerable increase in earned income that comes with age as it did before. Analyses on such equality in educational opportunities as well as discussions on the security of educational opportunities have emerged partly owing to Japan's poor scholarship policy (e.g., Kobayashi, 2009; Yotoriyama and Fukushikokka Kōsō Kenkyūkai (Research Society of Welfare State Plan), eds., 2012). The weight of the educational expense burden on households needs to be recognized as an increasingly important issue.

(3) Small Public Spending on Education and People's Attitude Reflecting this Fact

Many studies have shown that the percentage of the Japanese government's public spending on education relative to its economic scale is small compared with other countries. Its education spending is also at the lowest level among developed countries. Figures Intro-2 and Intro-3 prove that public spending on education in Japan is very low relative to its economic scale. The percentage of educational expense in the overall public spending is also small. Particularly for higher education (OECD statistics mainly include universities and colleges, excluding vocational schools), Japan is almost at the lowest level. This scenario has not changed for a long time; however, the growing educational spending per capita is attributed not to an improvement in public spending but to an unchanging public spending on education despite a rapid decline in birth rate.[5] This is seemingly reflected in recent policies such as making high school education free, which was implemented as a result of the change in administration to the Democratic Party of Japan (DPJ).

These figures might promote the view of "focusing more on education as the cornerstone of the state and directing more public funds there." Further, these data might also increase support for raising and caring for children, which has been considered inadequate under the welfare policy in Japan. The core policies of the DPJ, which replaced the Liberal Democratic Party (LDP) in 2009, included those that focused on childcare and education. However, a slightly disenchanted reality contradicts these sentiments.

For example, the morning edition of *Asahi Shimbun* on August 30, 2010 published the results of an Asahi/University of Tokyo Joint Survey. A year after taking over the administration, the DPJ was defeated in the House of Councilors election. This defeat created the condition called "Divided Diet" where the party in control of the Lower House does not control the Upper House. Among the contributing factors to this defeat was the Hatoyama administration's mismanagement of various issues, from the Prime Minister's own issue of "politics and money," to the issue on the Marine Corps Air Station at Futemma, and to the policies they listed as election pledges that were not implemented. Hence, voter ratings remained low despite the DPJ legislators gaining high satisfaction from the DPJ's featured policies on child allowances and household income support system for farmers, which were implemented albeit with limitations due to financial constraints. According to the poll conducted immediately after the inauguration of the Hatoyama administration and published on September 18, 2009 by the *Asahi Shimbun*, 71% of the respondents supported the administration (14% did not), whereas 60% said the child allowance policy should be implemented and 30% said otherwise.[6] Thus, although the expectation for the DPJ administration was high based on the September 2, 2009 opinion poll, which was conducted immediately after the inauguration of the administration, only 31% supported to abolish spousal deduction for income tax and provide child allowance, whereas a greater number (49%) opposed it. Those opposed accounted for 37% of the

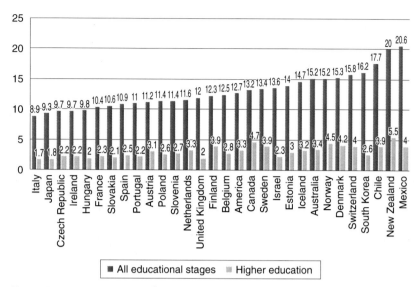

Figure Intro-2 Percentage of Public Spending on Education in Overall Public Spending (%)

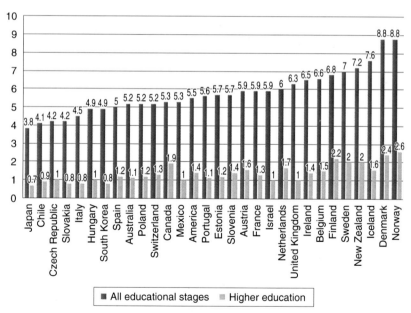

Figure Intro-3 Percentage of Public Spending on Education to GDP (%)
Source: Both figures were prepared based on Table B4.1 in "Total public expenditure on education (2010)" (OECD, 2013: 218).

people who voted for DPJ candidates in the proportional districts for the House of Representatives election (43% supported) and more than half of those who voted for other parties. These figures indicate that the change in regime did not necessarily occur because of people's preference for DPJ's featured policies, such as child allowance and free highways.[7] In fact, the administration was even criticized for "throwing money away" in addition to addressing the lack of funding sources for the policies, including child allowance and free high school tuition.

An even harsher reality has been pointed out by Masakazu Yano. According to the study conducted by Yano and others, those who believe society should bear the cost for university education are the minority; 80% believe it should be paid for by the individual or family. Moreover, he states that there is no relationship between this tendency and respondents' demographics, such as educational attainment (Yano, 2013). An analysis based on the International Social Survey Programme (ISSP) data yielded similar results.[8] Figure Intro-4 shows the results of the four-point scale responses to the question on government responsibility as regards "giv[ing] financial help to university students from low-income families" under the Role of Government IV section in the ISSP. The data in the survey are tabulated and show that the respondents with a larger score (to the right) believe it is the responsibility of the government and the ones with a smaller score (to the left) believe it is not the responsibility of the government. Japan (JP-Japan) is listed in the third row from the top, the second column from the left. The shape of Japan's

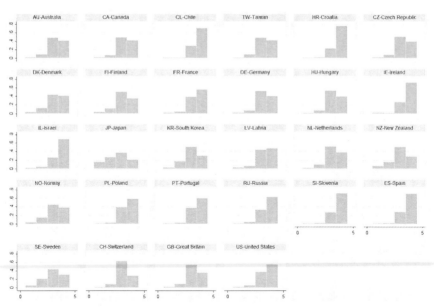

Figure Intro-4 Distribution of the Responses on Covering the Expenses for Entering University in the *International Social Survey Programme* (ISSP)

Note: Tabulated by the author based on ISSP 2006–Role of Government IV graph is spread on both sides with a large variance and shows a number of respondents to the left, indicating that a considerable number of people are opposed to this opinion. Japan seemed to be the only country where a certain percentage of the population opposed such opinion. The percentage of naysayers (two left bars) is small in most of the other countries and is insignificant in certain countries. For instance, the percentage of opposing opinions is extremely small in the United Kingdom (GB-Great Britain) and United States (US-United States) (found in the last row, the third and fourth columns, respectively), the countries often associated with neoliberalism.

As the implementation of policies usually reflect people's opinions, policies such as tuition assistance for college students or making school free of charge would then be considered unpopular even without touching the issue of funding sources; these unpopular policies do not earn votes for politicians. Meanwhile, this attitude might have been formed by past circumstances surrounding the burden of tuition in Japan for it could not have been formed instantaneously. In other words, the tradition that individuals (family/parents) pay for college tuitions turned into a fait accompli and became established as a common understanding that "it is something to be done as the individual's (family/parents) own responsibility" (Yano, 2013). Such data alone could not tell to the extent such attitudes reflect contemporary beliefs. The data also could not tell whether people have partly given up and accepted that individuals have no other choice but to pay tuition on their own as they foresee an unchanging reality brought about by such factors as the Japanese government's financial circumstances, although they recognize that education expenses impose a significant burden on households. Available data have shown that the opinion of holding the government responsible for educational expenses is probably not as robust as expected by those involved in education, including researchers.

Nevertheless, education expenses are weighing heavily on household finances: an issue that cannot be left unaddressed. Further, the anticipation of costly education expenses could become a factor preventing people from having children. For example, Fumihiro Maruyama said that tuition increases certainly do not immediately lead to outcomes such as deciding not to enroll in school, even while such increases occur annually. Households can manage their finances, as they may have already made (upon childbirth or, in other cases, before childbirth) long-term life plans, including preparations for college enrollment in anticipation of tuition fee increases. Considering these circumstances, cutting down on other expenses rather than those for education becomes a rational choice for families with children. For those who wish to have children in the future, reducing the number of children or not having children at all would be a more rational choice given the conditions, including educational expense burden (Maruyama, 1998). Of course, these decisions perceived to be most rational from a personal viewpoint are irrational at the macro level as social security and welfare policies are maintained on the premise of the country having a certain level of working-age population. However, people often do not consider the broad perspective in their decision making. Even while they recognize the problem, their decisions would probably be based on their current living environments. A problem might be apparent in the current situation, but it will not be easily resolved until a political party promoting increased public spending on education wins the majority through election. As a premise of the debate over public spending on education, accepting the fact that people have such an attitude toward educational expenses is necessary. The following questions are crucial: Why people do not believe in increasing public spending on education even while such spending is considerably lower than that in other countries; and why many Japanese do not consider providing school enrollment support to economically poor families, a position considered as a matter of concern in other countries.

(4) Issue of National Burden

Placing more financial burden to the government is not plausible without addressing the current issue on Japan's financial resources. The DPJ took over the administration by advocating waste reduction and drew the media's attention to budget review and prioritization. However, the financial crisis worsened because the budget review and prioritization were not done for financial retrenchment. The DPJ's calculation was also too optimistic.

Everyone understands this situation in theory, but when the government implements a program requiring a large expenditure, the funds do not materialize by themselves; ultimately, the people must bear the burden in the form of taxes. Sourcing funds, hence, becomes a difficult task. One solution is to reallocate funds currently allotted for another item to education. Where reallocation is not possible, increasing the national burden is the last resort. Japan's national burden is small relative to its economic scale (see Figure Intro-5), and people are beginning to recognize this fact. "National burden" can be divided roughly into (1) tax burden, such as national and local taxes; and (2) social security burden, such as pension and medical insurance. Figure Intro-5 shows the sum of these two.[9]

I will discuss the national burden further in Chapter 3. The low level of Japan's national burden is nothing new. This level has been consistent since the end of WWII. Employee benefits and women working under the gender division of labor are among other factors that have compensated the shortfall created by this low burden. In recent years, however, a trend to cut down on employee benefits has emerged as women's social advancement increases and corporate competitions intensify owing to globalization. The difficulty currently facing society is in deciding whether to build a system that will allow the government to assume employee benefits and the functions that have been fulfilled mainly by women since the end of the war.

If the direction of not expanding the functions of the government continues, the likelihood of societal instability increases as social ties connecting individuals loosen and disparities expand. Meanwhile, people would probably want the current society to remain stable. Unless people are extreme anarchists, then they would expect the government to contribute in maintaining the status quo. A notion prevails that a society might fall apart unless supported by institutions and systems. Filling the gap left by the institutions and systems is, therefore, necessary.

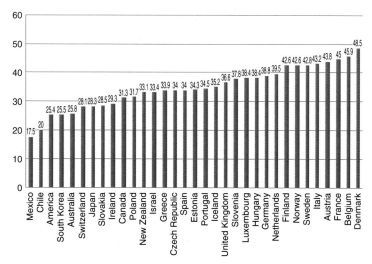

Figure Intro-5 Percentage of the National Burden Rate in OECD Countries (compared to GDP, 2010)
Source: Website of the Ministry of Finance
(http://www.mof.go.jp/budget/fiscal_condition/basic_data/201303/sy2503o.pdf)
Among 34 OECD countries, Turkey was excluded. The data for Australia and New Zealand are as of 2009.

Neoliberals, hence, prefer a smaller government that emphasizes ideals such as familial love and patriotism. The decision to emphasize such emotional connections is often made to maintain social ties without incurring financial costs.

Going back to the main discussion, the Japanese national burden is not heavy compared with other countries; in fact, it is deemed rather manageable. Nordic countries are often mentioned as model welfare states; without exception, these countries have a heavy national burden. The principle is that a citizen obtains welfare services in exchange for carrying the burden. In contrast, the United States, which has a strong emphasis on freedom, self-responsibility, and minimal government responsibility, has a lower national burden. Japan is similar to the United States in terms of national burden.

Many people tend to remain unconvinced even after seeing the above objective data. This is because the objective data do not always directly reflect people's subjective (actual) perception. I will examine this scenario in Chapter 5. At any rate, people probably become frustrated because they cannot receive their expected benefits. The likelihood is high that people will understand a heavy national burden only if they reap the appropriate benefits that would provide them with peace of mind. At this point, the core issues are the extent of people's expectations from the government and the amount of burden they will pay for these expectations.

People who criticize the government, particularly the neoliberals, have a strong distrust of the government. The idea is that a free market yields better results than the government's artificial policies, which are seen as often wrong and leading to inefficient results. Based on this idea, then welfare states, such as Nordic countries,

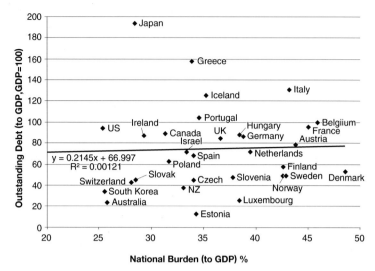

Figure Intro-6 Relationship between National Burden and Outstanding Government Debt (2010)
Source: OECD (2012) *Economic Outlook* No. 92

which have big governments, should have managed their economies inefficiently and be on the verge of bankruptcy. Figure Intro-6 shows, however, that the national burden rate and outstanding government debt are not correlated. A regression line was drawn to test the data, but the determination coefficient is almost zero.[10] Thus, there is almost no relationship between the scale of government and its outstanding debt. The problem lies in the people's expectation on the balance between the scale of government and national burden. If their expectations are contradictory such that they believe the government has to fulfill certain roles and functions but they resist an increase in the national burden (rather than creating a small government along the veins of pursuing non-governmental/self-help efforts and other options that ease the national burden), then there will be no revenue–expenditure balance, and the debt will bloat. While leaving this issue unaddressed may pose more crises, no decisive measures have been taken to date.

Neoliberal ideas are probably difficult to implement, although many people have taken this position. Living without the assumption of a welfare state system is almost impossible since it is prevalent in people's lives. Moreover, having an aging population has placed Japan in an inevitable position of requiring increased government spending, especially on social security. Therefore, status quo requires that a discussion on welfare and educational services enhancement goes hand in hand with increasing the national burden. The DPJ administration's failure to identify wasted spending and find financial resources indicates that the budget has been limited and the government could not afford to cut down on other items to redirect the funds to educational expenses.[11] Spending on public works, which used to be criticized, has been greatly reduced. The adverse effect of the sudden reduction has become noticeable in recent years.[12] This means that the root of the problem lies in the budget. In response to this situation, a review of viewpoints such as "how to reevaluate the way people view tax and their attitude as taxpayers" and "how to ask them to take on the national burden that is reasonable for the services that they demand" is ongoing (e.g., Miki, 2012: 216–219; Ide, 2013, etc.).

This book shares a similar awareness of the issue. As we live in a modern society, provision for equal educational opportunities is of absolute importance. I believe that not being able to access the opportunity to pursue further education owing to various situations is undemocratic, unfair, and absurd; it is a problem that must be resolved. I believe that people would widely accept such value of equal educational opportunities as a common opinion in contemporary Japan. However, the key is in properly drawing people's attention to this type of problem and eventually solving it.

2. Can We Increase Public Spending on Education?

I have observed a strong tendency among education-related researchers and people involved in education who are highly aware of these problems to criticize the government regardless of whether the problem is a result of government inaction or the government representing the interest of the wealthy. The same people merely demand the government to increase public spending on education. I highly criticize their take on the issue.

The government is not a monolithic body. We say "the intention and will of the government," but this phrase has unclear implications when closely reviewed. It is common for two central government agencies to have conflicting interests, and it is not unusual for different ministries and agencies to hold inconsistent views (Imamura, 2006).[13] The government certainly has tremendous power; people in the government could possibly abuse their power to implement a policy that does not reflect the people's intentions (demands). Hence, a critical look at government actions is indeed imperative. However, we can also demand indirectly from the government through our voting behaviors, which is a pillar of democracy. Unlike in a dictatorship, policies and businesses carried out by the Japanese government cannot be completely independent of the public's demands and opinions.

First, a simple plead to the government will not resolve the problem on increased public spending on education, for instance. Second, Masakazu Yano lamented a lack of economic perspective among educators (Yano, 2001). As pointed out earlier, Japanese people do not seem to share the opinion that the government should cover educational expenses. A significant change to a situation is difficult to achieve unless people's demands evolve. While the opinion of promoting equal educational opportunities through enhanced scholarship programs is growing among certain people in a society with widening disparity, the voice is occlusive. The issue might have gained ground among certain people, but it is surely not widely shared by the public. Thus, the demands to increase public spending on education have to reach not only the government but also society and the general public. This book's mission and objective are to provide materials to initiate a discussion for such a progression.

Below I explain the structure and content of this book.

The book consists of two main parts. The first half examines the situation surrounding the education policy in Japan by comparing the policy with other subject areas as well as with those in other countries. In the first chapter, I employ sociological theories to examine the social role of education by examining the functions of education in society. School education is a system that was established at the beginning of modern times. In sociological terms, this system has occurred in parallel with modernization processes, such as bureaucratization of organizations and social division of labor. In addition, society's central foundation shifted from the naturally occurring ones of family, relatives, and communities to artificial organizations (e.g., administrative and for-profit organizations, such as companies); the separation between residence and workplace has widened. Under these circumstances, education was given two functions that have completely different directions. One is the human development that enables people with different roles to coexist; second is the allocation of people with different abilities to various positions in society. Other functions of education include proving a person with appropriate abilities for a given position in a modern society where people can choose an occupation as long as they have the ability for such. To justify this function, the screening process needs to be transparent and convincing to people. While the written test-oriented education system in Japan has achieved this to a great extent, it has made people perceive competitions as fair. This perception, in turn, made inequality in educational opportunities less apparent despite its continuous existence. This resulted in a reinforced self-responsibility argument. I will point out the possibility that the perception "Japanese education and screening systems are fair" creates the notion that educational choice, particularly at the higher level, is simply a private matter; this further makes it difficult to increase awareness among the public even while the issue requires public support.

In Chapter 2, I examine education that plays a social function as reviewed in Chapter 1 and its relationship with the state and government. In general, the education community is wary of governmental intervention in education; this is understandable considering Japanese history, particularly during the pre-WWII period. Nonetheless, the education system is closely related to the existence of the government because it is more or less financed by taxpayers' money. First, I examine the justification for the government to maintain the education system in this way. I look at how the formation of the educational system had been sociologically examined during the establishment phase of the modern state. Then, at the end of the chapter, I briefly touch on neoliberalism, which is said to have a strong influence on the state, tax, and field of education in recent years.

In Chapter 3, I will discuss social security and welfare as programs and services that the government undertakes in the same way as education. I describe how opinions are divided on where to position education: either as part of welfare or something completely different. I take this issue and review its financial aspects from the perspective of international comparison. Social security in Japan places a considerably disproportionate emphasis on pensions and medical care for the elderly while ignoring or downplaying other policies. Further, the function of education varies between primary/secondary education (which emphasizes equality) and higher education (which emphasizes the difference from others and the assignment of positions). This causes confusion when looking at the relationship with welfare policies. Therefore, I look at the historical data on why Japanese welfare policies came to overemphasize the elderly and medical care while neglecting social security in other areas. I confirm that the Japanese-style welfare system has reached its limit owing to the globalization of the economy and women's social advancement, even while it has a scheme to incorporate private sectors. I use an international comparison of financial data to explain the characteristics of the Japanese welfare system in terms of its relation and positioning in policies in other areas as well as in Japan within the global context.

Chapter 4 explains the structure of people's attitude, which is the basis for forming and maintaining the social security and welfare system explained in Chapter 3. First, as a fundamental problem, I discuss the remarkably low level of trust that Japanese people have for the government. Although it is not easy to identify a causal relationship, this lack of confidence and difficulty in raising taxes or the large outstanding debt generated because of the inability to raise taxes, are deeply related. Second, I explain that while expansion of the government's role would presumably involve an increased tax burden, the connection between an increased burden in personal areas and the overall scale of government spending is weak according to the Japanese perception of education and social security system in general. This seems to indicate that Japanese people consider the method by which taxpayer money is spent as a more important concern than wanting a smaller government. I will further show that this does not imply that they want the scale of welfare to further expand and that the overall consensus to maintain the current state is strong. The discussion will also reveal that the attitude to public spending on education is not very different from that in Scandinavian countries (where the level of public spending on education is already high) even though the level of public spending on education is low based on the world standard, whereas the level of support for increasing public spending on education is relatively low compared with other countries.

In Part II, I focus on the financial aspects of the characteristics of Japan in relation to other countries. I examine the reasons why and how Japan has been shaped this way. In Chapter 5, I review the overall characteristics of Japan's financial and budget system. I briefly touch on educational finance as well as children's schooling expenses. In particular, I examine the function of the government's fiscal investment and loans fulfilled under the financial structure of Japan and how it has led to the present budget deficit and the sense of tax burden among people. The key is to reevaluate the functions of the state and government. I argue the importance of the "public" that connects the state authority with ordinary individuals, families, and companies.

In Chapter 6, I summarize the various trends related to the increase in tuition and school expenses by focusing on the post-WWII period. After the war, junior high school was established in Japan as a completely new system. As junior high school became compulsory education, developing high schools was prioritized. As a result, public spending on higher education did not increase significantly. The government then adopted the beneficiary-pays principle during the crisis. This idea became accepted by the general public. Consequently, the soaring education costs were perceived as a responsibility that parents must endure but not for society to bear.

In Chapter 7, I point out that the glaring issue regarding the national burden. There is a need to find the necessary financial resources to implement social policies when economic growth slows and income growth becomes sluggish, which was the case after the bubble economy collapsed. As the idea of jointly providing support or the idea of public good remained less popular when life became seemingly comfortable and equality in life conditions became available, individuals had become responsible for their own outcomes. Consequently, recipients of public assistance became a target of attack for the middle class. People interpreted educational attainment as personal investment and achievement without considering the social benefit aspect. I discuss this perception among Japanese people by specifically considering attitudes to several policies that the DPJ administration had presented. In addition, I will review the significance of the DPJ administration's policies, the methods by which these policies were communicated, and the notion on education and government involvement.

In Chapter 8, I examine the cause of the recent strict stance that Japanese people have taken against the government (government employees) through an organizational sociology lens. I describe why bureaucratic organizations tend to move away from the public opinion as well as why the criticisms against bureaucratic organizations are likely related with the neoliberal standpoint. Then, I argue that political parties need to set forth a responsible public pledge that includes a financial source; when they do, voters' choices will be presented. I further explain how the DPJ had a decent level of support based on voting behavior through the 2010 House of Councilors election according to the results of a panel survey, albeit limited to the younger segment. However, a considerable number of those who had consistently voted for the DPJ voted for other parties in the 2010 House of Councilors election. In addition, I look at the favorability of political parties to show that it was not only the security issue (in which the difference in ideology between parties was clear) but also the attitude to welfare and social security that distinguished the favorability of parties.

Based on the above points, I enumerate in the final chapter the key issues needed to be discussed in expanding the debate over public spending on education.

NOTES

[1] In addition to Kenjo (2004), Hori (2009) similarly criticized the theory of collapsing pension. The feature story on pensions published on the October 31, 2009 issue of *Weekly Toyo Keizai* summarizes the theory of collapsing pension and points out the issues.

[2] The Ministry of Education (currently Ministry of Education, Culture, Sports, Science

and Technology) used to conduct this survey every other year. The Japan Student Services Organization (JASSO) has taken over the survey.

3   Although scholarships are normally provided as benefit (the Longman Dictionary of Contemporary English, for instance, defines it as "an amount of money that is given to someone by an educational organization to help pay for their education"), nearly no scholarships had been provided as benefits in Japan; the loan-style scholarship provided by the Japan Scholarship Foundation (current JASSO) has historically been recognized as a "scholarship." Based on this information, I will use quotation marks when referring to the word scholarship. As a note, OECD statistics categorize scholarships in Japan as "student loans."

4   Students in the high-income bracket do not have a repayment obligation after being employed as they do not need a "scholarship." Many children do not "repay" the tuition paid by their parents. However, student loans or the borrowed money via the "scholarship" of the low-income segment students could follow them for a long time after graduation. Further, a student's income bracket and the ranking of the university that he or she enrolls in correlate; the problem becomes acute when individuals in higher income brackets are more likely able to enroll in universities that have competitive advantage for graduate employment while those in lower income brackets are more likely to enroll in universities with less advantage.

5   According to the OECD (2013: 178), when the year 2005 was set as the base, expense (spending) per person in 1995, or 10 years ago, was only 78% because although the total public spending on education in 1995 was 97%, the number of students was to 1.24 times the base value. The educational expense per person increased by 1.09 times in 2010 because the educational spending increased by 1.04 times even though the number of students declined to 96% in 2005.

6   As a note, many opposed the policy on making highways free of charge: 24% supported and 67% opposed.

7   The issue of children on the waiting list of nursery schools was becoming serious especially in urban areas owing to cash payments, such as child allowances; subsequently, a stronger clamor for improvement in childcare environments emerged (Nihon Saiken Inishiachibu, 2013: 173–180).

8   The ISSP data were obtained by downloading from the ISSP website made available by GESIS (social science data archive in Germany).   http://www.issp.org/index.php

9   The national burden rate is calculated by adding the tax and social security burdens together and dividing the total by the national income. This indicator is often used in Japan but it is rarely used in international comparisons. See Naruse (2001) for more information on this issue. The current statistics published by the Ministry of Finance (MOF) include not only the traditional figure divided by the national income but also the figure divided by the GDP. As the nature of social security is the receipt of benefits in the future, discussing it only as a one-sided burden is problematic, although this method is possible with taxes. Naruse pointed out that individuals typically cover their own social security expenses unless provided by the government.

10   At 0.035, Pearson's product-moment correlation coefficient was also at the level where a no correlation conclusion is feasible.

11   For example, arguments such as "cut and redirect defense spending to education and

welfare" were often heard during the Cold War period. These ideas may be ideological, but it is difficult to imagine that many people will indeed support them when the recent situations are taken into consideration. The judgment on whether spending is wasteful varies depending on the people's viewpoints. As such, obtaining consensus on cutting budget items is difficult.

[12] Japan had many roads built all at once during the high economic growth period. This means that their useful life will end almost at the same time. In fact, numerous piers and tunnels are said to have exceeded their service life and become dangerous in recent years. The fallen ceiling board accident that occurred in the Sasago tunnel on the Chuo Expressway in December 2012 is still fresh in people's minds. The need for seismic reinforcement work on many old buildings should be recognized as well, in light of the increased disaster prevention awareness following the Great East Japan Earthquake in March 2011. A huge budget is needed to invest in these infrastructures.

[13] For example, the Cabinet Office, the Ministry of Economy, Trade and Industry (METI), and the Ministry of Agriculture, Forestry and Fisheries (MAFF) have estimated the impact that the TPP (Trans-Pacific Economic Partnership Agreement) will have on the GDP, and while the Cabinet Office and the METI estimated a large benefit, the MAFF estimated a large loss, resulting in a difference that amounts to the order of trillions of yen (the morning edition of *Asahi Shimbun*, October 23, 2010). In addition, there is a fierce discussion between the MOF and the Ministry of Education, Culture, Sports, Science and Technology (MEXT) over the budget of the MEXT. Refer to Chapter 3 for more on this topic.

PART I

PEOPLE'S ATTITUDE AND THE STATE OF POLICY REGARDING EDUCATION SPENDING

CHAPTER 1
Reconsidering the Social Role of Education

1. Society where Education Takes Root

Education takes place in a variety of settings. It begins at home with our parents (or guardians) taking the role of teacher during our early formative years. Most children enroll in elementary school after a communal life experience in kindergarten and nursery school. Children experience school education as attending elementary and junior high schools, which is generally mandatory. Schools are the central place for education after enrolling in an elementary school, but other places to gain education include the home and local community. Individuals may choose to continue to an advanced school and obtain employment after graduation. At the workplace, employees often undergo in-house training. Continued learning is essential as technological innovations continue to evolve rapidly. A number of employed individuals even return to universities and technical colleges to continue their learning beyond graduation. Others find new hobbies or attend public lectures at cultural centers and local governments. As the phrase "lifelong learning" indicates, educational opportunities in public places for people, regardless of age, will certainly increase when people's life courses diversify.

Popular notion holds that education takes place under public organizations and systems (e.g., school system) and has been considered important; this notion has become a standard since the modernization of society. Leading a normal social life in a modern society requires having skills aside from basic knowledge of reading, writing, and arithmetic. Moreover, the importance of knowledge is increasing. Then again, knowledge acquisition is not necessarily confined to school attendance. The school is not a place where we merely absorb knowledge. As we spend most of our childhood and youth in school, we also learn from extra-curricular activities and school events, which are considered important in school life in Japan. In fact, many people have these as their fondest school life memories.

Schools are found throughout the country. At present, a world without a school is no longer imaginable. Even with a declining birth rate, the number of teachers in 2013 was over 417,000 for elementary schools, over 254,000 for junior high schools, over 235,000 for high schools, close to 9,000 for junior colleges, and close to 179,000 for universities.[1] These figures add up to over one million educators. Apart from the mandatory schools, there are vocational schools and private educational institutions, such as cram and prep schools. As such, school education has become a major source of employment as a major industry.

If school was for simply gaining knowledge, we could say that the need to outsource education to institutional schools is fading owing to such factors as advancement in communication technology. Denying the existence of school is considered an extreme albeit valid opinion. As various problems emerge and debates are ongoing, people continue to believe in schools and seek improvement measures; we do not hear opinions such as "reevaluate the existence of schools where problems are piling up" (unless the individual is unconventional or has an extreme view). In other words, any discussion on education cannot ignore the existence of institutions and schools.

Institutional authorities (such as both the national and local governments) typically manage the school system. Even when the operation itself is performed by private citizens, a certification to establish a school is issued by the government; an example of such certification is one that ensures the school's legitimacy. However, school-like organizations and institutions could exist independently from the state and the government. Studying at a school gives life profound meaning, although in the case of studying in private school-like spaces, the meaning may not be recognized by society. Graduating from or completing one's schooling has a social meaning only when the government has certified or established the school. Regardless of how we argue about the details of school education, we need to recognize that this type of institutional foundation is founded through education.

Although I mentioned that education takes place in many settings, I will limit the discussion to education in public school systems. This limitation also supports the book's main subject, which is looking at the dimensions of school education where going to school is costly even while there are public schools. Moreover, although the government certainly has immense power over individuals and private organizations, it cannot suppress and control the people under the democratic system of government. In theory, a government that reflects the people's will is maintained through the voting system. Therefore, the government's direction is not completely independent of the people's will; certain policies also reflect the people's aspirations even if only partially. In Japan, limiting the state's power was a major concern as the country strived to build a post-WWII war democratic society, partly because state power was out of control and led to tragedies during the pre-war period. Consequently, the state and individuals were perceived as opposing parties, with the means to protect individuals from the state becoming the focus of discussion. Further, the concept that the state has been created for the purpose of protecting individual rights rather than certain authorities, who control the world as they please, has gained popularity (Omoda, 2013: 13–14). The call to "be vigilant watchdogs of the government" is meaningful to an extent because the state and bureaucracy indeed have the power over individuals, with many instances where individuals had no control over state power. Although the power of the state is tremendous, the present relationship between the government and the people is not necessarily one-sided where the government suppresses the people. In another point of view, citizens (the people) pay for the government services, which include education, social security, and welfare. In other words, the government collects money from the citizens and then reallocates the funds in the form of direct human services or money. Hence, the operation of public school education is paid using such funds, which were mainly sourced from the people's taxes.

To an extent, we are inclined to believe that the government is collecting tax from us against our will; the government's existence, however, is completely independent of us, and its responsibilities include providing such services as education and welfare. Although such viewpoint is understandable given that taxes may not always be spent according to our priorities, it is still a superficial and problematic idea. I believe that the tendency to look at the state and individuals as opposing parties became strong after WWII as a response to previous circumstances; people were concerned about the state authority imposing its ideologies that strongly reflected the dominant political party's agenda during the pre-war period. Nonetheless, school education was established under state authority. As long as the education system is organized under state authority, its curriculum and educational materials will never be neutral. Thus, it is necessary to examine school education critically with consideration for the possibility that the government and organizations could move away from the will of the people and become uncontrollable. At the same time, the demand, which is a legitimate one, has often been to make educational services free or inexpensive. It might sound rude, but I view it as making a demand to a certain type of authority: "We will not allow any intervention, but pay out the money." It would be different if Japan was under a dictatorship that does not reflect the will of the people; however, as long as we advocate for a democratic nation, we need to realize that a complaint to the government is also a complaint to the people (citizens). If we increase public spending on education, we need to collect funds from the citizens in certain forms to be allocated to education. We would have to reallocate the funds used for other purposes to education; if we cannot afford to do so, we have to increase the national burden. In this system, it is inadequate to show open hostility to the government and merely demand an increase in education spending as if the government is a dominative existence standing remotely from us. The intention of the government is not always unilaterally imposed on the people. It is possible, albeit indirectly, to correct the methods of the government through personal involvement. Therefore, it will be necessary to increase public awareness on why larger education spending is necessary and to have such advocacy reflected in political parties' public commitment. By increasing public awareness, it might be possible to encourage people to support political parties that lay down such policies, thereby shaping people's voting behavior.

2. Modernization and Education: A Sociological Look at School Education

(1) Function of School Education in a Modern Society

What is the social meaning of education?

Socialization in the post-modern era society, compared to that in primitive society, is complex; the spaces for children to grow up and adults to work are separate. The historical development pertaining to this, as detailed in *L'enfant et la vie familiale sous l'ancien régime* by Philippe Ariès in France (1960, translated into English as *Centuries of Childhood: A Social History of Family Life* in 1962 by Robert Baldick), is well known among education specialists. In summary, it states that the modern era produced the notion of "childhood" as a growth stage as well as a pure and innocent existence to be protected and shaped by "adults." The development of such views on children is deeply related to the establishment of the modern school system.

As the urban concentration of the population intensified and factory labor developed into large-scale operations during the industrial revolution, adults' workplace and children's living space became separated. Consequently, the place for children to learn as well as master technology and knowledge by observing how adults work was lost. Organizations themselves became complex after the modern era, a wider perspective and more experiences were required at the workplace. In sociology, we typically ask "what is modern era?" as among the main research subjects. In many cases, Émile Durkheim from France and Max Weber from Germany are studied. In particular, Durkheim personally taught educational science courses at the Sorbonne (University of Paris) and proposed educational science to shed light on education-related phenomena as social facts. He is regarded as the founder of educational sociology (Aso et al., 1978).

Durkheim perused the history of school education in France and found its origin in Christian Sunday school. Religion functions as a mechanism for social integration that cohere individuals. Christian schools did not only communicate knowledge but also imparted holistic values that are consistent with the Christian doctrine; they instill these values so that people practice them in their lives. Schools, therefore, were created as a result of popularizing such religious beliefs. While local churches and temples had played a major role in maintaining the sense of unity among people, societal development eventually led to the creation of an organization called the state, which is regarded above communal societies that are spontaneously created, such as settlements and villages. Durkheim's argument is that the function of popularized school is to educate people to become members of the state (Durkheim, 1938, trans. 1966).

As these spontaneous communities shifted to a society centered on organizations and institutions regarded as artificial, people's way of communicating (solidarity) also evolved.[2] In French society, which had been unstable since the French

Revolution owing to frequent changes in the administration, building a stable and peaceful society was an urgent concern. Under such circumstances, functional differentiation of the entire society advanced after the Industrial Revolution and individual differences were emphasized. Consequently, people in a simple communal society led self-sufficient lives. They communicated with only the people around them; the types of available work were limited (roughly divided into farming and hunting as work is basically for securing food for survival). When problems arose, people addressed them on their own. Durkheim likened spontaneous communities to annelids. Annelids or ringed worms, which appear to be connected by joints, are characterized by their ability to connect because their "joints" have similar features. In the case of a spontaneous community, such community is composed of individuals who share many similar elements and, through kinships, one can handle an issue when it arises (i.e., regardless of who handles it). Durkheim likens individuals in such society to machine parts; that is, broken parts could be easily replaced so that the machine will operate again. As such, he called the people's connection in such society a "mechanical solidarity" (Durkheim, 1893, trans. 1989).

However, it became impossible for a limited number of people to perform everything in a modern society where economic activities had become brisker and complex. In addition, communities had expanded geographically. This process is in line with the increased bureaucracy, which Weber listed as among the characteristics of modernized organizations (Weber, 1956, trans. 1960). The division of labor (functional differentiation) within an organization inevitably increases as businesses expand; one person can only handle so much. In large organizations, a large job can be accomplished by assigning a range of roles to individuals rather than having one person perform everything. In manufacturing, likewise, the division of labor largely improves productivity and reduces the cost of training workers. The so-called Ford system was created based on this idea. The above example shows that the overall productivity of a society in modern times increases when people work together and perform their own roles. Durkheim calls such dominant connections of people in modern society as "organic solidarity." Modern society is like a biological organism; it has internal organs with their own functions and a particular organ cannot replace another. Surviving as an advanced biological organism becomes possible only when organs with different functions are combined. This "organ" is a metaphor for the various professions in a society. While each individual has their own profession and is devoted to a particular type of work, the overall performance of a society improves when individuals fully perform their roles corresponding to their own professions (Durkheim, 1893, trans. 1989). However, when a large society is formed by combining different individuals, people usually do not think of undertaking joint work by cooperating with others who seem to be different from themselves because each individual's views and interests are limited. This is when education becomes important. The main role of education is to plant seeds and nurture certain physical, intellectual, and moral states in children as required by society as a whole and by a part of a special environment within such society. This means that one's education would help him or her reach a certain position that society requires all of its members to achieve. Moreover, education helps a person master the skills and knowledge necessary to belong to a particular group where he or she would perform a role. This point of view corresponds to the function of compulsory education that helps individuals master the minimum skills and knowledge required to live; the function of higher education and vocational/technical education, meanwhile, is to help individuals master advanced and specialized vocational skills and knowledge. Durkheim coined "methodical socialization (*socialisation méthodique*)" to refer to the process of guiding individuals to demonstrate their own abilities so that they take roles and function in a society (Durkheim, 1922, trans. 1976: 58–59).[3]

(2) School Education in the Emerging Society in America
A similar discussion has been developed in the United States by John Dewey, a distinguished philosopher and education scholar. He said "a modern society is many societies [that are] more or less loosely connected" (Dewey, 1916, trans. 1975: 42). In fact, a modern society is composed of independent communities, such as families and relatives, local societies, occupational groups, and clubs. As geographical movements become active along with the development of commerce, communication, and transportation, among others, people and groups with different backgrounds begin creating even larger communities and societies. For children, learning through imitation of their parents might be sufficient in uncivilized, relatively homogeneous local communities. However, in a society composed of people with a variety of backgrounds, education facilities that offer a balanced environment become necessary for people to master skills for carrying out community life with others from all walks of life. Thus, it is essential to have schools as an institution to educate and train children with a purpose (Dewey, 1916, trans. 1975).[4]

Unlike Europe, America started from a blank slate where there was no social class system (except for the existence of Native Americans), and the availability of vast frontiers promoted equality. In contrast, Europe needed a revolution to achieve equality because of the existence of a solid social class system. Thus, various types of effects (reactions) occurred as a result of the revolution. Alexis de Tocqueville's *Democracy in America*, a book written on the premise of the difference between Europe and America, has been a must-read classic even today to understand how American society evolved (Uno, 2007). According to Tocqueville, among the English immigrants to America, Puritans who settled in New England were originally from a wealthy educated class; they abandoned their assets in their homeland and moved to the America with their wives and children. In England, they were persecuted for trying to practice their strict Christian faith. They traveled to America in search of a land where they could live freely and practice their religion. In America, their individual roots and social class were of no importance. Many parcels of reclaimed lands that produced products would have been necessary for the aristocracy to work. As such a concept did not exist in primitive America, they only needed their own efforts. In contrast, Europe's political realm (especially in France) assumed a scenario where information traveled from the upper echelon right down to the bottom of society. America took the opposite setup where everything started with the communities, which formed counties and then the Federation. It can be said that the Puritans had to adapt to America's setup when they settled in New England. However, it may be that humans could have a type of unhealthy freedom stemming from ignorance. This is a threat to a peaceful life, and God is opposed to such freedom. God wishes for us to have civil liberties and moral freedom. Therefore, according to Tocqueville, to obtain the knowledge provided by our ancestors to create the foundation that leads to obeying God and, thereby, realizing these civil liberties, people must establish schools in every community and require parents to send their children to school. To maintain the community's philosophy, they created complete legal and civil service systems and imposed obligations on membership to society (Tocqueville, 1888, trans. 1987: Vol. 1, Chapter 2).[5]

Tocqueville's *Democracy in America* was originally written for French readers. The European societies at the time, including France, were in transition from a class to an equitable society (albeit at a slow pace). However, European societies were rooted in the aristocracy, and the nature of the aristocracy included inequality in the system. As the only way to reduce inequality was to reject the old power that maintained the aristocracy, it led to a violent revolution. Europeans, who believed in the ideals of equality, carried out the democratic revolution. However, they fell into a paradox where self-indulgence increased as equality was achieved; this paradox made it difficult to achieve a free society (Tocqueville, 1888, trans. 1987: Vol. 2, 534–552). As such, achieving both freedom and equality is an extremely difficult task even though both ideals often go together as among the basic human rights.

Although freedom and equality are also ideals often presented in relation to education, pursuing one tends to sacrifice the other. David F. Labaree classified the objectives of education into three points, namely, democratic equality, social efficiency, and social mobility (Labaree, 1997). These points represent people as citizens, taxpayers, and consumers, respectively. Hence, the first point refers to the idea that schools should strive to develop good citizens. The second corresponds to the notion that schools should develop individuals to become useful to society as workers. The third applies to the idea that people participate in friendly competitions for specific and limited positions so that only competent talents are chosen. Through competition, people could secure opportunities available in whatever profession they choose regardless of their roots. While all of the three points are frequently noted as the objectives of education, it is impossible to achieve them all at the same time.

The first objective of education during the initial developmental phase of society would be to have all residents achieve a certain level of literacy. By doing so, people gain the ability to think, determine their paths, and make choices on their own. Having the opportunity to express opinions or undertake work alone would not do much unless the individual can take advantage of such an opportunity. Education thus provides a person with the minimum capabilities to survive in society.

However, as education becomes widespread and ubiquitous in a society, and the content of study also becomes advanced, differences in abilities and preferences among people naturally become evident, and their needs diversify accordingly. The educational level and the specifics of study subjects that the labor market requires also diversify. The education system responds to these needs to save people from the risk of unemployment; however, there will be differences in wages and salaries in the labor market based on job description and social status. The function of education at this point is to highlight the differences in abilities and skills among people rather than bring everyone to the same level. On the one hand, this is generally described in a positive picture when emphasizing the aspect of bringing out the differences in abilities. On the other hand, it has a negative image when these differences are directly linked to, for instance, disparities in salary in the labor market.

We cannot overlook education's disadvantageous aspect, which differentiates individuals by salary; however, the notions such as "instilling similar values and knowledge within the same community" tend to be emphasized in education. The contradiction in the objectives of education is evident in these aspects. If education helps people obtain a desirable social status, people will try to obtain a higher education. Common phrases such as "others cannot do this, but I can" and "I graduated from a more prestigious school than others" are applicable to situations where education and educational attainment are useful at the individual level. High wage and status are guaranteed because the person has advantage over others. As such, people compete to get into prestigious schools. In certain cases, a school's overall quota for new students is increased in an attempt to loosen the admission criteria because of fierce competition. However, another criterion would be created, and the competition once again becomes fierce for that small quota. This is what happens in the ever-changing nature of competition in Japan. Everyone aims for the same kind of affluent life and strives to go to college, as college education is valued. This attitude intensifies the competition in college entrance examinations, leading to the negative effect that the college admission quota is increased to solve the problem (i.e., the enrollment rate increases). Choosing another college becomes the next problem. If such competition is unavoidable, surviving the competition becomes a serious concern for the education-obsessed middle class. The middle class concern basically lies in the desire for distinction rather than achievement of equality. As people in the middle class are considered major taxpayers, they demand an education that is suitable to their needs, claiming that they are taxpayers. This is, however, contrary to the principle of equality. While public schools have focused on creating the first common and equal education, those in the middle class who are disappointed with public schools, which fail to meet their needs, opt to attend private schools. As such, it is possible that those who attend private schools become increasingly dissatisfied with paying taxes for public schools as they do not benefit from such schools directly. The current educational reform focuses on the efficiency aspects and consumers of education services; we are faced with a difficult question as to how we maintain the democratic equality of public education while responding to the demands of the middle class (Labaree, 1997).

(3) American-Style Liberalism and the Education Philosophy
In the United States, there are dynamic discussions over freedom, a concept rooted in their history since the country's founding. Opinions on the government are divided as well in terms of whether the form of government leads to oppression of or a means to freedom. Liberalism is applied in the opposite way in Europe. Policies against laissez-faire, such as aiding the underprivileged or the so-called welfare, are considered means to guarantee freedom and promote the formation of a group of Democratic Party supporters. This is the idea of liberalism (Watanabe, 2010).[6] This means that while we tend to perceive being liberal entails blocking the state from interfering with individuals, the United States government takes a role to ensure the freedom of every citizen. From this standpoint, freedom is not merely self-indulgence or being selfish. In financial terms, it is true that the spending on welfare initiatives is small in the United States; the country might not qualify as a welfare state. The United States also often takes a stance to minimize regulations on economic activities. However, as pointed out by Shogo Takegawa, the United States is characterized by its extreme sensitivity to equal opportunity and numerous regulations that strictly prohibit discrimination against demographics, such as race, gender, age, and people with disabilities (Takegawa, 2007: 42).

Establishing regulations may cost less than offsetting manifested disparities through redistribution. However, the laws and regulations for equal opportunity are not necessarily inadequate in Northern European countries with a big government. Rather, thes differences in stance indicate the differences in philosophies on freedom and equality among countries (or societies). Although it depends on the definition of a welfare state, saying that the United States is not a welfare state by only looking at its financial output could be a hasty conclusion. While a regulatory welfare state and a welfare state with generous benefits are not necessarily in a trade-off relationship, issues in Japan are clearer when we explore Japan's standpoint through an international comparative view.

The idea of public management where a modern state governs and understands all citizens—i.e., the idea to try to prevent problems and diseases, such as the concept of public health and public education—emerged in Europe and later came to the United States. However, Americans have been very cautious of state control since gaining independence; freedom has been highly celebrated.[7] It was not until around the mid-19th century when public education was established as a system. Horace Mann, who played a central role in the common school movement in America and became the education secretary in Massachusetts, believed that humans intrinsically had a moral conscience, and education systems should be developed to help children exhibit such conscience. He reasoned that it was necessary to finish forming their personality before children become adults because adult minds are considered "iron molds" and lack flexibility (Tanaka, 2005: 194–213).

Being successful in American society is linked to an economic advancement. As many Americans work at companies and public institutions, instead of profiting from personally managed stores and farms, an economic advancement (obtaining profit through work) does not always result directly and immediately in personal happiness. Being successful on the job means helping the company's profit increase and moving up the social hierarchy of the company. However, devoting oneself to work for this purpose does not always coincide with the goal of spending time and developing a good relationship with one's family.

Meanwhile, the characteristics of individualism include maintaining one's difference from other people and isolating oneself from family and friends. While individuals might be able to create a small society according to their own tastes, this behavior tends to make them indifferent to outer society. In this way, individuals are trapped in their own minds. Such a contradiction exists between the personal pursuit of economic interests and individualism. According to Robert N. Bellah and others, participation in religion and voluntary democratic activities amends the contradiction between the two. Moreover, those organizations and activities move against the tendency of the centralized government to tighten its regulative and administrative controls (Bellah et al., 1985, trans. 1991: 26–45).

In the United States, a conflict between establishment and populism over visions for the public good emerged during the period between the 1880s and the First World War. The establishment was associated with the elite group, which built a network by providing funds to private institutions, such as universities, hospitals, and museums. Meanwhile, populism stressed an egalitarian ethos. According to the populism of Thomas Jefferson, America's third president, citizens have the wisdom to decide on their own. Both sides, however, recognize that the industrial as well as enterprise economy community needed to be included in public morals and order. Progressivism, a political reform movement in the early 20th century, attempted to build a community by borrowing visions from both sides. This movement thought that government intervention was necessary for public interest because market fundamentalism, which would widen the disparity and divide public society further, could not be trusted. As such, people expected the government to improve the healthcare and education sectors as well as regulate large corporations for public interest. They emphasized rationality and science to advocate for public management, such as social engineering that will promote a more efficient national society.

Subsequently, visions such as new capitalism and welfare-state liberalism emerged from the enterprise economy, which collapsed owing to the Great Depression. Under new capitalism, which Reagan later emphasized, the government's purpose is to protect peace and security necessary for people to engage in economic activities for their own and their family's benefit. Welfare-state liberalism, a movement rooted in Franklin Delano Roosevelt's New Deal policies that allowed government intervention in the market, considers sharing the benefit of economic growth as a public good. This means that the government must promote economic growth and ensure a fair opportunity for people to reap its benefits. Both welfare-state liberalism and new capitalism believe that the government exists so that individuals could pursue their personal agenda. Welfare-state liberalism, however, lost its credibility owing to the recession during the 1970s. Low-cost new capitalism was preferred as there was not much difference between how both viewed the role of government.

New ideas such as government-managed society and economic democracy emerged as a response to the recession. Both ideas criticized new capitalism and welfare-state liberalism, saying that these represent the interests of specific groups. New capitalism focused on increasing the safety of individuals and distributing economic growth to bring social harmony among various unequal populations. This could be achieved when people in various sectors collaborate while the government's administrative agencies engage in management based on technology and expertise. Once the mechanism starts to work and generates benefits for the wider population, it is highly likely to result in an ironic ending by retrogressing against social harmony because people often assume an even more personal attitude. As capitalistic activities (excluding the process until obtaining benefits) are for one's self and family, people are prone to think that the benefit they obtain is attributed to their own achievement and performance. Meanwhile, welfare-state liberalism emphasizes the empowerment and enabling of citizens to participate in new systems while questioning the government-managed style in the context of bureaucracy restricting freedom. Nevertheless, both new ideas ended up relying on experts because the important question of whether the people have proper management skills remains; in terms of being expert-dependent, both are similar (Bellah et al., 1985, trans. 1991: 310–327).

Americans are fundamentally skeptic toward the government's power because of historical events since the country's independence. Therefore, it was rare for them to grant public authority or objectives to the government. For example, the introduction of Medicare, a publicly funded health insurance for the elderly and disabled, saved many people. However, the federal government was faced with the need to reevaluate its priorities as regards healthcare facilities as well as implement various adjustments because taxpayers criticized the abuse of the system. This is among the reasons the United States federal government collects various data. The government is supposed to make a new decision based on data; however, when there is no common moral foundation on which people base their decisions, it becomes difficult to only hold a public debate over such matters as what is the objective of such a system, who pays for it, and what parts should be regulated (Bellah et al., 1991, trans. 2000: 24–26).

Looking back on the history of how such individual freedom and the nature of the public are balanced, we can see that individual demand is especially growing in recent years. This growth shakes the viability of the common foundation in society. James Coleman summarized and identified four elements of the equality of educational opportunity, a concept that has been shared by Americans for a long time. The first element indicates that anyone can receive an appropriate education to enter the labor market at no cost. The second posits that anyone can take classes under the same curriculum regardless of social background. Third, individuals with different backgrounds learn in the same location at the same time. Lastly, as long as public education is paid from the taxes, the same education is to be made available in the given area (Coleman, 1968).

As mentioned earlier, there is a strong trend that educational policies and reforms are based on the market-oriented principle. These policies and reforms try to restore confidence and improve public schools to fulfill fundamental individual demands. Despite respecting the free choices of individuals, it prompts a question of why such schools must be paid using public funds. The principle of public education includes important objectives such as forming the foundation for a common community. This particular objective, however, does not fit into the economic aspect of utilizing education in the labor market. This is related to the third and fourth elements of Coleman's definition. Thus, schooling (especially basic education) needs to be provided publicly and operated using public funds. Education is one of the few services in the United States that people consider should be provided for free (operated using public funds). It can also be interpreted that this reasoning is valued all the more because American society is composed of people with various backgrounds. Introducing excessive market principles would naturally lead to considerable disparities and, as a result, could create social divide. I have mentioned earlier that it is impossible to achieve simultaneously and adequately the three objectives of education listed by Labaree (democratic equality, social efficiency, and social mobility). Ultimately, the only way is to find the balance among the three while maintaining the premise that we are all standing on a common social foundation; promoting one thing could distort the way education should be.

(4) School Systems and the Societal Role of Education

The establishment of educational institutions has become an essential requirement for the modern state. Schools under a state are the mechanism and institution for instilling common knowledge, skills, and morals, among others, to its members. At schools, people socialize as citizens of the state through a common language for the purpose of promoting social control (Mori, 1993; Takegawa, 2007: 225–226).

In Europe, connecting people beyond the social class system and forming a society took time even while it was possible to unite social classes and professional groups based on similar interests through the school institutions that had been developed early on. The main purpose of education at the time was to communicate religious doctrine, but school was not the only means for education.[8] The first compulsory education system was established in Prussia in 1717; according to Ikuo Amano, it was strictly for the purpose of developing loyal subjects to the state and king, and it was separate from the secondary education for training elites. Separating primary from secondary education in this way was similar with the case in France (Amano, 2006: 94–97).[9] The idea that one can gain knowledge through education and use this to obtain higher status and economic benefits did not appear in these circumstances.

The United States, meanwhile, was different from Europe in that the former started by building a single-track education system available to all. This was because educational institutions from primary and secondary to higher education, which were not directly linked to the social class system, was already established under the philosophy of economic success (Kariya, 2004: 62–69).

Takehiko Kariya examined the educational ideology of Lester Frank Ward, one of the founders of American sociology. Kariya identified an indication for the view "there is no relationship between specific social categories (race, gender, etc.) and genetic abilities," an idea widely shared in today's education community. At the time, the opposite view that race, gender, and class were genetically related to intellectual ability was dominant. Today, such a view is seen as discrimination. According to Kariya, Ward denied the differences in ability by social category and adopted the environment theory: differences in ability by individual exist, but the ultimate difference in intellectual ability is overwhelmingly affected by the environment.

Ward believed that the apparent difference in intelligence by class, race, and gender is due to the difference in the environment in which people are placed, rather than a difference in genetic ability; thus, educational intervention is not useless (Kariya, 2004: 132–144). To guarantee the freedom of choice allowing individuals to become anything they want, common education, rather than a profession-specific apprenticeship, must be provided for as long as possible. Education also helps individuals consider and discover their identity. Education in America evolved through a repeated trial and error in an attempt to achieve the values of freedom and equality, which at time come in conflict (Kariya, 2004: 340–348).

Although the difference is gradually fading in recent years, school education systems in Europe and the United States differed previously. A multi-track school system fully corresponds to the structure of external social hierarchy by branching off to multiple courses at the early stage upon admission so that the range of schools one can advance to is determined based on one's course. However, in modern times, education cannot be divided into courses at the primary school stage where common education is provided. A relatively common system is the branched type where the schools for advancing to college are clearly separated from those for obtaining employment; this separation occurs at the secondary education stage, which comes after the compulsory education. Germany and pre-WWII Japan are examples of countries that applied the branched school system. The United Kingdom had previously used this type of system as well. Meanwhile, a single-track school system allows individuals to advance to a higher level regardless of schooling stage as long as they want to advance and then pass the exam. This type of system is applied in the United States and post-WWII Japan.

Ralph H. Turner noted that the range in which competition and social mobilization can occur is extremely limited under the multi-track and branched types because the competition takes place within particular classes or among those who advance to higher education as a matter of course. Turner called such mobilization patterns "sponsored mobility." In contrast, in "contest mobility" under the single-track type, competition is always open to all classes, and it is easy for competition and social mobilization to penetrate throughout society, including its adverse effects (Turner, 1960). Such differences in education systems reflect historical backgrounds; people's views on school education and expectation on the function of school education are also based on such historical backgrounds.

3. Reconsidering the Social Function of Education

(1) Equalization and Human Resource Allocation

Education was once regarded as the symbol of hope among people. This is because obtaining education was a means to rise in a society when the entire society was poor. In fact, this is still true in poor societies in developing countries. Many private organizations are providing a variety of aid to help build schools and spread school education. However, such knowledge was reexamined in a society where school education became ubiquitous. In the modern era, going to school has become mandatory instead of a choice. Managing a school attended only by those who want to attend is relatively easy. As students consist of individuals who are highly motivated to learn to begin with, it is not necessary to question the rationale for learning. Students' strong desire to learn even overpowers the teachers' shortcomings. However, as Teruyuki Hirota stated, school education in post-modernization has become a tool for forcing all children to learn whether they like it or not. Therefore, it became necessary to design teaching techniques that will rouse interest and motivation among unmotivated students. The tendency to consider popularized school education as commonplace in today's educational settings presents us with extremely difficult tasks. The emerging educational issues are not necessarily simple, such as the deteriorated leadership of teachers (Hirota, 2009: 96–98). Leaving these issues unaddressed will cause people to lose confidence in school education.

Paradoxically, school education is a mechanism not only for equalization but also for differentiation from others. Those who perceive education in a utopian way tend to ignore this differentiation function. Through education, people can increase their income or obtain a higher position from the advantage of receiving better education or graduating from a more prestigious school. Without this aspect, people would have never realized the importance of the role and function of education. In the field of pedagogy, we are used to discussions that critically view how school education facilitated the choices of whether to pursue higher education and what occupation to pursue. However, school education would not have become popular if education did not have such a function (Hirota, 2004: 12–14). Moreover, if education did not have the sorting function that allocates people to various occupations when modern society evolved to a society of division of labor, then school education in society would have no reason to exist (Kondo, 2001a). The criticism on the sorting function of school education was strong that it restrained, if not creating a taboo, the questions on the relationship between education and occupation in Japan. As a result of this criticism, schools stopped actively pursuing vocational education, and the perception that knowledge taught in school education is useless widely spread.

People's attitude to disparities and class structure as well as awareness of the problems would certainly differ between a society with many poor people who struggle to put food on the table each day and a society where people lead a moderately comfortable life, notwithstanding social disparities. Empirically and statistically, it is not that there are many people who are recreating the occupational class in the true sense (i.e., an individual is taking up exactly the same occupation as his/her parents). Although disparities are much debated, questions such as "why is it important to eliminate disparities?" are being raised but only a few people address it. In the field of social hierarchy research, scholars commonly posit that inequality in education opportunities by social class still remains in Japan. However, many people in Japan believe that the issue of structural inequality and disparity is not accurately understood or even not socially necessary to be resolved. We are faced with the need to examine the cause for such a view as well as the structure and mechanism of people's social perception (Kondo, 2001a).

(2) Japanese People's Sense of Injustice as regards Educational Attainment
According to Hiroyuki Kondo (2001a; 2002), who analyzed the Social Stratification and Social Mobility Survey in 1995 (the SSM Survey)[10] data, many Japanese believe that there is unfairness in Japanese society based on educational attainment. Many people have said it is unfair that "life is largely determined by what kind of school you graduated from." Meanwhile, others find it absurd to think that educational attainment, which is merely one indicator, is overrated and used for determining everything in life. What about opinions such as "educational attainment fairly reflects the person's ability" and "academic performance and educational attainment depend on how much effort the person put in"? Normally, it would make sense to think that determining a person's life based on the school he/she graduated from is unfair because "educational attainment does not reflect [one's] true ability" and "whether the person put effort does not matter." Thus, those who believe that there is unfairness based on educational attainment should more likely oppose the latter two opinions. Yet, the responses to both of these items did not differ whether they thought there was unfairness based on educational attainment: 40% agreed with the former whereas about 60% agreed with the latter.

Kondo found that being unable to continue education owing to the economic environment at home was a common occurrence as the disparity between the rich and the poor in Japan was larger at the time. Therefore, the story about being unable to pursue education even though the person is adept was frequently heard. The perception that "educational attainment does not equal capability" was also widely shared. However, as most people now attend high school and those who do not continue their education after graduating from high school are becoming a minority, cases of being unable to continue education despite personal capability have become exceptions and are unlikely to be perceived to occur universally across societies. As the perception that educational attainment reflects personal capability becomes more common, we need to recognize the possibility that people are gaining a sense of educational attainment-based unfairness from a different angle. A further review of the same SSM Survey data in terms of status and allocation of economic resources showed that highly educated young people are becoming more likely to believe that performance should be emphasized; more than half of university graduates think this way. In the past, highly educated people were more sensitive to social inequality. (They were also more knowledgeable and aware of Japan's social inequality. During those times, it was easy to identify the people who were unable to pursue education because of the clear disparity in wealth.) As such, it would have been difficult for them to conclude that performance should be emphasized. Meanwhile, those who were not highly educated might say "look at the true capability (performance) rather than educational attainment, given the cases [where] people could not pursue education despite having the capability." However, such perception will no longer work once the view that "educational attainment equals performance" becomes dominant. Hence, the number of those who support the emphasis on performance will not increase among the less educated people (Kondo, 2001a; 2002).

The specifics of equal opportunity are not straightforward when fairness of competition is considered. When we say "provide equal opportunities," we tend to imagine doing so in the exact same manner. Although not inherently incorrect, it usually refers to the condition where a system is established to guarantee opportunities for everyone without discriminating based on race, origin, age, and gender. In the case of entrance exams, it would mean that everyone has the right to take without conditions (except for completion of a certain school level). Further, the entrance examination system in Japan has been using a method of administering a simultaneous written test in a fairly uniform and controlled environment (although it has become more diversified). While the entrance exam is a type of competition, extensive considerations have been given to ensure that the conditions of the competition are completely identical.

In reality, however, students have countless differences in their respective backgrounds. These include the differences in the type of home environment one grew up in, educational resources the parents have provided to the child, and quality of education one has received. These differences could work against the students entering the competition. The simultaneous written exam masks these differences in the students' previous environmental conditions while giving a strong impression of equality among exam takers. As a result, the exam's outcome is seen as a reflection of the person's capability and effort. It would not be surprising if the so-called winners in Japan's educational attainment-oriented society overlook their own privileged circumstances and believe that they "win" because of their effort and talent and that those who "lost" are responsible of their own defeat. Hence, winning a competition becomes one's own merit and losing a competition becomes one's own responsibility. This perception might be spreading as people enjoy a seemingly comfortable life. It has become difficult to see the differences in people's lives. This standpoint could also be among the reasons for the indifference of people to debates over disparity in society.

According to Takehiko Kariya (1994; 1995; 2004), "equality" in the context of educational settings in Japan means "equal treatment"; conversely, providing different treatments in an educational setting results in discrimination. Although resistance seems to have faded, especially when classes are held separately according to one's academic ability in the same school or students who are behind in class are chosen for tutoring sessions, people viewed it as "providing special treatments to particular students" or "discrimination because it has been embarrassing to be seen as an incapable child." Arguments such as "entrance examinations should be completely abolished" and "an integrated selection system[11] should be introduced" emerged in the education community in the past to eliminate the difference in treatment as well as the sense of discrimination triggered by such differences. In such a society, equal outcomes refer to the state in which the differences in treatments themselves or the systems that create differences in treatments are eliminated.

In American society where people have diverse backgrounds, equal outcome is achieved when social attributes are taken into consideration and the difference in school enrollment and graduation rates based on social category (e.g., race and gender) is eliminated. Many systems, such as affirmative action,[12] had prompted various debates over the opportunities needed to achieve such equal outcomes. More debates on how these specific measures achieve equal outcomes also emerged.

However, the above standpoint on achieving equal outcomes has not yet reached Japan's general public. As people are concerned with implementing entrance exams under the same conditions, examination estimations or data are unavailable for examining whether students' background and environment are equal. People also tend to focus on shallow discussions such as aiming for a reduction in the competition and consideration of a wide range of personalities as regards entrance examination reform. As such, people perceive equal outcome as "providing standardized education service"; arguments such as "this type of 'equal outcome' violates equal opportunity (i.e., takes away the opportunity from capable students)" thus go unchallenged (Kariya, 2004: 349–354).

(3) Equality Debates and Public Education that Accounts for Individual Potential

Further, if we consider the capability approach conceived by Amartya Sen, we can understand that treating everyone in the same manner in an educational setting does not necessarily signify equality (Miyadera, 2006: 5–7).

Sen's argument can be explained in the following situation. Assuming there is an extremely poor village and we provided home appliances to them as aid. However, electricity is not available in the village or no one can explain how to use these appliances. In such a situation, the aid becomes useless. Therefore, before providing such aid, it is necessary to first make the electricity available and provide education to enable them to explain how the items can become useful. Simply handing them whatever we think is good for them will not immediately provide benefits. Unless we understand the environment and situations of the recipients and provide aid based on such understanding, the benefits would be wasted.

As such, providing a place where anyone can take the exam would not guarantee equal education opportunity. In an extreme example, making arrangements for an identical examination venue for blind people to take the same test as people without disabilities and then saying "we provided an equal place" would be completely irrational and hardly acceptable. Examinations for students with disability are administered by providing appropriate measures (assistance) while still following the standard testing conditions. This scenario would hardly be considered unfair or reverse discrimination.

Nonetheless, providing formal equality could actually lead to discrimination in certain cases. The full meaning of equal education in educational settings in Japan is often not discussed in depth. The way schools in Japan handle children of newcomers (different ethnic groups that newly came to Japan) ended up highlighting the issue of superficial equality in education in Japan. Misako Nukaga compared schools in Japan and the United States, with a focus on the difference in how teachers handle students from ethnic minorities. The resources provided by teachers (school) include physical ones, such educational materials, cultural ones related to the lecture style, and relational ones that relate to students' sense of belonging to the school, motivation, and friendship. In the United States, ethnic minorities often have difficulties with the language and the diversity. At the same time, the pressure to improve academic abilities is increasing in each school in America; students with ethnic minority origins need to show results efficiently within a limited time. Hence, teachers focus first on the physical resources; they interact with the students individually under a limited scope while focusing on providing educational materials suitable to their needs. This practice is partly driven by the curricular and educational reform in the United States in recent years. However, we can presume that it strongly reflects their philosophy on equality, which is providing what is suitable to one's need and personality with respect to individual differences.

In contrast, teachers in Japan pay attention to how those minorities blend into the group of school children. Teachers focus on allocating the relational and cultural resources by arranging a setting for classmates to support the minority student on purpose or mentioning the home country of the minority student, among others. However, the allocation of cultural resources is considered limited as the pace of lessons does not change at all; minority students participate in group activities with natural-born students. Further, the same teaching materials are provided to both minority and other students. This indicates that the teachers would not provide any special treatment noticeable enough to other children because, in Japan, it is of foremost importance not to be left out from the group; relationships among school children are emphasized. Special teaching materials are not provided because the allocation of physical resources would be noticeable as differential treatment. However, while keeping the same physical resources, teachers device various plans to help minority students obtain scores that are not far from those of other students. As Japan's school culture values relationships among children, these types of responses by teachers and schools are not necessarily unreasonable (Nukaga, 2003). This study, hence, poses the question whether affirming (not recognizing) the difference as a difference and insisting that formal equality is truly fair.

Of course, there may be cases in which this formal equality has been successful.

For instance, being thorough on institutional equality resulted in making people psychologically feel that everyone can access higher education. Although entrance exam competitions were often considered negative, they might have increased the overall school enrollment rate in the country and raised the overall education level of Japanese people. In addition, Japan is characterized by a small variance in scores even while international comparisons of academic abilities tend to always look only at average scores. This indicates that there are no (or very few) outliers in both directions. It might be related to the assessment that we lack creativity in the sense that there are only few exceptionally talented individuals. The fact that only a few are exceptionally untalented is directly linked to the confidence that the level of knowledge and skills of the general public has met the standard set by employers; it might be that producing a high-quality labor force has contributed to Japan's post-war economic growth to a certain extent.

This slightly digresses from the issue but is nonetheless worth discussing. Japan's percentage of spending on education relative to its GDP is not necessarily low when the data are limited to primary and secondary education, although it is still generally small. Indeed, the success in focusing on primary and secondary education played a role in Japan's post-war economic development. The return on investment of primary and secondary education is high because, in general, the level of society as a whole likely rises when education becomes well established from the bottom up as well as when secondary education is emphasized over higher education, and so on. Therefore, the policy to allocate more of the limited resource to primary and secondary education is, in fact, valid (Ichikawa, 2000: 11). Emphasis on primary and secondary education could be evidence of the Japanese philosophy that "everyone is to be treated the same" in a broad sense.

There is the possibility that the Japanese education system, which tirelessly pursues equal treatment, affects the public perception of education. For example, the examination system, with which we are obsessed in making uniform and identical to the point of neurosis, tends to attribute success as one's merit and consider failure as one's responsibility. That is, the student is responsible for whatever outcome of the exam given that everyone has taken the exam under the same conditions. When the trend is to recognize even a slightest difference in treatment at school as "discrimination (special treatment)," it is only natural that parents would want to provide their own child the same education as others. In fact, we often hear this statement from parents: "I am doing this for my child because other families are doing it as well." This type of psychological pressure to provide a treatment similar to that given to other children expanded education and created a mass education society in Japan after WWII (Kariya, 1995; 1998). Such circumstances created a moral tone that it is a standard or a parent's obligation to strain themselves to pay for school and allow their children to pursue education. As a result, statistics show that we are in an era where anyone can pursue higher education; therefore, whether one is able to advance to higher education or student performances differ, the individual is responsible for obtaining the best education. In addition, as pursuing higher education is paid using private funds and this makes the person think that "I paid for it on my own," people are led to think that it is appropriate to attribute the merit to the individual. Further, educational choices are also regarded as a private matter and the public meaning becomes less visible under an overall privatization trend.

Many people, hence, understand the social meaning of education only in theory. However, there are not many situations where one sees such social meaning in Japan.

(4) The Meaning of the Government's Involvement in Education

The following discussions are educational administration scholar Isao Kurosaki's summary on the public nature of education as discussed in the field of educational administration and general pedagogy in Japan. Education is not originally a state's monopolistic business; it was widely recognized as citizens' freedom. However, as the educational activities of the organization called the school have an extreme impact on national society, the state and local public organizations are held accountable for school education activities. Schools are also established only by the state, local public organizations, and school corporations. This is the public nature of education in terms of legal interpretation. Meanwhile, the private nature of education is also emphasized with consideration for the historical risk of education being placed under state control for political purposes. Therefore, people begin claiming that they (or their guardians) can determine on their own, with appropriate provision of information, which school to attend. Public and private education do not necessarily conflict each other; rather, the public is responsible for establishing a foundation that will allow the people to accomplish private educational endeavors. Developing such philosophy further leads to the conclusion that "public education is an institutionalization of private matters," as proposed by prominent pedagogy scholar Teruhisa Horio. It is a pole for building a new public nature rather than leaving private matters private. Receiving the type of education that allows people to achieve these private matters would be regarded as a human right.

Although the board of education system modeled after the American one was adopted after WWII, the popular election system, which was the popular control principle of the board of education, was abolished. Subsequently, "reactionary" movements gradually became conspicuous. The field of educational administration in Japan led by Seiya Munakata called themselves "anti-educational administration." This administration was more inclined to the legal interpretation and rights arguments in opposing the unfair intervention in education by the State and the Ministry of Education; its approach blocked substantive analyses. However, "public education as an institutionalization of private matters" has fallen into simplistic dichotomies, such as "democratic education vs. reactionary education" and "education movement vs. education policy." These dichotomies simply indicate that democratic education and education movements are good because they were launched by parents and the people, whereas reactionary education and education policy are bad because they are imposed by the state, the Ministry of Education, and the government. For example, the movement for creating joint nursery facilities as a form of shared custody is an embodiment of the idea of institutionalized private affairs; it is also considered an act of exercising the right to choose an education that is desirable from the parents' perspective. However, when the policymakers proposed it as the introduction of school choice system, people interpreted it arbitrarily; they opposed the idea and regarded it as privatization of education in which people merely consume simple educational services, however similar the idea was with the joint nursery creation movement in which parents could choose their own child's education (Kurosaki, 1999).

Such an argument works on the assumption that there is a certain public entity other than the state authority and that education is realized when the entity becomes independent of the state (Miyadera, 2006: 192–194). However, questions arise on the nature of the public entity that rises above the state and the process by which a certain entity other than the state and government could possibly collect resources from people to operate schools. In theory, however, volunteers could gather and establish a school, but the operating income of such schools must rely on tuition. In such a case, these entities would have to increase tuition drastically to collect the amount of money required for labor and school operation. Hence, people's opportunity to go to school depends on their ability to pay. As sending all children to school is a matter of principle in a civilized society, it is not realistic to collect huge tuition from individuals (especially with respect to variety in individual backgrounds). At the core of the issue is whether it is logical to share the burden only among beneficiaries or among members of society in general, given that the overall running cost will be the same as long as school education exists. If it is unreasonable to share the burden only among beneficiaries, the only way to operate is to use funds such as taxes. When this happens, no agency other than the state (government) seems capable of systematically collecting taxes and reallocating funds.

Further, there is no guarantee that a school the citizens themselves create would become valuable to society. Those involved in such a school-launching movement are often people from a higher social class enjoying social privileges. While it might meet their interests, there is no guarantee that it will result in creating a school that upholds the common public interest. The school management must be centered on a group of guardians who take charge. This type of civil movements that criticize schools should not assume "strong children" of "strong citizens" (Hirota, 2004: 37).

In Japan, people are sensitive to the issue of state control over education because of circumstances in pre-WWII education. It seems futile to look at the state and the government as the enemy as if the leaders live completely isolated from the general public and operate the country with completely different values from those of the general public.[13] The debate over education spending also seems to claim that the government, which is considered separate from public existence, should assume more of the burden. However, the source of funds for public education is tax paid by the people; how the fund is spent is determined completely independently of the people's needs. Although this is not limited to education spending, people have a strong inclination to think that financial affairs are somebody else's problem despite advocating democracy. I will reevaluate this issue in

Part II.

In addition, the center of the debate over Japan's current education spending revolves around higher education with expensive tuition. When the higher education enrollment rate is low, those who completed higher education are more highly valued in the labor market, as graduating from higher education has a high social value. Thus, they are more likely to receive preferential treatment in terms of wages than those who did not complete a higher education. Further, as the opportunity to pursue higher education itself varies by social hierarchy, individuals from a higher social class have an advantage over others. Therefore, directing public funds toward higher education and making school expenses a public burden can be interpreted as moving the tax money collected from those who do not (cannot) advance to higher education to those in a higher social class (see Wilensky, 1975, trans. 1984: 77). This means that a policy that is completely the opposite of correcting disparities and redistributing income is implemented. However, this does not imply that we do not need to do anything; rather, we study how we can expand the opportunities among those in the lower social class to advance to higher education.[14]

Once the school enrollment rate increases and pursuing higher education becomes common, the disadvantage rather the advantage of not pursuing higher education becomes noticeable. Nevertheless, as it still does change the fact that there are disparities in opportunities to advance to higher education based on social class, certain assistance to ensure sufficient opportunities will be necessary.

Moreover, higher education institutions such as universities are generally positioned not only as educational institutions but also as research institutions; the results of this research development will be returned to society. As economies become borderless and globalized, the return on investment to society are not limited to economic and monetary ones. As higher education institutions are exposed to the pressure of competition, government support, among others, becomes necessary for them to be able to compete. Producing Japanese researchers who might be chosen for international academic awards, such as the Nobel Prize, or athletes who might win a medal in the Olympics do not generate monetary/economic benefits for the general public, but it is also not easy to measure their impact on society. However, it would certainly give pride to the people living in that society.

Moreover, society could "produce people who achieve success to become a driving force to attract talented people and, if such a cycle of attracting human resources becomes successful, the overall level will further increase." This is called "externalities in higher education." Although the concept of externality can be understood, it is not easy to measure its actual degree of impact. If public aid is provided despite insubstantial benefit, it will be considered an excessive investment. There are those who question externalities by saying the number of universities is increasing in recent years (Yano, 1996: 92). I will touch on this in Chapter 4. In the present discussion, opinions that support public spending on higher education are not necessarily strong in Japan compared with other countries. The perception of the general public regarding higher education policies is unsympathetic; higher education is regarded as a personal choice that benefits only the individual.

Although I highlighted education and employment (labor) here, on-the-job training (in-house training) may be sufficient education for the purpose of obtaining employment. In fact, the true meaning of public education may be to study liberal arts and general subjects that are not directly linked to jobs (Jinno, 2007). As this type of knowledge cannot be applied immediately, it tends to be considered useless. There are also limited circumstances where one can make use of this knowledge (there may be many individuals who cannot recognize it). However, human life does not consist only of work and economic activities. Subjects such as literature, art, history, and natural science may not produce outcomes immediately. However, people's lives have humanness because of these types of activities. In fact, many people must have experienced instances where they felt like engaging in a cultural activity and picked up a new book even though it is not directly connected to their work; they might even had an "aha" moment. The government's role becomes meaningful because these moments are not generated by simple economic activities (market mechanism). It might be bold to say that the meaning of public education, in truth, lies in providing elements that do not become useful immediately.

As such, a debate on the correct amount of public funds that must be allocated on education is imperative given that people's lives today are not always easy. Resources do not automatically materialize by themselves. As we move forward, it is important to obtain a consensus that we need to share the burden and continue providing public education rather than merely criticizing the government. Japan is currently faced with a financial crisis, and there are also strong demands to expand the social security budget as the aging population further grows. The challenge is to find a basis to overcome those constraints to be able to expand public spending on education as well as ways to convince the general voters and taxpayers (Ichikawa, 2000: 70–72).

NOTES

[1] All based on the *Basic School Survey* by the Ministry of Education, Culture, Sports, Science and Technology.

[2] In sociology, there are certain pieces of literature that can be considered as classics on the changes in the methods of such organizations and groups. *Gemeinschaft and Gesellschaft* by Ferdinand Tönnies is particularly famous (Tönnies, 1887, trans. 1957). It examined how human will can be classified into spontaneous "essential will" and calculative, profit-seeking "arbitrary will"; he also examined how society (community) shifts gradually from one ruled by the former (which he called *gemeinschaft*) to that ruled by the latter (which he called *gesellschaft*).

[3] *Education and Sociology*, translated into Japanese by Sasaki, uses the term "systematic socialization" instead of "methodical socialization."

[4] It was because he had such a sense of purpose that Dewey emphasized allowing children to learn by socially associating what they are doing. However, as mentioned in Chapter 19 of *Democracy and Education: An introduction to the philosophy of education*, it

was not that Dewey followed the simple dichotomy of "professionally useful knowledge (utility)" vs. "knowledge merely for enjoyment (culture)" and valued only the former. We need to pay attention to the warning that such a dichotomy leads to a half-hearted compromise in curricula and that utility and culture cannot be easily separated; further, there are concepts that do not necessarily contradict one another (Dewey, 1916, trans. 1975: Vol. 2, 98–104).

5   The history of communities in the United States is short because the history of Europe where they came from had been cut off. Individuals who were completely unrelated gathered and built communities from scratch. Therefore, they had a sense that they were voluntarily participating in the communal society in one form or another and shared the pride of creating prosperity with their own hands. In this way, the community's prosperity became the individual's prosperity and the community's fate became the individual's fate. This is the foundation of patriotism formed in the United States. Tocqueville explained this by comparing the scenario to his home country of France in the context of personal and national interests, which appeared to be in conflict, to foment unity that would produce patriotism (Tocqueville, 1888, trans. 1987: Vol. 2, 138–143).

6   Based on the reasoning that it is merely coincidence that a person is born with a particular talent under a given environment and conditions, John Rawls argued the principle of disparities that individuals would ultimately make a choice to maximize the benefit for people who are the most disadvantaged if they are surrounded by the "veil of ignorance" (the state in which they have no idea into which environment they were born). Rawls is often cited by leftists. His take on this issue is the reason he is called a liberalist.

7   We can surmise that behind the birth of the idea of free education by Jefferson was an urgent situation for trying to resolve the social situation in America at the time (Tanaka, 2005: 160).

8   "School education spread gradually in some rural villages where people realized the importance of practical knowledge" in France during the second half of the 18th century. However, the French revolutionary government was not keen on organizing primary education to impart knowledge to the common people. The authorities were instead interested in elite education to carry forward the republic and became committed to secondary and professional education. Although France is similar to America in terms of adherence to "freedom" and "equality," both countries applied different approaches during the early days of the education system (Amano, 2007).

9   The case of the United Kingdom is examined in Chapter 2.

10 *The Social Stratification and Social Mobility Survey* has been conducted by sociologists in Japan once every ten years on years ending in five since 1955. It is referred to as the SSM Survey, from the initial letters of "social stratification" and "social mobility." It is one of the few national surveys of Japan that are known internationally.

11 This is among the high school entrance examination systems used by a number of local governments. It was introduced to reduce the entrance exam competition for entering certain schools for preparation to university. Under the normal entrance examination system, students would directly apply to the school and take the test. Under the integrated selection system (although with variations), students take a test for a group

of schools. In such a case, multiple schools belong to one school group. The number of applicants who will fill the total quota of a high school in a given school group would pass the exam. Entities such as the board of education would randomly determine (in a way that it will not result in different levels of academic ability) which high school the applicants would actually attend. In this way, the apparent gap in academic ability is "corrected."

[12] Affirmative action has evolved while being torn on how to views the two issues of equality and minority's disadvantages. The views can be divided into traditional and proactive non-discrimination. In the former, exactly similar treatment is provided regardless of a person's personal attributes. The latter believes that equalizing only the formality will merely preserve the disadvantages created by previous discrimination because the disadvantages certainly occurred as a result of intentional treatment, given that minorities have historically been subjected to a variety of discrimination types. Thus, that affirmative action should first provide preferential treatment to fill the gap that has been created artificially (Pedriana, 1999).

[13] There is an old concept called "the iron law of oligarchy" that is well-known in sociology. Proposed by Robert Michels, it says that once a group of people enter the position of authority, they have no choice but to rule for a few individuals even if they originally advocated a democratic agenda. This, in turn, eventually creates a gap in perceptions between them and the general members, and then results in an opposing relationship. A democratically created organization is initially operated partly because the philosophy is shared; however, leaders inevitably become bureaucratic once the organization expands and likely to forget their original philosophy over time. This perception is based on the premise of a scheme of power politics.

[14] On the basis of the perspective on effectively using limited resources, public funds cannot be directed inexhaustibly to higher education even for the purpose of equalizing opportunities. This raises the question of how opportunity to pursue higher education is increased (i.e., how much increase in school enrollment rate will be made) when public funds are used. According to Yano's estimate (1996: 93), the tuition must be reduced by 42,000 JPY to raise the application rate by 1% and, as the increase in school enrollment rate is only 6.1% even if the tuition is eliminated, it is problematic in terms of cost-effectiveness.

CHAPTER 2
The State/Government and Education

1. Education from the Perspective of the Government

(1) The Role of the Government in Education from the Perspective of Economics
The norm that "the government (the state and local government) must take on the responsibility of public education" is not obvious in theory. People are beginning to recognize the value of the public nature not only in education but also in areas such as welfare. Under the present situation, private organizations are getting involved in both school education, which was started as a national project, and various welfare and social security services. As mentioned in Chapter 1, the movement to reevaluate the public nature under such circumstances seems to assume the existence of public spheres that are not intervened in by the state. The sense of resistance and caution against the state authority's intervention in education is particularly strong. Therefore, the view that "educational undertakings should be implemented in a form that is independent of the state" is generally dominant, actually making "public education" a concept that is opposed to national education (Miyadera, 2006: 192–194).

Nevertheless, this book will not deal with the contents of education, i.e., "what the state (government) teaches," which tends to draw attention when the relationship between education and the state is discussed. It will simply look at the role of the government by focusing on its financial concerns. In public economics, the role and function of the government are always discussed first.

Richard Musgrave, a well-known financial scholar, divides the government's budget policy targets into three categories: (1) adjustment of resource allocation, (2) distribution of income and wealth, and (3) stabilization of the economy (Musgrave, 1959, trans. 1961: 6–40). First, allocation is the function of purchasing goods and services that are socially necessary but not produced in the market, as well as providing them to the public. For example, the government would cover the cost of school education and then provide that service to the public (children), since school education is not something that readily results in monetary benefits. Distribution is a matter of how to divide the collected goods among the people again. In other words, the government collects wealth in small increments in the form of taxes and then redistributes it to the disadvantaged, such as the elderly, people with disabilities, and the unemployed who no longer have an income. This is a so-called income redistribution policy. Stabilization is an attempt to suppress price fluctuations and maintain full employment as much as possible.

Discussions on public economics are primarily related to (1) and (2); however, there is the further matter of handling market failure as a particularly important government function. According to Joseph E. Stiglitz, market failures can be divided into the following six types (Stiglitz, 2000, trans. 2003: 95–106).

The first is the failure of competition. Goods and services are efficiently traded in the market and at the optimal price because there is competition. "Full competition" refers to the state in which there is fierce competition among companies to produce the goods and services preferred by consumers; however, when there is only one company (monopoly) or only a few companies (oligopoly), they can manipulate the price as they like, and consumers lose the ability to trade at the optimal (the lowest) price because there is no price competition.

The second is the presence of public goods, which are goods and services that are socially necessary but not supplied in the market, or else they in extremely short supply when they are, in fact, supplied. Furthermore, although the cost of producing normally traded goods and services incrementally increases with the number of beneficiaries, this does not apply to public goods. Conversely, while there are people who will definitely receive benefit from the supplied goods and service, even if some have not paid for any of the cost, they cannot be excluded from usage, even on such basis; in other words, when left to the market mechanism, everyone would become a free rider.

The third is externality. As mentioned in Chapter 1, externalities are roughly divided into positive and negative, with the former considered applicable to education. In effect, although each individual that receives education (i.e., enrolls in school) may be driven by personal desire, we can think of a scenario such as the following: "when individuals with such desire get together and devote themselves to study, the intellectual level and productivity of the entire society improves to facilitate economic development and contributes to the establishment and maintenance of democratic systems." In other words, there are effects beyond the transaction between the involved parties. Such costs and benefits not related to the transaction itself are not taken into consideration in the market mechanism. For example, environmental issues are often cited in relation to negative externalities.

The fourth is incomplete markets. Insurance and loans are often mentioned as examples. Goods and services supplied at a cost that is lower than the price individuals are willing to pay should always be available in a normal market. However, the market mechanism does not work well in an incomplete market because the suppliers of goods and services, as well as the consumers wanting these goods and services, have information that is too biased or inadequate. In the case of insurance, insurance companies would want to determine the premium by estimating the risk; however, the premium would become too expensive and no one would purchase the insurance if the risk were overestimated; on the other hand, if the risk were underestimated, the insurance company would incur a large loss because they would face the actual risk more frequently.

The fifth is the failure of information. The market mechanism works on the assumption that both the supply and demand sides will openly provide accurate information to allow details to be compared.

Finally, the sixth are macroeconomic disturbance factors such as inflation and unemployment.

With respect to the finance of public education, the market failures that are especially important are the second and third issues. However, the fourth issue also comes into play in relation to education expenses.

Considering the functions of public education as mentioned in Chapter 1, only teaching what people want would not be enough to inform a curriculum for school education. Furthermore, although everyone understands the need, it is difficult to maintain a school education system with only those who receive education paying for the cost, because the amount is large. In particular, charging tuition fees for elementary and secondary education which everyone goes through would be at odds with the compulsory system, and it would be almost impossible to effect in reality. In other words, unlike the normal trade of goods, it does not follow that not paying the fee (tuition) would eliminate the student in the case of public education. Creating individuals who did and did not attend school at the elementary and secondary education stage would result in a disparity at an early stage that is beyond the will of the children themselves. It might also promote a social divide, increase the risk of unemployment and insecurity, and ultimately increase social costs. Therefore, basic elementary and secondary education, in particular, has the nature of being a public good provided free of charge.

Furthermore, in order to provide decent education, the quality of educators must be maintained, and in order to do so, a certain level of remuneration for teachers must also be maintained. Because such costs cannot be lowered, the amount would be enormous if the parents sending their children to school were to cover it all. It is not realistic to make the parents bear all of that burden. Moreover, if we did, there is no doubt that the declining birth rate would drop even further because the economic burden imposed on individuals (parents and guardians) would become too heavy. In addition, the social benefit of spreading education throughout society is large since it provides broad and basic knowledge and skills to the people (relating the issue of externality). Another concern is that those who want to receive a higher level of education would need obtain a scholarship or education loan. In the case of loans, in particular, lenders usually assess the borrower's repayment capability. However, it is highly likely that the typical borrowers of education loans stemming from a more difficult family background would have no collateral. In that case, it is improbable based on market logic to loan money to these people. If this is left unaddressed, a higher level of education will become something that only privileged people can receive (raising the issue of an imperfect market). This is why there is room for the government to intervene.

It is true that there is a private education industry, including cram schools and distance learning. Private education has played many roles particularly in higher education in Japan as well. Therefore, there might be doubts as to whether it is really necessary for the government to provide education. However, cram schools and distance learning presuppose the existence of the public school system. As for private schools (which I will also touch on in Part II), the reality is that they are in a difficult situation, as they are expected to operate only by means of tuition revenue. At the same time, tuition is extremely expensive from the perspective of students. The private school subsidy program was created for the purpose of improving such a situation. Considering the above, we can see that completely leaving it up to the market is unlikely to work in the world of education. Hideyuki Takechi positions education, healthcare, welfare, housing, and pensions as quasi-public goods under partially working market mechanisms. He argues that it is necessary for the government to intervene because quasi-public goods may have an inadequate market scale and require the demand level to be increased; otherwise, consumers may not be able to take correct consumption actions in the market (Takechi, 2000).

(2) Introduction of Quasi-Market Reform
Nowadays, a reform that incorporates the market mechanism is often implemented in the education community as well. This has been examined in detail by Hidenori Fujita, who focuses particularly on the trends in the United States (Fujita, 2003). Here, let me introduce a part of the reform based on Fujita's explanation.

The characteristic of school and education reforms in recent years commonly observed not only in Japan but also in the United States and the United Kingdom is based on the premise that promoting competition among schools by emphasizing the freedom of choice, founded on the logic of self-determination and self-responsibility and letting people choose schools freely, will make socially efficient education possible, as well as improving the overall quality of education. However, the operating expenses of schools are paid by public funds in not all but most cases: it is a "quasi-market style" in the sense that it only introduces market mechanisms and is not completely privatized.[1] There are five examples that Fujita discusses as quasi-market reform: school choice system, educational voucher system, alternative schools, charter schools, and schools operated by for-profit companies.

The school choice system virtually eases or eliminates the regulations on the school district system; and the voucher system is a more radical version of the school choice system. Although both presuppose being publically funded, the voucher system differs from the school choice system by the fact that it also includes private schools. The voucher system was advocated by Milton Friedman, who is known for popularizing the argument for neoliberalism. The voucher is a kind of ticket to cover educational expenses. In short, the system works by distributing vouchers to children (or guardians), who freely choose a school and submit their vouchers to it. The schools that collect more vouchers will receive more government subsidies.

Alternative schools aim to attract school children and their guardians by implementing unique educational programs within the framework of the public school, providing a traditional, uniform curriculum and education without being restricted by such uniformness. Some alternative schools are schools called "magnet schools," which were created to draw students—like magnets—from outside the school district by offering a unique curriculum and various advantages through cooperation with universities.

Charter schools are schools established by teachers and volunteer guardians who—also dissatisfied with the existing public schools—get together and sign a contract with the Board of Education (with the authorization granted by the Board of Education referred to as a charter). Although volunteers establish a school based on their own educational philosophy, it is publicly funded. Therefore, there are stipulations such as not to use social attributes and academic achievements as requirements for children to be admitted to the school. The founders are further held accountable for performance, such as improving the children's academic abilities. According to Fujita (2003), moreover, it could be a for-profit company, rather than volunteering teachers and guardians, that signs a contract with the Board of Education.

Though I will not discuss these quasi-market style of reforms any further because that is not the aim of this book, the increase in the type of schools that does not fit into the traditional framework prompts discussions such as the level of educational expenses that should be covered by the government and what its role in education should be. While these reforms that define the role of the government in a limited way are observed frequently, especially in Anglo-Saxon countries such as the United States and the United Kingdom, Japan is also following such a trend.

For example, the renowned economist John Kenneth Galbraith deemed any measure or regulation that prevented or may prevent the American society from providing or producing more of better things to be a society of manufacturing supremacy to be opposed no matter what. Only private manufacturing is considered important under such manufacturing supremacy, which he believed to result in an increase of national welfare and wealth. On the other hand, he considered the existence of public services to be harmful, or at best a necessary evil, because public services provided by the government represented a burden, and private production might stagnate and decrease if this burden became too large. What people needed was food, clothing, shelter, and an orderly environment in which these items could be provided. Most of the food, clothing, and shelter had normally been secured in a voluntary matter, without relying on the power of the government and state. In contrast, since the order provided by the state cost money and, in some cases, took away the means of living from people in the name of keeping the order, or was even used as a means for a person in power to fill their own pockets, the government was inherently untrustworthy. For this reason, economic liberalism in the 19th century considered a state that provided trustworthy order at low cost without requiring anything else to represent the ideal.

However, once food, clothing and shelter became available to some extent, people would begin to seek goods and services of a higher standard to be provided universally. This would include many items that are collectively necessary, such as infrastructure, education, public health, police, and military, which must in any case be provided publicly. This is because they are not economically viable unless publicly provided, and nobody in the private sector would provide them. However, even when the government eventually provides these services, they will get a bad reputation as untrustworthy, incompetent, reckless spenders, intrusive, and as posing a threat to freedom. In this way, the inclination to respect things that are private and look down on things that are public becomes stronger and stronger (Galbraith, 1998, trans. 2006). As a result, those who can afford it will buy services provided by the private sector and those who cannot will have no choice but to rely on what is publicly provided. Once such a flow is created, those who receive public services are perceived negatively, and the differing relationship between the government and its service recipients and that of the private sector and its service recipients becomes even more evident, widening the gulf between the two.

Let us apply this trend to the subject of education. As the entire society becomes more affluent and lifestyles become more personalized, freedom of choice is emphasized. Therefore, the education provided by public schools with tax money becomes too uniform to bear for some people, and the preference for the private sector (i.e., private schooling) that provides a flexible service increases. People who choose the private sector are often financially well-off. Furthermore, since the service level they require is also high and the school needs to respond to that need, this ultimately creates the ranking consciousness that the private sector is better than the public service. Such a chain-reaction actually assigns the meaning of a certain social stigma to choosing a public school (Takegawa, 2007: 110–111).

According to Charles Taylor, the fact that Americans do not try to rely on the government can be attributed back to the movement for American independence. The American Revolution was characterized by the need to realize a republican society in order to fight against the authority of the mainland (i.e., the British) monarch. It aimed for sovereign independence in which public society is gradually pursued by each individual and finally enjoyed equally by every single person. The evangelists of this philosophy, who were gentlemen from the relatively upper classes, thought that the leader should be a fair and disinterested individual who devotes himself to the public good. And so sovereign independence became a reality through high economic growth, the expansion of the domestic market, industrial development, and the pioneering frontier. They are thought to have left their family, broke off with their community, and also cut traditional connections to step out onto the new road of self-reliance. Here, although only the part concerning the breach with traditional ties tends to be highlighted, at the same time, they created a new individualism extolling those who work diligently, behave patiently, and can depend on themselves. This maxim and moral principle gradually built a new order and connections among people.

These people later brought an enormous economic interest, which became the foundation that supported society. Ultimately, it was sought to promote virtue for the entire society rather than dividing it. In other words, the American society is one where individuals who are characterized by being independent, self-disciplined, having an entrepreneurial spirit, and being able to live a self-reliant life in good faith are considered free and worthy of the utmost respect and praise. Such Americans also came to be socially recognized by creating charity businesses while generating wealth and assuming leadership positions (Taylor, 2004, trans. 2011: 212–217). While it might be true that the financial role played by the government is small, such a culture of donation by individuals and corporations who have generated enormous wealth has taken root in the United States. We should highlight a little more of the fact that a certain percentage of finance is supported by private companies, organizations, alumni, etc., at universities in the United States (Tani, 2006: 46–58).

2. Establishment of Modern States and Development of Education Systems

(1) State and Bureaucracy

The state is an organization created by humans. While this may seem obvious, Kan'ichi Fukuda states there was some debate among Japanese people in response to the notion that "Japan had lost the previous war," for example, that "the country remained," and that "as long as there is a national land, Japan has not perished." However, they did perceive this as a denial (or collapse) of the national organization (or national polity) at the time. In fact, it is not self-evident that the state came to be regarded as an organization (Fukuda, 1970: 101–105). The picture of the modern state that we imagine when referring to the "state" may go all the way back to an absolute monarchy in Europe, and its characteristics can be attributed to the installation of bureaucracy and a standing army. Absolutism, a patrimonial state in which the state itself is considered the private property of the monarch, is a society in a certain region conquered by force that has turned into a power structure. So, bureaucracy emerges to deal with how to maintain the finance of this patrimonialism and gains even more power as it becomes a public means of political authority. Then, a standing army is also organized to enforce that authority. However, since authority cannot be exercised well by merely repressing the people one-sidedly, public welfare and people's well-being come to be addressed through the strategic use of religion. That is to say, in terms of the Reformation, there were multiple religions instead of one, and the authority began choosing one. The authority then forced people to believe in a given religion and created a state church system in which the state and religion were tied together. They strengthened absolutism by using religion, since not believing in this would mean that the individual was unpatriotic (Fukuda, 1970: 74–79). In this regard, the first case of building the picture of a modern nation out of an absolute monarchy was the United Kingdom, and its historical development cannot be ignored.

According to Anthony Giddens, a well-known British sociologist, a postmodern nation-state is characterized by the fact that the well-organized administrative power is centralized in an area, referred to as territory, that is based on a clearly defined boundary (or border). Furthermore, since the activities of such a nation-state require necessary information to be collected, initiating the compilation of so-called "official statistics" would also appear to be an important characteristic of the beginning of a modern nation-state (Giddens, 1985, trans. 1999: 55–64, 208–210). It was the *Northcote and Trevelyan Report* in 1854 that first clearly defined the characteristics of civil servants in a modern sense, such as working in a government office, or as people who worked in an administrative organization as government employees. It mainly stated that official positions were divided into senior positions (intellectual, management works) and junior positions (routine, blue-collar works), with candidates hired on the basis of an open competitive examination administered by an independent committee; promotions were merit-based; and staff members were transferred as needed for purposes such as staff placement and the unification of government affairs, etc. (Burnham and Pyper, 2008, trans. 2010: 9–10).[2]

The details on public services found in the *Northcote and Trevelyan Report* agree with the characteristics of bureaucratic organization that Max Weber examined. According to Weber, governance structure in society transitions from traditional domination and charismatic domination to legal domination based on a legal system. The form of domination in modern times is democracy, in which representatives are chosen each time by election rather than a certain influential individual hereditarily passing down the authority. In order to operate such a modern state, bureaucrats with expertise are essential, and functional differentiation based on each expertise in the organization increases. Furthermore, a democratic society means that it must be guaranteed that anyone can get a government position regardless of origin, as long as the individual has the relevant expertise. The diploma, therefore, was used in order to indicate that an individual had the expertise. As it then became a prerequisite to obtain a government job, it turned into economic benefit; and with it, the social prestige of education began increasing (Weber, 1956, trans. 1960: 135–138).[3]

The modern era is the time in which functional differentiation of every social institution and system progresses in this way under a legal authority to drastically complicate such institutions and systems. Weber referred to it as bureaucratization, considering this to be an unavoidable phenomenon in modern society. When we hear "bureaucracy," we generally think negatively, such as this representing "an inflexible organization with a silo mentality." However, the term here is used neutrally, merely to indicate the characteristic of an organization.[4] The management of the modern state is made orderly, and the scope and duties of the authority are also stipulated by the law (or rules). And such a bureaucratic organization rules not only the government offices but also the private economy, fully developing under the modern state and capitalist society. In other words, the characteristics of a bureaucratic organization can be summed up by the presence of the authority based on rules, hierarchical government positions and a promotion system, red-tapism, the principle of separation of public and private, and the specialization of duties, etc. (Weber, 1956, trans. 1960: 60–62). The advancement of specialization and division of labor makes it necessary to complete a well-defined curriculum and obtain professional qualifications, which become a prerequisite.

In a society that has become complex, it is impossible for one individual to be well-versed in all policies or to formulate and implement a policy from scratch, no matter how competent he/she is. This is why those at the top create appropriate departments, have professionals to prepare a draft plan, and then oversee those plans. Doing so also clarifies the scope of roles of each department and makes it easier to define the required competencies for individuals to work there. It allows one to identify the field one should study in preparation of assuming a particular position and also makes it easier to develop human resources. Therefore, personal aptitude must be evaluated or education must be provided to train individuals who are suitable for a particular position. A modern society with bureaucratic organizations will always require qualification systems and develop examinations to judge the qualification as well as school systems to provide the preparatory education. And the school system itself will also gain characteristics as a bureaucratic organization.

(2) Bureaucratization of the Education System

While examining the establishment of a school system in Boston, Michael B. Katz, who specializes in American education history, summarized the characteristics of school bureaucracy in terms of the following six points. The first is the centralization of control and supervision, which refers to the control by an education agency, such as the so-called Board of Education, and the central government agency. The second is the differentiation of function. The differentiation of duties, the department system, the differentiation of specialized subjects, and the birth of a grade system fall under this category. Furthermore, a hierarchical structure (involving differentiation of job titles) emerges within the school organization, and the disparity of salary also increases along with it. The third is the requirement of qualifications for the job. This refers to appointment and promotion based on objective eligibility requirements, which means that examinations are administered based on standards developed in advance and managed professionally, and whether to hire an individual is determined on such basis. The fourth is objectivity and expertise pertaining to how professional government officials begin undertaking reforms and making administrative decisions, so that arbitrary decisions by amateurs such as individuals who are merely influential in the local community will no longer go unchallenged. The fifth is accuracy and consistency. Duties used to be executed at a whim; however, statistical data began to be collected as a required reference for standardizing duties, so that administrative decisions came to be made based on the data, and decision-making that put to use a consistent procedure became possible. The sixth is cautiousness. Personal information is protected in a way that when the work behavior of people employed by the organization (in this case the school) is evaluated, the evaluation results can be accessed only by some of the top executives, for example. At the same time, this led those in power such as managers to further strengthen their authority to manage and appropriately place their subordinates (Katz, 1975, trans. 1989: 118–131).

It was probably England that first systematically developed an education system. Thus, let us briefly review the process in which the education system in

England was developed by the state. According to Tomiji Nagao, although there were signs that they were aiming to establish a school with public funds in England during the period of the Puritan Revolution, the Clarendon Code (1661–1665) passed after the Restoration of Imperial Rule expelled nonconformists from public offices and prompted the Puritans to spread to the New World as well as in the business community (rather than in the political community). When the control over nonconformists slightly loosened after the Glorious Revolution, they eventually developed private schools called the Academy. However, it seems that England preserved the existing education system and left it to natural selection rather than rapidly developing a national system, because the country subsequently stabilized its political system and succeeded in colonializing a vast land. Schools aiming to provide religious education to the lower classes must have emerged under such circumstances, and the need for the 3Rs (reading, writing, and arithmetic) among these people gradually came to be recognized (Nagao, 1978: 74–81).

While pinpointing the establishment of a public education system in the Kingdom of England is an issue that also relates to how this should be defined, there are several interpretations. Although it is generally attributed to the Elementary Education Act of 1870, it was not the case that this Act was swiftly implemented; various processes had existed in prior phases. For example, while he acknowledges a certain rationality in the interpretation that attributes the origin of the public education system to the Act of 1870, Ichimaro Matsui claims that it is not necessarily appropriate because there were already many education-related laws enacted by the state prior to 1870 (Matsui, 2008). In addition, Haruo Yanagi positions the year 1833, when the Treasury of the Kingdom of England began subsidizing school construction expenses, as the beginning of state intervention in education (Yanagi, 2005: 67).

Once the Industrial Revolution took place and a massive labor force became necessary during the period between the end of the 18th century and the beginning of the 19th century, the idea that it was dangerous to teach sophisticated knowledge and skills to people in the lower classes, who would become wage workers in the future, emerged. Therefore, the ruled were required to further improve their work ethics and respect the rules and orders while the state tried to promote education for the purpose of maintaining security. This is how it all started.

However, basic education for the working class had been provided mainly at private schools backed by religious organizations. The state became involved through the Parochial Schools Bill of 1807[5] and began providing state subsidies in 1833. According to Haruo Yanagi, this can be regarded as the state making good use of the organized schools that had been expanded nationwide by two private religious organizations called the National Society and the British and Foreign School Society, which had developed the so-called monitorial system. The monitorial system, which is a teaching method that happened to be developed by two completely different private organizations at around the same time, can broadly be considered the prototype of the simultaneous teaching method found in today's classrooms or lessons in school education. When there are many students and few teachers, how does one efficiently teach simultaneously? Teaching assistants are chosen from among the competent students to aid the teacher. While many students gather in a large room to perform tasks according to the teacher's instruction, teaching assistants communicate that instruction and monitor the students while they perform the task.

While the individuals who devised this system were Andrew Bell and Joseph Lancaster, their supporters created organizations called the National Society and the British and Foreign School Society, respectively, in order to popularize this type of school system.[6] The schools they invented were a novelty and could not be created without affiliating with these organizations. Seeking to popularize schools by using these private organizations, the British government made it possible to apply to construct a school by becoming affiliated with one of the two societies and also paid the subsidy (half of the construction costs) through these private organizations (Yanagi, 2005: 66–68).

Upon the realization of this subsidy commitment system, they attempted to establish a central, national agency to control the education system, placing an education committee under the Privy Council and a secretariat under the Committee in 1839. The first secretary of the Committee, James P. Kay-Shuttleworth, was called the "father of British public education."

However, Naoko Ota positions the slightly later Revised Code of 1862 as the introduction of modern public education. Ota reasons that, even though one might call it the beginning of state intervention, the education system prior to that had been limited to the subsidy system, based on religious education rather than secular education, and mainly aimed to give the working class religious and moral indoctrination. She focuses on the fact that this Revised Code introduced by Robert Lowe established a pay-for-performance system to check school performance based on the 3Rs, allocating the subsidy based on the results. This implies that the foundation for basic education as a nation shifted from religious education to secular education that included the 3Rs. Lowe was a believer of Adam Smith, who disapproved of making teachers government employees in *An Inquiry into the Nature and Causes of the Wealth of Nations*. Therefore, although teachers had been paid their salaries directly by the state, this was changed by the reform so that teachers established an employment relationship with the school administrator. Nevertheless, this did not diminish the nature of public education. Rather, the important point is that this clearly laid out a system of pay based on students' performance rooted in secular education, organized a systematic teacher training system and a school inspector system that was based on it, and gradually strengthened state control from the top (Ota, 1992: 30–33, 73–75).

Meanwhile, education movements by workers themselves aiming for personal development and liberation also appeared due to the effect of the so-called Chartist movement. It was here that the idea of education being guaranteed by public funding saw the light for the first time. Because the demand for knowledge of science also spread widely due to the Industrial Revolution, mechanics' institutes were established as well.[7] The compulsion of basic education coincided with the expansion of democracy. In particular, it became a key point that the right to vote expanded to include many workers after the home ownership restriction had been abolished by the Representation of the People Act 1867 (the Second Reform Act). Lowe thought that the state should mandate and provide basic education rather than leaving it to the parents' initiative, because he believed the voter should receive education to become someone who could make his own decisions. And so a debate unfolded as to how to build a nationwide education system based on the Revised Code, and because the Liberal Party took the power in 1868, the Elementary Education Act 1870 was enacted, which later became recognized as the foundation for the development of British public education (Ota, 1992: 84–87).[8]

What is important here is the significance of the mandatory schooling system being made "compulsory as an institution" based on the Elementary Education Act 1870.[9] This is because, in reality, many children had already been attending some kind of school, which raises the question of the purpose for which this Elementary Education Act was enacted, given that to be the case. It can be said that the Act was enacted because the meaning of "mandatory schooling" as stated here was not limited to merely sending children to school; it meant sending children to a "good school" that embraced standardized basic secular education, as stipulated by the Revised Code for 1862, accepted the pay-for-performance education system, and accordingly accepted the state subsidies and inspections (Ota, 1990). Using subsidy as a means, the state impelled disparate schools to proactively change according to the demands of the authority, making the school side choose the standardized style on their own. In this way, a modern school system, which was subsequently imitated by neighboring countries, was gradually established in the United Kingdom.

(3) Introduction of the Modern Education System in Japan

In Japan, Confucianism (especially Neo-Confucianism) is sometimes considered to be the basic ethos for education since people had a great regard for it during the Edo period. The basics of Confucianism (the belief in the innate goodness of man) can be explained as thoughts on morality that represents principles for how humans should live and behave in society. And these principles are understood to be rooted in the nature and destiny bestowed on humans. Furthermore, Confucianism is based on the logic that fully developed individuals who have mastered the moral principle will extend it to the family, the country, and the world at large, in a stepwise manner. It indicates that since human nature is consistent with the natural order (because it was granted from above), the natural order persists in groups of humans as well (Tsujimoto, 1990: 4–6). Sokou Yamaga who was affected by but criticized Neo-Confucianism aimed to create consistent social norms by improving customs, i.e., civilizing common people, in addition to cultivating the minds of those in power. *Chikyō Yōroku (Governance and Education Digest)* was written to present a vision of a nationwide school system as a theory of organization serving such purpose. It is the prototypical idea of pre-modern public education, as it were (Kaneko, 1967: 8).[10]

Yamaga deemed a samurai's duty to include not only defense preparation but also moral education of the three classes of people, namely, the farmer, the artisan, and the merchant. This is because the meaning of the social existence of samurai, who were originally warriors, was questioned during the stable Edo period and they were ultimately asked to adopt an ethos worthy of a ruler. Behind this premise were the work ethics that reprove idling one's time away and endorse the value that one must work for a living. In addition, there was already a concept called "calling" in Confucianism, intending that the highly virtuous were to govern people on behalf of divine will according to such virtue, whereby this calling was distinguished from a general occupation. However, Tekisai Nakamura, a Confucian scholar at around the same time (17th century) deemed that everyone born into this world has a calling to supplement what divine will lacks,[11] so that striving to perform one's own duty will contribute to the evolution of the universe. This vocational view later gained traction among the Japanese and was passed on in the vocational views of Baigan Ishida's *Sekimon-Shingaku* (teachings that combine Buddhist, Shinto, and Confucian ethics), which became popular among the merchants. Although this vocational view assumes the domination of the samurai, it practically created a foundation to accept hereditary identification as destiny (Hiraishi, 1997: 46–50, 82–85).[12]

The development that signals the beginning of the modern school education system in Japan during the Edo period, according to the explanation by Masashi Tsujimoto, can be summarized as follows. Under Neo-Confucianism, which was considered orthodox during the Edo period, schools were positioned as a means of edification, since the purpose of education was the edification of the common people. Therefore, sovereigns (feudal lords) reasoned that since their education was the foundation for the edification of the *han* (feudal domain), they needed to be particular about the academic sect and follow Neo-Confucianism, which did not recognize different studies. In this way, the orthodox education spread among *hanko* (feudal domain schools) and even among *terakoya* (private elementary schools), which were places for common people to study. Therefore, the establishment of the academic sect became paramount in Neo-Confucianism, and edification at so-called "school" came to play an important role. Shunsui Rai, a Confucian scholar who worked for a feudal lord during the mid-Edo period, encouraged the general public to also attend *hanko*, created schools for townspeople, intervened in common people's education at *terakoya*, and so on. In this way, *han* began implementing policies to protect and control education (Tsujimoto, 1990: 219–229).

Because of its inflexible nature, Neo-Confucianism in general tends to receive the negative evaluation of having prompted the stagnation of Confucian thoughts. However, it has been thought that Neo-Confucianism, which does not regard common people as inherently ignorant, can enlighten and improve them, not only ethically but also intellectually. There was a viewpoint similar to the philosophy of the European Enlightenment that common people were actually the subjects who needed to be enlightened, so that they would not be misled by illusions. This partially made it easier to accept the way of modern Western thinking. Such rationalism is thought to have led to the logic for samurai to unite and create a political system. As a result, *hanko* became necessary for the purpose of edification serving the needs of samurai education.

The significance of the popularization of Neo-Confucianism and the prohibition of heterodoxy in the Kansei era in the history of education lies in the fact that 1) there was a logic (i.e., being particular about the academic sect) that proactively contributed as an ideology to integrating the state (feudal domain); 2) the practical goal to promote the proactive edification of the minds of the people was clear, and it therefore provided a reason to develop public education for the common people by cooperating with the public authority; and 3) samurai education in particular had a dual structure, in which they learned the elementary basics including Neo-Confucianist morality before acquiring knowledge in various specialized disciplines, so that it became easier to absorb practical sciences in various studies. We can say that these formed the basic characteristics of the way that politics, academia, and education have related to each other in modern Japan since the end of the Edo period (Tsujimoto, 1990: 237–255).

In February 1868, the new government after the Meiji Restoration appointed three Japanese classical scholars, including the Judicial Officer of the Secretary of Divinities, Kanetane Hirata, and the Assistant Judicial Officers of the Department of Home Affairs, Misao Tamamatsu and Harumichi Yano, to School Officers, ordering them to investigate the school system. As a result, they formulated and submitted a proposal for a higher education system called *gakusha sei*, which appears to have been based on *daigaku-ryo* (an ancient formal educational institution for training public officials). According to Terumoto Kaneko, the driving force for such a movement was Tomomi Iwakura, who stemmed from a court noble family. Being at the center of the regime, he was concerned that Japan was subservient to the foreign policies of Western countries. Meanwhile, there was also a circle of people trying to modernize Japan from the Western standpoint in the new Meiji government, leading to the appointment of Rinsho Mitsukuri, Masao Uchida, and other scholars of Western studies as school system investigation officials[13] in October of the same year. Subsequently, this force gradually gained power and began eliminating the Imperial Way Faction. It is said that as Iwakura also came to recognize the growth of colleagues advocating Western modernization within the regime, they began favoring the unified school system, including elementary school, junior high school, and college (Kaneko, 1967: 22–29).

The modern school system had a completely different structure from *terakoya* or private academies that had existed in Japan up until then. It is known to have therefore encountered a lot of resistance, such as the destruction movement, when a new school system was introduced (Mori, 1993: 63–76). At the time, Japan was aggressively incorporating Western styles in an effort not to lag behind the West. Needless to say, as Hidehiro Sonoda points out, rapid Westernization did not necessarily incorporate such systems uncritically due to an adoration of the West; there is the view that Japan came to recognize the importance of identifying and training talents for the military, science, and technology after selecting and applying Western information as needed (Sonoda, 1993: 89–95). However, the fact that the education systems and school mechanisms every country introduces are all relatively similar, considering the diversity of the world culture, suggests that the spread of school education cannot be explained merely from such functional aspects.

3. Development of the State Mechanism and Its Spread in the World

(1) Spread of Institutional Isomorphism and the Modern Education System

We have reviewed the infancy of the modern education system in the United Kingdom and Japan in some detail. Besides the United Kingdom, where the system was first created, the ruling class at the time sent people to Europe and brought in so-called "hired foreigners" to actively adopt the European style.

If one rereads the theory of bureaucratic organization by Weber, the logic that works there is a type of manualization and standardization. It becomes less difficult to launch a nationwide school chain—such as the spread of British schools—once normalization advances, because it becomes easier to convey the system to third parties. Mass training of human resources also becomes possible. We can see from these points how essential the flow of rationalization, standardization, and normalization is to modernization. These types of new organizations and systems must have looked very innovative in the eyes of the people of that time. Although sometimes met by strong resistance, the new does not take long to be established when it is clear that adopting it will result in some sort of advantage (or at least that it will not result in any significant disadvantage).

I covered the economic significance of public education at the beginning of this chapter. While its economic significance is probably true, there are some parts of the education system that do not sit well in terms of social significance. There remain deep-rooted criticisms, such as, "what is the point of what we learned in school education?" and "things learned in school are completely useless in society," particularly among the Japanese people. There are also those who respond by arguing for education theories, saying, "it might be necessary to link school education and professional aspects of society to impart knowledge that is as practical as possible." This represents an argument that the education system should be based on certain goals and objectives.

In contrast, there are people who insist that the school system was not installed to impart useful knowledge to people in the first place. John W. Meyer and Francisco O. Ramirez, who are in this camp, present empirical data to demonstrate that education systems were not necessarily installed with a functionalist sense of purpose. According to them, although people tend to think that the state created a school system because there was a substantive objective, the fact is that there are systems and institutions that any decent modern state should have, and a school system is just one of them. Conversely, their logical construction asserts that a state creates a school system because a society that does not even have a school system cannot be regarded as a legitimate state (Meyer and Rowan, 1977; Ramirez and Boli, 1987). In other words, we can look at the fact that the new Meiji government scrapped *terakoya*, which had been functioning, albeit imperfectly, and relentlessly insisted on establishing Western-style schools in the face of strong resistance, and interpret this to have been due to a compelling feeling that the state would not otherwise earn recognition unless they established such schools.

Looking at schools from the functionalist perspective, it is natural to expect school education to spread once modernization advances and society becomes highly industrialized because knowledge becomes necessary. If that is the case, we can expect a correlation between the level of economic development and the level of school penetration (e.g., enrollment rate, etc.). However, a study by Meyer and colleagues overturns this expectation (Meyer et al., 1992). Moreover, popularized schools are similar all over the world, although their forms, lecture methods, and lecture content (curricula) have a variety of cultural backgrounds. This is partially because self-legitimacy is confirmed by imitating the systems of leading countries. Paul J. DiMaggio and Walter W. Powell referred to such a movement as institutional isomorphism (DiMaggio and Powell, 1983), by which is meant that these systems were installed for the convenience of the national mechanism, and we individuals are making choices within the constraints of that system (i.e., at the mercy of the system).

Based on the discussion by Meyer, Masashi Fujimura explains that since mass education is ultimately the foundation of national formation that includes all people across social groups such as religion, ethnicity, gender, and class within the framework called the state, it becomes clear which countries lag behind in the implementation when the level of popularization is understood by various statistics worldwide. If that is the case, an education system is introduced and popularized through a sense of competition between states, apart from any reasoning as to whether it is useful or not. That is to say, a country where education is not popularized could be internationally perceived as a backward country that does not provide opportunities for children to be educated. Since such a system is imitatively introduced, the gap between the real-world culture and the system widens, and it is only the formality and framework that spread rapidly without a good understanding of matters such as the original philosophy of the education system (Fujimura, 1995: 162–166). Based on this framework, it can be understood that "the legitimacy as a modern state is first proven by the completion of an education system, and then the education system grants people who study there the characteristic of being citizens of a modern state," rather than explaining it with the reasoning that "knowledge is accumulated among people, and the organization of society is promoted once an education system is created."[14]

Such a movement is not limited to the education system. Then again, it is questionable whether all systems are really the same, as emphasized here. For example, as mentioned in Chapter 1, school education has the function of assigning status, and the school system is heavily involved in that process. In other words, the differentiation of school types is closely related to matters such as the way that social mobility and employment operates among people in that society as well as customs in the labor market. Labor practices are also related to the social security system. Though I will examine it in detail in the following chapters, the common view is that this type of social security system and welfare will not converge even when the economy develops. In other words, while isomorphic systems in some cases spread in the way explained by such institutional theories, they could also in other cases be established in a way that adapts to the society.

(2) State and Tax

Although it is said that individualism has spread, a human cannot live alone; he/she has no choice but to have a connection to a community or society somewhere in order to live. Local community, relatives, and family used to represent such ties. Although I do not think that the inclination to emphasize family has not weakened considerably, partly due to privatization and the popularization of the idea of privacy, it can be said that connections with relatives and community that go beyond the framework of family have weakened in general. Schools and companies are the alternative institutions. In addition, childcare and nursing care, which used to be performed mainly by family members, have come to be fulfilled by other agencies due to changes in the social situation. Welfare states were born out of such trends (Hashimoto, 2013). In short, services such as childcare, education, and nursing care themselves will never go away. It is a matter of who takes the burden if it is too much for individuals to handle; and in such case, the state and government would be the most rational choice under the current situation.

However, since maintaining a state naturally costs money, tax must be collected from the citizens in order to secure funds for the expense. The ways of thinking about such tax payments to the government are roughly divided into people's rights and obligations. In the United Kingdom, where civil society began expanding early and had an affluent economic foundation, paying tax had a strong role as the right to position the market mechanism in the center of its economic activities and proactively reduce the burden of compensating the cost required to maintain such a society. Here, the idea that the pursuit of personal gain ultimately results in gain for the entire society took deep root. Meanwhile, lagging behind in Europe, Germany needed to artificially form a unified nation first, and then build a society in a planned manner through top-down control, since it could not otherwise catch up with leading countries such as the United Kingdom and France if left to its individual activities. Therefore, in contrast to the British idea of an accumulation of individuals creating the state, the state ended up controlling individuals from the top, and people came to perceive it as a sort of common destiny. In this way, paying taxes became an obligation to be fulfilled to a state that shared the same destiny with them.

The German approach in which the state had to take the lead in developing this kind of capitalist economy society is also related to the fact that the country produced financial scholars such as Lorenz von Stein, Adolf Heinrich Gotthilth Wagner, and Albert Eberhard Friedrich Schaffle. In Japan, it is said that Hirobumi Ito idolized Stein. This is probably because there were some overlapping characteristics between the way that Germany tried to compete with the United Kingdom by promoting state-led modernization because they were a latecomer country and the post-Meiji Restoration direction of modernization in Japan. It can be said that the fact that Japan's first state-led financial system was established after modernization has also had great significance in the formation of the people's perspective on taxation (Morotomi, 2013: 59–61, 96–100).

The government undertakes a variety of activities by using the taxes collected as a main source of funding. Such government activity, viewed from the monetary perspective, is financial administration. The functions of financial administration can be generally summed up by three elements: resource allocation, income redistribution, and stabilization of the economy. And the main means of financial administration is the budget—usually an estimate of revenue and expenditures for one year—which is managed and controlled through the approval of the Diet. The rules, procedures, and customs in a series of budgetary planning steps, from preparing the budget, obtaining the approval of the Diet, and enforcing the budget, to settling the accounts, are called a budget system.

When the fiscal deficit expands and the current account balance drops to trigger a currency collapse and interest rate increase, structural reforms aimed at reducing the fiscal deficit become inevitable. Typical examples from the past have been fiscal restructuring in countries such as Sweden and New Zealand. In addition, a change in regime could also be a factor promoting fiscal restructuring in the sense of responding to the expectations of voters by revoking the policy of the former regime and starting structural reforms. This is characteristic of the United Kingdom, the United States, Australia, Canada, and the Netherlands. In the case of Japan, however, until now there have been almost no economic crises, changes of regime, or external political pressures, even though the ever increasing fiscal deficit has historically been considered a problem. This has therefore led to a situation whereby we are forced to increase taxes or cut spending in order to implement fiscal restructuring (Tanaka, 2013: 49–64).

(3) Under Neoliberalization

Ultimately, the framework of the modern state will not collapse and the issue remains of how far the government should bear the burden of people's life security. So-called neoliberalism criticizes such a bloated government. While the government, in theory, has the economic legitimacy (or reason) to intervene in the market, this does not mean that everything will work out well when they do. A failure on the part of the government is certainly possible. And even though social security and welfare are very expensive, one cannot easily revise them, far less abolish them, since people's behavior is premised on the existence of these systems once they are in place. Economic growth slowed down especially around the 1970s in Japan, despite the growing demand for welfare and social security, making deficit-ridden finances a problem.

Therefore, neoliberalism considers cutting government spending to be the number one priority. Considering that the role and function of the government must be accordingly reduced, there is a reason for neoliberalists to be nationalists or conservatives who idealize the picture of so-called "typical" family: to make up for what is cut in the spirit of nationalism and with personal expenses paid by the family. And since this might still be insufficient, they advocate the argument of complete self-responsibility at the same time. This is why it is also emphasized in education that individuals, rather than society, should compensate for their own failures, and that the individual must be strong enough to be able to do so.

Since the collapse of the Cold War structure, the debate over social security and welfare can no longer be simply understood in terms of the dichotomy of "individuals vs. the government" or "whether to save the disadvantaged." The government finances have become tight, but the national burden cannot be easily increased. Because public scrutiny of the usage of government spending has increased, it has become difficult to pay out benefits without careful consideration (even if the individual is socially disadvantaged). In short, it means that "since taxes are collected from those who work, the ones who receive benefits should show sincerity to some extent; it is shameless of them to obtain benefits for free." Therefore, in the United Kingdom, the country that was once touted as a model welfare state with the phrase "from cradle to grave," education was advocated as the most important policy and its budget was eventually increased when the Blair ministry of the Labour Party was formed. Although those in education-related industries, including the field of education sociology, are inclined to argue that "education spending is being cut by neoliberalism," such logic is a little too simplistic; it is necessary to recognize the fact that there is actually a side to neoliberalism that utilizes education as compelling evidence to cut social security (Iwashita, 2013). The fact that the trend in the field of education to assess education spending from the taxpayer's perspective is growing stronger must be understood from a broader perspective, such as the one shown above.

Studies that critically interpret education as the apparatus of power by citing Michel Foucault and others were frequently seen in the past. However, such studies have become less common in recent years. This might be partially due to the fact that criticism against power structures is becoming predictable and losing its novelty because the storylines generally become similar from the standpoint of research. In addition, there is another side to the welfare state wherein it tries to keep the people under power by throwing in rewards called welfare. It is clear without even listing examples such as the establishment of a social insurance system by Otto von Bismarck in Germany that for those in power, welfare is a measure to prevent revolutions by socialist and communist ideologies as well as an ingredient to make the public unite in war against foreign countries. Although it is hard to imagine in today's Japan, the development of social security and welfare is so deeply connected with war that it cannot be discussed separately from it; in fact, there was an overt intention for the state power to control the people.

However, the debate over small government in recent years is making the story of control by such power feel less real. Whereas neoliberalists often stand by their conservative thoughts, people in the education community in many cases support deregulation and liberalization. There is a movement among people who used to be critical toward state control over education but who have now become wary of such a stance to try to defend public education. And as the increased cost of social security becomes a problem, education is used as an expedient to cut social security spending. In short, the position adopted is along the lines that "benefits are paid only to those who receive education such as vocational training," rather than providing benefits for free. Those who refuse or are unable to receive such an education for some reason will end up being excluded by society (Nihei, 2009).

Furthermore, once commercialization divides people into those who can afford private services and those who cannot, the rich will probably be more inclined to buy what they prefer on their own and avoid what is publically provided. Then, it is likely that they will feel that the large burden (of tax payments) is unfair because they are no longer the direct beneficiaries of public services. While there is an issue that extreme advancement of social disparities itself promotes a social divide, it could also make the maintenance of public services difficult, thereby further escalating the social divide (Sandel, 2009, trans. 2010). Under such circumstances, how will education be positioned as a state policy? It is not possible to understand this by looking at education policies alone. It will become necessary to position education as services provided by the state, while examining its relationship with other social security and welfare.

NOTES

[1] This is used in the fields of medical care and welfare as well. The discussion on quasi-market reform by Julian Le Grand is well-known in the United Kingdom. See Akutsu (2008) for a commentary on this discussion.

[2] In reality, however, it took time for this to be implemented as stated, during which time the government role expanded. Then, fiscal deficits and inefficiencies associated with the bloated role of the government became an issue in 1968, and the *Fulton Report* was published to state that the government services were moving away from the people as amateurism became prevalent and the adverse effect of bureaucratic organizations became conspicuous. While the *Fulton Report* prompted a huge debate, many of the reform proposals presented in it were deadlocked after meeting with strong resistance from government employees (Burnham and Pyper, 2008, trans. 2010: 12–13).

[3] Weber uses "whether people acquired expertise through education" as one of the key criteria when explaining social class categories and social standing (Weber, 1956, trans. 1960: 207–217).

[4] That said, the negative aspects of bureaucracy that we can easily think of, such as a silo mentality and standardization (or formalism), have already been noted by Weber as well.

[5] However, this bill was discarded later. Subsequently, all bills relating to education for the general public were dissolved until the Elementary Education Act was enacted in 1870. This Parochial School Bill was different from other bills in the sense that it at least passed the deliberation of the lower of the two houses (Matsui, 2008: 76).

[6] The circumstances surrounding this are detailed in Yanagi (2005). According to Yanagi, the National Society and the British and Foreign School Society were incompatible because the former was backed by the Church of England and the latter advocated nonsectarianism. The National Society which had put Bell up front and tried to popularize the Church of England was advantageous at the beginning. Although much was made of Lancaster's schools, Lancaster was expelled from the operation of the British and Foreign School Society due to personal troubles. In order to compete with the National Society, he then streamlined and standardized schools to enable easy expansion in the manner of a national chain. It is said that the schools managed by the British and Foreign School Society, which became popular among the wealthy, gradually became more stable in the end than the schools of the National Society, which was absorbed with its religious doctrine.

⁷ Nevertheless, because mechanics and workers lacked basic education, mechanics' institutes often continued as schools that were more open to the middle class than the working class. The so-called grammar school also differentiated into schools centered on practical sciences, such as modern natural science, technology, and business, as well as schools that mainly provided classical liberal arts education (Nagao, 1978: 129–132).

⁸ According to Ota, this Elementary Education Act alone is not something to be recognized as the foundation of the modern public education system in the United Kingdom; rather, it should be recognized as something that institutionalized basic secular education throughout the nation by taking the Revised Code of 1862 into consideration and settling the chaotic history of basic education in the United Kingdom (Ota, 1992: 128–129).

⁹ The mandatory schooling system only applied to the school districts in which an academic affairs committee elected by public vote was established per Article 74 of the Elementary Education Act of 1870; therefore, it had not yet been introduced throughout the nation at the time. This was because "good schools" that abided by laws and regulations were then still short in supply, and it was thought that the supply of "good schools" would be guaranteed in districts with a school board directly elected by the citizens (Ota, 1990).

¹⁰ Another individual who had a considerable impact on the shogunate politics by criticizing Neo-Confucianism, as Yamaga did, was Sorai Ogyu. He disagreed with Neo-Confucianism, which deemed human nature to be innate (the belief in the innate goodness of man), as well as with Yamaga's argument that human disposition changes, thinking that it was possible to bring out human abilities that are socially valuable (innate personality) through education (Kaneko, 1967: 9–13).

¹¹ This originates in the phrase "the sovereign ruler is to establish orderly moral principles and promote justice in the world to teach people to help feed each other" found in the Overall Image section of the Pervading Hexagram in *I Ching*. It refers to an undertaking of a saint with a virtue as large as the world to realize the stability of people's welfare by helping the evolution effect of heaven and earth to grow all beings (Hiraishi, 1997: 48).

¹² As a side note, it was Robert N. Bellah, who pointed out that this vocational view of *Sekimon-Shingaku* shared some commonalities with Calvinism. Needless to say, there is *The Protestant Ethic and the Spirit of Capitalism* by Weber behind Bellah's analysis (Bellah, 1957, trans. 1996).

¹³ Arinori Mori, who later made a significant contribution to the establishment of the modern school system in Japan, had also been appointed to this duty (Kaneko, 1967: 27).

¹⁴ Therefore, although there could, in theory, be individuals who have already mastered the knowledge and skills without learning them at school, whether they have graduated from school is questioned first in the real world, and if they have not completed school by studying in formal programs, a situation could occur in which their knowledge is not socially trusted.

CHAPTER 3
Relationship between Education and Social Security/Welfare

1. Education as Social Policy

(1) The Difference in the Scope of Social Policy
In the previous chapters, I have examined from the perspectives of sociology and historical development why education is borne by the government (public). I have also made it clear that defining the role and function of education is difficult because it can be understood to have two sides: the perspective of the welfare state, namely, the resultative relationship in which education fulfills part of welfare measures, and the paradoxical relationship that actually conflicts with the egalitarian principle (Hirota, 2013).

Jutta Allmendinger and Stephen Leibfried noted that the positioning of education policy differs between the Anglo-Saxon countries and continental European countries such as Germany (Allmendinger and Leibfried, 2003). They refer to quotes by Thomas H. Marshall, who is a prominent social policy scholar in the United Kingdom, and the 1942 Report on Social Insurance and Allied Services by William Beveridge, asserting that education is positioned as part of social policy and that education reforms are mentioned more often than social security reforms in the Anglo-Saxon countries. For example, general information manuals and texts on social policy and welfare in the United Kingdom list education along with elderly care, health and medical care, family policy, and so on (Lewis, ed., 1998; Glennerster, 2003; Glennerster and Hills, eds., 2003; Annetts et al., 2009).[1] The education sector has considerably evolved in the United States as well; according to Allmendinger and others, the level of publicly provided education is good enough to call the country a pseudo-welfare state. In contrast, education policy is usually regarded completely separately from general social policies in Germany

(Allmendinger and Leibfried, 2003). As for Japan, as Shogo Takegawa observes, there was a time when social policies were listed side by side with labor policy (Takegawa, 2007: 6).

Arnold J. Heidenheimer pointed out that the course (or order) of development of public education and social security in Europe was completely the opposite of that in the United States, suggesting that education, or social security, is linked to the labor market in quite a different manner (Heidenheimer, 1981). Karl G. Hokenmaier took this into consideration, examining the relationship between education and other social security from the viewpoint of public spending. The results showed that education and social security were to some degree in an opposite (or trade-off) relationship in terms of expenditure, indicating that education spending as a percentage of public spending was relatively large in countries with a liberal regime, followed by countries with a social democratic regime, and then by countries with a conservative regime. Whereas upper secondary education was centered on general education under liberal regimes, vocational education was actually the mainstream under social democratic and conservative regimes (Hokenmaier, 1998).

Hans Pechar and Lesley Andres state that, under the so-called welfare state regime, liberal regimes put considerable effort into policies like education that strengthen human capital in exchange for spending a very small amount on benefit-oriented social security; on the other hand, a decent level of life security is guaranteed under conservative regimes even if people do not obtain higher education because vocational education in such countries is extensive at the secondary education stage. In other words, higher education and social security are in a mutually exclusive relationship in both types of regimes. However, such a negative correlation is not found under social democratic regimes in the Nordic countries, where a certain scale of spending on education is basically observed (Pechar and Andres, 2011). In short, this means that the phenomenon whereby government spending increases linearly from liberal to conservative to social democratic regimes, as seen with general social security and welfare, is not observed with education.

Returning to the subject of regimes, here, they are based on Gøsta Esping-Andersen's theory of welfare states, which—it would not be an exaggeration to say—is invariably cited in today's international comparative studies on welfare states (Esping-Andersen, 1990, trans. 2001). This states that even though the theory of unilinear development has traditionally prevailed, indicating that the welfare system is gradually enhanced as the economy and society develop, this is not actually the case. Furthermore, looking at the Western industrialized countries in particular, they can be roughly classified into three systems. The keyword here is de-commodification, which is an indicator for the extent to which workers (labor force) are free from being traded as a commodity on the market. To put it simply, the labor force is de-commodified when there is a system in which the government compensates income for workers who fall into a situation of not being able to work in the labor market for some reason. And depending on the degree of de-commodification, welfare states can be roughly divided into liberal, conservative, and social democratic regimes.

Typical examples of liberal regimes include Anglo-Saxon countries such as the United States and the United Kingdom. Since they basically value the market economy and consider social security almost as if it were something provided for people who have lost in a competition, their governments tend to be the smallest in term of national finances. On the other hand, the Nordic countries, which are often referred to as model welfare states, are considered to have a social democratic regime. There, social security policy is in effect in every corner, and equality is aggressively promoted. Their governments are likely to become large in terms of national finances. Conservative regimes, which are positioned between the two, include countries in Continental Europe such as Germany and France. There, because entities such as professional associations are influential, even though they are not states, social policies are tightly associated with them. In addition, there is a tendency for the community of family and relatives, rather than the private sector or the state, to take responsibility for the social welfare function. In terms of the scale of national finances, they are often at the middle level. Thus, we can expect a certain relationship between the scale of government and the type of welfare regime.

(2) Who Receives More Benefit from Education?

While education and welfare are both undertakings of the government, there are various debates over their positioning, as described. Education and welfare would have similar functions from the standpoint of the welfare state theory that presupposes the equalization function of education. On the other hand, education is considered to have a function to create new discrimination and disparity when the allocation function of education is emphasized. According to the economic point of view examined in Chapter 2, primary and secondary education have strong characteristics as public goods. However, as Harold L. Wilensky stated, higher education is unlike other policies in the field of social security and has a different nature in terms of actually providing more benefits to the rich. This is because, statistically, those who advance to higher education are often (the children of) wealthy individuals. While insurance and welfare are so-called income redistribution policies contributing to the absolute equality of society, the equality of opportunities for higher education is not intended to realize equal outcome in the first place, even when equal opportunities for higher education become an agenda. And if everyone is paying tax uniformly, it means there will be regressivity to allocate income to high-income earners because those who benefit from higher education are the rich. This is what particularizes education according to Wilensky (1975, trans. 1984: 38–42).[2]

Then again, as Ulrich Beck observes, we might be at the stage where there are excessive supplies of educated individuals today. Nevertheless, there is almost no chance in the labor market without pursuing higher education. Even though education was intended as a means to pave the way to the labor market, it merely now provides the right to get the opportunity for employment. While a diploma is essential in order to obtain the opportunity to work, that alone is no longer sufficient. As a result, new qualifications and requirements are added. In any case, because the formation of classes based on impoverishment or through a community created on the basis of social status is no longer possible due to the penetration of the welfare state policy, our times are characterized by the fact that it is no longer realistic to share, think, and explore some kind of standpoint based on status or class (Beck, 1986, trans. 1998: 167–168). Meanwhile, people who have lost their chance to receive an education are considered not to have not put in enough effort (because, on the surface, it looks as if they were offered equal opportunities). They then lose the opportunity to jointly raise the issue within society, and wind up being left behind and excluded from society as a whole.

As discussed in Chapter 2, from the government's perspective, education can actually be used as an expedient for cutting social security spending under circumstances in which social security spending is becoming tight. This attitude is one which views merely providing benefits as throwing money away, while providing subsidies is acceptable to some extent if the recipients are to receive training. This would also make it easier to obtain consent among the voters (taxpayers). While the sorting and allocation functions are more greatly emphasized than the equalization function once education passes a certain level, equality of opportunities must be maintained in order to justify such allocation. Therefore, when education and welfare are linked, policies to secure equal opportunities for education tend to be focused.

Under these circumstances, there are people who have carved out a field called "education and welfare studies." Toshio Ogawa at Nagoya University is one of them. There, issues that fall under both education and welfare—that is, issues concerning the right for children subject to social and child welfare to receive education—have been studied as the subject area of education and welfare studies. In response to the increased social advancement of women, the scope has subsequently been widened to include issues such as expanding nursery schools and kindergartens as places of infant development and guaranteeing lifelong education (Ogawa and Takahashi, eds., 2001). In addition, a seminar named "Education and Social Work" has been established at Hokkaido University, and studies focusing particularly on poverty issues have been undertaken mainly by Osamu Aoki and colleagues (Aoki, ed., 2003; Aoki and Sugimura, ed., 2007; Aoki, 2010). These studies that take field studies into consideration are valuable references aimed at the relevant issues.

That said, this book will focus more on policies at the macro level, particularly on the allocation of the national budget, than policies that center on these particular segments. It is not that these individual efforts are useless—in fact, they are extremely important given the recent situation; however, as I have discussed thus far, education policies are closely related to social security and welfare policies, rather than coming into effect by themselves.[3] In terms of finance, the state has a range of items they should spend money on, and the resources are allocated to some of them based on a certain intention relevant to strategy. Individual policies on education and social security are implemented as a result of such resource allocation. When discussing issues such as child poverty that have emerged in some areas in recent years, where this occurs and sufficient measures have not been taken to address it, it is necessary to examine its overall relationship with other policies, including social security and welfare as a matter of course. Within such process, it is also probably necessary to consider how Japan positions education in relation to other policy areas.

In Japan, where the degree of de-commodification—an indicator of the welfare regime—is low, trying to merely mandate work or promote women's employment without thoroughly deliberating their relationship with policies and systems in other areas could result in an increase in non-regular employment and the one-sided imposition on women to bear the burden of housework and childcare, further exacerbating the declining birthrate (Miyamoto, 2013: 108).

(3) The Ways of Positioning Public Education Expenditure and their Problems

As mentioned in the Introduction, Japan's public spending on education relative to the GDP is at the lowest level among the OECD countries (see Figures Intro-2 and Intro-3). Conversely, Japan is ranked high among the OECD countries in terms of personal defrayment. While this has the effect of forcing individual households to bear an excessive burden, it may further mean that the total cost for education is too high. In fact, it is necessary to scrutinize the breakdown and calmly examine how far the government should cover the expense, which does not mean blindly trying to increase the public burden. As mentioned on the Introduction, opinions may be divided as to whether public spending on education is small or large, because how one assesses the figure is subjective; however, many people are not exactly enthusiastic about increasing the public burden of education costs. Furthermore, while the argument that the public burden should be increased is based on an assumption that raising the percentage of the public burden would considerably reduce that of the personal burden, according to Kaori Suetomi, an analysis based on time-series data shows that the level of personal burden does not decrease at all; the personal burden for both school education and education outside of school has actually been increasing simultaneously with public spending on education (Suetomi, 2010: 67–83).[4]

The reality is that the personal burden has increased to a considerable level even when such situations are taken into account. For example, although the compulsory education phase is free of charge, a considerable amount of expenses are personally defrayed, including school lunch and school education (teaching materials other than textbooks, etc.), a variety of extracurricular activities at school, participating in school events, athletic wear, and uniforms, etc. (Ozawa, 2012). Furthermore, the MEXT outright objected to the Ministry of Finance's (MOF) claim, based on the same OECD statistics during the FY 2010 budget compilation process, that "Japan's public spending on education is at the top level among the G5 countries (the United States, the United Kingdom, France, Germany, and Japan), considering the number of children and the scale of the entire government expenditure." MEXT countered that Japan's public spending on education was low compared to other countries, further pointing out that it was peculiar that Japan's education expenditure was not growing while other countries tended to drastically increase theirs as international competition intensified, despite being additionally faced with a declining birthrate.⁵

Furthermore, according to the Japanese government's statistics and the opinion of Takuji Ishii, who examined in detail the classification of the OECD statistics, public spending on education had been overestimated in the government report (intended for the Japanese), because the items that should have been classified under private education in the statistics for international comparison were classified under public spending on education. The OECD's statistics on educational expenses are classified based on who pays, which feels right to some extent. In other words, while public education expenses are something to be completely covered by the national and local governments, the statistics by the Japanese government include school-specific revenues such as admission fees and tuition fees as well as the self-generated income of national schools. MEXT takes expenses such as the admission and tuition fees paid by beneficiaries and classifies them under personal expenses when submitting the data to the OECD. Therefore, even though MEXT seems to have at least countered the MOF's argument in order to fight against the move to cut education expenses, they ended up allowing for a double standard by using different classifications for aggregating government statistics and international comparison statistics (Ishii, 2012).

In addition, a significant percentage of children are receiving out-of-school education at cram schools or other places. Since the burden of such tuition fees is also heavy, it is an expenditure that households with children cannot ignore. Furthermore, because higher education institutions are clustered in certain areas and individuals from rural areas need to relocate or travel, this naturally adds to the expenses, for example, relocation expenses, commuting expenses, and living expenses once accommodated. In other words, associated expenses must add up to a considerable amount in addition to the direct expense of tuition fees. According to Hiroyuki Kondo, the results of a study on income disparity related to college enrollment opportunities, which he conducted using the MEXT's *Survey on Student Life*, showed that disparity had increased again in the 1990s due to a steep rise in tuition fees, although there had temporarily been signs of a reduction in disparity during the 1980s (Kondo, 2001b).

Suetomi (2010), who summarized the burden of education expenses by using the two axes of "freedom—equality" and "welfare—efficiency," claims that Japan's public spending on education has consistently maintained the efficiency—equality principle. In other words, the principle of providing compulsory education free of charge to ensure equal opportunity of education and the passive principle of equality based on the principle of defrayment by the establishers are the only legally required areas of responsibility. Out-of-school education, upper secondary education, and higher education fall entirely under the area of free choice, meaning that each household has defrayed the cost to improve the level of welfare for their children (Suetomi, 2010: 17–27). However, in today's situation where one cannot expect to increase one's income, the household burden is finally approaching its limit. In addition, while it is generally overlooked in discussions of this type, we should bear in mind that the level of Japan's public education spending compared to other countries can be considered passable only for elementary and secondary education; the level of public spending on pre-school education is quite low compared to other countries.

2. Education Policy in Japan and the Welfare System behind It

(1) Establishment of a Japanese-Style Welfare System

As has been pointed out many times, Japan is at a stage where it is not even remotely feasible to call it a welfare state, both in terms of history and international comparison, due to its national finances (Kenjo, 2001; Kenjo, 2004). Public spending on social security is at the lowest level among the developed countries. However, Japan was not necessarily a country with an extremely large economic disparity up until the collapse of the bubble economy in the early 1990s. Increase in disparity had been minimized by establishing the so-called employment security system built on the male breadwinner model that was based on the division of labor by gender role. In fact, although it had not changed significantly from the previous income redistribution to the latter redistribution,[6] the Gini coefficient had been relatively small compared to other countries up until the 1980s. This is because abundant employment was suppressing the number of households with a significantly low income (Miyamoto, 2009: 40–44).

Figure 3-1 shows social security-related spending in each of the OECD countries as a percentage of general government spending (2009).[7] Looking at this, we can see that the Nordic countries, which are usually regarded as welfare states, are not necessarily ranked at the top, although the European countries allocate a substantial amount of their government spending to social expenditure. We can also see that the percentage of social security-related expenditures in Japan is not necessarily high compared to other countries.

Social security policies in Japan focus disproportionately on elderly policies such as pensions. In other words, although Japan's social spending for family, vocational training, and unemployment is extremely low, the spending for pensions and medical care is actually at the same level as Sweden. If the levels are high for pensions and medical care when the social expenditure is at the lowest level to begin with, it is no surprise that other policies are underserved. Furthermore, if the population were to continue aging farther in the future, we can imagine that this expenditure will increase but never that it will decrease. Indeed, while social spending levels might be low, the scale of spending has been increasing naturally because spending for pension and medical care had to be increased given the demographics. In that sense, Japan is gradually becoming a mid-level welfare state based only on spending levels (contrary to the perception of the general public) (Tanaka, 2013: 238–241). Although uneasiness about pensions and medical care and complaints about benefit levels are often heard among the Japanese people in general, just maintaining the current state is already quite a challenge. Under such circumstances, it must be very difficult to increase social spending on other items. How did we come to this point? Taro Miyamoto sums up this course of development, making it short and easy to understand. With reference to this, the relevant developments are briefly outlined here as follows (Miyamoto, 2008; 2013).

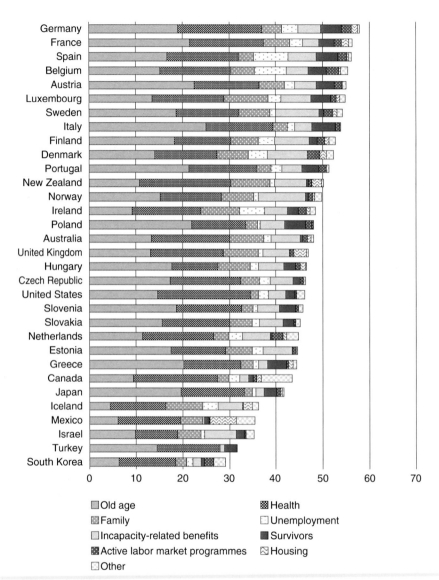

Figure 3-1 Social Security-related Public Spending as Percentage to Total Expenditure (2009)
Source: OECD StatExtract (http://stats.oecd.org/)

The so-called "three-law welfare system" was established in Japan after the Child Welfare Law and the Disabled Persons Welfare Law were established in 1947 and 1949, respectively. The (new) Livelihood Protection Law declaring the guarantee of the right to minimum standards of living was subsequently established in 1950. However, because the disparity was widening even between people who were involved with large companies and able to enjoy the corresponding benefits and others like primary industry workers, small and medium-sized company workers, and those with unstable employment after the high economic growth period began, solving this problem was becoming a political issue. Then, since the Democratic Party of Japan (DPJ), the other party at the time of the conservative merger of 1955, had declared for the first time in its charter to be a welfare state, the Liberal Democratic Party (LDP) also followed suit by aiming to establish a welfare state. And so the universal health insurance and the universal pension were established as early as 1961, albeit unintegrated with each other and insufficient.[8] However, after Hayato Ikeda took over the administration, Japan was steered to the so-called "income-doubling plan" to increase the pie itself rather than focusing on the redistribution. This, in turn promoted public works in the form of the development of the industrial infrastructure, followed by the development of social capital, leading to Kakuei Tanaka's later plan of remodeling the Japanese Archipelago.

In the meantime, although people's lives became more affluent, problems such as pollution due to rapid growth during the period of economic boom emerged and the LDP began losing support, especially in urban areas. Local government heads who were backed by the DPJ or the Japanese Communist Party (JCP) highlighting their commitment in welfare were elected one after the other in the urban areas, especially to the Tokyo Metropolitan Government, therefore becoming a threat to the LDP.[9] In 1973, Prime Minister Kakuei Tanaka consequently implemented free medical care for the elderly and increased employee pension benefits in order to maintain the LDP's approval rating, which had been on a downward trend for quite some time. While this year became known as "the beginning of the welfare era," various systems to guarantee employment for the working generation had already been established, and the movement to essentially shift social security to the second half of life had already been solidified by this time (Miyamoto, 2013: 116–119).

Meanwhile, Kakuei Tanaka's remodeling of the archipelago led to job creation in the rural areas. The LDP aimed to make use of this to save their approval rating, which was declining in the urban areas, through gaining support in the rural areas. A policy to protect small and medium-sized companies was also advocated, while employee benefits were developed for the large companies behind the high economic growth. In other words, in Japan, large companies operating on the basis of long-term employment organized employee benefits backed by the power of their enterprise, while small and medium-sized companies and the construction industry formed an employment regime based on a completely different scheme. The former guaranteed a minimum standard of living by sporadic government intervention under the market mechanism. As for the latter (including the self-employed and farmers), the mechanism worked in a way that guaranteed their livelihood in exchange for supporting a given political party. Therefore, both were potentially in a tense relationship. However, such tension was unlikely to surface, partially because small and medium-sized companies, the self-employed, and farmers were able to stay competitive during the high economic growth period thanks to government intervention. In short, the low unemployment rate in Japan was achieved by creating a scheme in which companies could not easily go bankrupt because of their connections within industry, public works, and protection and regulation measures, rather than by public services and a wide range of social security systems. We could even say that, despite being in a tense relationship, the existence of two different employment regimes actually served the function of shifting income from the high- to the low-productivity sectors, or from the urban to the rural areas, when these were functioning well.

At the same time, however, the unemployed and the elderly had been excluded from such employment regime systems. The unemployment issue did not manifest until the 1980s since these systems were functioning. As for the elderly, since rapid aging of the population was certain, the government had no choice but to increase spending on pensions and medical care for them after the 1970s. And because the rapid increase in social security expenditure worsened the fiscal deficit, this led to administrative reforms and welfare programs being cut one after the other.

These situations became conspicuous at the beginning of the 1980s, with the Thatcher and Reagan administrations of the United Kingdom and United States, respectively, often taken to exemplify neoliberalism. Because the state activities are suppressed under neoliberalism, the gap is filled by traditional values (conservatism, such as the family principle) and the market function to increase economic activities (i.e., liberalism). This is common to all ages and all places; however, while welfare reevaluation was built upon anti-welfare ideologies such as monetarism in the United Kingdom and the United States, that was not necessarily the case in Japan. Since there was no doctrine to fundamentally attack the concept of the welfare state, Japan positioned itself as "an original welfare state that emphasizes self-help, family ties, and mutual aid" rather than denying it altogether (Shinkawa, 2005: 107–109). Thus, there is no political party that openly criticizes or insists on cutting welfare policies; by contrast, all political parties emphasize welfare. However, anti-welfare subjects such as self-help and familism have been discussed as if they were pro-welfare in the history of social security policy in Japan (Takegawa, 2007: 125).

As the economy is globalized and maintaining business foundations becomes difficult, large companies have increased their non-regular employees while stabilizing the employment foundation among regular employees to build a large company-specific labor-management relationship, thereby moving away from government control. Meanwhile, once the interests of rural areas, small and medium-sized companies, and farmers began conflicting with those of large companies, criticism actually intensified that public works would begin malfunctioning. Dissatisfaction with disparity is not always caused by accurately recognizing its objective situation (Inoki, 2012: 116–118). In fact, Japan is no longer necessarily a country with low economic disparity when compared to other OECD countries. However, once the employment situation became unstable in the late 1990s, the difference in compensation *within* closed industries and employment systems amplified the level of anxiety, and even though the disparity was by no means small, people began criticizing "excessive egalitarianism" and "over-the-board equality" (Miyamoto, 2008).

(2) Welfare Systems that Rely on the Private Sector

Based on Esping-Andersen's welfare regime theory, Japan can be considered a borderline case: it is close to a conservative regime in Continental Europe in terms of the hierarchy and role of family in its social security system but can also be classified under a liberal regime in terms of the level of benefits and the effects of redistribution (Esping-Andersen, 1997). This welfare regime theory is easier to understand when one thinks of the idea of the market and family replacing the function of the government. Considering it to be a conservative regime if the family has a function to substitute the government and a liberalist regime if the market (private sector, i.e., employee benefits) bears that responsibility, the way family and corporation reinforce each other is not something that we see in the West. On the other hand, it can be said that this is a form of late-starter welfare state that had no choice but to address welfare by mobilizing existing resources without waiting for the formation of public systems under high economic development. Furthermore, this type of welfare state was formed by the ruling party and state bureaucracy working together (i.e., led by the state) rather than being created as a result of political competition among different political forces (Miyamoto, 2013: 96–98).

Thus, Japan historically does not have any era in which it can classed as a welfare state in terms of the fiscal spending of the government. It would seem that Japanese people feel that they have achieved excellent economic performance to the extent of even being considered exceptional, with large private companies leading such performance, and employee benefits and welfare supported by those large companies; or they feel that the private sector has historically supported people's lives without really relying on the government. Such perception must be part of the reason why people feel emotions such as distrust and unreliability toward the government.

In addition, as shown in the iconic example of Japan National Railways, the image that what the "public" provides is inefficient and old-style has spread widely among the people, namely, that it is more wasteful than the private sector, repeatedly falls into a large deficit, has staff with arrogant attitudes, and has uncompromising labor movements, which seem (in the eyes of civilians) just plain selfish, etc. (However, in the case of Japan National Railways, problems such as politicians forcibly laying local lines that are certain to lose money and constructing the planned new bullet train lines are probably more fundamental reasons for the deficit symbolized by the term "self-seeking.") As these factors became increasingly entangled in complexity, the tendency to distrust the government became a normal state of mind. Moreover, distrust in the authorities was exacerbated when the media reported, one after the other, on the government's collusive relationship with certain industry organizations, their squandering of money, and the appointment of retiring government officials to important posts in industries controlled by their former ministries, etc. As a result, the image of government failure was established along the lines that "the public sector is lazy and inefficient when the private sector is working so hard," instilling a sense that increasing the national burden through measures such as increasing tax is absolutely out of question in the case of such a government.

Furthermore, this began incentivizing politicians to use such discourse to criticize government employees for the purpose of gaining votes. They then began turning irresponsible proposals without proper evidence or basis into campaign pledges and then later into election manifestos. Even though Japan is already at the lowest level among the developed countries in terms of labor force participation rate and the percentage of government employees' wages of the total government expenditure (Pilichowski and Turkisch, 2008), politicians began attempting to gain votes by listing campaign pledges indicating that cutting government employees would result in a reduced amount of waste. The situation of the DPJ administration taking over the regime in exchange for such a manifesto, serving as a kind of "contract" with the voters, and then profoundly betraying that expectation is an extremely grave one in the sense that they have yet farther spread political distrust and resignation among the voters. There is a clear need for them to humbly inspect and reflect upon this situation.

We can say that this book's underlying awareness of the problem is to be found here. That is, it might be that only the feeling of evasion with regard to the defrayment of taxes increased for certain reasons in the perception of the Japanese during the history of the postwar development of Japan, while the image remained that the government (the state) is something that automatically provides service. The foundation of public service is the defrayment of taxes by the people; without it, public service is not possible. This means that only the perception that the government is not worth paying taxes to was reinforced. Even though the national burden is now more necessary than ever for aspects such as social security, in reality increasing the burden (i.e., obtaining consensus) has become extremely difficult. And if the government tries to obtain consensus, people will support something that they can personally benefit from but otherwise deny its need by saying that it is either useless or the individual's own responsibility.

Though this is an issue covered in Part II, i.e., the second half of this book, as a precursor, let us say that it all comes down to the debate over the type of burden. Considering the current fiscal deficit situation in Japan, no-one would probably think that there is no need at all to increase the national burden in the future for a while. The problem is how: whether to set up direct taxes centered on income tax as a foundation, as we have done, or to impose indirect taxes such as consumption tax as the basis. However, as we can see from the fact that it has taken considerable time to introduce and increase consumption tax and that the resistance is particularly strong in Japan, the tax system, which is closely related to systems and mechanisms for the entire country, is not easy to change.

According to Kimberly J. Morgan and Monica Prasad, the United States and France are at opposite ends as far as the tax system is concerned. The speed of industrialization is faster in the United States, while the centralization of the government has been more advanced in France. Also, whereas the tax system in the United States is mainly based on direct tax (progressive income tax), that of France mainly operates on the basis of indirect tax (regressive consumption tax and value-added tax). Since industrialization was already advanced in the United States at the beginning of the 20th century, industry asserted that the government should be funded by income tax rather than imposing tariffs. On the other hand, France preferred to impose tariffs on agricultural products from abroad since the agriculture segment was strong, but the industrial sector was not yet at a stage to be able to discuss the abolishment of tariffs at that time. It also found itself in the circumstance that despite needing to create a government system to track individuals' income in order to introduce income tax, this did not work out well because the French had a strong sense of vigilance toward the asset survey by the central government (Morgan and Prasad, 2009). Such differences in the process that formed the foundation of the tax system continue to have an influence even today. Japan had forecasted the aging population at an early stage and considered introducing a consumption tax; however, its implementation was quite difficult (Kato, 1997; Ishi, 2009). Furthermore, it is common knowledge that a somewhat one-sided negative view of the consumption tax has also widely been shared among the people following its introduction, making it difficult to raise the tax rate.

(3) Beneficiaries of Social Security

In terms of social security and welfare policy, two approaches are relevant: selectivism (targetism), which is the idea of selecting individuals who deserve a given service and narrowing down the target population; and universalism, which is the idea of trying to have as many people as possible as beneficiaries by aiming to avoid making such a selection in so far as possible. As in the case of the tax system, this difference is a point that should also not be overlooked when considering social security and social welfare policy.

Needless to say, universalism cannot be practiced unless the scale of public finance is large in the first place. Under Swedish-type welfare, employment and social security have always been tightly linked. Its difference from the workfare seen in countries such as the United States is that it presupposes employment and is mainly based on the de-commodification policy that allows people to leave the labor market as needed. What is particularly important is the income replacement principle, where the purpose of publicly provided income security in the case of unemployment, medical care, childcare leave, etc., is to maintain the citizen's current income rather than guaranteeing the minimum income. Therefore, securing employment and raising the level of income would result in a higher level of benefits. It is true that the level of benefits also increases with the income in Japan. However, while the amount of contribution also increases in Japan, the difference lies in various benefits directly increasing employment and income security in Sweden because the employers pay the social insurance premium. Conversely, the level of minimum income guaranteed outside the labor market is significantly lower. These systems in Sweden were created by considering the incentive to work in addition to work ethics in order to obtain votes from the middle class. In fact, although Sweden is considered to have generous social security, the percentage of social assistance[10] such as welfare is extremely low (Yumoto and Sato, 2010: 161–176). Therefore, Taro Miyamoto states that starting with the question, "Why would the middle class support such a large government?" is not only wrong but nonsensical: the correct understanding is that the government voluntarily became big in order to obtain support from the working middle class (Miyamoto, 2013: 42–43).

On the assumption that financial resources are scarce, as in Japan, it is inevitable that policies to enhance the re-distribution function must rely on selectivism. However, this creates a gap in treatment between service recipients and those who are one-sidedly forced to take on the burden of paying tax. It means that the latter—the majority of whom are middle class—would almost never find themselves in a situation of experiencing the direct benefits. According to Walter Korpi and Joakim Palme, the method of selectivism that appears to create results by cutting costs would result in strong opposition by the middle class, which constitutes a large section of the population; and that, in turn, would have the paradoxical result that it becomes difficult for society as a whole to gain benefit, since the burden only increases and it becomes even more difficult to obtain support (Korpi and Palme, 1998). Today, poverty is frequently pinpointed as an urgent issue (Iwata, 2007). At the level of research, it has been pointed out that many individuals are not receiving the benefit of the public assistance system in Japan because the procedures of claiming benefits are troublesome and the eligibility requirements are very stringent (Hirao, 2002). By contrast, there has recently been some negative news coverage on public assistance and many people are casting a critical eye in response. This probably reflects the situation that those in the middle class in Japan are dissatisfied with the fact they are not receiving any benefit even though they are defraying the costs while the income level remains low.

3. Globalized World and Social Policies

(1) Economy that Goes beyond the Framework of the State

Peter Taylor-Gooby states that the following four stages have occurred in the transition to a post-industrialized society.

First, women's social advancement increased and participation by men in the labor force began decreasing. This made it necessary to earn a double-income in order to maintain a living. Therefore, demands for women's equal opportunities in education and the labor market further increased. Second, the elderly population requiring social care increased, as did the corresponding cost to the welfare state of providing services such as pensions and medical care. Third, while the demand for highly educated individuals increased as the relationship between the labor market and education was strengthened, the risk of less-educated individuals becoming socially excluded increased. Fourth, in response to the movement to try to tighten national finance, private services, especially private pensions, increased.

Since those at risk were mainly the elderly and the unemployed up until then, the objective of these policies was clear, such as focusing on those who are not earning wages. However, there is now a wider variety of new risks and there is no choice but to target a wide range of age groups (or life stages). Not only that, but there is also a need to provide services to cater to individuals rather than uniformly allocating resources. Specifically, examples of services may include assistance for work-life balance, education, and training (Taylor-Gooby, 2004).

In a sense, the transition to globalization makes the framework of the nation state meaningless. In particular, economic activities that span the world "export" work in order to input labor force at a lower cost. In addition, thanks to the advancement of technology, goods can be produced anywhere by building a division-of-labor system in places around the world, as long as this does not cost too much. And large, transnational companies responsible for such activities aim to expand their business to places where the tax is the lowest and the infrastructure is fully developed, by escaping from countries where taxes are high and thereby removing employment from these locations. Not only that, but such companies choose among different locations as places to invest in, produce, pay tax, and live, making nation states compete with each other. By doing so, it becomes possible for the individuals at the top to live comfortably and pay taxes in places with the lowest tax rate. Because this creates problems such as tax havens, as briefly touched on in the Introduction (see also Shiga, 2013), it has become a vexing issue around the world. And this is not only something decided at the level of political discussion; it develops during the course of normal economic activities (Beck, 1997, trans. 2005).

This follows the same course as the problem pointed out by Ulrich Beck in *Risk Society, Towards a New Modernity* (1986, trans. 1998), namely, that although it appears as if a society that is rational and feels safe is built as modernization progresses, risks that are difficult to see (or difficult to sense) and at the same time infinitely difficult to predict, going beyond the framework of the nation state, will surface in reality. And these risks are not dependent on the circumstances that each individual finds him- or herself in. Moreover, people cannot realize the risk itself; rather, they come to recognize it having been being pointed out by some kind of expert (Beck, 1986, trans. 1998). Although it might be an exaggeration to say that the various systems created on the premise of the framework of the state would become meaningless as economic activities are globalized, it would even be difficult to control them.

(2) Social Exclusion and Inclusion

I have previously made use of the term "social exclusion." Welfare and social security policies were originally closely related to labor legislations, and improving their benefits was not independent of labor movements. As the state became a welfare state, the standard of living of the working class improved, reducing the incentive for it to unite as a class called workers to undertake a movement. Instead, people realized that women, minorities, and people with disabilities were not covered by these systems in the first place and began actively advocating their rights. In sociological terms, this is the beginning of the so-called "new social movements,"[11] or advocacy movements for minorities based on feminism, race, and ethnicity. These new social movements began raising awareness of various structures of discrimination that were not limited to the economic dimension. Arguments were made of the following kind: "merely throwing around goods until they are enough will not work for these people," "these people might have been excluded from the systems and communities in wider societies in the first place due to institutions and cultural criteria making it difficult for them to obtain employment and opportunities to connect with other people," and "encouraging social participation and building a system that can maintain such a custom might for this reason become all the more important." While the term "exclusion" is used in such context, "inclusion" is used as its counter-concept. Behind these assertions was the emerging need to respond to criticisms from the right wing regarding various social policies as social security put pressure on the national finances. In short, the criticizing right-wingers positioned themselves entirely as neoliberalists. According to their viewpoint, far from increasing the motivation to work, generous benefits therefore create dependency and actually encourage laziness. Therefore, the left-wingers who support these policies needed to show that the roots of the problem were deep and that these were not policies to merely provide money and goods (Kameyama, 2007).

According to Kengo Nakamura, the term "social exclusion" was first used in France and then later spread to the United Kingdom. However, the context in which it was used differs considerably (Nakamura, 2007). In France, the concept of "participation" was adopted as a counter-strategy in the Revenu minimum d'insertion (RMI) to promote social participation among long-term unemployed individuals. The term "participation" was used in the context of reconstruction of social solidarity under the republican tradition.[12] In the United Kingdom, on the other hand, the concept of inclusion was established as a strategy to counter the neoliberalist ideology touting that welfare makes people dependent on the state. The term "inclusion" was used to mean using welfare to facilitate excluded people in becoming active in society, i.e., connecting the needy segment with the labor market to help them become financially independent. This was a keyword presented by the Labour Party led by Tony Blair in 1994 in order to overcome the situation of poverty and inequality in the United Kingdom. Having taken the helm of state, the Labour Party then positioned social inclusion as one of the most important agendas of the regime. This idea of "inclusion" in the United Kingdom later affected the policies of the Democratic Party in the United States.[13]

The policy details of a conventional benefit-type welfare state were basically formulated in accordance with the vertically divided administrative organization, which is also centralized. However, when putting forth the effort to socially include people who might otherwise fall through the system's cracks, services cannot merely provide monetary benefits; provision of actual goods (or actual service) becomes necessary, and cross-functional cooperation becomes important. In other words, issues such as employment policy, social security policy, and education policy are no longer separate; whether these policies succeed or not depends largely on cooperation with each other and how they are combined. Implementing flexible services then becomes important, making it necessary for the local governments—rather than the centralized and vertically divided administration—to comprehensively govern services based on the actual circumstances of the community. Therefore, decentralization, strengthening cooperation across different agencies, and building a mechanism for mutual coordination becomes necessary; and such opinions do, in fact, begin surfacing, although taking the relevant actions is not as easy as it sounds. And if they fail here, the administrative organization itself is indeed deemed inefficient, as it is seen to be the government's fault, which might lead to reinforcing the neoliberalist argument for reducing the size of the government itself; therefore, the government is truly faced with a difficult situation (Miyamoto, 2013: 3–23).

4. The Relationship between Education System and Social Security/ Welfare System from the Perspective of International Comparison

(1) Complementarity of the Systems

As mentioned in Chapter 2, the theory by neo-institutionalists such as Meyer and colleagues on the global spread of education systems has gained a certain level of support and is often mentioned in the field of educational sociology. As I touched on there, neo-institutionalists focus on institutional isomorphism.

However, it is known that there are actually a variety of relationships between education (particularly the pathway of vocational education after secondary education) and the labor market. Such varieties do not necessarily occur completely at random. As stated at the beginning of this chapter, there is a mutual complementarity[14] whereby the affinity of the labor market for a given education system exists because the labor market naturally makes use of the existing education system (and vice versa). In other words, since various systems are intricately intertwined with each other rather than existing independently, it is difficult to make changes independently when a problem becomes apparent with one system. To be more precise, because there is a kind of institutional inertia, it takes enormous cost to make any corrections once a system is established. In this way, a path dependency is created in which newer systems and mechanisms are affected by the systems that are already in place. The mutual complementarity among systems is meaningful when its existence actually interacts with various systems; a reform is meaningful only when various systems are forced to change across the board (Amable, 2003, trans. 2005, 18–21; Aoki, 2008: 39–41).

This can be put in another way as in the following explanation. For example, given the opinion that the ideal economy of the 1990s would have had the Danish education system, Swedish technology and employment policies, the competitive environment of the Finish high-tech sector, and the American entrepreneurial environment, labor market regulation, financing system, and competitive environment, the question is whether the best model can be created by merely combining these Nordic and American systems. There is an infinite number of possible combinations of different institutions and systems (between different areas). And there could, of course, be more than one pattern rather than a very limited number of combinations that produce the best performance. Conversely, this means that randomly combining systems that have produced a partially good performance would not always result in systems that produce good performance. Basically, a given system running well means that it is in a complementary relationship with other systems, so that it might not work well if that relationship did not exist (Amable, 2003, trans. 2005: 79–84).

Bruno Amable, a regulationalist economist in France, divides systems in capitalist countries into five areas comprising product market competition, labor relations-related, financial sector, social security, and education. These systems were created as a result of conflicts and compromises among various groups within a given society. Each combination of systems was created based on the complementarity of each system rather than randomly linking them. Amable also states that the types of capitalist systems can be divided into five categories: market-based economics, social democratic economics, Asian capitalism, Continental European capitalism, and Mediterranean capitalism (Amable, 2003, trans. 2005: 136–142).

(2) Education under Social Policies

Let us turn to the method employed by Amable and explain it based on empirical data on the relationship between each policy. The method used here is called Principal Component Analysis (PCA).[15]

Here, I used the OECD Social Expenditure Database (SOCX) and looked at each country's public spending on *old age, survivors, incapacity-related benefits, health, family, active labor market programs, unemployment, housing,* and *education* compared to the GDP. Using these variables, I created a composite variable with high explanatory power, namely, that maximizes the variance of each original variable under the composite variable.

Here, in order to highlight the difference between the functions of higher education and non-higher education under social policy, *education* was divided into "primary and secondary education plus post-secondary education not included in higher education" and "higher education" for analysis. After conducting the PCA, the first and second principal components with a large contribution rate (ratio of eigenvalues) were used as the horizontal and vertical axes, respectively, to plot the factor loading of each variable, as shown in Figure 3-2. In PCA, the meaning of the derived principal components (the axes on the figure) is interpreted by looking at the relative positions of the original variables (i.e., factor loadings). Variables plotted closer to an axis have a higher loading for the corresponding principal component, making a higher contribution to the component of the axis (i.e., they have a high explanatory power for that axis).

The contribution rates are approximately 35% and 26% for Axis 1 (horizontal axis) and Axis 2 (vertical axis), respectively, and many variables are located to the right of the vertical axis (Quadrants I and IV). This implies that, based on the first principal component, there is a general relationship whereby the social expenditure items shown here increase as the ratio to the GDP increases. In particular, labor-related indicators and *health* are plotted very closely together and close to

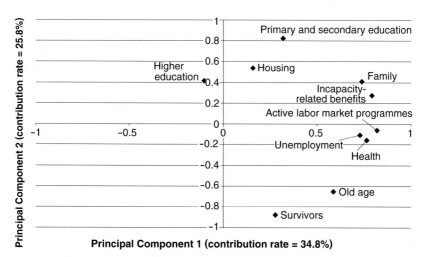

Figure 3-2 Factor Loading Plot
Source: OECD StatExtract (http://stats.oecd.org/)

the horizontal axis (Principal Component 1), while not contributing much to the vertical axis component (Principal Component 2). In other words, while labor-related and health expenditures largely contribute to the axis of the first principal component, based on the values on the horizontal axis, *incapacity-related benefits* and *family* equally contribute to the component of the axis. The contribution of *old age* is also large. In comparison, while the contribution of education is not large, it is noteworthy that *primary and secondary education* is found on the positive side and *higher education* slightly on the negative side. Therefore, it can be said that the first principal component is an indicator for the size of expenditure percentage for a wide range of welfare and social security in general, and *primary and secondary education* is positioned more or less close to these welfare policies.

As for the second principal component on the vertical axis, the positions are divided into positive and negative. Since those related to education and family are positive and *survivors* and *old age* are negative, it can be inferred that the second principal component might be a measure of determining whether the policy target is childcare or the elderly. In other words, it is an indicator for explaining whether the service's target segment is the children and youth generation or the old generation.

Based on the factors extracted for each country as a result of the above PCA, I can assign a score (factor score) to each country. These scores are plotted in Figure 3-3, which can be regarded as analogous to Figure 3-2. In other words, since variables such as *primary and secondary education, family*, and *incapacity-related benefits* are plotted in Quadrant I of Figure 3-2 and we can see the Nordic countries, the United Kingdom, the Netherlands, and other countries in Quadrant I of Figure 3-3, it can be said that these countries are characterized by their focus on primary and secondary education, family, and incapacity-related benefits' policies that are

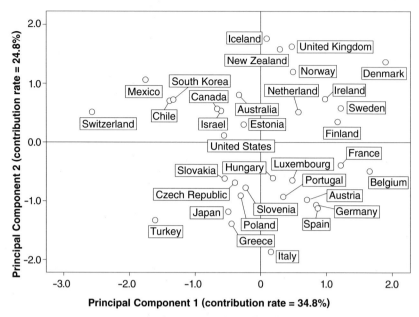

Figure 3-3 Factor Score Plot by Country (Social and Education Expenditure)
Source: OECD StatExtract (http://stats.oecd.org/)

plotted in very similar positions. Since the countries in Quadrant II are positive on the vertical axis, this indicates that their overall ratio of social expenditure to the GDP is small, although they focus more on policies for the younger than the older generation (only in a relative sense).

Looking at this in the same manner, the countries in Quadrant III are the ones where social expenditure itself is small yet focused disproportionately on the elderly policies. Japan is one of them. Quadrant IV shows that although the focus on elderly policies is the same, the size of social expenditure of these countries is large.

To summarize, we can see from Figure 3-2 that education is plotted in different positions for *primary and secondary education* and *higher education*. Although the explanatory power of the first principal component is not necessarily high, given that *primary and secondary education* is located on the positive side on the first axis while *higher education* is located on the negative side, we can see that primary and secondary education have an affinity with welfare and social security policies to promote equality, whereas higher education has a different vector. In addition, we can see from the components of social expenditure that Japan is close to some of the Southern European countries and positioned opposite the so-called welfare states in Northern Europe, as expected.

(3) Position of Education Policy in the Overall Public Expenditure

I intend to position education in a wide range of government measures rather than limiting it to so-called social policies. The data are sourced from the OECD database in the same way; however, in order to see the positioning within overall policies not limited to social policies, I used education as one item rather than dividing it into primary and secondary education and higher education to perform the analysis. As a note, items with a degree of contribution too small to compose the factor are often excluded from the analysis in PCA because they do not contribute to the overall factor component. (In such a case, the variable ends up coming close to the origin when plotted. In other words, its factor loading is close to zero under higher-ranked factors with a high explanatory power.) Here, too, *general public services* and *security maintenance* (police, etc.) were excluded from the analysis because their explanatory power (or factor loading) was small under the factors with a large contribution rate.

This may mean that every country had a certain level of spending on general public services and security maintenance and there was not much difference by country. "Expense items that constitute a factor in PCA" does not mean that these are large spending items; it means that they make a large contribution to constitute the axis or have a large variance (dispersion). Social security expenditure does not contribute much to the first and second principal components, although its increase has become a problem. This is probably because every country has a certain percentage of social security expenditure.

Now, looking at Figure 3-4, all items are on the positive side of the first principal component, except for *defense*, which is on the negative side. In other words, most items are in a completely opposite relationship with the percentage accounted for by defense expenditure (i.e., when the former is large, the defense expenditure is small, and vice versa).

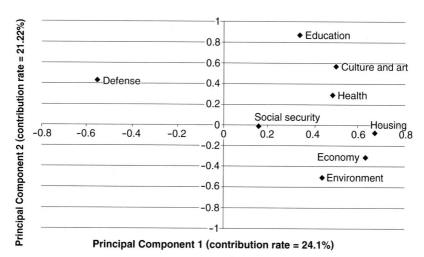

Figure 3-4 Factor Loading Plot for the PCA of Public Expenditure (to the GDP) (1)
Source: OECD StatExtract (http://stats.oecd.org/)
Data are for 2010, except for Canada (2006) and New Zealand (2005).

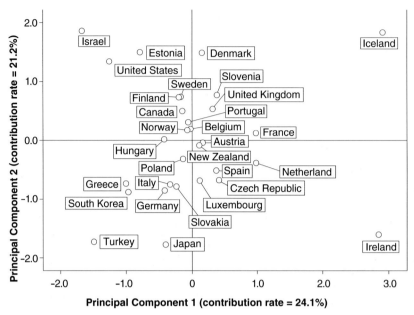

Figure 3-5 Factor Score (Principal Components 1 and 2) Plot (Public Spending to GDP)
Source: OECD StatExtract (http://stats.oecd.org/)
Data are for 2010, except for Canada (2006) and New Zealand (2005).

Figure 3-5 plots countries based on the first and second principal components in Figure 3-4. The ones that lie close to the origin are countries that are difficult to characterize based on these two principal components. Looking at the second principal component in Figure 3-4, *education* and *health* are on the positive side and *economy* and *environment* on the negative side. It seems that what we would think of when we hear the term "welfare" is found on the positive side of the second principal component. On the other hand, looking at Figure 3-5, the Nordic countries seem to be concentrated on the positive side near the second principal component axis.

The fact that countries such as Israel and the United States are found in Quadrant II, obviously reflects that their military spending (i.e., defense expenditure) is large. Continental European countries, including conservative regimes as defined by Esping-Andersen, are concentrated in Quadrant III. Japan is also included here. Japan's second principal component is found on the far negative side. Looking at Figure 3-4, *education* and *culture and art* are located on the positive side of the second principal component axis; therefore, the fact that Japan's public spending on education and culture and art is relatively small can be positioned in this way.

Since the contribution rates of the first and second principal components were not necessarily large in absolute terms and were on par with each other, I examined

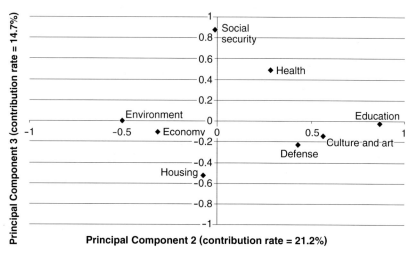

Figure 3-6 Factor Loading Plot for the PCA of Public Expenditure (to the GDP) (2)
Source: OECD StatExtract (http://stats.oecd.org/)
Data are for 2010, except for Canada (2006) and New Zealand (2005).

them by including the third principal component. The results are shown in Figure 3-6. When the data are plotted based on the second and third principal components, a completely different picture emerges.

Although it is difficult to interpret the second principal component, variables related to education and culture are positive, while those related to environment and economy are negative. Furthermore, these variables have a considerably low contribution rate to the third principal component. The third principal component is relatively easy to understand; the ones that are referred to as welfare or social security are found on the positive side. Even though *housing policy* is also usually counted as social security, however, it is found on the negative side, in contrast to *social security* and *health*. In addition, looking at this third principal component, education is found almost on the second principal component axis and not really contributing to the third principal component. Likewise, *economy, environment, defense,* and *culture and art* do not contribute to the third principal component. We can gain a glimpse of the uniqueness of *education* (as compared to *social security* and *welfare*) from these plots.

Figure 3-7 is a plot of each country's factor score for the second and third principal components. Based on this, we can see that Japan and the United States are exactly in the opposite position. Although this is partially due to the fact that not only *education* but also *defense* makes a large contribution to the second principal component, the United States and Israel are found on the positive side on the second principal component axis. In addition, while *defense* is in Quadrant IV in Figure 3-6, the United States and Israel are also in Quadrant IV. The fact that both of these countries focus on education in their own way is another characteristic. On the other hand, welfare states such as countries in Northern Europe are all

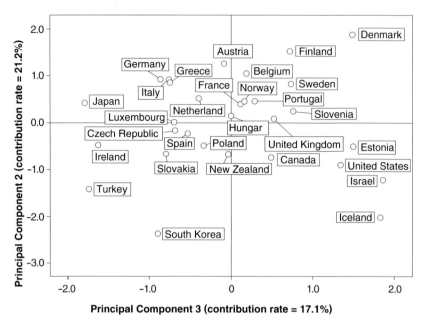

Figure 3-7 Factor Score (Principal Components 2 and 3) Plot (Public Spending to GDP)

Source: OECD StatExtract (http://stats.oecd.org/)
Data are for 2010, except for Canada (2006) and New Zealand (2005).

found in Quadrant I.

Japan is found almost at the edge of Quadrant II, where Continental Europe is concentrated. Japan is quite close to the positive side of the third principal component axis because it reflects the results as in Figure 3-1 that social security is shifting toward the elderly. Furthermore, given that *education* and *culture and art* largely contribute to the second principal component, we can see that Japan does not financially focus on these types of policies.

(4) Distance between Education and Each Policy Area and the Classification of Country Based on Distance

Based on the above, the proximity (or distance) of each policy can be measured by using the structure of social expenditure. At the same time, countries can also be classified based on a certain standard by using the breakdown of national finances. Looking at social policies, education policies can be divided into *primary and secondary education* and *higher education*; and it has been shown that *primary and secondary education* is close to the welfare and social security policies in general (Figure 3-2). The Nordic countries, which fall under the social democratic regime as defined by Esping-Andersen, are found relatively close to Continental Europe, which falls under the conservative regime. However, Anglo-Saxon countries, which are considered liberal regimes, are relatively scattered, so that the United

Kingdom and New Zealand are close to Northern Europe but far away from the United States, Canada, and Australia. While Amable defined the category "Asian capitalism," there is a considerable distance between Japan and South Korea, and they are not exactly similar in terms of social expenditure breakdown (Figure 3-3).

In addition, when the subject variables are expanded to cover the entire government expenditure, what we first see is that many social policy-related expenditures and defense expenditures are in the opposite position. *Education* and *culture and art*, which are found closely together, are in the opposite position to economic and environmental policies. Investing in education should lead to economic development of the society from the perspective of human capital; however, since higher education expenditure means lower spending on economic policies in terms of government spending, it does not seem that they are always in an affiliative relationship (Figure 3-4). *Housing policy* is also in the opposite position to *social security* and *health*, while *education* is positioned in between them (Figure 3-6).

Japan is considered to have been influenced by neoliberalism and has a small government; however, based on the structure of government spending, Japan is quite different from the United States and actually closer to Continental European countries, which are considered conservative regimes as defined by Esping-Andersen. This suggests that Japan is quite different from countries like the United States in terms of people's feelings toward the government as well as the country's historical development. Thus, I will continue by examining the perception toward the government from the standpoint of international comparison.

NOTES

[1] Works by Pat Thane, which have also been translated into Japanese, have separate sections for education items (Thane, 1996, trans. 2000).

[2] This mostly applies to higher education. According to Christiana Stoddard, who examined the background of how the United States came to spend public funds on compulsory education, the percentage of public spending on education was higher among states with fewer disparities when compared to those states with similar median assets. This also had the effect of increasing the school enrollment rate, particularly among the poor (Stoddard, 2009).

[3] In terms of territory of the government authorities, whereas school education falls under the jurisdiction of the Ministry of Education, Culture, Sports, Science and Technology (MEXT), family policies including child welfare fall under the Ministry of Health, Labour and Welfare (MHLW), for example. However, since childcare itself costs a considerable amount of money, especially from the standpoint of parents raising children, such vertically organized administration is only logical from the perspective of the government offices. Education policies that are disconnected from family policies are meaningless, and labor policies that ignore family policies are also unreasonable. It is undeniable that academics tend to lopsidedly examine a narrowly defined, specific area as specialization increases; however, as this chapter argues, how to relate education policies to social security and welfare policies needs to be examined from a broader perspective because it affects how society thinks of education.

4   However, the rate of increase has been slowing down in recent years.
5   The claim made by the MOF can be viewed by accessing the following document as of January 2014: http://www.mof.go.jp/budget/budger_workflow/budget/fy2010/bunkyo.pdf
The counter argument by MEXT can be found on the following website: http://www.mext.go.jp/a_menu/yosan/h22/1287930.htm
6   This implies that the effect of inequality correction by income redistribution is not very large.
7   This is the OECD's public social expenditure data as a percentage of the total general government expenditure. The latest comprehensive data available as of February 2014 are for the fiscal year 2009.
8   Although they had some difficulties and issues, establishing the universal health insurance and universal pension in 1961 was quite early compared to other countries; in particular, universal health insurance had only been implemented in three countries in Northern Europe (Miyamoto, 2008: 66–67). In that sense, the assessment that asserts that there was no sign of welfare is somewhat too extreme. However, in terms of the scale, it was insufficient.
9   For example, free medical care for the elderly over the age of 70 introduced in 1969 by the then Tokyo Governor Ryokichi Minobe later spread to other local governments throughout the nation, prompting the Tanaka administration to decide to make medical care free for the elderly nationwide. This case is often cited as an example in which local policies affected the national policy.
10 This refers to the policy measure of using tax money to provide cash to individuals whose income is lower than a certain level.
11 Sociologically, they are said to have started with a movement that Alain Touraine in France argued to have emerged to replace class conflict.
12 However, according to Nakamura, although the term "exclusion" is used in the political setting in France, it is only mentioned carefully as an unconvincing concept in the field of social science (Nakamura, 2007).
13 In Northern Europe, employment support has been provided through active labor policy. Furthermore, the national and local governments have traditionally taken the responsibility for improving childcare services. This means that national governments in particular were already implementing welfare state policies incorporating the concept of inclusion in the sense used in the United Kingdom.
14 "Complement" is the opposite concept of substitution. If the demand for Goods A increases when the price of Goods B rises, Goods A has become a substitute. Conversely, Goods A is a complement if its demand decreases when the price of Goods B rises. For example, if more people begin eating rice when the price of bread rises (i.e., they avoid consuming bread that has become expensive), rice is considered to be in a substitutional relationship with bread and becomes a substitute. On the other hand, bread and jam are in a complementary relationship where the demand for jam to put on the bread declines when the price of bread rises (causing fewer people to eat the expensive bread), but it increases when the price of bread drops and more people begin eating bread, so that jam is referred to as a complement of bread. To have mutual complementarity means one system exists on the premise of the existence of the other system and they are hence in a

relationship to complement each other.

[15] See Ueda (2003) on PCA.

CHAPTER 4
The Structure of Japanese People's Attitude toward Education and Social Policies from the Perspective of International Comparison

1. Attitude toward Welfare Policy and Social Security

(1) Rationale for Focusing on the Attitude

The way the so-called welfare regime theory is discussed varies because it is relevant to various fields. The cohering principle among them is that the theory implies a rebuttal against the viewpoint that there is a unilinear relationship between the economic development stages and welfare system development, such as that welfare systems and social security services develop as industrialization and modernization advances (Uzuhashi, 1997). In other words, welfare institutions and systems can be seen to vary even among countries exhibiting similar economic development.

For example, as an indicator of the development of the welfare system, public expenditure or the proportion of social security expenditure to the economic scale (GDP) is sometimes used. I have conducted an analysis by partially following the method also of Chapter 3. While this is something seen in the aforementioned work by Wilensky as well as Fred C. Pampel, John B. Williamson, and Francis Castles, among others (Wilensky, 1975, trans. 1984; Pampel and Williamson, 1988; Castles, 1989), we need to be aware that such a viewpoint has the following pitfalls.

The Thatcher administration during the 1980s is generally regarded as the vanguard of neoliberalism. However, looking only at the facts, the overall public expenditure actually increased, especially for social security-related items, even though neoliberalism indeed seems to have had an impact on cutting government spending on items such as housing and education (Takegawa, 1999: 67–70). When the unemployment rate increases, its cost is passed on to social security-related expenses. Conversely, if a state of close to full employment is realized, the cost is reduced regardless of the welfare system. The Japanese government is not in the least bit big compared to its economic scale. However, as we can see from the demographic composition of Japan, the social security benefit cost is destined to increase. Pension and medical care account for 50% and 30% of the total social security benefit cost, respectively; and the social security benefit cost as a percentage of GDP has consequently increased four-fold in 40 years. The overall social expenditure as a percentage of GDP, which is 23%, has also doubled in the past 30 years. This increase is significantly larger than other countries, with the percentage of social expenditure to general government spending already having reached the European level (Tanaka, 2013: 238–241). In other words, while social security expenditure could increase due to rapid population aging, it will never decrease (unless some kind of binding power comes into play). In that sense, although it might not feel that way, Japan will become more of a welfare state in terms of government expenditure.

In addition, although the scale of social security benefit tends to attract all the attention, the roles and functions of the state (or government) are not limited to resource allocation. As Shogo Takegawa points out, we also need to pay attention to the aspect of the welfare state as a regulatory state. In general, the United States is rarely considered to be a welfare state; however, that is when mainly considering benefits; and this does not mean that the United States has been indifferent to the value of equality. In fact, discrimination based on race, gender, age, disabilities, etc., is institutionally strictly prohibited. Deregulations in the United States are mainly related to economic activities; however, when it comes to aspects such as equality of individual freedom and opportunities, the American society pays extremely close attention and deploys strict regulations (Takegawa, 2007: 42).

In short, as shown in Chapter 3, we are beginning to understand the way the welfare system differs considerably even among developed countries. The education system—also a large undertaking that the government is involved in—is not independent of the welfare system. The question is what explains the difference in these regimes (or systems).

While numerous factors can surely be hypothesized, the people's voice (or public opinion) cannot be ignored in a democratic society. This is because the people in a democratic country are supposed to have the opportunity to realize their own will and desire through their voting behavior. While it does not have to be perfect, a policy that does not at all reflect the will of the public is unlikely to be realized. In addition, although the explanation here sounds as if there were a causal relationship whereby a policy is realized through politics because there is the will (or desire) of the people, the actual relationship is not that simple. In the case of social security policy, society begins to consider it a matter of course for beneficiaries to receive benefits once a system has been put into place, so that further expansion of the program might become necessary in some cases. In other words, it seems that there is tendency to no small extent for policy to rouse the demand.[1]

In this chapter, I will continue looking at the issue from the perspective of international comparison and examine to what extent people recognize education, along with other social security and welfare policies, as the government's role by focusing on attitude toward the public burden of education costs.

(2) Competing Interests for Public Spending on Education
The need for services provided by the government is basically increasing more and more. Meanwhile, the government must secure funds to accommodate that need. While this is a common problem among developed countries, it is not easy to secure funds. Tax avoidance behavior is becoming conspicuous, especially among high-income earners, as economic activities become more globalized and the competition to reduce corporate tax continues worldwide in order to attract companies that ultimately bring employment. Under such circumstances, the only option that can ultimately surface in an attempt to somehow secure funds is to persuade the people, or the taxpayers, on an increase in tax.

However, generally speaking, higher taxes tend to be considered as an increased burden. Therefore, the idea is unlikely to gain support, while politicians are unlikely to advocate such policy for which it is difficult to gain support because they could face tax revolt and be defeated in the next election if they did.

Japan is currently in the midst of such difficult circumstances. Ideologically, the appropriate information is supposed to be provided in a democratic society for individuals to refer to in order to make a decision to vote for a political party or candidate he/she considers suitable. However, it is difficult to judge the appropriateness of the information to begin with. There are also various positions regarding tax increases, and the reality is that each party is communicating the information that they consider to serve their own purpose. Unless one has the expertise, it is difficult to judge the appropriateness of the information. Systems related to social security and welfare are particularly complex and require a considerable amount of knowledge. Even experts sometimes state their opinion from completely opposite positions. At the end of the day, it is unreasonable to assume that everyone has the same detailed knowledge on these systems. In addition, an extremely biased image and understanding could become popular, and people might in some cases vote based on such misconception.

According to the analysis by Taylor-Gooby and others, although relatively accurate information is prevalent in the United Kingdom regarding services such as the National Health Service (NHS) that everyone can receive, there is a tendency to overestimate the cost for income redistribution policies targeting specific segments (such as the unemployed and single-parent households, in particular). Furthermore, the highly educated as well as relatively affluent segments such as the middle class are more likely to have this knowledge. In terms of type of policy, those such as the redistribution policy that are beneficial to the low-income segment are more likely to be judged harshly. Not only that, but it is said that the segments that would benefit the most from the redistribution policy are more likely to vote on the basis of an inaccurate understanding (Taylor-Gooby et al., 2003).

To state it very simply, taxpayers consider an expenditure justifiable if they can see it benefit for themselves somehow but do not tend to support an expenditure for which they do not see any direct benefit. Everyone undoubtedly has experience of receiving education and should have enjoyed some of benefit at the personal level; however, the period in which people go to school is generally limited. In addition, those who pay some kind of personal cost for education are limited to families with children who go to school. Assuming that whether or not to have children is a personal choice, it is possible that some people consider the education cost incurred for children to be something that should be paid for by the individual because it is a consequence of their own choice at the micro level (i.e., the act of bearing and raising children itself). As for expenditures in areas related to social security, however, anyone may be at risk of falling into the position of having to rely on the benefits of medical care and the elderly pension, for example (and the possibility could be high or certain when considered over the long term). Therefore, these types of social security expenditures are issues for everyone. It can be said that policies in favor of welfare and social security in general can more easily get support because no one can avoid aging eventually. In that sense, education might be an area that people cannot fully appreciate. For this reason, we can also say that those in urgent need are limited.

As pointed out by Samuel H. Preston, the difference between the expenditure on measures for the elderly and the money spent for children and youth, such as education, is that while the implication of the former is more on consumption, the latter is not merely consumption but social investment (Preston, 1984). However, Kenneth S. Y. Chew states that policies to be supported from a long-term perspective—particularly public investments related to children—will have a hard time receiving support due to an increasingly individualistic orientation in addition to demographic factors such as the declining birth rate, high divorce rate, and aging population. In general, highly educated people tend to agree with direct public funds for education; however, this tendency weakens as people get older. This might reflect the fact that it is the elderly who have strong traditional values that parents should raise their own children (Chew, 1990).[2] It has been observed in the United States that people who are paying for education as parents are more likely to support public spending on education (Chew, 1992).[3]

In many cases, the demand for spending on elderly welfare and health ultimately increases while the demand for spending on the youth segment decreases in developed countries as their birth rates continue to decline and the population further ages. And as the service sector economy flourishes and women begin advancing in society, the instability of family increases and single-parent families, unstable employment, and unemployment manifest as new risks. Meanwhile, however, underfunding is also a common issue. The emergence of the problem of how to allocate limited financial resources reflects the beginning of the era of the post-industrialized society. In southern European countries and societies where the arrival of post-industrialized society has been late, expenditure on pensions tends to become disproportionately large, while education and family policies are overlooked (Tepe and Vanhuysse, 2010).

(3) The Low Level of Trust in the Government among the Japanese
The reason why the problems faced by Japan are extremely difficult to solve lies in

the complicated attitude of the public. In a democratic country, the policy direction is basically selected according to the interest of the majority. As for Japanese people, there is still an extremely strong sense of avoidance of increased tax and burdens, although the tendency appears to have somewhat weakened recently as they have become more acutely aware of the country's financial crisis. In fact, the call to cut down the amount of wastefulness has been receiving a certain level of support. It would be easy to understand the situation if such voices were coming from a so-called "small government orientation." Aside from whether or not one personally agrees, if the people persist in insisting on cutting the amount of wastefulness and not increasing tax because they strongly prefer a small government, and if that is the choice of the majority of the people, such policy must be implemented under a democratic system.

However, the problem is that it does not seem that many Japanese are thinking that way. It is somewhat questionable to what extent people commonly understand the fact that the Japanese government is considered one of the smallest among the developed countries in terms of national burden and number of government employees, and that we have already reached the limit at which there are no more wasteful departments to cut. In addition, many Japanese probably want a stable pension and healthcare system and are uncomfortable with the idea of entrusting everything to the private sector. In other words, it could be that a considerable number of Japanese remain convinced that "since there is still enormous wastefulness in Japan, increasing the tax is unthinkable until it is cut."

Therefore, we have a contradicting attitude structure whereby people do not wish to increase the burden even though they wish for a stable and extensive welfare society (and even though the national finances are in a deficit and the government is considered small enough in terms of the number of government employees and the rate of national burden). The situation has become difficult because there is no logic to views such as "we don't want to increase the burden because we want a small government" or "we will accept some increase in the burden because we want extensive welfare" (Miyamoto, 2008: iii–iv). I will touch on this later in this book as well . Economic crises in the Southern European countries such as Greece have often been talked about in recent years. It is said that people in these countries do not have much trust in others and their so-called public morality is low because of the fraudulent government and large underground economy. Since the trust in the government is compromised when public morality is low, it ultimately become difficult to support welfare state policies.

As for Japan, while there is a moderate amount of welfare and level of trust in others, the level of trust in the government is extremely low. It is not that all countries with extensive welfare (i.e., countries with a big government) have fallen into financial crisis. In the case of Japan, the level of trust in the government is extremely low relative to the range of roles that the government thinks it should play, and people have fallen into the reasoning that they do not want to take on any more burden.[4]

Figure 4-1, which was prepared based on Chapter 1 of the 2013 edition *Government at a Glance* by the OECD, shows the relationship between the level of

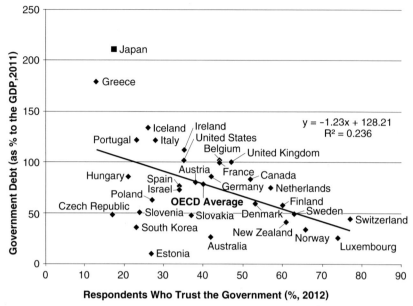

Figure 4-1 Confidence in the Government and Outstanding Debt
Source: OECD (2013) *Government at a Glance*: Figure 1.8 on page 32
The data on confidence in the government is based on the Gallup survey. The data on debt is from the OECD National Accounts Statistics.

trust in the government and the outstanding debt. This problem has been attracting so much attention that even the OECD has dealt with the trust between the government and the people in the reference work that they published. This only shows a simple correlation and does not indicate that there is some kind of specific causal relationship. That said, we can see the relationship that the larger the government's debt, the lower the trust in the government. Whether the government is not trusted because the debt is large or the debt has become excessive because people distrust the government and are not cooperative is unclear. Nevertheless, Japan stands out for the size of its excessive debt and for making a considerable contribution to support the relationship between these two variables.

This type of research that focuses on the sense of trust in the government has been actively conducted in recent years by several economists in France. According to Philippe Aghion and others, people tend to put more pressure on regulating the government when their general sense of trust is low (Aghion et al., 2010).[5] Furthermore, Yann Algan and Pierre Cahuc have pointed out that those who immigrated to the United States still have the level of trust they used to have in their home country, and that there is a correlation between the sense of trust among immigrants by ethnicity and the sense of trust in their home country. They also showed that this sense of trust contributes to economic growth (i.e., the higher the sense of trust in a given society, the more their economy has grown). Solely on this basis, it might seem that sense of trust is determined by the ethnicity-specific culture; however, such a correlation actually weakens and almost disappears among the second generation of immigrants (Algan and Cahuc, 2010). In other words, it shows that the sense of trust created through relationships with others in their home country could change as they live out their lives in the place to which they have emigrated as part of American society.

Toshio Yamagishi compared the sense of trust in Japan to that in the United States and noted that Japanese people tend to trust others as long as they are acquainted but become suspicious if they are not acquainted, so that the sense of trust toward complete strangers is lower compared to Americans. Yamagishi also notes that highly educated individuals are more likely to have a stronger sense of trust toward unacquainted third parties (Yamagishi, 1999). Furthermore, Algan, Cahuc, and Shleifer point out the importance of education in fostering a sense of trust. Attending many one-way lectures in which one only copies from the blackboard means that one will not have many opportunities to learn skills for interactive discussion and communication and cannot easily build cooperative relationships with others. In contrast, attending many lectures that emphasize discussion and group work allows students to actually develop skills for communication and negotiation, contributing to building social capital (Algan et al., 2013). In other words, these studies indicate that the level of trust is not necessarily invariant and fixed; it could sufficiently be changed depending on the social conditions.

2. Determinants of Social Policy

(1) Relationship between the Welfare Regime and Attitude

There must be certain factors that support the situation of each country if welfare states do not necessarily converge in one direction. If the role of the government is to realize the requests of the people who live there, the expectations of the people should be in keeping with the reality of social security and welfare, and their attitude toward social security and welfare policy should also change.

Using two ideas called power resources theory and welfare production regimes, Torben Iversen and John D. Stephens identified and classified the differences in the manner of investing in human capital by government into three categories.

The first is the model of "coordinated market economies with a proportional representation electoral institution without a strong Christian democratic party," which is observed in Scandinavian countries such as Denmark and Nordic countries such as Finland. It makes a high level of investment in the redistribution policy and public education and provides industry and occupation-specific education. In these countries, people are encouraged to acquire sophisticated knowledge to become (non-professional) technicians or skilled workers. Their societies seek to enable people to utilize their acquired skills and move between companies as a result. In addition, their public childcare systems are well-developed to enable parents to participate in the labor market. This makes a high birth rate and the provision of early childhood education possible, in turn, making it possible to maintain a wide range of welfare systems.

The second is countries that have "coordinated market economies with a proportional representation electoral institution with a strong Christian democratic party," like Germany and Italy, where investment in public education is relatively small, even though there is extensive social insurance and company and industry-specific vocational training. Although Christian democratic societies generally focus on skilled work, they are not very interested in non-skilled work and not enthusiastic about publicly absorbing the cost of early childhood and primary education. The biggest difference from the Scandinavian countries is that they are not eager for women's social advancement; in fact, they maintain a tax system to encourage women to stay at home.

The third is countries that have "liberal market economies with a majoritarian electoral institution" where investments in knowledge and skills are made personally and investments in public education and redistribution are modest. Education and training systems are not well established and the institutional linkage between schools and the labor market is not very common in these countries. The level of public burden for early childhood and primary education also remains low. The polarization between winners and losers increases, and there are not many opportunities for the middle class who are winners to sympathize with leftist assertions in these countries since people are expected to get good grades. Therefore, they are unlikely to have any incentive to change their voting behavior to improve these situations. The three economic systems presented here can be considered to roughly correspond to Esping-Andersen's welfare regimes of social democratic, conservative, and liberal regimes, respectively.

However, Mads Meier Jæger points out that many previous studies have indicated there to be no strong correlation between welfare regimes and people's support for and attitude toward public policy. He cautions that the variance of the relationship between regimes and attitude must also be observed rather than merely looking at the average level of support. In terms of redistribution policy, the average level of support gradually increases in the order of liberalism, social democracy, and conservatism. Looking at this based on variance, however, it increases in the order of liberalism, conservatism, and social democracy. In the case of liberalism, support for redistribution policy rarely becomes a political issue in the first place because it is not recognized as social problem when the support is not large. In the case of social democracy, there are not many people who advocate further increasing redistribution because extensive redistribution is already in place. The policy also tends to become a political issue (and thus a larger variance) because it is highly visible. Conservative regimes are basically inclined to set their "ideal" allocation at a high level (because they are in between liberal and social democratic regimes). They are also inclined to perceive the scope of redistribution within the same trade rather than for the entire society (because of their corporatism scheme); this might be the reason why the variance remains modest (Jæger, 2009).

Using the United States as a representative of the liberal regime, Sweden of the social democratic regime, and Germany of the conservative regime, Pil Ho Kim investigated where Japan falls based on people's attitude toward welfare. The results indicated that while political attitudes such as leftist and rightist ideologies and voting behavior directly affected the attitude toward welfare in the United Sates and Sweden, the effect was weak in Germany, and there was no significant effect in Japan. Thus, he concluded that Japan is close to Germany's conservative regime in the sense that political ideology does not affect attitude toward welfare (Kim, 2004).

When researching attitude, it is necessary to pay full attention to its context and surrounding environment because its nuance can be perceived in a completely different manner on such basis even if the responses to a survey are the same. For example, according to Jonas Edlund, people's distrust toward the welfare state policies in Sweden does not necessarily lead to their opposition of welfare state policies. Such distrust often concerns not providing sufficient services to meet expectations; the percentage of people who increased their sense of distrust because they agree with neoliberal small-government ideology (or due to the spread of such ideology) is not very large (Edlund, 2006). In other words, even if the number of responses indicating distrust in government policy increases, it is somewhat hasty to conclude that the number of advocates for a smaller government is increasing or that neoliberalist ideology is becoming common among the general public.

It is necessary to focus on aspects such as the tax system and whether to implement public assistance or social insurance in addition to looking at the welfare regime. For example, since the taxpayers are more likely to feel being heavily taxed in a country with a higher percentage of direct taxes, such as national income tax or property tax (due to the visibility of the tax),[6] anti-tax and anti-welfare movements are likely to occur in countries such as the United Kingdom, the United States, Japan, and Denmark. In addition, since public assistance and social insurance are systems based on completely different ideas, with public assistance considered "charity for the lower class," or income transfer in a manner of speaking, the sense of burden among the taxpayers increases when public assistance becomes conspicuous (i.e., the percentage becomes relatively high). On the other hand, because social insurance is a social security system for the middle class and only those who pay the insurance premium can enjoy the benefits, there is a sense of entitlement and relatively fewer objections. According to a theory by Sara A. Rosenberry, anti-tax and anti-welfare movements are likely to occur in the United Kingdom, the United States, and Denmark because the proportion of public assistance is high (Rosenberry, 1982). Furthermore, the existence of anti-tax and anti-welfare movements depends on whether labor organizations are strong or not. Regarding this, Toshimitsu Shinkawa concluded that there was no noticeable anti-tax and anti-welfare movement in Sweden, for example, where the visibility of tax is high and public assistance is relatively extensive because there is strong labor organization power to maintain the corporatism system (Shinkawa, 2005: 216–221).

What are the requirements to have these type of powerful labor organizations? According to Yoshikazu Kenjo, a country must have a high level of dependency on trade and a small population. By contrast, Japan has never met these requirements and is most likely never to meet them in the future. Capitalists under capitalism would normally advocate liberalism since it is not an option for them to support redistribution policy (because they would have to surrender their capital and income). Meanwhile, resisting these capitalists, labor organizations would put forward the value called equality to assert the value of their own existence and strongly support social security policies.

Small countries have small markets. Therefore, they have no choice but to rely on the development of an export industry if they want people's lives to improve. And so they would aggressively inject capital to leading companies and industries as a national policy and actually weed out noncompetitive industries by suppressing the investment demand. Once the openness of the economy increases, however, the economic structure becomes fragile and the freedom of domestic policy is lost because the country becomes susceptible to international economic fluctuations. The three parties—the government, workers, and employers—come to have a mutual interest in addressing such crisis and being able to deeply share awareness of the problem. They would then develop social security policies in response to the urgent need to set up a buffer against international economic fluctuation.

Moreover, because highly productive industries are protected and the rest of the industries are weeded out, the protected industries become enormous and centralized. As a result, giant corporations begin requiring a relatively homogeneous labor force in a wide range of areas. With strong homogeneity, the workers also become likely to share common awareness toward problems and create a highly organized labor union. Then, labor unions begin creating a national center and centralizing negotiations in order to gain an upper hand in negotiations not only with the employers but also with the government. At the same time, the national center sometimes exercises its power over individual unions to make them cooperate with policies that go against their own will, such as wage control, for example, when an inflationary impact arising overseas might affect the domestic economy. Having overcome the crisis, the national center would then demand compensation in return.

However, like the United States, the openness of the Japanese economy is very low.[7] In such environments, the possibility for a labor organization to grow that vigorously promotes the equality policy is close to zero (Kenjo, 2001: 126–136).

(2) Relationship between Personal Attributes and Attitude

Ultimately, social security and welfare divides people into those who can receive the service and those who cannot. As described in Section 2-(3) of Chapter 3, the conflict of social interest is lessened if the provision of government services is based on universalism; however, the difference between the beneficiaries and non-beneficiaries becomes obvious in the case of selectivism. Therefore, those who are eligible to receive the service are more likely to support social policies in a country with a small government that tends to target specific segments. In general, low-income individuals, those without a stable job, the elderly, and those prone to get ill, as well as women and parents raising a child in terms of family policies are probably likely to be in favor of social security and welfare services. As for education, the number of individuals who think it is the role of the government, or that the government should bear the cost, is naturally expected to increase in the parenting generation with children.

However, I have already mentioned that whereas other social security and welfare policies are characterized, if anything, by more of a redistributing, equality-type of policy, education—particularly higher education—has a slightly different characteristic. Individuals from a higher class are more likely to advance to higher education to begin with. On the other hand, because a lower cost would be welcomed even among those from a higher class, they might actually be more in agreement with having the government cover the cost.

According to Morten Blekesaune and Jill Quadagno, although public aid for unemployment, medical care, and the elderly are all likely to be supported by women and people who are familiar with egalitarian ideology, there is no difference in the level of support by an individual's employment status (i.e., employed vs. unemployed) for medical care and the elderly, probably because these tend to be perceived as a risk for everyone. Although the tendency to support public aid for the unemployed also increases at the country level along with the rate of unemployment, the level of support to provide public aid for medical care and elderly welfare is not related to the country's penetration rate of egalitarian ideology (Blekesaune and Quadagno, 2003).

Stefan Svallfors also examined the support structure with regard to the level of people's support for income distribution policies and their demographics by referring to Esping-Andersen's welfare regime theory and selecting countries that fall under each regime type. The results showed that the difference observed between these nations can be explained by the level of support (i.e., social democracy and conservatism had a higher level of support, while liberalism had a lower support level); moreover, the support structure [8] as to who among them was likely to support income distribution policies was similar regardless of the regime type (Svallfors, 1997).

3. International Comparative Analysis

(1) The Data Used and Angle of Analysis

Here, referencing previous studies and based on a questionnaire survey on attitude conducted in multiple countries simultaneously using the same questionnaire, I will examine 1) whether there is a relationship between people's attitudes toward social security, welfare, and education policies and the scale of the welfare regime and government; and 2) whether each policy tends to be supported by the supposed beneficiaries. Regarding 2) in particular, while there are many previous studies on social security and welfare policies for redistribution, the elderly, and medical care, there are no concrete results on education policy, and its support structure is also unclear.

Therefore, I will use the 2006 survey by the ISSP mentioned in the Introduction. The ISSP chooses a topic every year,[9] prepares a questionnaire on the basis of the topic, and conducts the survey simultaneously around the world. In Japan, the NHK Broadcasting Culture Research Institute serves as the contact and implementation entity. The data can be downloaded at no charge from a dedicated website,[10] as long as it is for research purposes (however, one needs to fill out a brief explanation about the research purpose in English). A survey on the role of government in particular has been conducted in the past as the ISSP project in 1985. Since its first iteration, the survey has been conducted three times in 1990, 1996, and 2006, which is the most recent at the time of writing. It is undeniable that the data feel slightly old, given that they predate the collapse of the Lehman Brothers and the effects of changes due to the financial crisis centered on Europe; however, they represented the best data currently available for the purpose of international comparison of attitudes toward the government role.

The major attitude questions that this book will focus on are as follows. The first is a question regarding government spending, formulated as: "Listed below are various areas of government spending. Please show whether you would like to see more or less government spending in each area. Remember that if you say 'much more,' it might require a tax increase to pay for it. (Please tick one box on each line.)" Although the question lists items A through H, I only examined *health, education, retirement*, and *unemployment benefits* in this book corresponding to its areas of interest, instead of including all items.[11] The choices were based on a five-point scale including "spend much more," "spend more," "spend the same as now," "spend less," and "spend much less."

Next, under the question "Here are some things the government might do for the economy. Please show which actions you are in favor of and which you are against. (Please tick one box on each line.)," I will only look at Item A, *cuts in government spending*, out of Items A through F. This is also based on a five-point scale comprising the options "strongly in favor of," "in favor of," "neither in favor of nor against," "against," and "strongly against."

Finally, I will look at the question "On the whole, do you think it should or should not be the government's responsibility to... (Please tick one box on each line)," examining the following five items: *Give financial help to university students from low-income families, provide health care for the sick, provide a decent standard of living for the old, reduce income differences between the rich and the poor,* and *provide a job for everyone who wants one*.[12] These items are rated on a four-point scale including "definitely should be," "probably should be," probably should not be," and "definitely should not be."

The ISSP survey in 2006 includes data for 33 countries. However, in order to take the scale of the national burden into consideration in the subsequent analysis, the countries without the data on national burden, including tax and social security as a percentage of GDP, were excluded from the analysis. Ultimately, 22 countries were included in the analysis. Such macro data were obtained from the OECD's statistics' website.[13]

(2) Relationship between the Attitude that Government Expenditure Should Be Cut and the Attitude that the Government Should Cover the Cost More

Cutting the overall government expenditure and increasing government spending on individual areas as shown in the title contradict each other. It is true that we often hear the phrase "agreed in general, but disagreed in the details." Moreover, there are many cases in which people say "Japan should eliminate wastefulness as a whole" and "the government should be able to cut their spending more" yet present a strong, deep-rooted argument against cutting spending by saying "it's a bad idea to cut it," as soon as individual policies are mentioned. I would like to examine such seemingly contradictory responses from the perspective of international comparison to see if this tendency is observed.

There is actually a considerable bias in response tendency: based on the original five-point scale, there are many cases in which extreme choices are rarely selected in some countries. In a quantitative analysis, the standard error of estimate increases when such rare cases are mixed in the data. Even though there are five levels here, the question ultimately comes down to three levels of choice, namely, increase, decrease, and unable to decide. Therefore, I have combined "much more" with "more" and "much less" with "less" and recoded them into three levels of choice. I subsequently ran crosstabs between the responses on attitude toward cutting the overall government expenditure and individual attitude responses as to whether to increase or decrease spending on four areas to determine the relationship between the two. The expected result was that there would be a tendency for individuals who think that "the government expenditure should be cut" to logically think "the spending on each area should be reduced."

Table 4-1 shows the results. The figures are the coefficients called Goodman and Kruskal's gamma (γ), which ranges from −1 to +1 and becomes zero when there is no association. Here, the cases in which the respondents think the spending on each area should be reduced while agreeing with cutting the government expenditure, or the respondents think the spending on each area should be increased while disagreeing with cutting government spending have no contradiction in response tendency so that the association is positive. Conversely, to think that the spending on each area should be increased while agreeing with the cut, or to think that the spending on each area should be reduced while disagreeing with the cut, would be considered a contradicting response tendency (even though it is of course possible when each argument is examined), and the association becomes negative.

When the absolute value of the gamma coefficient is below 0.1, it is almost impossible to see a clear tendency. A weak correlation can be identified once the absolute value exceeds 0.1 and a somewhat clear correlation emerges once the value exceeds 0.2. Looking at this, the country with a clear indication is the United States. The gamma coefficients are all positive, indicating that many respondents understand the relationship that the spending on each policy must be reduced if they were to carry out financial retrenchment. In other words, it is highly likely that the Americans are consciously choosing a small government. In contrast, looking at the gray-shaded line for Japan, the gamma coefficient is close to zero under all items. In other words, the relationship between the overall expenditure and itemized spending remains ambiguous under all policy areas. In fact, regardless of whether the opinion is in favor of the overall financial retrenchment or not, there is very little difference in the distribution of the opinions on whether to increase or decrease government spending on each area. We need to understand

Table 4-1 Relationship between Yeas and Nays for Cutting Government Spending and Yeas and Nays for Increasing Spending on Individual Items(Goodman and Kruskal's gamma coefficients)

	Education	Health	Retirement	Unemployment benefits
United States	.314	.320	.203	.267
United Kingdom	.197	.093	–.017	.048
Sweden	.075	.275	.026	.227
Spain	.119	.023	–.014	–.023
Slovenia	–.011	–.159	–.002	–.040
Portugal	–.090	–.009	–.277	–.093
Poland	.013	–.064	–.068	.101
Norway	.092	.008	–.136	–.012
New Zealand	–.020	.091	.044	.226
Netherlands	.178	.139	.053	.248
South Korea	–.032	–.075	–.044	–.004
Japan	–.001	–.031	.040	.059
Israel	–.372	–.382	–.245	.192
Ireland	.163	–.070	.170	.054
Hungary	–.152	.158	–.105	–.035
Germany	.030	.175	–.010	.141
France	.293	.143	.021	.429
Finland	.084	.291	.277	.310
Denmark	.147	.403	.166	.359
Czech Republic	.046	.051	.043	.145
Canada	.139	.176	.028	.150
Australia	.093	.119	–.012	.130

Note: The data is sourced from ISSP (2006).
These coefficients were calculated only for the countries included in the subsequent analysis.

this point first.

A negative gamma coefficient means that the relationship between the opinion on financial retrenchment and the opinion on increasing or decreasing government spending on each area is inversed. Israel has many such items. This is somewhat exceptional; and the basis and mechanism as to why it turns out that way is not necessarily clear. Other than that, it looks as if positive relationships are common in continental Europe in general. The country that stands out next to the United States is Denmark. Finland also shows positive relationships for all items other than *education*. While the tendency of Norway is not very clear, we can see positive relationships for *health* and *unemployment benefits* in Sweden. It is relatively easy to see the relationship between both variables in these Nordic countries with a social democratic regime as well. Other than that, France and the Netherlands also stand out relative to other countries. Besides Japan, it would seem that cases where there is no relationship between the two are often seen in South Korea as well as East and Central European countries. In addition, the relationship between these variables is not as clear in the United Kingdom, Canada, Australia, and New Zealand as in the United States, although they are grouped together with the United States as liberal regime. The United States actually looks like a special case.

Looking at the data by policy area, the relationship between these variables tends to be unclear regarding *retirement* which will almost certainly become relevant for many people once they age. In other words, it can be inferred that there are a relatively large number of individuals who advocate financial retrenchment but are uncomfortable if it affects pensions. As for *unemployment benefits*, there must be quite a few individuals who think that it is clearly targeted for a certain segment of people so that it is fine to cut it down.

(3) Basic Tendency with Attitude Responses

Figures 4-2 and 4-3 show the distribution of the questions of interest. As can be seen, the items on government responsibility (with four levels of choice) were also recoded into two levels: "government's responsibility" and "not government's responsibility."

First, regarding the government spending items, those who think it should be reduced are minorities in all countries, as expected (except for *unemployment benefits*). Many of them seem to believe that it should be increased or that the current level should be maintained; however, the opinion of a large number of individuals who think it should be increased does not seem to correspond with the type of welfare regime.

With regard to *education*, although public spending remains at an extremely low level in Japan compared to other countries, as mentioned many times, there are not many people who think it should be increased—it is almost at the same level or actually even lower compared to Scandinavian countries and Finland, where the percentage of public spending on education is already high. Although the number of people who think that spending should be increased is relatively small in France as well (though the number is still larger than Japan), with the exception of these Scandinavian countries, the number of people who think that public spending on education should be increased is large in the majority of countries. In that sense, we can say that Japan is in a somewhat unique position.

Looking at *health* and *retirement*, too, the demand of the Japanese people is not particularly high. There are actually many who think that the current level should be maintained. The number of individuals who think it should be increased is not large in comparison. As for the graph for "*Cut the Government Expenditure,*" there are many yea-sayers in European countries such as France and Germany in addition to Japan. There are actually many nay-sayers in the Nordic countries where the governments are already big. This is probably based on the understanding that it would become difficult to maintain the current welfare services if the government expenditures were cut.

112 *People's Attitude and the State of Policy Regarding Education Spending*

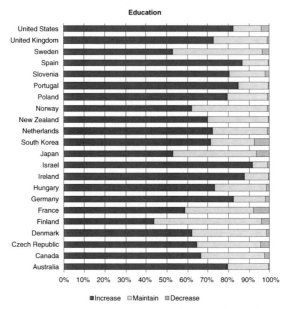

Figure 4-2 ISSP (2006) Tendency with Response —Whether to Increase Government Expenditure (a)

Note: Calculated by the author

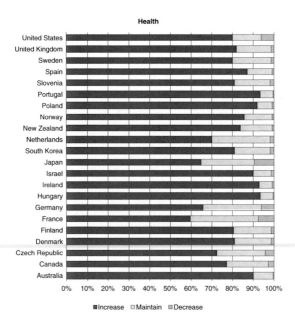

Figure 4-2 (b)

The Structure of Japanese People's Attitude

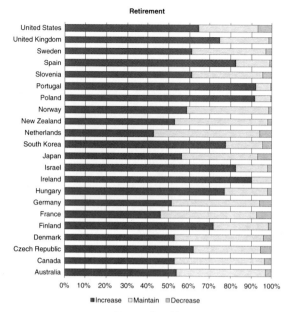

Figure 4-2 (c)

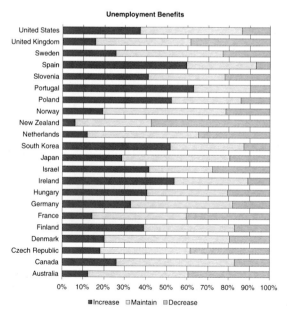

Figure 4-2 (d)

114　*People's Attitude and the State of Policy Regarding Education Spending*

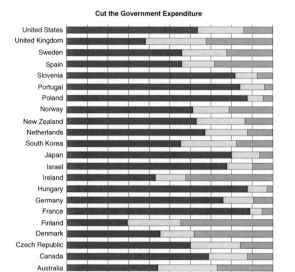

Figure 4-2 (e)

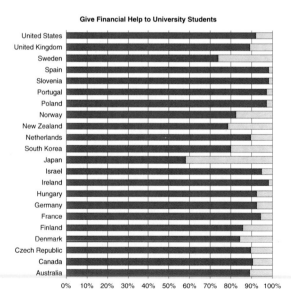

Figure 4-3　ISSP (2006) Tendency with Response—
Government Responsibility (a)

Note: Calculated by the author

The Structure of Japanese People's Attitude

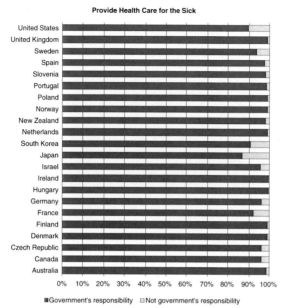

Figure 4-3 (b)

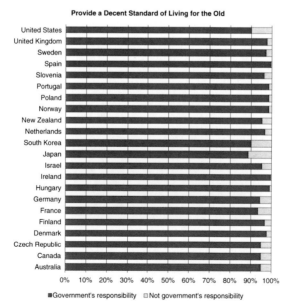

Figure 4-3 (c)

116 *People's Attitude and the State of Policy Regarding Education Spending*

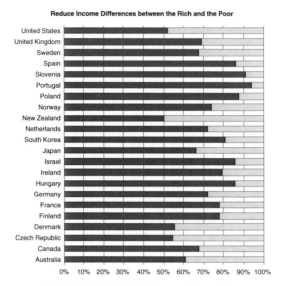

Figure 4-3 (d)

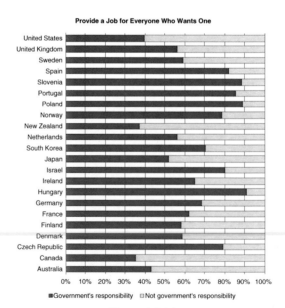

Figure 4-3 (e)

The reason for not being able to observe any relationship in Japan in Table 4-1 might be because people thought it was necessary to eliminate wastefulness in order to resolve fiscal deficit. This may have been based on three assumptions that: 1) social security is inadequate; 2) in contrast, there is considerable wastefulness such as in public works in Japan; and 3) meanwhile, the fiscal deficit had become a serious problem. However, they may also have believed that welfare, social security, and education were not wasteful and the fiscal deficit could be resolved by cutting public works and the number of government employees. In fact, because the DPJ had not yet taken over the administration in 2006, it might be that many people still thought there was considerable wastefulness in Japan and the fiscal deficit could somehow be addressed by eliminating it. However, this is just speculation (or a possibility) because attitude questions that ask about issues such as whether to cut public works were not included.

(4) Logistic Regression Analysis to Predict the Attitude toward Government Expenditure

In the following analysis, I have coded those who think that the government spending on each of the four areas should be increased as 1 and other respondents as 0, and those who agree with the opinion to cut the overall government expenditure as 1 and those who disagree as 0. Using these as dependent variables, I have conducted regression estimations.

The independent variables that are expected to predict the dependent variables are personal attributes such as gender, age, marital status, education, occupation, income, and whether the individual has children. The data set is in a format that has merged the results from each country into one. Needless to say, it is highly likely that the attitudes and behaviors are similar within a given country compared to the attitudes and behaviors of other countries. This kind of attitude of yeas and nays might also be related to the current level of social security policy implemented by the country. Therefore, explanatory variables to predict the dependent variables are divided into the factors that can be attributed back to individuals such as the ones listed above and the institutional and environmental factors at the national level. It clearly would not make sense to conduct the estimations using such institutional factors as explanatory variables at the personal level. In other words, the estimations should be conducted by separating explanatory variables into those at the personal level and those at the institutional and environmental levels. The type of analysis that has frequently been used in recent years based on such differentiation is called multilevel analysis.

$$\ln(p_{agree}/1-p_{agree}) = \alpha = \beta_k x_k + \varepsilon \qquad (4.1)$$

When the dependent variable is a dummy variable coded as 1 and 0, the estimation method called logistic regression analysis, as shown in Equation 4.1, is used. The dependent variable is the natural logarithm of the odds of yea-sayers and nay-sayers for each questionnaire item. α is the constant term, x is the explanatory variable, β is its coefficient, and ε is the error term. When there is no explanatory variable, α equals the log odds of yea-sayers and nay-sayers in the sample population. Normally, explanatory variables are plugged in here. When α and β get large, it means that the number of yea-sayers in comparison to nay-sayers has correspondingly increased. At the time of interpretation, one would use the exponentiated β (exp (β)) and read it as "when the explanatory variable increases by 1, the odds of the dependent variable also increases by exp (β) times."

The above equation (4.1) is based on the assumption that the variance of the survey sample population is random. However, as described above, it would be reasonable to assume that the distribution of samples in a given country would cluster somewhere (because they are likely to have similar opinions), and the data for another country would cluster somewhere else. Since the α on the one side of Equation (4.1) is expected to differ by country, we can formulate the following equation:

$$\alpha = \gamma + \upsilon \qquad (4.2)$$

γ is the log odds of each country and υ is the error between the countries. It is also possible to add (national level) explanatory variables to this Equation (4.2) when such log odds at the national level differ by environmental factors (e.g., national policy, etc.). The same can be said about the coefficient of the explanatory variable; if there is a hypothesis that the size of the coefficient itself varies by country, the coefficient can be decomposed as in Equation 4.2 to further include explanatory variables at the national level.

Although I used a software called HLM for the estimation, it has in recent years become possible to use various software for such analysis. For more detail, books by Ita Kreft and others (Kreft and de Leeuw, 1998, trans. 2006) translated into Japanese are easy to understand. For readers comfortable with English, the book by Stephen W. Raudenbush and Anthony S. Bryk is highly rated (Raudenbush and Bryk, 2002).

Table 4-2 shows the estimation results.[14] The ones with a large constant term indicate that there are more applicable individuals relative to non-applicable individuals. As can be seen from Figure 4-2, the coefficients of constant terms get larger for *health* and *education* because the number of individuals in favor of increasing the spending has become large in general. As for cutting the government expenditure, it shows that yea-sayers are not necessarily in the majority.

Looking at the increase in each area, we can see that there are more yea-sayers for *retirement* among older individuals. This is an understandable result, considering that the elderly are the beneficiaries of pensions. While *level of education*, *occupation*, and *income* are the variables for so-called class, the one that is particularly noteworthy is *level of education*. While highly educated individuals (university/graduate school graduate or higher) tend to oppose increased spending on social security and welfare policies, they are in favor of increasing spending only on education. Looking at the junior high school graduate level, which is a disadvantageous position in terms of level of education, they are likely to agree with *retirement* and *unemployment benefits*; however, they rate *education* negatively (the

Table 4-2 Estimation Results on the Multilevel Logit Model for the Attitude Toward Government Expenditure and Spending Cuts

	Increase spending on education		Increase spending on health		Increase spending on retirement		Increase spending on unemployment benefits		Reduce government expenditure	
Fixed Effect (Level 1)	Coefficient	S.E.	Coefficient	S.E.	Coefficient	S.E.	Coefficient	S.E.	Coefficient	S.E.
Constant term	2.526	.565***	3.418	.458***	.918	.388*	1.640	.603*	-.679	.598
Female	.106	.034**	.198	.037***	.147	.037**	.079	.026**	-.026	.047
Age (increment of 10)	.006	.014	-.020	.012	.107	.027**	.011	.011	.055	.016**
Single or widowed	-.033	.041	-.059	.025*	-.016	.029	.127	.037**	-.110	.039**
Junior high school	-.094	.040*	-.044	.051	.208	.064**	.184	.033***	-.014	.057
Junior college	.015	.048	-.129	.040**	-.016	.049**	-.135	.039**	-.042	.034
University/ graduate school	.201	.054**	-.286	.058***	-.436	.061***	-.252	.049***	-.181	.065*
Professional/manager	.026	.037	-.121	.034**	-.165	.054**	-.202	.040***	.106	.034**
Self-employed	-.216	.077**	-.165	.062**	-.019	.066	-.208	.072**	.293	.062***
Farmer	.168	.054**	-.134	.056*	-.271	.094*	-.219	.069**	-.028	.080
Skilled worker	-.029	.038	-.025	.064	.108	.042*	.034	.040	.005	.041
Semi-skilled/ unskilled worker	-.009	.036	.035	.060	.150	.039***	.213	.039***	-.058	.042
Unemployed	-.175	.041***	-.018	.044	-.083	.047+	.087	.064	-.010	.046
With children	.293	.051***	.031	.030	-.100	.034**	.005	.038	.042	.035
Income (below the 50th percentile)	.053	.037	.060	.038	-.137	.034***	-.213	.056**	-.035	.040
Income (above the 50th percentile)	-.052	.049	-.016	.043	-.264	.054***	-.426	.055***	.062	.060
Income (above the 25th percentile)	-.002	.052	-.181	.061**	-.385	.051***	-.587	.057***	.111	.056+
Income (non-response)	-.021	.042	-.101	.062	-.149	.049**	-.229	.061**	.002	.045
Fixed effect (Level 2)										
National burden as percentage to GDP (in the unit of 10%)	-.496	.135**	-.518	.127**	-.143	.099	-.606	.150**	.281	.159+

+p < .10 *p < .05 **p < .01 ***p < .001
Random effects are included in the italicized coefficients and S.E.
S.E. is robust standard error; N(Level 1) = 30149, N(Level 2) = 22
The reference categories: the level of education = high school; occupation = clerical worker, income = below the 25th percentile

results are all in comparison to high school graduates, which is the reference category). Education is supposed to be beneficial to those who receive it even if they are from a lower class; however, they do not necessarily support increased funding. That said, given that this is a cross-sectional survey and many of the respondents have already completed their schooling, those in the less educated segment in particular have had that much shorter a period of education, potentially making it difficult for them to appreciate the benefit of allocating public funds to education. It is actually natural that they would direct their attention to their current life and risks as well as issues after retirement. On the other hand, one might think that this variable would not necessarily become statistically significant if people were motivated for their children to receive education even if they themselves were less educated. However, the result is actually completely the opposite for *education* and other items.

Although *occupation* and *income* do not show consistent trends as does *level of education*, there is a clear tendency for people to oppose *retirement* and *unemployment benefits* as their *income* increases relative to those with the lowest level of income. In addition, respondents with children are significantly more likely to be in favor of increasing spending on education, indicating that this is also likely to be supported by the beneficiaries.

Looking at the fixed effect at Level 2, three areas other than *retirement* are negative and significant, and there is a clear tendency for populations that are in favor of increasing spending on pensions for the elderly to be small in countries with a large national burden relative to the GDP. In other words, it reflects the fact shown in Figure 4-2 that the ratio of those who agree to increase spending is not relatively high in the Nordic countries.

As for the model to reduce government expenditure on the far right column, university/graduate school graduates are significantly more likely to oppose this (compared to high school graduates) when looking only at the level of education. This does not necessarily mean that those from a higher class are in opposition, as professionals and managers, the self-employed, and those in the highest income bracket are significantly more likely to support cutting government expenditure compared to clerical workers. It is possible that people in these occupations and those with a very high income feel that the benefits received are small relative to the tax they pay, which is considerable as based on the progressive tax system. However, it seems that it is the highly educated who reflect more deeply about concerns such as the relationship between the size of government expenditure and the extensiveness of social security services. It could be that these situations result in a tendency for the highly educated to oppose cuts to government expenditure.

(5) Logistic Regression Analysis to Predict the Attitude toward Government Responsibilities

Next, I would like to examine the attitude toward the responsibility of the government in the same manner. The dependent variable is coded as 1 when the respondent thinks it is the responsibility of the government and otherwise as 0 in order to estimate the multilevel logistic regression model in the same way. The results are shown in Table 4-3.

In terms of education-related financial help for the low-income segment to go to college, the difference from other areas is the level of education, as might be expected; university graduates are particularly likely to think it is the responsibility of the government, which may be because it is/was relevant to themselves. This is a trend that differs from other areas. Somewhat consistent is the *income* variable: regardless of the area, the higher the income, the less likely the respondent is to think of it as the responsibility of the government. Looking at *occupation*, blue-collar workers also have a strong tendency to think of it as the responsibility of the government, regardless of the area.

However, unlike Table 4-2, which showed tendencies that could be considered opposites between education and other areas, the results here are not as clear. In fact, as far as the policies listed here are concerned, the results are all similar. The dependent variable *financial help to university students* in Table 4-3 can be regarded as more of a redistribution policy that guarantees a certain segment of people the opportunity to go to college than asserting it to be the government's responsibility on education itself in general terms. It may be more appropriate to consider this to be the reason why the results turned out to be similar to other social security policies.

(6) Public Education to Increase Support for Public Spending on Education

In reality, it is difficult to increase social expenditure such as social security without public confidence in the government. Further, although it is a popular view that Japanese people only expect services by the government and do not think about defrayment because they are strongly dependent on the government or have the attitude that everything should be left up to the authorities (and I cannot say that this would be completely mistaken), looking at the attitude toward increasing government expenditure and the role of the government, the demand is not as high as other countries—many items actually remain at a low level. Naturally, the implications of such an attitude would be completely different depending on whether it purely represented support or were more indicative of a sense of resignation to the apparent reality of the current state of affairs. In addition, even though people are not expecting government expenditure to actually be increased, it might be the case that they wish for it at least to be maintained at the current level. However, given the actual financial situation of Japan, there is no other way to think about the issue than that of being a burden, because just to maintain the current level—which is low by international standards—is considered difficult.

For example, as shown in Table 4-1, there is some inconsistency in the attitude toward increasing and decreasing government expenditure. Since this is by no means an issue unique to Japan and does not include policies in areas such as public works, which have been criticized by some advocates, it is entirely possible for the underlying idea that "since the Japanese government is generally wasteful and most of it has to do with public works, we can cut down public works and use the money for welfare and education" to take root. However, the notion of public works accounting for a high percentage of the budget of Japan is becoming a thing of the past;[15] it actually seems that adverse effects and concerns related to extreme reduction have become apparent in recent years. In the case of Japan, the issue of an increased national burden cannot, after all, be avoided because social security-related costs should naturally increase as the population ages. Therefore, it is necessary to consider the issue of burden as a given problem, assuming that the cost will increase just to maintain the current standard for social security, welfare, and education.

Although there is no obvious relationship at a glance between the type of welfare regime and attitude, there would appear to be some kind of association.

Table 4–3 Estimation Results on the Multilevel Logit Model for the Attitude toward Government Responsibilities

	Financial help to university students		Health care for the sick		A decent standard of living for the old		Reduce income differences		Provide a job for everyone	
Fixed Effect (Level 1)	Coefficient	S.E.	Coefficient	S.E.	Coefficient	S.E.	Coefficient	S.E.	Coefficient	S.E.
Constant term	1.644	.907 +	2.939	.638 ***	2.322	.388 ***	.617	.421	1.142	.504 *
Female	.045	.031	-.083	.030 *	.071	.037 +	.253	.035 ***	.291	.380 ***
Age (increment of 10)	.063	.020 **	-.014	.009	.004	.018	.049	.009 ***	-.015	.015
Single or widowed	.111	.025 ***	.041	.029	.026	.033	.098	.037 **	.123	.036 **
Junior high school	.030	.041	.009	.034	-.010	.040	.273	.030 ***	.217	.036 ***
Junior college	-.001	.044	-.021	.041	-.148	.045 **	-.154	.040 **	-.212	.045 ***
University/ graduate school	.151	.059 *	-.051	.059	-.229	.044 ***	-.136	.069 +	-.240	.064 **
Professional/manager	-.110	.039 **	-.076	.026 **	-.029	.037	-.212	.039 ***	-.180	.035 ***
Self-employed	-.171	.070 *	-.011	.087	-.647	.049 ***	-.053	.061	-.218	.060 **
Farmer	.192	.071 **	-.072	.065 ***	-.214	.051 ***	-.044	.086	-.055	.057
Skilled worker	.116	.038 **	.185	.046 ***	.150	.060 *	.142	.044 **	.155	.044 **
Semi-skilled/ unskilled worker	.055	.033 +	.244	.032 ***	.121	.052 *	.259	.048 ***	.230	.056 ***
Unemployed	.024	.041	.123	.042 **	-.034	.086	.044	.045	.142	.053 **
With children	.192	.033 ***	.055	.027 *	-.053	.029 +	.056	.026 *	.032	.028
Income (below the 50th percentile)	-.197	.041 ***	-.047	.022 *	-.071	.029 *	-.116	.050 *	-.155	.045 **
Income (above the 50th percentile)	-.315	.041 ***	-.117	.026 ***	-.127	.035 ***	-.374	.065 ***	-.351	.055 ***
Income (above the 25th percentile)	-.369	.044 ***	-.317	.040 ***	-.276	.052 ***	-.653	.084 ***	-.592	.058 ***
Income (non-response)	-.209	.045 ***	-.155	.031 ***	-.086	.039 *	-.251	.054 ***	-.191	.040 ***
Fixed effect (Level 2)										
National burden as percentage to GDP (in the unit of 10%)	.014	.228	.019	.173	.159	.105	.072	.115	-.102	.126

+p < .10 *p < .05 **p < .01 ***p < .001
Random effects are included in the italicized coefficients and S.E.
S.E. is robust standard error; N(Level 1) = 30149, N(Level 2) = 22
The reference categories: the level of education = high school; occupation = clerical worker, income = below the 25th percentile

Nevertheless, even though we are inclined to recognize such association as something unchangeable and specific to a given culture when interpretatively linking differences in regimes with cultural differences, this does not mean that there is no room to change these attitudes, as previously mentioned. It is true that a country-specific institution is difficult to change because it is naturally embedded in various systems; however, this does not mean that change is impossible. In addition, as seen in the study by Algan and colleagues, the possibility that education plays some kind of role is undeniable.

According to Rüya Gökhan Koçer and Herman G. van de Werfhorst, highly educated individuals begin recognizing the existence of income disparity in society because they gain a broader and more objective view once becoming highly educated (though the possibility that it is individuals with such a view that advance to a high level of education cannot obviously be refuted). In addition, the variance of opinions on whether to accept economic inequality or not becomes smaller in countries where education focuses on vocationally oriented materials. However, when the education system itself is branching out (i.e., as a school system in which one chooses at the secondary education stage to prepare to advance to higher education or to obtain employment), people begin accepting the existence of economic inequality and the variance of opinions on redistribution policy also increases.

According to Tracey Peter, Jason D. Edgerton, and Lance W. Roberts, when the difference in academic performance between schools was examined based on the Programme for International Student Assessment (PISA) conducted by the OECD, the largest was among the conservative regimes and the smallest among the social democratic regimes. For countries with a social democratic regime, education is a requirement for the equality of citizens. For liberal regimes, it means more equal opportunity as well as social investment. However, conservative regimes are distanced from all ideologies and often use the so-called branching education system. And this education system is associated with the labor market structure and social protection systems (Peter et al., 2010).

While opinions often vary in conservative regimes as typified by Germany, this is because the education system in such countries tends to branch out. That is, the branching type of education system tends to promote opinions that diverge. Koçer and others suggest the possibility that diverging opinions might be reduced even in those countries by implementing vocational training (Koçer and van de Werfhorst, 2012).

As summarized by Alan C. Kerckhoff, an education system that branches out is suitable for vocational education because it enables specialized education in a specific area. In that sense, it tends to promote a smooth transition to the labor market (Kerckhoff, 2001). However, there used to be deep-rooted criticism in Japan that specialization in upper secondary education (or the high school stage) turns education into a subcontract of the labor market or merely strengthens the function of reproducing the hierarchical social class structure. Such circumstance led to the establishment of a predominantly large number of general education courses for high school in post-war Japan while not often providing vocational training. Meanwhile, it is said that the transition from education to the labor market has been effected smoothly in Japan even though its education system is not the branching type, because there are employment system customs unique to Japan (Kariya and Rosenbaum, 1995). Yet, since such an employment system has no longer consistently functioned well in recent years due to a difficult labor market, problems are beginning to be pointed out (Brinton, 2008). Therefore, it seems that we can expect to move toward reevaluating vocational training in Japan in the long run. Moreover, the voice calling for vocationally useful and practical education appears to have been becoming particularly strong in recent years. While it seems necessary to think a little deeper about what being useful and practical means, there is no doubt that we are at a point where the relationship between education that is merely for community members who live in the same society and the path of vocational training should be thoroughly reconsidered.

NOTES

[1] Clem Brooks and Jeff Manza examined in detail the effect of the causal relationship in both directions—a policy is determined because there is a certain attitude, and a certain attitude is aroused because there is a specific system—and concluded that the latter effect does not exist. (Brooks and Manza, 2006).

[2] The possibility certainly cannot be denied that the primary concern among the elderly is their own life in their golden years rather than education since they are already freed from raising children. However, this cannot be confirmed without looking at panel survey data.

[3] However, Chew concluded that the individual's political ideology has a larger effect on public spending on education, although being a parent or not is also an important factor (Chew, 1992).

[4] In the article "*Nihon wa Nan'ōka Surunoka?* (Will Japan become like the Southern European countries?)," Kotaro Tsuru took these current situations into consideration, sounding a note of caution as to whether it is advisable to continue bashing government officials and employees to diminish the credibility of the government, ultimately allowing the citizens to get away with taking the burden (Page 21 of the morning edition of *Nihon Keizai Shimbun*, June 21, 2012).

[5] Aghion and colleagues also examined the association between the trust relationship of labor and management and minimum wage regulations. They indicate that the labor-management relationship is good and the level of regulation is low in Northern Europe such as in the Scandinavian countries because a cooperative relationship is established between labor and management, an environment in which to directly communicate and negotiate is created, and the rate of labor unionization is high. In southern European countries, on the other hand, labor-management relations are poor, the unionization rate is low, and an environment in which to negotiate is not well-established because they do not trust each other, for which reason they must resort to relying on regulation. This suggests that there is a possibility that this ultimately affects labor performance (Aghion et al., 2011).

[6] This is based on the aforementioned suggestion by Wilensky.

[7] There is a strong perception that Japan is a trading nation that became a major economic power by exporting industrial products; however, the dependence on foreign trade is by no means large. For example, the export dependence in 2010 was 14.1% and this trend has not changed much for a while. As a point of reference, the figures for the United States and the United Kingdom are 8.7% and 18.3%, respectively; and the figures are 34.4%, 31.8%, and 31.1% for Sweden, Norway, and Denmark among the Nordic countries. See the Ministry of Internal Affairs and Communications Statistics Bureau website (http://www.stat.go.jp/data/sekai/pdf/09.pdf).

[8] Specifically, white-collar professionals are unlikely to be in support compared to non-skilled workers; and unemployed individuals and women are likely to be in support

compared to employed individuals and men, respectively (Svallfors, 1997).

[9] They cover a wide range of topics, including social network, social inequality, family, and gender-based division of labor.

[10] http://www.issp.org/

[11] Other items include *environment, law enforcement, defense,* and *culture and arts.*

[12] Other items include *keep prices under control, provide industry with the help it needs to grow, provide a decent standard of living for the unemployed, provide decent housing for those who can't afford it,* and *impose strict laws to make industry do less damage to the environment.*

[13] OECD's StatExtract website ("http://stats.oecd.org/Index.aspx"). Given that the survey was conducted in 2006, I used the macro data for 2005.

[14] As a side note, when the standard error at the national level is expected to be larger than the error at the individual level, υ in Equation 4.2 is incorporated into the model at the time of performing the multilevel analysis. This υ is called the random effect. Ideally, one should assume that there will be a margin of error at the national level for all coefficients as well as the constant term; however, it is basically better to estimate a simpler statistical model. In addition, since a multilevel logistic regression analysis is complicated to estimate, setting a complex model could prevent the results from converging. Therefore, only the random effects that were significant at the 0.05 level were left for the estimation. The italicized coefficients in the table incorporate random effects into the model.

[15] On the other hand, some would say that the percentage of public works in the general account is not very large, and what lies behind this is the fiscal investment and loan program that drastically increased and was used exclusively as public investment. I will touch on this in Chapter 5. We also need to closely monitor the situation, as these movements could change again after the establishment of the second Abe administration of the LDP—the Komeito coalition based on the results of the 2012 general election.

PART II

WHY HAS THE PUBLIC BURDEN OF EDUCATION NOT INCREASED?

CHAPTER 5
Public Finance and Education in Japan

1. Causes of Government Deficit Financing

(1) Sociology of Fiscal Crisis

In the first half of this book, up until the end of Chapter 4, we used an internationally comparative perspective to examine the relationship between education and government-provided services, particularly social security and welfare policy. We further looked at the stances vis-à-vis social and education policy in Japan. Henceforth, I examine how and why Japan built the current type of relationship between government and the people, and how and why the public education expenditure has continued to proceed at a low level, unchanged.

Current public finance in Japan is in an extremely difficult situation. Japan's level of fiscal debt is the worst in the world, even among the developed countries. Under these circumstances, demanding a further increase of the percentage of public expenditure allocated for education costs alone is not that simple. The problem of deficit financing is not new. In the 1970s, the public finances of Western countries deteriorated, and this problem was pointed out by both the political right and left. Economics of public choice by James M. Buchanan and Richard E. Wagner concludes that the linking of so-called Keynesian economic policies with democracy will "inevitably" bring about the consequence of an unstoppable expansion of fiscal deficit. What exactly does this mean?

Essentially, to maintain a budgetary equilibrium and create a budgetary surplus it is necessary to maintain a balance between raising the real tax rate and lowering the real public expenditure rate. However, in order to extend or increase the budgetary surplus, there needs to be some means by which to do so, such as raising taxes. Hence, such measures come with an immediate cost—the reduction of disposable income. But if attempts are made to maintain fiscal equilibrium at a time when reducing disposable income is not possible, a reduction in public services will be the inevitable result—this would mean a drop in the quality of services. In other words, the maintenance of fiscal equilibrium and budgetary surplus does not fundamentally result in anyone benefitting from this at the level of the individual citizen. Although there is an indirect benefit in that a budgetary surplus plays a role in safeguarding against inflation, this benefit cannot easily be felt directly by the citizens. Therefore, in a democratic form of government, the possibility of the citizens supporting a budgetary surplus policy is low. If there is justification for a budgetary deficit that provides for expenditure without taxes by deficit-covering government bonds, the citizens do not lose out from this and can therefore easily support deficit budget policy. In a representative democracy, the opinion of citizens is formed by giving a mandate to politicians. However, as politicians make their "livelihood" from this, it is basically in their own interests to be reelected. An inevitable consequence of adopting a democracy is that if politicians espouse an increased burden that is fundamentally disliked by the citizens, this will increase their risk of losing the next election. Consequently, politicians do not take this risk. If we link this to the expenditure habits and deficit creating habits of the state, it brings about a catastrophic consequence. This is the basis of Buchanan and Wagner's argument that deficit financing is inevitable (Buchanan and Wagner, 1977, trans. 1979).

How best to respond to Keynesian policy guidelines is considered to be to choose either of the following two ways: 1) as the populace essentially supports Keynesian policy guidelines for the aforementioned reasons, a situation occurs in which democratic government brings about policy failure—consequently, democratic government is negated and government is made more autocratic; or 2) if maintaining a democratic society is given precedence, Keynesian policy is repudiated and different policy principles are thought up. In this situation, Buchanan and Wagner state that priority should normally be given to 2), which represents a negation of "big government" (Buchanan and Wagner, 1977, trans. 1979: 6).

On the other hand, Jürgen Habermas and Claus Offe write that in societies in late capitalism, although governments fundamentally provide social infrastructure by means of taxation, a problem emerges in that the securing of tax revenue becomes difficult due to the slowing of economic growth and the aging of society. Against such a backdrop, the populace makes demands for even more services from the government. The populace's acceptance in paying taxes is on account of their commensurate returns (or merits). Generally, however, when the populace begins receiving services, it leads to demands for even higher levels of service. When the securing of tax revenues reaches a threshold, however, there is a mismatch between the quality of services and the expectations of the populace. This leads the populace to strengthen their mistrust of government. When collecting taxes from a greatly mistrusting populace, the state's legal force is highlighted, and this gradually alienates the hearts of the populace from the government. In response, the government strives to respond to the demands of the populace, which are increasingly strengthened, and the gap between the demands and the reality widens. In turn, the depressed mood of the populace worsens, the tax collection function weakens, and as a result, the quality of services drops. From this emerges an unstoppable negative cycle whereby a drop in the quality of services leads to deterioration in the populace's trust in the state. This is a common problem for late capitalism (Habermas, 1973, trans. 1979; Offe, 1987, trans. 1988).

The ideological position of Habermas and Offe is completely opposite to that of Buchanan, but they commonly raise the same points as problems. However, although the problems stated here would seem to fit the crisis currently faced in Japan, these are problems that have already been discussed for more than 30 years in the West.

(2) Causes of Fiscal Deficit

The modern state is unable to survive without taxes. However, as taxes are not produced naturally, they must be procured under the authority of the state from private assets. Although this produces resistance from the citizens, the modern state at least does not procure taxes by legal force; rather, it only collects taxes by persuading the citizens and by reaching consensus among them (Morotomi, 2013: 13). Theoretically, when implementing a redistribution policy by the government, the following can further be summarized about the relationship between the method of procuring this fiscal resource and the people's share of the burden. Specifically, measures targeting all members of society are funded using general taxes. Clarifying the relationship of privileges, namely the benefits and burdens, with respect to a part of the members of society are the insurance premiums. Also, special purpose taxes are used to optimize the distribution of the cost burden of special groups in society. What to do regarding the percentage share of the burden of these third parties is a problem to which no optimal solution has been found (Naruse, 2001: 26)

The cause of Japan's fiscal crisis is fundamentally a shortage of tax revenue rather than excessive expenditure. Specifically, the repeated lowering of taxes carried out since the 1990s has caused an imbalance with expenditure and a noticeable decrease in tax revenue. Japan's level of tax revenue is conspicuously low among OECD countries. What needs to be noted here is that the fundamental cause of the fiscal crisis is not the size of public finance allocated by the government. For example, in northern European countries, the size of public finance is large, in keeping with their image of the welfare state, and the tax revenue to GDP ratio is high. The size of their sovereign debt, however, is very small. In other words, the fiscal soundness of public finance is not related to the size of government; rather, it is largely dependent on tax revenue procurement capability (Ide, 2012: 9–10; 2013: 32–34).

Although debate has been extensive as to whether Japan falls into the category of "big government" or "small government," there is a certain degree of consensus among experts that Japan has quite a small government if judged from the public finance aspect or by the number people actually working in government (number of government employees) (Kenjo, 2001; 2004, OECD, 2013, etc.). The problem is that despite this, the politicians run on a platform of "removing the excesses" and "decreasing the number of government employees and lowering their pay," and this is met with a certain degree of support. In terms of actual sentiment, citizens probably either feel that there is a strong influence of government service on many fronts, or they do not really feel that these efforts of the government are serving a useful purpose. For example, Shogo Takegawa writes that when big government and small government are discussed, the focus of attention should not necessarily be only restricted to the public finance aspect—rather, attention should also be given to the regulatory aspect (Takegawa, 2007). Looking at the aspect of cost, the securing of financial resources is not simple. Therefore, when the government wields authority at a low cost, the provision of regulations becomes the most simple. Specifically, the numerous regulations place constraints on citizen activities, and it cannot be denied that this serves to conceal the smallness of the work activity of the bureaucrats (i.e., public servants).[1] The fact that it is the strength of Japan's regulations that gets pointed out is probably reflective of the smallness of the public finance size of Japan's government. Moreover, affiliated organizations and industry organizations that are considered part of the private sector, have strong ties with the associated government authorities; and there are also some organizations whose actual founding was based on the influence of the will of ministries and agencies. People who observe this situation probably feel strongly that the strength of the government service is substantial (Iio, 2007: 69–71).

The matter of trust toward the government has been previously explored in Chapter 4, but this strength of the regulations probably informs the perception of government authority and fosters an attitude among people of leaving it up to the authorities. Hideaki Tanaka regards transparency in budgets and public finance in Japan to be at the worst level among the OECD countries. Not all of the large amount of fiscal deficit and outstanding debt can be explained by indicators of transparency in budgets and public finance. Nevertheless, it is possible to observe a negative correlation whereby the lower the transparency of the budgets and public finances gets, the higher the outstanding debt becomes. If there is no transparency in public finance, the true shape is concealed and opportunism runs rampant. A lowering of trust in the government even spreads to the financial market and interest rates rise. Moreover, even if the targets are achieved on paper, if this is due to accounting gymnastics, then naturally trust will diminish. Hence, it is essential to ensure there is transparency in attestation concerning achievement of targets and compliance with rules. But simply ensuring transparency is not good enough—even then, if the targets are too high or the rules too strict, it invites accounting gymnastics. If accounting gymnastics are allowed to flourish, it is possible that this will cause a lessening of trust. According to Tanaka, Japan has a clear problem when it comes to the transparency of budgets and public finance. He thinks that this is a major cause of deficit financing having become a constant practice (Tanaka, 2013: 129–132).

2. Public Finance and Budgets

(1) Idiosyncrasies of Public-Finance Activities in Japan

To learn about the mechanism of public finance, it is best to refer to documentation dedicated to the matter. Nevertheless, in this book, I wish to reflect a little on the fundamentals.

The public finance activities of the Japanese government can be categorized into general public finance, and fiscal investment and loans. General public finance is made up of the General Accounts, the special accounts, and the government agencies (Yumoto, 2008: 17–30). We will first turn our attention to the budget of the General Account. Figure 5-1 shows the trends of the percentage share of the budgetary allocation of each of the expenditures on a time series using a unit scale of five-year intervals. Ideally, the budget should be processed by the government in a single account for all revenue and expenditure (the single annual budget principle). However, for specific projects it has become possible to establish special accounts, such as in cases when carrying out operations where specific funds are held or when there are specific revenues and it is better to distinguish from general revenues and expenditure by allocating specific expenditure in line with the objectives. As of February 2013, the government held 18 kinds of special accounts.

The general account budget of the fiscal year 2012, including revisions, was of a size that exceeded 100.5 trillion yen. In the general account expenditure, payment

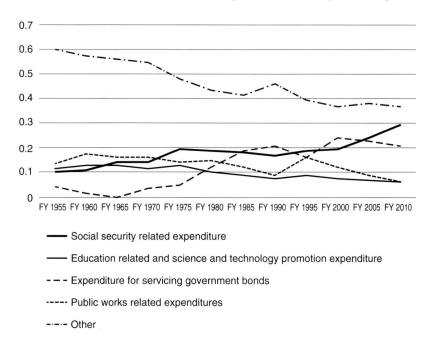

Figure 5-1 Trend of Expense Categories in General Accounting Budgets
Source: Ministry of Finance

of principle interest on government bonds, social insurance related expenditure, and distribution of local allocation tax made up 70% of the total. Note that for general account expenditure such as social security related expenditure and public works related expenditure, rather than paying it directly, the money is often transferred to a special account first and then paid from there. Looking at Figure 5-1 while taking such details into account, there is a gradually increasing trend for social security-related expenditure, the growth of which is particularly large after entering the 2000s. Moreover, looking at the long-term picture, there is a gradual increase of expenditure for servicing government bonds. There is a trend of gradual decrease for education-related and science and technology promotion expenditure. Moreover, public works-related expenditure also appears to have been decreasing in recent years. However, in reality, when looking at the government's public finance activities, placing attention on only the general public finance could invite a misleading conclusion.

Including revisions, the budget for special accounts in the fiscal year 2012 was approximately 394 trillion yen, which is actually much larger than the general public finance. However, as mentioned above, this includes items that are recorded in both accounts, such as transfers from the general account to special accounts (more than 50 trillion yen). Therefore, simply aggregating the amounts of all of the accounts is not a reflection of the scale of the government's public finance activities. Note that these special accounts contain reserve funds of large amounts, and at the time of the closing of accounts for the fiscal year 2011, the size of these amounts was 167 trillion yen. This is what is referred to as the "buried treasure." Of this, 133 trillion yen is a slush fund for future pensions of the people, and 21 trillion yen is in foreign currency denominated funds. As this buried treasure is fundamentally allocated for future risks, judgment of its size depends on the sense of values of the advocate. However, the management of special accounts is fundamentally entrusted to the respective governing agency, and a large portion of these special accounts are criticized as hotbeds for the inefficient use of funds in projects involving incorporated administrative agencies and public interest corporations. However, if this buried treasure is used, it can only be used once, and once gone, there will be nothing that remains. Therefore, it cannot become a means for fundamentally resolving Japan's deficit financing (Yumoto, 2008: 178–179). First and foremost, a substantial cause of Japan's deficit financing relates to the increase in ordinary costs from the steep increases in social security expenditure and the aging population.

Moreover, an area to pay particular attention to when looking at Japan's public finance is fiscal investment and loans. The sector that has been often portrayed as an emblem of excesses in Japan's public finance is public works. Public works-related expenditure is the expenditure target of construction bonds as stated in the general budget provisions. Fiscal investment and loans refer to the government's accommodation of funds for government-affiliated institutions and local self-governing bodies and the implementation of the public investment of these funds as financial resources. Hence, this is not entirely synonymous with public works. In reality, however, fiscal investment and loans has effectively been categorized into public works' categories of buildings and construction. Looking at the general account only, from the budget of the fiscal year 1974, social security-related expenditure began to rise above public works-related expenditure; but, in fact, since the situation of the 1970s, the fiscal investment and loans have been increasing at a pace clearly exceeding the public works-related expenditure and the social security-related expenditure of the general account (Ide, 2013: 42–44).

The difference between fiscal investment and loans and general public finance is that while general public finance is a world of subtraction and addition of actual funds, fiscal investment and loans is a world of lending and borrowing—in other words, a world of financial transactions (Yumoto, 2008: 22–23). In the initial budget for the fiscal of 2012, the size of fiscal investment and loans exceeded 17 trillion yen. The effect of such fiscal investment and loans on Japan's overall public finance policies will be revisited later.

As one can understand from the discussion thus far, problems with public finance are extremely difficult for the layman to understand due to the complexity of its actual content. While, on the one hand, this is unavoidable due to the scale of the country, on the other hand, the existence of both the general account and special accounts does make it easy to conduct some accounting gymnastics between the two accounts. Not only that, but the revised budgets, which are carried out when there is a high level of intrinsic urgency, end up being allocated every year as if they had been planned all along, which also results in the difficult-to-understand nature of these matters and the accounting gymnastics that occur (Tanaka, 2013: Chapter 4). The complexity of the system causes different interpretations by advocates and confusion among laymen. Democracy fundamentally reflects the will of the people, but it greatly depends on the people being informed by accurate information. However, when the opinions among the experts present views that are completely opposed to one another, it causes problems for the public finance, taxation, and social security systems. This state of confusion can surely be linked to the lack of trust in the government that was mentioned earlier in Chapter 4.

(2) Mechanism of Budget Compilation

The compilation of budgets in Japan does not take the form of cramming in the content after deciding the apportionment for each field. Budgetary adjustments inside each ministry and agency accumulate as the budget advances to each division and bureau. Each ministry and agency then negotiates with the MOF concerning this accumulation of adjustment items (whereby each ministry and agency repeatedly engages in back-and-forth discussion with the MOF a significant number of times).

During the high economic growth period up until 1970, on account of the growth in expenditure, it was the Meeting of Budget Examiners in the MOF that finally performed the adjustments of the budgetary allocation. It can therefore be said that the authority of the MOF was very strong. From the latter half of the 1970s, however, the government issued deficit-covering government bonds. Moreover, by establishing a limit on the preliminary budget request (i.e., a ceiling) to constrain expenditure, the budgetary allocation limit was effectively passed on to each ministry and agency. It thus became possible to see the existing level before the preliminary budget request. For this reason, before the preliminary budget request to the MOF, the refining of the budget inside each ministry and agency rose in importance, while the significance of the requested budget given to the MOF and the examiners' assessment became comparatively weaker. Although the budgetary adjustment by this method of accumulation brought about a sense of stability, the situation also made it difficult to instigate much change to the public finance budget overall (Iio, 2007: 56–59).

The ceiling that prescribes the preliminary budget request limit (or criteria) is treated strictly, which is also the case all over the world. The strictness of this ceiling, however, can be viewed as the cause of the large public finance deficit. When the ceiling was first adopted, it was limited to the initial budget of the general account. Then, since the 1990s, throughout the special accounts, the size has continued to increase and the limit for the revised budget has also been expanded. In other words, because the ceiling in the general account was too strict, it caused a backlash within the LDP, and there was a strengthening of pressures, led by influential members of the Diet, to increase the items and their amounts as exemptions to the ceiling. The MOF negotiated partial concessions with the politicians and enacted special limits to allay the discontent, while he continued to maintain the ceiling as it was. However, in effect, the applicable scope of the ceiling was limited only to the general account, and it did not serve the role of cancelling the public finance deficit, which comprised the total budget (Amou, 2013).[2]

Now if we look at the specific procedures of this budget compilation, first, beginning in mid-April, all the governing divisions of each ministry and agency set about creating a draft with the chief of their general affairs unit in charge, which is examined by the general affairs division inside the respective agency. Then, budget negotiations are conducted inside each agency between the general affairs division and each of the divisions in charge, and a budget proposal for inside the agency is decided on. Next, negotiations begin between the general affairs division of each agency and the division-budget division of the ministry; and by repeating this process, a budget proposal for the ministry gets prepared. Using the ministry budget proposal that has been prepared in this way, the ministry then enters into negotiation with the MOF (Omori, 2006: 146–147).

Although, from the start, the ultimate objective of the MOF has been to control the state's public finance, this does not entail control of the fine budgetary details of each ministry and agency but rather control of the size of the overall budget. The objective is also to adhere to the establishment and maintenance of the ceiling. Since 1961, the MOF has decided on the budget growth rate by comparing it with the time of compilation of the previous fiscal year, and each ministry and agency has submitted a preliminary budget request that is in line with this. On the other hand, once the budget is created, the MOF is disinterested in its control and the executed budget is often different from the planned budget (Kato, 1997: 62–65).

Among these, the Ministry of Education has traditionally contained clearly sectionalized bureau units, and each of these has the particular characteristic of possessing numerous associated institutions directly linked to the daily lives of the people (such as the education committees of elementary, junior high, and senior high schools in the case of the Elementary and Secondary Education Bureau). According to Masahito Ogawa, as it is not possible to execute policy without taking into consideration the voices of society, such as schools, the policies have been formed with importance given to a bottom-up type of consensus.[3]

Specifically, according to Ogawa (2010), the public finance for education directly after the war was influenced by the bureaucrats and the minister of the Ministry of Home Affairs before the war. The fact that the Ministry of Home Affairs controlled Japan's domestic portion of public finance and the pre-war Ministry of Education established institutions for local education with public finance was the reason that the influence of the Ministry of Home Affairs still remained. The local public order (i.e., police) was also the jurisdiction of the Home Ministry. Accordingly, the education policy at that time was to take control of education from the perspective of public order and efforts were put into controlling the local area. On this point, the Minister of Home Affairs and other members of the education policy tribe observed and attacked the socialists and the Japan Teachers' Union, which was a significant ideological move in support of the ruling party. From the 1960s, however, even from inside the LDP, the education policy was debated as "policy," and it became a politicized issue. It was from this that the modern image of the *bunkyozoku,* the education policy tribe, emerged. At that time, The Education and Science and Technology Division was established beneath the General Council, and while power was strengthened there, power was correspondingly weakened in the Ministry of Education government offices. One thing that is often pointed out is that Diet members were able to collect votes based on subsidies for agriculture and forestry, construction (land and transport), commerce and industry (trade and industry → economy and industry); thus, they wielded power in the LDP and enjoyed popularity. However, the education policy tribe had difficulty getting access to these subsidies and votes. Conversely, because there was no relationship to votes, the tribe included many Diet members with a strong ideological streak, characterized by a will to execute education policy to realize their own political beliefs and stance.

With globalization and the collapse of the Cold War, however, the relative position of education policy changed dramatically from the 1990s, and the character of the MEXT underwent inevitable and dramatic change after this reorganization of the Ministry of Education and the other ministries and agencies. In particular, with the introduction of the single-seat constituency system, the political voice of politicians became relatively strong, and this strengthened the cabinet's functions. The reason that this led to MEXT having a stronger influence is because political power is necessary. In other words, when there is no political power, it is not possible to extend the budget.

It is written above that the political voice of politicians was strengthened with the single-seat constituency system. This refers not to the individual politician but to the appeal of policies as a political party. Rather than an individual politician running a campaign on the strengths of a specific policy, it is necessary to appeal to a wide spectrum of policies. It is for this reason that the aforementioned tribe of Diet members lose influence. Sometimes, the voices of these tribe Diet members are criticized as being "vested interests" and "forces of resistance;" and, paradoxically, they sometimes use this to their own advantage during elections. A typical example of this was the Koizumi administration's reform of the postal system, which is one example of a cabinet's strong authority effectively working. Accompanying this, the organization inside MEXT also placed importance on adjustment by the Lifelong Learning Policy Bureau (Policy Division) and the Minister's Secretariat Policy Division that dissects horizontally through the ministry, and there was a strengthening trend for final decisions to be made further up the hierarchy (Minister's Secretariat and Minister) (Ogawa, 2010).

(3) Composition of Education-Related and Science and Technology Promotion Expenditure and Child Learning Costs

Figure 5-2 shows a breakdown of expenditure categories in "Education-related and science and technology promotion expenditure" in the general account budget (including revisions). As can be seen, the share of expenditure of the National Treasury's compulsory education contribution is significantly decreasing. At present, it has been cut by 30%. In its place, the expenditure that has increased the most is that of education promotion grants. The reason for this is that up until the

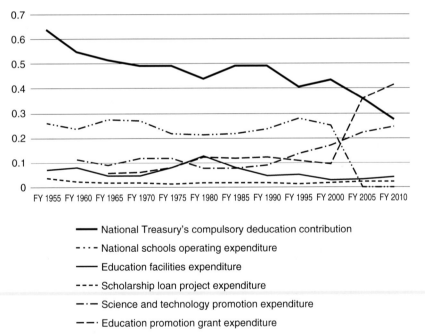

Figure 5-2 Trend of Expenditure Categories in Education Related and Science and Technology Promotion Expenditure of the General Account Budget
Source: the Ministry of Finance

budget of the fiscal year of 2003, transfers to the national schools' special account were classified separately. Moreover, as the national schools' expenditure came to be understood by the same mechanism as grants to private schools due to the incorporation of the national schools, it came to be included in the education promotion grants. This is why the expenditure for education promotion grants rises sharply from 2005. In addition to these grants to schools, the expenditure required to distribute educational materials such as textbooks is also included in this expenditure. The share of education facility expenditure shows a gradually decreasing trend; and in its place, science and technology promotional expenditure shows an increasing trend. Scholarship loan project costs have proceeded at a consistently low level.

If we comprehensively look back at the results of the "Survey on Local Educational Expenditures" conducted by the MEXT, the declining population was reflected in each of the educational fields. In recent years, the percentage of distribution to total expenditure has proceeded steadily at around 27% for elementary school expenditure and at around 15% for junior high school. In the fiscal year of 2010, expenditure for schools for special needs' education, showing a gradually increasing trend, was 4%, while senior high school expenditure, showing a decreasing trend, was in the lower 12%. Higher education expenditure has shown an increasing trend, and in recent years it has been around 15%.

In March 2010, the DPJ Government established the Act on Free Tuition Fees at Public High Schools and launched the High School Tuition Support Fund Program. This budget proposal is reflected in the fiscal year of 2010. As Figure 5-2 shows a trend using a time series of five-year intervals, it is somewhat difficult to discern, but compared with the fiscal year of 2009, there was a growth in expenditure exceeding 300 billion yen—the highest in the past 30 years (approximately 5.9% of the MEXT budget). The expenditure for the Free Tuition Fees at Public High Schools and the High School Tuition Support Fund Program is included in this expenditure for education promotion grants.

However, as already mentioned many times, the public finance education expenditure itself is low in Japan by international comparison. Looking at elementary and junior high school education alone, the international ranking is not that low, but the overwhelming share of the expenditure here is for teacher salaries. In other words, the expenditure spent on items other than teacher salaries (educational material costs, school equipment costs, and building maintenance costs, etc.) is only a little more than 10%, whereas the OECD average is about 20–30% (Ishii, 2012). Therefore, while education is compulsory in Japan, the actual situation is not one in which people do not have to pay for their children's education. The schools operate by collecting funds and donations from the parents and guardians for various accounts such as PTA costs and classroom activity fees. For example, according to the "Child Learning Cost Survey" (in the fiscal year 2012), conducted biannually by MEXT, even for public schools that do not impose tuition fees, the annual costs were found to be 55,197 yen for elementary school, 131,534 yen for junior high school, and 230,837 yen for senior high school (for all "school education costs"). Figure 5-3 shows the trend of the total

140 Why Has the Public Burden of Education Not Increased?

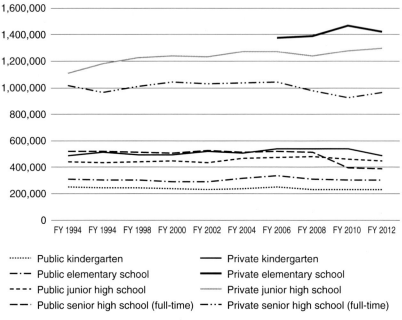

Figure 5-3 Trend of Total Child Learning Costs
Source: MEXT "Child Learning Cost Survey"

amount of learning costs (including extracurricular education) (unit: yen) based on this "Child Learning Cost Survey." Apart from kindergartens, private schools cost the most at the elementary school level and less as the level of schools becomes higher. Private elementary and junior high schools exceeded 1 million yen, and private senior high school costs were close to 1 million yen (there having also been a period in the past when they exceeded 1 million yen). The sudden decrease in the cost in the fiscal year 2010 corresponded with the introduction of the Free Tuition Fees at Public High Schools and High School Tuition Support Fund Program. The cost for private schools also decreased in the fiscal year 2010, but as costs rose noticeably in the fiscal year 2012, the impact of the Free Tuition Fees at Public High Schools and the High School Tuition Support Fund Program is more difficult to observe than is the case for public schools.

Figure 5-4 shows the percentage share of total learning costs for "curricular education costs" and "extracurricular education costs." The costs in "curricular education costs" include lesson fees, school event costs, PTA costs and student association costs, textbooks, other books and equipment, excursions, uniform, and commuting costs, among others. The costs in "extracurricular education costs" include costs and monthly gratuities for private coaching colleges, home tutors, equipment and books for study at home, and arts, sporting, and other experiential activities. The dark line indicates curricular education costs and the faded line extracurricular education costs. The continuous line signifies public schools and

Public Finance and Education in Japan   141

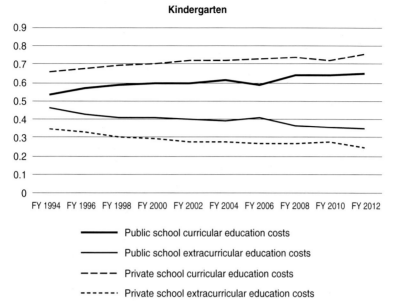

Figure 5-4 Trend of Percentage Share between Curricular and Extracurricular Education (a)
Source: MEXT "Child Learning Cost Survey"

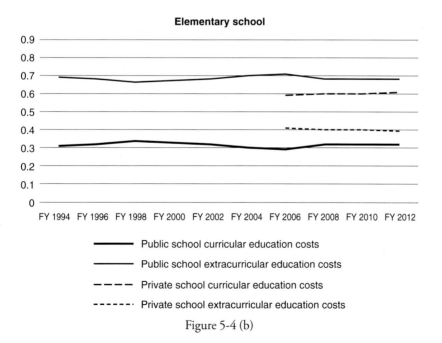

Figure 5-4 (b)

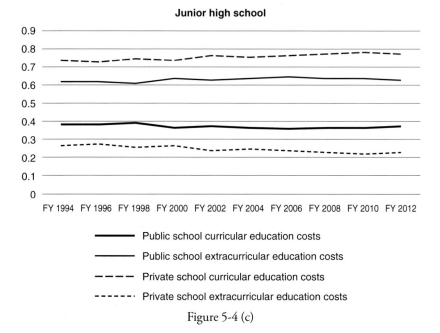

Figure 5-4 (c)

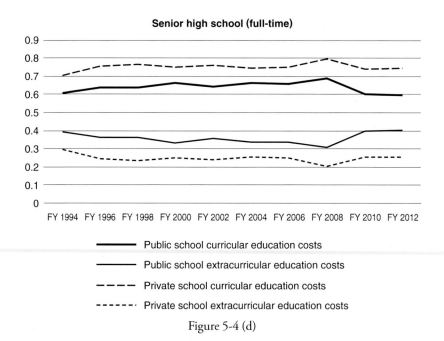

Figure 5-4 (d)

the dotted line private schools.

The comparative difference for elementary schools and junior high schools proceeds stably, but there is a large change in the comparative difference for kindergartens and senior high schools. With regard to kindergartens, there is not a large change for the total learning costs, but the percentage share of curricular education costs is creeping higher, overall. Looking at this breakdown,[4] there are no obvious trends that can be observed concerning particular increases for any of the cost categories. However, the public finance burden on pre-primary education, which tends to be overlooked as an education expense problem, is also at a low level among the OECD countries. In the first place, not all children attend pre-elementary education (in recent years, the percentage has proceeded at around 60%). Therefore, even though there is a certain level of choice regarding whether or not to enter kindergarten, according to this survey, the fees required will be a little more than 70 thousand yen for public kindergartens and a little less than 240 thousand yen for private kindergartens. As parents with kindergarten-age children are in younger adulthood, some parents might find this a heavy burden.

In social stratification research, it is often pointed out that one's social stratum of origin affects education achievements and school performance. In order to weaken that effect, early-stage measures are considered to be important. For example, in the United States, the Head Start Program, which was initiated by the Democratic Johnson (Lyndon B. Johnson) administration based on a "War on Poverty" campaign, was truly a program that addressed this problem. However, in Japan, such public support for the early stage of education and child rearing is extremely weak, and with respect to the point that the cost of school education itself includes numerous costs, measures of some kind probably need to be considered.

On the other hand, although change has been significant for senior high school, the percentage of curricular education costs in particular has lowered due to the Free Tuition Fees at Public High Schools and High School Tuition Support Fund Program. The introduction of this program has effectively reduced household expenditure by at least 100 thousand yen, which is definitely not a small impact. One would think that if the burden of tuition fees were simply reduced, this portion would shift to a different education costs (such as extracurricular education, etc.). In particular, one might expect this to be observable in data for private schools,[5] where one assumes there to be many cases in which tuition fees are high, and the pupils who attend them are hence likely to be in the high-income class. Just from looking at the data alone, however, this trend cannot be observed. As can be described with reference to Figure 5-3, the educational cost burden of families overall has been alleviated, and fundamentally, a large increasing trend can no longer be observed in recent years.

In the case of the compulsory education stage of elementary school and junior high school, the percentage share of curricular education costs used for public schools is becoming lower. To express this the other way around, the fact that the tuition fees for private elementary and junior high schools are that high is the cause of this result.

3. Balance between Burden and Benefit

(1) Sociology of Public Finance

Public finance is really governance by money, and public finance policy is always at the center of the political system. It differs depending on who the significant actors are and the establishment of the target of analysis (whether it is the budget policy itself or public finance policy for an individual region).

Moreover, this changes depending on the historical context. The choices that actors make, depending on the system, decide the direction of that system. Moreover, depending on the incentive for an individual actor to strengthen his/her own political power, his/her choices will be swayed; and what ultimately controls these choices are the immediate political situation, the response of the market, and the attitudes of the people that holds sway at that time. Furthermore, the system not only prescribes the conduct of the actor, but half of what the system is made up of represents the aspect of reaffirming the habitual state of affairs.

The central theme of the "sociology of public finance" is an investigation into the relationship between public finance and the state. This is in the words of Rudolf Goldsheid. According to Horst Jecht, who adopted Weber's theories, the sociology of public finance attempts to explain public finance by its relationship with overall societal and economic constructs. To show this more concretely, he centers on the establishment of target, which is the process by which intentions are formed relating to public finance policy, and the historical system theory, which conceptualizes the state as an autonomous agent and narrows down the focus of analysis to the relationship between the system and the actor. According to Naohiko Jinno, the contemporary study of public finance, while heavily influenced by German thought, can be categorized on the one hand into a group of thought following on from Musgrave (Chapter 2), who can fundamentally be positioned along with neo-classical synthesis, and on the other hand, into the tradition of the sociology of public finance that attempts to analyze public finance phenomena inside the flow of society as a whole. The sociology of public finance can be categorized as follows: the neo-Weberian sociology of public finance of John M. Hobson, who builds on the contribution of the historical sociologist Theda Skocpol, who emphasized the autonomy of the state; the historical sociology of public finance of W. Elliot Brownlee; and a systems theory-based sociology of public finance that gives importance to the decision processes of government in public finance (Jinno, 2002: 61–70).

The state mentioned here can be regarded as a functioning principle and system that has been artificially created based on the constraints of time and space. Its exercise of fiscal authority can be organized into three parts: 1) there is a flow of administration and control from state authority toward the people, and meeting this in the opposite direction is a flow of support and consent by the people vis-à-vis the state authority; 2) based on the assumption of 1), there emerges a flow of tax payment, or taxation, from the people, and this becomes a resource of monetary, physical payment that flows from the state authority to the people; 3) furthermore, against the backdrop of trust in state authority, the lending and borrowing of money between the government and corporations and between the government and the household, and the financial distribution of money through public finance are added (Oshima and Ide, 2006: 245–252). Although 1) is particularly important in modern-day Japan, I wish to review the relationships between tax and the state, and tax and the people in 2), which constitutes the premise for 1).

The biggest objective of the tax system is to effectively secure tax revenues. It is possible to carry out economic policy of some kind through the tax system (for example, environment tax, whereby a tax is imposed on fossil fuels to protect the environment, etc.). However, the purpose of such action cannot be seen as anything but secondary. If that be the case, in recent years, the effective securing of tax revenues has become a challenging task for all countries. For example, although there is a progressive tax system whereby high-income earners are burdened with higher taxes, in recent years the level of progression has weakened and there has been movement toward a flatter system. As an argument against the progressive tax system, it has been asserted that it hinders high-income earners' motivation to work. Empirical data to support this, however, is practically non-existent. Rather, it is the various acts of tax avoidance by high-income earners[6]—mentioned in the Introduction—that are becoming a problem.

In today's globalized world, high-income earners are willing to shift their income overseas to a country or territory where there is hardly any income tax. The same applies to corporations. Due to the high corporate tax rate, if a corporation shifts to overseas, the number of jobs also decreases as a result. In fact, currently, competition seems to have arisen to lower the corporate tax rate in order to attract corporations to a country. Therefore, there appears to be a limit to what is possible concerning the establishment of a progressive tax system for income tax and securing tax revenues by increasing corporate tax if one considers the relationship with the tax systems of the neighboring countries. The concentration of attention on consumption tax is not unrelated to this global trend (Morotomi, 2013: 238–246).

Moreover, the problem with the Japanese tax system is that it has a narrow tax base. In order to collect tax revenues, a tax base and a tax rate are applied to determine what tax to take from what income. In other words, setting a broader tax base would make it possible to have a lower tax rate, and conversely, narrowing the tax base forces the tax rate to be that much higher—otherwise, it would not be possible to collect the equivalent amount of tax revenue. Fundamentally, the world trend in tax reform is to safeguard fairness by getting as many people as possible to share the burden (broadening the tax base) and to achieve economic efficiency and vitalization through the associated lowering of the tax rate.

Since the tax base in Japan is small to begin with and tax-lowering policies to kick-start the economy out of a recession have been broadly implemented, the tax system has ended up taking the form of a "narrow tax base and low tax rate." According to the estimations of Shigeki Morinobu, Japan's scale is only half of that of the United States, which is often cited as a typical example of small government (Morinobu, 2010: 92–95). In particular, Japan has a system of many exemptions in its income tax. Such exemptions are a big cause of the lowering of the tax base.

(2) Public Works that Utilize Fiscal Investment and Loans

The subject of fiscal investment and loans was mentioned earlier, but according to Eisaku Ide, a particular characteristic of the public finance policies of postwar Japan, colloquially referred to as the "construction state" policies, is that they have been maintained and allowed to function through active use of fiscal investment and loans in the following ways: 1) lowering the tax burden by utilizing fiscal investment and loans; 2) gaining support from the middle class, small- and medium-sized business owners, and the self-employed by the reduction of taxes; 3) using public works to secure the employment of the low-income class while stimulating the economy; 4) thereby converting the low-income class from recipients of public assistance into tax payers; and 5) enabling payment of insurance premiums by providing employment opportunities (not recipients of public assistance) and placing many people inside the framework of social insurance. Of course, these are temporary effects, and we probably ought to give credit to the fact that there was a period when it functioned well. However, as the population structure has since changed, the percentage of the population living in urban areas has risen, the public finance deficit has rapidly increased, and criticism toward local public works has become severe.

This has led to a situation where, despite never enhancing the social security system, "wasteful" public works have been sharply cut to reduce the deficit, spousal special deductions have been abolished,[7] and tax reduction measures have been curtailed or abolished (effectively resulting in an increase in taxes). This has led to a loss of local employment opportunities. The economic activity of Japan as a whole has stagnated, and it has become politically impossible to advocate any further tax increases. As a result, the already inadequate social security system has been further reduced, the discontent of the people has deepened, and a negative cycle has been perpetuated (Ide, 2012: 232–233). Moreover, the only thing that is now emphasized is the reduction of excess, and the scrutiny of the people is becoming ever more forbidding. In recent years, the media has repeatedly given attention to stories on the illegal receipt of public assistance in the form of livelihood protection, and so forth. Consequently, society has been given the impression that welfare fraud is increasing. As a result, a more suspicious and tougher level of scrutiny is directed at the vulnerable of society, and the people are showing a less generous spirit.

Clearly, it is becoming increasingly difficult for Japan to continue borrowing money in the same way that it has up until now. This means the budget system must now undergo reform. And as to be expected from a democratic state, this reform must have the consensus of the people. If consensus is obtained, the politicians cannot but be moved by it. The reason Japan's public finance deficit has accumulated so high is because the politicians, the bureaucrats, and the people have been avoiding reform (Tanaka, 2013: 250–251). The people, while being the tax payers, also hold the voting power to select politicians. However, as already mentioned, this public finance system and the bureaucratic organization is too complicated for the people to pass judgment accurately. It is not realistic to expect all members of the voting public to learn such complicated knowledge and pass judgment accurately. Therefore, the experts, both in the government and among the people, are expected to play an important role (Nakabayashi, 2004).

Looking back at post-war Japan, we can understand that Japan's public finance system that has produced the current public finance deficit was already established by the end of the high economic growth period. Hayato Ikeda who proposed the so-called "doubling of income" was originally a tax expert who learned the ropes in the tax bureau, and his policy efforts were focused on balancing public finance and reducing taxes. He believed it was important to be as thrifty as possible in the country's expenditure to deliver a cheap government in order to reduce the burden on the people as much as possible.

At the time of the formulation of the budget of the fiscal year 1957, when Ikeda was Minister of Finance, there was a large increase in tax revenue due to the effects of high economic growth. This prompted not only the proposal of aggressive policy measures, but also the proposal to change the tax rate for income earners (who had sharply increased in number) and to introduce broad tax lowering policies. Then, when a policy was proposed to fix the income tax burden of the people's income at about 20% and to turn excess tax revenues into tax reductions, it became partly set in stone. In this way, the fundamental deduction, deduction for dependents, and the spousal deduction system, which was established in the fiscal year 1961, were established. These deductions were applied to adjust the tax rate for the middle- to low-income class. Meanwhile, the tax rate for small- and medium-sized businesses was slightly reduced and special taxation measures were expanded.

Despite these tax reduction measures, tax revenue was generated from the high economic growth, and this generated a virtuous cycle in which further growth caused by tax reductions continued. The tax reductions were benefitting the people's livelihood and corporate activities, and at the same time the people began putting leftover income into savings. The places where these savings swelled were postal savings and postal insurance. The government utilized these savings to carry out investment activities, and these funds became a large financial resource for expanding public works. In other words, the funds that could be generated under a low tax burden were used to carry out investment for providing social capital; and through such investment, employment was created in regional areas as well. Hence, the fiscal investment and loans system can be said to have created a framework for Japan's public finance operation. Another reason why the people readily accepted the assertion that tax reduction was tax reform—it collected votes through tax reductions and increased tax revenues by the policy of economic stimulation—was because of the memories that the people held during post-war Japan.

Jun Saito, who himself participated as a DPJ Diet member, summarizes the LDP governments that continued for a long time in the post-war period as follows. The LDP, through its relationship with local support groups and industry, has received support in return for bringing forward these parties' interests. This "pork barreling" style of politics carried with it a dilemma: if politicians ignored the opinions of supporter groups and industry, they would not receive any support from anyone; but, conversely, if they delivered on these demands too quickly, that might also weaken the support structure. For large public works, such as the expressways and the *shinkansen*, construction promotion associations involving local government agencies were formed, and these were able to function as vote-collecting systems. However, once the large infrastructure is completed, its benefits can be enjoyed irrespective of which political party or candidate one decides to support. Therefore, although large public works' projects of ambiguous necessity were started one after the other, it cannot be denied that these public works generated a certain level of employment locally, that income was generated from this, and that this provided a certain contribution to tax revenues, and so forth. On the other hand, the increase in civil engineering works of ambiguous necessity and purpose, such as land improvement and dams and land reclamation, generated particular distrust among influential people in the urban areas, and they also resulted in a huge fiscal burden being left for future generations. Such vast fiscal debt has unquestionably placed huge constraints on the freedom of policy needed to take Japan forward. (Saito, 2010: 16–17).[8]

Nevertheless, by proceeding with public works, this in some way enriches social capital. Consequently, ordinary people begin contemplating the future risks to their own livelihood, and their chief concern becomes pensions, nursing care, medical treatment, and so forth. However, when refocusing on concerns such as these, one notices that the mechanisms for socially supporting such concerns are pretty weak in Japan. With respect to welfare programs, large corporations in particular have been providing such mechanisms (presupposing the role of women as wives that become dedicated homemakers), but through globalization, companies have increasingly less leeway to maintain such welfare programs. Hopes can no longer, then, rest on the husband for raising enough salary to pay for the large education costs of the children with the wife continuing to be a dedicated homemaker. Putting aside the obviously shaky basis for such sense of values concerning gender-based division of labor, when the wife (regardless of sense of values) considers the education costs of the children, it gives rise to a situation where seeking a job becomes necessary.

The working population (i.e., the tax payers) agglomerates in the urban areas. Meanwhile, there is an unavoidable strengthening of criticism over who it is that will benefit from large-scale public works in regions with decreasing populations. When people take a dispassionate big-picture view of their life's course, they are faced with making extremely weighty decisions concerning having and raising children under the given circumstances, considering how much it will cost.

As already mentioned, Japan's social security schemes are extremely skewed toward care for the elderly. If looking only at the level of benefits paid to the elderly, Japan does not pale in comparison even to the northern European countries such as Sweden. However, the levels of Japan's benefits paid to the working generation, including benefits paid to families and those paid to persons with disabilities, particularly benefits in kind, are the lowest of any developed country. The reason for mentioning this is not to say that the working generation is making the sacrifice so that the elderly can have it easy (in fact, this is unlikely to be the case).

However, the degree of imbalance is such that one may get this impression. Hence, the working generation, who are the chief tax payers, will actually feel they only have burdens and no sense of benefit. As a consequence, this situation could also cause what is referred to as generational discord (Ide, 2013: 155–163).[9]

(3) Considering the Balance between Tax Burden and Received Benefit

The government procures funds to carry out various activities. As mentioned in the Introduction, the burden of the people is that of tax and social security. Although the social security burden is compulsory (it is compulsory to contribute to social insurance in Japan), unless insurance fees are paid, it is not possible to receive the benefit. In other words, individuals can easily see the merits of paying. However, in the case of tax, the government forcefully collects it and, from the perspective of the taxpayer, possesses gratuitousness in that the consideration in return for that payment is unknown. Such compulsory nature and this perception of gratuitousness undeniably underlie some of the causes of opposition toward tax.

However, as pointed out by Naohiko Jinno, it has come to be known that rather than a strong discontent being held toward the government, the sense of contentedness among the people is high in countries with a large burden on the people, particularly the tax burden. As one line of thought, Jinno (2013: 83–94) points out that it is possible that the Japanese consciousness toward the "public" causes a warped consciousness and understanding toward tax, which is the cause of discontent. Specifically, although it is popularly said that the Japanese have a strong awareness of authority, the concept of "public" has not sunk in, and instead there is confusion about the difference between "public" and "government service." For example, when describing a public school, it is first and foremost recognized as a school established by the authorities (government), and it is hardly likely that anyone holds the image of it as a school that operates jointly based on the burden that is each and every person's tax money. In other words, Japanese have a weak grasp of the idea of "public" as something used by everyone rather than belonging to one person, and as something that is jointly controlled through the provision of a share of the burden by everyone. Therefore, if the slogan "*kan kara min e*" (meaning: from government service to the private sector; translated as: "from public to private") is advocated by the Japanese government, since the distinction between "government service" and "public" is unclear, people will become concerned over the idea of joint control and inadvertently interpret it to mean entrusting the domain of the public to the private domain made up of individuals and corporations.

The government is a device for governing a society by providing special authority to it for the time being to give stability to society, which could otherwise fall into a state of anarchy if merely left to individual private interests. In this way, it enables people to live in security. However, as there is the potential for a person, once given the authority, to unexpectedly seize power, and to either practice tyranny or govern against the will of people, a mechanism has been put in place that reflects the public will in the form of elections. Therefore, the government is bestowed with the quality of enforceability, which is a strong power, as well as with the quality of publicness, which is the means to reflect as much as possible the will of the people living there; and its formation can be said to depend on the balance of both of these.

However, in the case of Japan, as it rapidly imported Western mechanisms, particularly when it was constructing the modern state, it immediately went ahead with replicating the systems themselves, but the intention and attitude behind them could not easily take root among the people. This is because the import of this "alien" Western system sometimes causes large opposition, all the more so due to its unfamiliarity (see Chapter 2). Therefore, the government or the state becomes one of two alternatives: something that is governed unilaterally and tyrannically, or something to be resisted and opposed.

The left-wing parties of Japan have a tradition of criticizing tax increases as bullying the vulnerable and have long been in opposition to it. Looking back at the history of thought control in pre-war Japan, it is not impossible to understand this as a prudent stance in opposition to the government and state power. However, socialism and communism are originally the ideology of controlling economic activity, and for this to occur, it is necessary for the government to intervene. Moreover, if one contemplates delivering services to the whole of society, then that necessitates a broad burden. In other words, people do not think in the following way: "First, please take the burden in the form of broader taxation for the time being, then the same amount of this portion will be put back into services, and the government will perform this intervention." Instead, it becomes more like regarding a specific "ruling class" as the enemy, with the idea that the government, who is in collusion with a segment of the greedy fortune-building wealthy, is exploiting the people. This weakens the concept of "public" in which everyone participates, in its place creating an "enemy" inside society, which ends up perpetuating an attitude that urges the government to make those people who have money pay more. Of course, there are some people who accumulate wealth that may be excessive and not proportionate to their contribution and work in society; however, these people aside, frankly, this stance has not received any wide-ranging sympathy in modern-day Japan, where a decent standard of living is maintained (in fact, such opinion has not earned a high level of support in post-war Japan). Moreover, because the universalism of public service implies mutual support by everyone, the posture of looking for the enemy within society causes fragmentation, and it is incompatible with the concept of universalism.

Conversely, in recent years, there have been claims that the left's assertions are simply selfish. This appears to be the viewpoint of conservative factions claiming that the post-war education, which has taught only rights and ignored obligations, is to blame. However, these are also put forward as a reaction against the aforementioned leftist assertions. This view can easily lead to the opinion that the state should have stronger power, in which the conceptualization of "public" is also somewhat simple. Hence, this view runs the risk of leading to an idea that the power of the state exists in absolute terms and that the individual should be sacrificed for the state, skipping over the concept of "public," as was the case in pre-war Japan. It misses the level of thought that inquires into the real purpose of the organ that is the government. The concept that the individual makes a sacrifice for the government can only be described as getting one's priorities the wrong way around.

For example, if one loyally intends to fulfill the tax burden corresponding to one's income (i.e., progressive tax), then it is essential to supplement one's income. As a cost arises here, a system needs to be built whereby the government can accurately ascertain income in order to suppress these costs. For this purpose as well, investigations need to be made into introducing a taxpayer numbering system or suchlike (Morinobu, 2010: 140–161). This is because without such a system, mistrust will ultimately emerge as to who is not actually properly paying their taxes, leading to a loss of trust toward the tax system and the government itself. However, not only is there concern that unilateral control of personal information is problematic, but there also seems to be resistance, which is strongly rooted among the people, toward the powers that be, i.e., the Japanese government, unilaterally controlling such a system. In particular, the adoption of socialist policies would make it necessary to expand the functions of government, and such a system would be essential. Yet the resistance to a unilaterally controlled system in Japan is probably stronger on the left side of politics. Although it is not necessarily clear whether this is because of the "memory" of the history of the pre-war Japanese government's rule, there are some reasons for the strong resistance against giving unilateral authority to the state power and government in Japan, where the concept of "public" is weak. This relationship tied in with the complex emotions of the Japanese surrounding "government service," "public," and "private" seems to be the reason why it is difficult for the government to establish public services.

NOTES

[1] To be sure, depending on the regulation, the cost of monitoring whether a regulation is being violated is also considered. In this sense, when looking at the total, there is no general rule as to which is the cheaper cost.

[2] Hideaki Tanaka also writes that because the budgetary system is too strict, it has made it easier to perform various accounting gymnastics aimed at presenting superficial coherence (Tanaka, 2013: Chapter 4).

[3] In a statement relating to a particular characteristic of the Ministry of Education by the current bureaucrat Kihei Maekawa, he mentioned that sectionalism was clear and that the mainline of policy decision making was an accumulation of the needs out in society (Maekawa, 2002).

[4] This book does not present a breakdown, but it can be viewed in the statistics' section of the MEXT website.

[5] To be sure, whether or not there is a clear tendency for people in a high stratum to go to private schools with high tuition fees would seem to differ significantly depending on the region, and it is not possible to make a blanket statement that this assumption is correct.

[6] The prime example of the overseas transfer of income for tax avoidance is the existence of tax havens. According to Shiga (2013), tax havens are countries and territories

without decent tax systems that have tough confidentiality protection laws but are lacking in legal systems, notably financial regulations. Some high-income earners and corporations, while enjoying the benefits of civilized society, move their income to these tax havens to evade their tax burden. Considering that civil society is maintained by the payment of tax, it may be said that this is a serious problem.

7   This was implemented from January 2004. Spousal deductions consist of spousal deductions and spousal special deductions. When a spouse's part-time work income is 1.03 million yen or less, a spousal deduction of 0.38 million yen is applied. For the spousal special deduction, there are two frameworks. The first is made applicable to incomes of 1.03 million yen or less: for the first 0.70 million yen, a fixed-amount deduction of 0.38 million yen is applied, but when it is more than that, the deduction is reduced in amount until it becomes 0 yen once the income exceeds 1.00 million yen. The second is the case in which income exceeds 1.03 million yen: as in the case of the first, 0.38 million yen is set as the initial value, and the deductible amount then continues to be reduced until an income of 1.41 million yen (this is not applied after the income exceeds 1.41 million yen). Here, the abolition of the spousal special deduction refers to the former.

8   Actual proof of this lies in asking why there was action to split off from the LDP, when the LDP split in 1993, why some Diet members who had split from the LDP rejoined, and what the intricate relationship is between this action and the level of provision of large-scale infrastructure (*shinkansen*) in certain regions. In the regions where there was an insufficient provision of infrastructure, there are many cases where Diet members stayed in the LDP, or returned to the LDP (Saito, 2010).

9   If attempts to rectify this imbalance are made in the current situation, where there is strong distrust concerning the pension system, by mindlessly reducing benefits paid to the elderly without increasing the burden on the people, distrust toward the pension system will probably strengthen further.

CHAPTER 6
Post-War History of Rising Education Costs

1. Foundation of Post-war Democratic Education System and Burden of Education Costs

(1) The Gap between the Center and the Local Areas
Creating a new education system and then implementing it was an extremely important issue in the establishment of the post-war democratic system. In particular, a new junior high school system was established after the war, extending the compulsory education age until 15 years old (which had previously stood at 12 years of age). This means that the field of work that children could enter after completing compulsory education was no longer limited to agriculture. There was also a rapidly expanding employee class centered on manufacturing. Moreover, changes in the industrial structure accompanying the high economic growth resulted in an influx into the urban areas of young people from agricultural backgrounds. To begin with, the employee world of the cities was one that valued academic records; and as a result, this led to the rapid explosion of the rate of students going on to the newly established senior high schools. Takehiko Kariya called the society in which there was this post-war, rapid educational expansion the "mass education society" (Kariya, 1995; 1998).

From the start, the Ministry of Education realized the necessity of strengthening the independence of education administration from the general administration in the area of public finance. However, in the Basic Act on Education (which came into effect in 1947) and the Ordinance for Enforcement of the School Education Act, no rules related to the public finance system were necessary in order to enforce the school establishment criteria that had been (somewhat loosely) prescribed. Later in 1949, the Act for the Establishment of the Ministry of Education was established, and more or less in parallel to this, bills related to the minimum criteria for the provision of educational conditions and the public finance transfer system for securing financial resources required to implement this were drafted (Yotoriyama, 2012: 36–39).

From before the war, teacher salaries were the greatest problem in the public finances of the local areas. In the pre-war period, it was mainly the municipalities that bore the cost of teacher salaries. The differences in these public finance capabilities were directly linked to the teachers' salaries. A system that prescribed the National Treasury's share of the municipal compulsory education costs, established in 1918, stipulated that the government bore a portion of the teacher salaries. This indicates that there was an intention to eliminate this problem. In reality, however, under the public finance of education, there was practically no function for promoting equal opportunity (Ibuka, 2004; Kariya, 2009). After the war, it was no longer tolerable to neglect this problem (due to the championing of the ideals of democracy and equality). However, establishing the new junior high school system caused a difficult situation for the issue of public financing of education.

The former Kokumin-gakko system (ordinary [jinjo] elementary schools) and the former middle schools, girls' middle schools, and secondary technical school organizations became parent organizations for the new elementary school and senior high school systems, respectively. However, there was no school system that was a predecessor to the new junior high school system. Nevertheless, it was compulsory education. Therefore, priority had to be given over everything else to the establishment and provision of the new junior high schools. However, in reality, this was not easily realized, and there were examples of making do with classrooms in elementary schools and setups in corridors, and sometimes, of temples and private residences being borrowed. Notwithstanding, there still appeared to have been insufficient funds on the books of expenditure to create the facilities for the new junior high school system.[1] For example, in the plenary session of the House of Representatives on April 26, 1949, Nobuemon Oka (LDP) stated the following:

> As you know, our country has thrown away shield and sword and announced to the world that we are a state that is peaceful and cultured. I think we all agree that the foundation of this new culture lies in education. However, when I compare the percentage share of the total budget of the post-war state allocated to education, I see the pathetic figures of 1.8% in the fiscal year 1946, 4% in the fiscal year 1947, 6.3% in the fiscal year 1948, and 5.1% in the fiscal year 1949.
>
> Then, when I look at the ratio of expenditure on the 6 : 3 System construction government subsidy and the public works expenditure, which at the moment are problematic, in the initial year, 1947, it was 4.7%, and it was 10.2% in 1948. However, even though there were unavoidable circumstances, it is still utterly deplorable that the construction budget is nil for 1949, the completion year. ("Diet Record" Plenary session of House of Representatives 5–22.)

According to the result of the "Survey on Local Educational Expenditures" conducted in 1950, about 80% of educational costs were used for compulsory education. Moreover, 11% of financial resources were donations from parents or guardians in the form of "6 : 3 System contributions" and "PTA contributions," whereby the ratios for kindergartens and senior high schools were particularly high.[2] Kokichi Kakuta of the then Liberal Party (the ruling party) raised the following issue on February 6, 1951, in the plenary session of the budget committee:

> The 6 : 3 System is considered as some kind of donation, donation is somehow associated with the PTA, and in the current 6 : 3 System, things are being covered by donation. This mindset still resides in farming villages. Moreover, we are developing and being brought up by the PTA, and even hold such feelings. The public finance of the local areas is in extreme trouble. Although there are equalization grants, rather than allocating these to education, they go immediately to civil works, and when there is a disaster, they go toward that. We even feel that the PTA in farming villages has been developed and fostered through the donation culture. That is the current situation.
>
> I read in the newspaper that according to a survey by the Ministry of Education—assuming this is right—according to a survey of a selection of 16 prefectures, 72% of the education budget at elementary schools is covered by the PTA and other contributions. In the junior high schools, 66% is covered by contributions, which, according to the newspaper, is also a survey by the Ministry of Education.
>
> ("Diet Record" House of Representatives' Budget Committee 10–8)

According to Kyoko Tokuhisa, in the immediate aftermath of the war, through the intention of self-examination regarding the war and the establishment of the cultured state, the schema of an ideologically opposed left and right had not yet formed. (This later became entrenched following the post-war period of high economic growth.) Thus, issues concerning the establishment of the new education system were to a degree commonly shared regardless of political position. In particular, after self-examination regarding the war, the Ministry of Education strongly advocated education's independence from the general administration and neutrality of education. However, this did not match the policies of the Civil Information and Education Section (CIE) inside the General Headquarters (GHQ); and the MOF which controlled public finance, was also in opposition. Moreover, the pre-war system prescribing the National Treasury's share of expenses for compulsory education was abolished and replaced with the Local Public Finance Equalization Distribution System. Because the supplementation measures were insufficient, local public finance noticeably deteriorated and it was no longer possible to secure education budgets. The Local Autonomy Agency, aiming for total administration, supported the Local Public Finance Equalization Distribution System;[3] and the MOF was in opposition to a system prescribing the National Treasury's share of expenses for compulsory education, which had the very real potential to hinder the equalization of public finance. However, because of the strong demands from public opinion, the system prescribing the National Treasury's share of expenses became essential to maintaining compulsory education and the 6 : 3 System required for democratic education. The then Liberal Party therefore changed its attitude to also supporting it.

In this process, although the policies of GHQ's control over Japan were initially focused on establishing democracy, due to the presence of the threat from the Soviet Union and the infiltration of socialist/communist ideologies as well as the teachers' unions embracing this ideology and union movements becoming gradually radicalized, the focus of control was turning to political stabilization. An undeniable effect of this was that the policies of neutrality and independence in educational policy consequently weakened, and there was no longer talk of removing interrelationships with other policy from the public finance of education, which became more susceptible to the influence of other budgets (Tokuhisa, 2008: 286–292).

Concerning the system prescribing the National Treasury's share of expenses for compulsory education, the expenditure for compulsory education was separated from the Local Public Finance Equalization Contribution that had been implemented before that, and the guaranteed minimum compulsory education expenditure was written down in law. From this, the local burden ratio was estimated and the resulting difference was intended to be entirely borne by the National Treasury. The compulsory education expenditure occupies a large percentage of local public finance, and the purpose was to stabilize local public finance that was made independent from contributions, thereby further clarifying the fiscal responsibilities for compulsory education of the country.[4]

For the local government agencies, their spirit of local government and decentralization of power would retaliate strongly if the autonomy of the local public finance were lost by a so-called strings-attached public finance of only the National Treasury's contribution to compulsory education. Furthermore, concerning the scope of the National Treasury's share of the expenses, the Ministry of Education intended to include teacher salary expenditure, school maintenance expenditure, and facility expenditure. However the MOF and the Local Public Finance Committee were inflexible in their assertion that they would not recognize anything other than educational personnel salary expenditure, and the then ruling party, the Liberal Party, made only the educational personnel expenditure from among the maintenance expenditure the National Treasury's share of expenses. A compromise plan was therefore made, whereby a framework for issuing construction bonds would be secured for the facilities' expenditure, and the interest payable on those bonds would be borne by the National Treasury.[5]

However, later on, opposition by the Local Public Finance Committee and the MOF continued, labelling the plan as something that oppressed the local autonomy. In the end, on June 18, the bill was passed by the House of Representatives as proposed by the MOF, and the next day, it was passed by the House of Councilors. With this, the National Treasury's Contribution System for Compulsory Education was established. In order for this bill to take effect, the Compulsory Education School Employees Act that made the education department public servants into national public servants was submitted on February 19, 1953.

However, according to the Japan Teachers' Union side, the gradually intensifying clash between leftist and rightist ideologies reflected the conservative forces, such as the Liberal Party, placing limitations on political activities by teachers. On the other hand, the conservative forces thought that the Japan Teachers Union held overwhelming power at the time and that a biased education that favored socialist ideologies was being taught. The opposition parties and the Japan Teachers Union expressed strong opposition to the central control of education by the government. Even among the Liberal Party, cautious opinions were expressed, and deliberation was left unfinished over what is referred to as the "Bakayaro Dissolution."

Moreover, it was clear that if the system for the National Treasury's share of expenses for compulsory education had been put into effect as it was, the government's public finance would have been inadequate. Hence, a "Special Bill on Compulsory Education Expenditure" was also submitted to cut out the National Treasury's contribution to wealthy municipalities, such as Tokyo, Osaka, and Kanagawa. However, this bill was also met with strong opposition and rejected. As a consequence of the passing of a budget amendment bill established in 1954, the following year, the National Treasury's share of the expense of compulsory education was distributed to these wealthy municipalities; and for the time being, this system for the National Treasury's share of expenses was settled.[6]

In the United States and other countries, teachers' salaries were calculated as the cost incurred for one student, on which basis the deployment of teachers was consequently decided. Kariya (2009) gave this the makeshift name of the "per-head world." Based on the per-head concept, if 40 students in one class are taught for 3 hours in one day, this is calculated as 120 person hours taught. This is regarded as equivalent to 30 students in one class being taught for 4 hours. Moreover, if we make the share of one teacher 120 student hours for 1 day, the desired lesson time for 30 students in one class would be calculated as 4 hours. Therefore, based on this per-head concept, the number of teachers is calculated from the number of students at a school; and based on this, the school grades are compiled and the class teachers assigned. Moreover, based on the per-head concept, the teachers can meet the requirements of the individualized curriculum and teaching method. Such were the assumptions of this system.

Japan, on the other hand, adopted an extremely special method: first the maximum students in a grade are established; from this, the number of classes is derived; and then, the number of teachers is divided up into the classes. Kariya called this the "standard law[7] world." Under this system (which for the policy makers was an unavoidable choice, considering the tough fiscal situation at that time), the instruction by teachers and the unit of education can be thought of not as students but as classes. Moreover, ultimately, this largely contributed to the establishment of the concept of providing a common education with a national standardization of class size (representing equality of education).

In addition, the first baby boomers were of school age; but later on, the number of children would sharply decrease. Initially, it was not uncommon to have classes of 50 students or thereabouts. When this baby boomer generation passed, the plan of the system was not to dismiss the teachers; instead, the plan was to ultimately reduce the number of students per class and achieve improvement in the educational environment in terms of class size.[8] If Japan had stuck to the per-head concept, then a decrease in the number of teachers would probably have accompanied the decrease in the number of students (Kariya, 2009). However, by not doing so and maintaining the "standard law world" instead, Japan did not have to later settle with a low global ranking for public education expenditure for the primary and secondary levels.

(2) Tuition Fee Rises Directly after the War

Given these conditions, after the war, the public finances were strained. The newspaper reported that the Ministry of Education had a policy of increasing tuition fees at government controlled schools by 2–3 times (and also increasing the tuition at private schools by 5 times to match this) from April 1948, soon after Japan's defeat.[9] Finally, at the end of May, the Ministry of Education announced a report that the tuition fees of national universities, higher schools and colleges, and junior high schools would be raised by 3 times.[10] The operation of private universities at that time had to be covered entirely by tuition fees, and the difference between public and private universities was extremely large. In particular, those universities with science and engineering faculties, such as Nihon University, Waseda University, and Keio University, were in a state of "management hardship." Compared with the total budget of Waseda, which included 10,000 students, the total budget of Nagoya University, which had the lowest budget of the national universities at that time, was much larger.[11]

Although opposition to the raising of tuition fees did not abate, the Ministry of Education and the MOF put forward a proposal to further double the tuition fees of national schools. It was reported that this would raise the new- and old-system national universities to 3,600 yen, the old-system higher schools and colleges as well as preparatory university courses to 2,400 yen, the new-system senior high schools to 1,200 yen, and the private universities to about 10,000 yen.[12] During the period of reconstruction when there was no public finance base, as already mentioned, compulsory education had been extended by 3 years. Hence, in education policy, the highest priority issue was the provision of new-system junior high schools. This meant that there was practically no available public finance to be put into higher education.

These sharp increases in university tuition fees were naturally regarded as a problem among the new generational mindset of the time that was seeking democratization of education. Regarding the scholarships,[13] also referred to as the Japan Scholarship Foundation scholarships, there was an opinion from among the conservatives that this was a benefit system, not a lending system.[14] However, the Ministry of Education, rather than describing these as borrowings, preferred to see them as loans for the next generation. It further expressed the opinion that loans were appropriate because by spreading the money thinner and wider, this enabled more people to benefit.[15]

In 1955, Waseda, Keio, and other private universities significantly raised their tuition fees, and in step with this, many more private universities decided also to raise their own. The cost upon entrance at university, which had been 38,000 yen for humanities and 45,000 yen for science in 1954, became as high as 45–50 thousand yen. For example at Waseda, humanities cost 20,000–22,000 yen, science cost 25,000–28,000 yen, and the separately charged facilities' fee was 5,000–8,000 yen and 8,000–11,000 yen for humanities and sciences, respectively. At Keio, the admission fee and the facilities' development fee were 5,000 yen each. However, the former became 20,000 yen and the latter 10,000 yen, which was a total increase of 20 thousand yen.[16] This situation attracted scathing views from the media, decrying the university fees as too high and printing headings such as "The Poor Cannot Enter," "Suffering for Only Private University Students," and "Only Rich Kids to Become Graduates."[17] On the other hand, on January 21, the then president of Hosei University, Marxist economist Hyoe Oouchi, presented a strong argument supporting the necessity of raising the tuition fees of private universities.[18]

Because there had been a continuing rise in the tuition fees of private universities, in 1960, an estimation by the Ministry of Education showed there was a disparity of about 300 thousand yen between national and private universities with respect to the burden over 4 years of higher education enrollment.[19] Moreover, it was reported that the MOF had a policy of raising the tuition fees of national universities (which had been left untouched since 1956) from 9,000 yen to 12,000 yen, beginning with the students entering in the fiscal year 1963.[20] Early in 1963, the *Asahi Shimbun* reported an observed trend in rising prices from kindergarten to university, citing the rise in the cost of living for other livelihood materials and the wave of reform to public servant salaries. It also reported an observed upward trend in education costs that were difficult to perceive as anything but tuition fees (materials costs and extracurricular education costs).[21] In the fiscal year 1964, because of the growing fierce opposition to fee increases amid the overall rising cost of living, many public higher secondary schools and national universities left the tuition fees as they were. Yet, on the other hand, the difficulties regarding public finance were being pointed out.[22]

Although many prefectural governments had incorporated the price rises in the tuition fees of national senior high schools, many prefectural governments postponed price rises, following the government's lead of making no changes to the public fees. However, the government's directive had no efficacy on the private senior high schools. In response to a question by Yoshio Domori of the Social Democratic Party of Japan, the Minister of Education, Hirokichi Nadao, responded as follows:

> Although the trend of the cost of living and the like are related, I think that constrained circumstances are gradually emerging in the operation of each school. Accordingly, although I think that it is mainly the private schools at present, there seems to be a strong mood to raise tuition fees from the next fiscal year.
>
> I do not know the details, but this atmosphere appears to be present. In the public schools as well, we are hearing several cases of this type of mood, but we do not know the details. For the national schools, we would consider increasing

the size of the budget for school operations to respond to any shift in the situation. We have no plans that involve the raising of tuition fees. Concerning this problem of tuition fees, I think there has been varied discussion on the issue. However, the Ministry of Education has no plan to raise tuition fees within the category of the public fees referred to at present. When the circumstances arise that make it necessary to raise tuition fees, we will take the view that it will be unavoidable. Accordingly, it is not at all our wish to see the tuition fees of private schools rise. However, when it is unavoidable in order to run the school, there is little that can be done except accept it with a reluctant heart.

("Diet Record" House of Representatives' Budget Committee 46–3, January 30, 1964.)

With this answer, Hirokichi Nadao gave tacit acknowledgement that there would be a rise in private school tuition fees, which had been rising on par with the soaring cost of living in society.

Education commentator Keiichi Shigematsu,[23] points to the following connection at the time between the hard-pressed education costs and examination competition.[24] Basically, because education costs are fees decided with respect to other living costs, no matter what kind of household setting, there is not a large difference in the amounts to be paid. Moreover, when looking at the breakdown, it is not the rise in the expense of the direct payment to schools, but rather the rise in the expenses not paid directly to schools, such as reference books and extracurricular education costs, that is by far the larger of the two. This is because there are disparities among the schools, and as part of the excessive competition to get into the prestigious schools, efforts are directed toward preparation for these entrance examinations. If this situation is left as it is, a clear relationship emerges between the family's capacity to pay and academic capability, and it becomes a threat to the basis of the modern school system. Moreover, the problem is that it leads to the prevalent situation in Japan of a warped sense of responsibility toward education, based on the notion that it costs money and it is the duty of parents to pay for it. In particular, the level of post-retirement social security in Japan is meager, and the transferal of property and goodwill to fulfil any sense of duty of supporting a child is also doubtful. Many salaried workers consider that a "school record" is all that parents can pass on to their children. In other words, this ordinary citizen's investment in education is a way of replacing the dim expectations of an insecure old age. It is worth noting that the issue of the large private share of burden directly linked to education and that of the weakness of Japan's social security system, which are issues relevant even today, have been a topic of discussion since as early as the mid-1960s.

From the above, we can understand that the public finance base of Japan's government has been extremely weak since directly after the war. Because the education budgetary priority was to put funds into elementary and secondary education, ultimately the budget allocation for higher education became extremely small, which is a situation directly relevant to the present.

2. Education Costs from the High Economic Growth Period to the Stable Economic Growth Period

(1) Student Movements and the Rise in School Costs

When one searches for articles related to "school costs," "education costs," and "tuition fees" in the post-war newspapers, several peaks are apparent. The first peak is around 1953. This was the time in which there was an overwhelmingly large number of articles related to the establishment of the system for the National Treasury's share of expense for compulsory education. Later, from about 1960, one can see articles here and there concerning the protest movement in opposition to rises in tuition fees at universities.

Although there are probably a wide range of views concerning the movement by the All-Campus Joint Struggle Committee (in Japanese, *Zenkyoto*), as will be mentioned later, one of its bases of was Nihon University. As this is the largest university in Japan, it contributed a great deal to the mass popularization of universities in the country. On the other hand, its lack of study environments, its tuition fees being out of kilter with such insufficiency, and the non-transparent nature of university management caused discontent. This discontent was undoubtedly one of the main reasons for the student movement. Performing a search in the Asahi Shimbun Article Search Engine "*Kikuzo*," there is a peak of articles related to protest movements (or conflicts) concerning the rise in tuition fees (i.e., school costs) in 1972, which was the end of the 1970 campaign against the Japan-U.S. Security Treaty.

The notable period of the movement in which the tuition fees of the private universities were significantly raised was from around the end of 1964. Then, in 1965, a movement in protest against fee rises at Keio University broke out.[25] This movement turned into a boycott on lectures. However, these protests against fee rises were not limited to Keio. The actual operations of private universities were really struggling, the bulk of which was running on tuition fees alone. However, many of the private universities were arduously continuing to operate by accommodating an over-capacity of students of 170%, and the education environment at private universities was deteriorating. Moreover, the salaries of the teachers at private universities at that time were low. As a result of operating at overcapacity, situations occurred in which, for example, it would not be possible to perform an experiment, or there would not be enough seats for all students when there was full attendance.[26]

Later, this movement in protest against rising school costs continued at Takasaki City University of Economics, Senshu University, and in the following year, at Waseda University. Looming in the background of the rise in tuition fees at private universities was a big problem with personnel costs, which had had to be raised to meet an increase in the base salary of teachers at the rival national universities. Moreover, it was also a problem that the government did not contribute practically anything to the operation of private universities. On the other hand, while it was true that university management was experiencing hardship, there was still a continuing rush to increase facilities for universities, faculties, and departments by making large investments. The lack of transparency related to university management caused suspicions about what it was actually doing, and this mistrust has been pointed out as a large reason why the movement occurred.[27]

In the end, the budget bill of the fiscal year 1967 left tuition fees for national universities as they were. However, the MOF, thinking that one of the reasons for the increasing protests and riots against the rise in tuition fees at private universities was the disparity in tuition fees between private and national universities, formulated a policy to definitely raise the tuition fees of national and other public universities in the fiscal year of 1968.[28] In that year, the conflict at Meiji University intensified. The Head of the Economics Department in the Faculty of Economics and Political Science committed suicide and students were arrested en masse. Meanwhile, at Chuo University, the respective policies of the Board of Trustees and Faculty Council vis-à-vis what action to take in response to a student barricade were opposed to each other, but to avoid bringing in the riot police, the policy of raising tuition fees in the fiscal year 1969 was abandoned. This was scathingly criticized by other private universities as sending the wrong message, namely, that if the students mobilized a strong movement, the decision to raise tuition fees may be retracted.[29] Concerning the incident at Chuo University, it was pointed out that the increase was very large, and students took advantage of the weak grounds for such an increase.[30]

As mentioned before, the point that the university operation was in a slump is a well-known factor concerning the conflict at Nihon University. The obfuscated accounting of the Board of Trustees at the time was also one of the causes of this incident. On November 10, 1968, a parents' association meeting was held at a lecture hall at Nihon University in which all of the serving members of the board resigned, and a resolution was passed claiming that the Chairman had committed a breach of trust and embezzlement.[31] With this succession of conflicts, many private universities decided against raising tuition fees for the following year.[32]

The student movement by the university students peaked from 1969 to 1970. The private universities (excluding the fine arts universities) also thought that the disparity in tuition fees compared to the national universities had widened to such a degree that it was not possible to raise tuition fees any further, and consequently fees hit the ceiling in 1970.[33]

(2) Introduction of Beneficiary-Pays Principle and Increase of National University Tuition Fees

In the period up until the 1970s, the provision of the compulsory stage of education had, to a certain degree, settled down. During the high economic growth period, due to the high enthusiasm for academic advancement among the generation referred to as the first baby boomers, senior high schools were newly established throughout the country. However, when the first baby boomer generation graduated from senior high school, there were naturally fewer students than there was capacity. Hence, even if no new senior high schools were established, it was still possible for many of the junior high school graduates to enter senior high school.[34] This meant that, finally, there was room to shift the gaze a little from the concerns of compulsory education and senior high school education. Moreover, it was not denied that the weak higher education environment was one of the causes of the campus riots. In the mid-1960s, it finally became possible for higher education to receive more attention in the public finance of education (Ichikawa, 2000: 9).

According to a report by the Central Council for Education made in June 1971, commonly referred to as the "46 Report," everyone had signed off to "Third Education Reform," upon which they had focused considerable attention.[35] The major points of this included: 1) trialing education system reform such as the 4:4:4 system; 2) enhancement of preschool education; 3) reform of teacher training and improvement in teacher compensation treatment, such as the establishment of a graduate school of education for existing teachers; 4) diversification and provision of higher education; 5) reform of administration and operation of universities; and 6) conversion to private school policies.

The conversion to private school policies of 6) was tied in with a system of providing subsidies to private schools. It was based on the assumption that it was going to be difficult for private universities to raise tuition fees any higher than their current level. Hence, even if the government were to assist the private universities, there was no room in the public finance to provide the assistance needed to bring the private university tuition fees to the level of the national university. Hence, from the second half of 1970 onward, the Ministry of Education and the LDP began attempting to raise the tuition fees of national universities. Their grounds for doing so were that there was a poor balance compared with other public contributions, and that the tuition fees of national universities were unreasonably low in price.

In 1965, deficit-covering government bonds were issued. These were explained as being necessary for the rationalization of expenditures, particularly in the MOF. Among this flow of events, a "beneficiary-pays" principle was put forward at a Fiscal System Council Interim Report in 1965. The crux of this report was that amid a fiscal crisis, it was selfish to receive only benefit while the tax burden was low. Therefore, if benefit was to be obtained, a suitable share of the burden was necessary. This share of the burden should be held by the people who become the beneficiaries. Of course, education is one investment. The recipients of the return of this investment were both the individual and society. Nevertheless, the level of tuition fees of national universities that were "unreasonably low" were leaving no room to support private universities. However, the private universities could not be left in their current state. The situation here can be interpreted as a negotiation involving two sides: one advocating the merits for education of "subsidies to private schools," and the other side emphasizing fiscal pressures to raise the tuition fees of national universities. The raising of tuition fees of national universities can be understood based on this social context (Ibuka, 2004: 349–358).

An example of the above argument at the time can be seen in the content of the question by LDP member Yōhei Kōno during a House of Representatives' Standing Committee on Education and the subsequent responses in February 1972.

I believe that the assistance to private universities is based only on a wish to bring them onto a level with national universities. However, looking at the national universities, if we take tuition fees as one example, I hear debate from here and there questioning whether it is a little too cheap in price compared with social commonsense. At any rate, the recent period has been one of strong public opinion that social commonsense should be given more importance in politics. On this occasion, the need to constrain public contributions has been given as the reason for postponing the raising of the tuition fees of national universities. Although there is absolutely no need for action that will play a role in further raising the cost of living, we need to consider things from social commonsense. If we make the current level of tuition fees the base of national universities, then it will be very hard for private universities to match this base. This is because these tuition fees of national universities are not anywhere near rational. Therefore, I think it is important to see this not as a fee rise but as an action to change the fees to appropriate tuition fees. I therefore think that we cannot allow these efforts to change to appropriate and rational tuition fees to be considered only as a measure to constrain public contributions, as we will end up moving forward without properly having this conversation. On the one hand, in special education and the like we have an extremely modest bunch of people working really hard at their jobs. On the other hand, we have allowed these irrational tuition fees for national universities to continue to this day. This cannot be accepted as social commonsense. I ask the Minister what his opinion is regarding these points.

In response to this, the Minister for Education, Michita Sakata, replied as follows:

This fiscal year, it is true that we will desist from raising the tuition fees of national universities. However, we hold a deep interest in the question of whether the current tuition fees of national universities are indeed appropriate, and we believe we must set a little more appropriate level of tuition fees that will meet with the acceptance of the general public. We would like to give a little more consideration to the period and the method. In actual fact, we are already considering the matter. When considering whether these tuition fees are appropriate or inappropriate, it should not be a viewpoint that only considers simply the cost of living or simply a comparison with private schools. While incorporating a scholarship system for Japan's university system and the recent report released on university reform,[36] I would like to give careful consideration to appropriate tuition fees. Therefore, if a stance is taken where the cheaper the university fees, the better, as you have just talked about, I think even students will not be able to understand this kind of view. I think the issue requires comprehensive consideration from various aspects, and it is time for examination in order to form one idea on what is a suitable level of tuition fees.

Continuing on from this, the Chief of the University Academic Bureau, Ministry of Education, and member of the policy committee, Matsuo Murayama, replied as follows:

> Since the school system was established in the Meiji period, the education system in our country has always been a system where tuition fees are collected even for national schools. From this rationale, national educational facilities are the buildings built and run by the state, and because these buildings are being used, there is a view that the beneficiary should take a share of the burden in the form of a service fee or user fee.[37] However, when it comes to discussing what is the appropriate amount to be collected, various debates will arise in whatever times we are living in, and no constant clear line has been established. It may be commonsense for the beneficiary to take a share of the burden, but only to the degree that the burden does not become excessive. Hence, the amount appears to have been decided naturally, as consideration has been given to both the education and public finance sides. Lately, tuition fees for national universities have been left alone for a considerably long period due to various circumstances. During this period, as the cost of living and the tuition fees of private universities have risen, from a commonsense point of view, there is a view that things should be relative to each other. There is also the view that tuition fees at national universities appear to be cheap.
>
> Moreover, when one looks globally at the various viewpoints, views toward the tuition fees of universities vary considerably depending on the country. There are countries with views that it should approach the level of paying for the required costs. There are also countries, including not only socialist states but also liberalist states, that take the stance of not charging tuition fees for national universities.[38]

While avoiding a detailed commentary of this argument, one can be sure that it was not necessarily the parents or guardians who judged the tuition fees of national universities to be irrational or unsuitable. "Acceptance by the general public" and "social commonsense," as mentioned in the reply by the Minister of Education, were perhaps references to the people involved in private higher education that competed with the national universities. For those involved in private universities, private universities cannot possibly hope to compete with national universities in terms of tuition fees, because their operation would not be possible if their tuition fees were at the same level as national universities. In other words, even if assistance were provided to private universities in the form of subsidies, it would be pretty much impossible for this alone to cover the disparity in tuition fees with national universities. As it is difficult to think of any significant differences between national and other public universities and private universities with respect to the public function of university in a broad sense, it does not make sense for only the tuition fees for private universities to be unreasonably high. In accordance with the principle of the beneficiary-pays, by raising the tuition fees on the national university side, it will correct, if only by a little, the disparity between the national and other public universities and the private universities.

The student conflicts quietened following what is referred to as the Todai (the

University of Tokyo) Conflict. At the end of the fiscal year 1970, although tuition fees were raised at small private universities, there was a movement of struggle in opposition to another rise in education costs by large private universities including Doshisha, Waseda, and Hosei Universities. Although the MOF asserted that there should be a rise in tuition fees at national universities on the grounds that there were problems regarding fiscal resources and the disparity between national and private universities, the Ministry of Education was afraid of a flare-up of the campus conflicts that had subsided. It therefore expressed opposition to these rises. The reason for the MOF's strong request was because the disparity in tuition fees between national and private universities had become even more pronounced. The rise in tuition fees had been postponed by many private universities because of the conflicts, but university operations became increasingly deadlocked. Consequently, in 1970, private universities, including Waseda, Sophia, Aoyama Gakuin, Kansai, and Nanzan University, had implemented fee rises.[39] Ultimately, at the end of 1971, there were struggles in opposition to the raising of tuition fees at 15 universities in Tokyo. In response, the Japan Association of Private Universities and Colleges requested that the government provide significant National Treasury assistance.[40]

Originally, there had been practically no difference between national universities and private universities with respect to tuition fees before the war. For example, around the period of the 1920s, tuition fees were first raised for national universities, and then Waseda and Keio Universities set their tuition fees slightly above the tuition fees of the national universities. Then, to equalize this difference, the national universities once again raised their fees. This cycle was repeated several times. Moreover, although most of the private universities followed the lead of Waseda and Keio Universities with respect to tuition fees, there was not the difference between national universities and private universities that exists today (Kaneko, 1987). Furthermore, many of the private universities specialized in humanities (or social sciences), which did not require large facility investment, and the smallness of resources was supplemented by a method of obtaining profits from special courses and preparatory courses in addition to the core courses. After the war, however, the criteria for the establishment of universities were loosened, and the number of private universities rapidly increased. However, many of the private universities established in this period had even fewer basic assets than those established before the war; and as there was no assistance from the National Treasury, these universities had to rely solely on student payments, mostly in the form of tuition fees. Ultimately, the expansion of higher education in Japan brought about a contradictory situation in which there was a tendency for people from wealthy backgrounds to prefer to go to the national universities that strove to achieve opportunity equalization, that were cheap, and that were highly competitive and difficult to enter, rather than to go to the private universities with high tuition fees (Maruyama, 2009: 62–63).

In a commentary in the newspaper at the time, Shogo Ichikawa wrote that the students going to cheap national universities were often wealthier than those attending private universities, and with a situation in which the rate of advancement to university was at about 25%, it was wrong that taxes were being used to pay for the full amount.[41] In the end, an LDP Education System Survey Committee found that there was no significant difference between the social roles of national and other public universities and private universities, reaching the conclusion that it was appropriate to raise the tuition fees by 2–3 times on the grounds of a "shrinking disparity between national and private."[42] Later, at a joint conference including the LDP Education System Survey Committee and the Education Subcommittee, the conclusion was presented to agree to a rise of tuition fees at national universities under the condition of enhancing scholarships and expanding exemptions.[43]

In 1972, the LDP and the Ministry of Education agreed to raise the undergraduate tuition fees of universities by 3 times (from 12,000 to 36,000 yen/year).[44] The Ministry of Education initially expressed concerns that there would be a reoccurrence of campus conflicts. However, at that time, the student movements were abating, and as a fee rise was inevitable at some point, the decision was made to move while the current situation was calm. Moreover, in exchange for compromising with the MOF on this occasion, the Ministry of Education was said to have the strategy and intention to focus on an expansion of scholarship funds and subsidies to the private schools presented in the report by the Central Council for Education, as mentioned above. Then, just as the Ministry of Education feared, the protest movement in opposition to university tuition fee rises spread to 86 universities as of January 18 (and barricades were set up at six universities).[45] However, that spring, 106 private universities decided to considerably raise tuition fees, and differences in tuition fees by university and faculty started to become prominent.[46] As there was also a sharp rise in the price of the cost of living, in the second half of 1972, some of the private universities apparently began considering the introduction of a sliding tuition fee system to keep fees in proportion with the cost of living.[47] Moreover, looking at the average amounts of private university student payments in the fiscal year 1973, it was about 200 thousand yen for humanities, about 300 thousand yen for sciences (and a little more than 400 thousand yen for pharmacy), and more than 1 million yen for medicine and dentistry.[48]

In 1973, the first oil shock occurred and sharp inflation became a social problem. In April, substantial fee rises were applied not only to universities but also to the educational material costs and the school lunch costs of elementary schools.[49] In response to the turmoil surrounding the fee rises, the Ministry of Education decided to establish a "Private School Promotion Survey Committee" and start an examination into the National Treasury Subsidization System for private universities.[50]

Against this backdrop of inflation, it became unavoidable for private schools from kindergartens through senior high schools to considerably raise tuition fees.[51] In April 1974, consumer goods rose by 3.5% compared to the preceding month. Although the Economic Planning Agency explained the sky-rocketing vegetable and education costs in April as being due to seasonal factors, the rise in public contributions continued thereafter as well.[52]

More than 70% of the expenditure of private universities amounted to personnel expenses. Hence, they were highly vulnerable to inflation. When an attempt is made to maintain the level of teachers' salaries, either tuition fees must rise or the student enrolment limits must increase; the latter option, in particular, worsens the education environment and could cause the problem that previously triggered the student movements. At the end of January, 1975, it was reported that Waseda University's cumulative deficit had risen to 2.8 billion yen; and even if fees were raised, the deficit was set to grow.[53] Private universities in regional cities were particularly hard hit, and it was reported that by 1975 it was already becoming more difficult for them to attract students. Against this backdrop, tough survival measures such as the sale of campus land or creation of sideline businesses were the only option.[54] Finally, when this time came, there was criticism that some universities had become leisure lands, and questions were asked as to the validity of pouring any more of the taxpayer's money into them.

According to a theory by Suetomi, the turning point for education costs in Japan, when there was a dramatic increase in the share of the burden of private costs, was in the years 1971 and 1975. The former, 1971, was the year of the Central Council for Education report that clearly became the grounds for the creation of the policy to strengthen the beneficiary's share of the burden. In the latter year, 1975, the Act on Subsidies for Private Schools was revised in an attempt to increase public contribution grants to private schools. At the same time, measures were taken to correct the discrepancy between national and private university tuition fees by sharply raising the tuition fees of national universities (Suetomi, 2010: 60).[55]

3. Institutionalization of the Heavy Share of Education Cost Burden

(1) Soaring Education Costs Before and After the Introduction of Subsidies for Private Schools

Suetomi (2010) compiled the following information from newspaper articles showing a change of interest concerning education costs among the general public. The 1950s was the period when the system by which the National Treasury bore compulsory education costs was established. The problem of education costs (and particularly public education expenditure) points exclusively to this issue, as reflected in the number of newspaper articles. However, after that system was established, the articles sharply decreased in number. Replacing that issue, the issue of household education costs began appearing here and there. In other words, it was from about this period that the size of the private burden of education costs became an issue. Then, entering the 1970s, proposals for measures to reduce the largeness of the education cost burden of private schools (particularly universities), and measures to reduce the education cost burden, such as assistance for kindergartens and tax deductions for school expenses, became prominent. In the 1980s, following the same trend, attention was drawn to the heavy burden of private education costs, specifically the general education costs included in household expenditure outside school costs (such as cram schools). This trend continued up until the first half of the 1990s. Then, from the period of Japan's economic recession from the second half of the 1990s, the growth of household education costs hit a ceiling, and since then, there have been articles that have even mentioned a slight decline in household education costs. However, many of these articles point to the economic recession as the main cause and state that the burden of the education costs continues to be high.

In amongst all of this, one can see a scathing opinion, particularly concerning the increase in costs for higher education, which is especially notable from the 1970s onward. On the one hand, up until that time, systems related to education costs were still being set up to some degree; on the other hand, the livelihood of the people overall had become affluent and there was greater participation in advancing to higher education. Hence, higher education was not special anymore—it had become ordinary. Consequently, there was a prominence of criticism that there may have been an overestimation concerning the public function and effect received from universities, and that perhaps there was a surplus of universities (criticism of whether or not the social function and contribution that could be expected from universities was really being fulfilled) (Suetomi, 2010: 167–181).

According to the analysis of Masakazu Yano, investigation into the trend of the average percentage share of household expenditure used for education costs revealed that at about the time of the first oil shock of 1973, the percentage share turned around from a declining trend to an increasing trend. The percentage share decline before the oil shock was because incomes were increasing more than the rise in education costs; hence, educational costs were relatively low. However, after the oil shock, not only was there a slowdown in income but education costs also increased more than the income. The soaring education costs were not just rises of tuition fees for higher education. Preparatory education required to advance to higher education (i.e., extracurricular education such as cram schools) was becoming commonly utilized. Moreover, it was also due to the fact that private schools were considered advantageous for advancing to the high ranked universities, and the lowering of the age of entrance examinations proceeded. Furthermore, students were going to university far away from their family homes, and once these expenses were included, the burden on the household budget was considerable (Yano, 1996: 44–56).

From around 1975, rises in the tuition fees of national universities were no longer an uncommon occurrence, and each rise was substantial. Private universities continued to suffer fiscally, and protest movements erupted in opposition to tuition fee rises. However, there was also an increase in protest movements opposed to tuition fee rises at national universities from that time. However, at the time, the aftermath of the Lockheed Scandal put the Diet in disarray, and it was not until the autumn of the fiscal year 1976 that the tuition fees for national universities rose.[56] On the other hand, discontent on the private university side was not entirely because of the disparity in tuition fees; the distribution of development funds was also overly biased toward the national universities. For example, although scholarship amounts also increased in response to the rises in tuition fees at national universities, there was no such response to the rises in tuition fees at private universities. Moreover, hiring rates were also biased toward the national universities.⁵⁷

For many private universities, a system of advanced payment of tuition fees was adopted to prevent those who had passed admission (and later passed admission to a national university) from absconding to a national university. In exchange for the rises of tuition fees at national universities, the Act on Promotion and Subsidies to Private Schools was put into force, and private schools began to receive official subsidies from the government. This resulted in private schools being subjected to an increased critical gaze from the public, and the Ministry of Education announced an abolition on advanced payments (in October 1975). Initially, there was a reaction of opposition from universities, excluding the influential private universities such as Waseda and Keio; but in the end, most of the private universities complied with this policy.

Although higher education began to receive a slightly greater share of the budget as a result of the private school subsidy system, it was not at all sufficient. Education costs were growing overall, and those for primary and secondary education alone were at a level equal to the other OECD countries. The problem was the budget for higher education: it was clearly at a low level internationally, and even though the advancement rate to higher education was about to reach 40%, there was no growth in the budget to reflect this. In other words, there were no signs of enhancement of substance to reflect the actual extent of quantitative expansion.⁵⁸ In a survey conducted by the Ministry of Education at the time, the household education costs for elementary and junior high school students, such as cram schools and educational materials, had increased by 100 thousand yen, which means it had doubled in the space of 5 years.⁵⁹ For private junior high schools and senior high schools in Tokyo, the annual initial-year school costs were higher than 500 thousand yen, and the cost of expensive private schools exceeded 1 million yen.⁶⁰ This was about the time when arguments were raised at the Fiscal System Council that there ought to be a difference in tuition fees between the faculties of national universities. Against this backdrop, the tuition fees of private medical universities and medical faculties as well as dental universities and faculties rose by a degree that could be described as exorbitant. Management of the medical faculties at private universities was unstable, and the obfuscated accounting that overemphasized school bonds and donations at the time of university entrance was regarded as problematic. Under guidance from the Ministry of Education, this was made impossible, and the face values of the amount of payments were considered to be out of reach of the ordinary household. Although the average was about 7 million for the initial year, there was an extremely big difference depending on the university. However, it was claimed that these universities and faculties would be unable to operate stably even if that amount were paid.⁶¹

In the spring of 1978, the tuition fees of national universities were again raised 1.5 times (from 96,000 yen to 144,000 yen). The newspapers ran features on these rising education costs. The estimation for the cumulative education costs from kindergarten through senior high school exceeded 5 million yen. If all schools were public, then the estimate was 2.36 million yen. If private schooling was used all the way from kindergarten through university, it was 9 million yen; and even if public schooling was used all the way, it was still over 5 million yen. Moreover, as the tuition fees at universities were continuing to rise, the costs were expected to continue to rise in the future. Education loans became a popular offering at banks, and there was a gradual emergence of new prevailing opinions like "what parents can give you is education only" and "rather than regretting it later...."[62] In illustration of this, a son of a farming family living in a remote island went to a senior high school in the city on the mainland; however, the family was unable to send him money under these circumstances. The family thus used its savings and took an advance on its postal insurance to move to the city, but the money ran out immediately and the father was unable to find work. The father quit alcohol and cigarettes, returned to the island by himself to earn some money, sticking to his firm commitment: "I want to give my children what I was unable to have myself." Education was difficult in the remote areas, and cases such as this increased.[63] Meanwhile in the case of both senior high schools and universities, there continued to be the paradoxical phenomenon that it was the children from comparatively affluent backgrounds that were going to the public schools. At the time, the average annual income of a household sending a child to the University of Tokyo was 5.17 million yen, the average annual income of a household sending a child to a national university was 3.76 million yen, for public universities it was 3.77 million yen, and for private universities it was 5.04 million yen. As the annual household income at that time was 2.81 million yen, one can see that the students of the University of Tokyo clearly came from rather high-income families.[64] The results of the "National Survey on the Actual Life of Citizens" by the Ministry of Health and Welfare pointed to glaringly obvious income classes in the education costs from preschool students onward.[65]

(2) Increase of Education Cost Burden on Families during a Restructuring of Public Finance

Entering the 1980s, the newspaper articles related to education costs and tuition fees decreased in number (however, this does not mean that tuition fee rises stopped occurring; it was more that they had become the norm). On the other hand, the argument that the parents' share of education costs was too heavy was continuing. In a survey conducted at the Dai-Ichi Kangyo Bank, Ltd., it was revealed that monthly expenses of 70 thousand yen were required by a university student in Tokyo (a little over 100 thousand yen if boarding), and this was putting families with housing loans in difficult circumstances.[66] In a survey conducted at the same time in Tokyo Metropolitan Government, including school, cram schools, and other extracurricular education costs, monthly education costs were on average 56 thousand yen, which was 20% of the household expenditure. Three quarters of survey respondents replied that the education cost burden was "heavy," and "pitiful" circumstances were reported of parents who replied "education is the only asset remaining."[67] Tuition fees at national universities rose 20%, from 180 thousand yen to 216 thousand yen in the fiscal year 1982.[68]

The government at the time made overcoming the deficit financing, which had become ongoing, a policy issue to be tackled through measures such as introducing a general consumption tax. However there was strong opposition in response to this, and in 1981 a Second Provisional Commission for Administrative Reform was established under the Zenko Suzuki Cabinet. Administrative Reform was then carried out on the basis of "public finance restructuring with no extra tax."

In a state of fiscal deficit, the MOF sought to reduce the subsidies to private schools by more than 10% in the budget of the fiscal year 1983. The MOF had intended to reduce the percentage of subsidies to universities that were at overcapacity, and senior high schools and universities with considerable improvements in their revenue earning status. However, the Ministry of Education and private-school interested parties reacted in opposition to the idea on the reasoning that, conversely, if subsidies were reduced (because they constituted 30% of ordinary expenses), this would likely create pressure to raise school fees, such as admission fees and tuition fees. In response to this, the MOF argued that over the past several years, the operations of private school corporations had considerably improved, their asset holdings had increased, and the level of teacher salaries at private universities had risen on average by 10% more than national universities, in some cases even 30% to 40%.[69]

In response to these reductions in subsidies to private schools, the trend of rising tuition fees in private universities once again took hold, and under the pretext of "correcting the disparity between national and private institutions," tuition fees at national universities once again began rising from 1984. Tuition fees rose by 25%, from 216 thousand yen in 1982 to 270 thousand yen in 1984; converted to monthly payment, they for the first time exceeded 20 thousand yen.[70] Moreover, according to the "National Survey on Education Costs" conducted by the Ministry of Education, the percentage share of expenditure for junior high school home tutors and monthly fees for cram schools had risen, now reaching 40% of household education expenditure. However, that figure of 40% also included students who did not go to cram schools, and the estimated cost paid by parents of children actually going to cram schools was at the level of 80% of the school education costs.[71] The reduction of subsidies to private schools also continued in 1984.

This trend of rising school costs persisted after this time as well. However, university student protest movements in opposition to tuition fee rises had gradually subsided. Then, when 1985 came around, articles declaring peace and quiet on the student front appeared. The voices raised in opposition to the fee rises were only at some universities, such as Meiji and Waseda, and all was calm on most campuses, with the dominant opinion among students being that "fee rises were unavoidable." Against this backdrop lies the fact that many private universities introduced school fees that followed a sliding-scale system fixed to the cost of living. This was to reduce the amount of fee rise every year. Moreover, as future revisions were taken into account at the time of admission, the system would contribute to mitigating the shock of fee rises.[72]

However, including the costs at university entrance, the expenses of university life over a 4-year period rose to as much as 8 to 9 million yen. In particular, there was a rising trend of a "rich lifestyle" for boarders and other students. It cost as much as 1.9 million yen a year for private university students staying at boarding houses; and even at national and other public universities the cost amounted to as much as 1.5 million yen. The children were living a rich lifestyle, but the parents were jokingly referred to as poor.[73] Under such circumstances, there were opinions at the Provisional Council on Education Reform that the public finance of education should be expanded, as might be expected.[74] On the other hand, there were also articles that stated there to be a lot of wastefulness in public finance. For example, there were cases of welfare pensions being paid to dead people, and there were 19 universities with household income criteria for exemption from national university tuition fees that were more lenient than the Japan Scholarship Foundation criteria. Moreover, the criteria for class work was mostly more lenient than those of the Japan Scholarship Foundation. There were even cases reported of repeaters being regarded as students of exemplary academic performance and receiving an exemption on tuition fees.[75] In the second half of the 1980s, Japan was passing through its bubble economic period. While there was an emerging societal problem of a mammoth education cost burden, it is very interesting that there were articles along the lines of inquiring whether this was simply a matter of increasing the public burden, and which suspected there actually to be a lot of wastefulness of public expenditure.

In research by Tokyo Metropolitan Government, based on an education cost survey conducted in 1986, data showed that education costs per household exceeded 70 thousand yen. In particular, in households in which the head of the household was in his/her 40s, it was an extremely heavy burden on the household budget. There were even examples of 40% to 50% of household expenditure being spent on education costs.[76] Tuition fees at national universities had risen 19% from 1987 to becoming 300 thousand per year, and the situation of tuition fees and admission fees interchangeably rising was persisting. Nevertheless, the MOF announced from spring of 1988, when admission fees were due to rise, that in order to narrow the disparity of tuition fees with private universities and to reduce the public finance burden, it was planned that tuition fees for science courses would rise by about 20%. In the case of science courses, they are highly staff intensive, and there needs to be special treatment for practical costs. This was an attempt to bring cost consciousness and the beneficiary-pays principle to these courses. However, because it broke the general principle that had been held since the Meiji period that tuition fees would be the same for all faculties, and because it would take away opportunities for people from low-income classes in particular to advance to a science university course, the Ministry of Education was strongly opposed.[77] In the end, agreement was given to raising the admission fee and the assessment fee (for the admission examination), and the fee rise to the tuition fees of the science faculties was postponed. However, the Fiscal Inquiry Council, an advisory organ of the MOF, officially set forth from that time to introduce faculty-specific tuition fees at national universities.[78]

The soaring tuition fees were affecting not only Japan's households but also international students as well. Specifically, the yen was sharply strengthening, and compared with the previous fiscal year of 1987, the number of persons eligible for exemption of tuition fees at national universities increased by 50% to 1,500 persons.[79] Moreover, from the fiscal year 1989, at the height of the bubble economy, tuition fees at national universities rose 12% to 336 thousand yen. Although there were changes in the lifestyle orientations of the students themselves, the housing circumstances also changed due to the impact of the bubble economy. In particular, the extreme inflation of accommodation costs for university students became a problem.[80] Furthermore, in order to go to private university, more than 2 million yen was required for the first year in the case of moving from the regional areas to Tokyo, and this was twice the cost that it had been 10 years earlier (with the average incomes of parents having but grown by 1.8 times). Nonetheless, this did not necessarily mean that the financial situation of private universities had improved. The number of universities with a deficit on the simple fiscal year balance sheet was 60 (out of the 96 schools in the Japan Association of Private Universities and Colleges), and the deficit was as much as 53 billion yen.[81]

(3) Trend of Education Cost Burden from 1990s Onward

At the beginning of the 1990s, the Second Baby Boomer Generation was entering university. Following this, the population of 18 year olds was declining along with the birth rate. The bubble economy had also ended, and Japan had entered a period of long-term economic recession. Nevertheless, the rising trend of tuition and admission fees continued after this. The MOF sought to further raise tuition fees for the students enrolling in the fiscal year 1995 on the grounds of public finance difficulty and correcting the disparity of tuition fees with private universities; and in the end, fees rose by 3 thousand yen per month to an annual amount of 447.6 thousand yen. Specifically, at that time, the MOF was planning to raise science-course tuition fees (through the introduction of faculty-specific tuition fees), and various debates were held centered on this issue.

The tuition fees at national universities rose to 469.2 thousand yen for students enrolling in the fiscal year of 1997.[82] After this, a sliding system was adopted for the tuition fees of national universities, starting with students enrolling in the fiscal year of 1999. Moreover, although tuition fees were applied from university admission to graduation from the fiscal year 1999, tuition fees would now change according to the new sliding system. (As a point of comparison, the tuition fees for students enrolling in the fiscal year 1999 were 478.8 thousand.)

Meanwhile, as the recession persisted over time, there were increasing cases of people finding it difficult to pay the school fees. In October 1998, there was an article stating that the rate of tuition fee payments more than 3 months in arrears at private junior and senior high schools had risen to 1.4%.[83] In Shizuoka Prefecture, the tuition fees for the prefectural schools were 9 thousand yen, but the number of students receiving full or partial exemption rose sharply to 1,855 persons (an increase of 479 persons from 3 years earlier). The number of students who left school on the grounds of economic hardship was 108 persons (an increase of 45 persons from 3 years before). The same trend was observed in all of the urban areas.[84]

Although the data are limited to regional areas, the Ashikaga Bank Local Financing Division conducted a questionnaire targeting 1,000 men and women in their 20s to 50s working in companies in Tochigi Prefecture, and more than half of the respondents answered that the "heavy burden of education costs" was the reason for the decline in birth rate. In particular, 70% of people in their 40s selected the "heavy burden of education costs" as the reason.[85] Moreover, according to a 1995 survey conducted by the Tokyo District of the Japan Association of Private Universities and Colleges targeting students studying at universities or junior colleges in the Greater Tokyo Area, while the amount of money needed to move from the regional areas to the capital and enter a private university in Tokyo exceeded 2.1 million yen, the annual income per household was beginning to decrease for the first time since statistics had begun to be collected. Moreover, it was clear that slightly over 30% of households were making do using borrowings.[86]

When the economic bubble collapsed and Japan entered a long-term recession, the effect gradually impacted the education budget. The National Treasury's contribution to compulsory education at that time was for the government to pay half of the costs. However, the bodies not receiving taxes allocated to local governments were considered a wealthy municipality and had their assistance unit price reduced. Meanwhile, tax revenues were declining due to the economic recession, and Kanagawa, Aichi, and Osaka Prefectures all became bodies receiving taxes allocated to local governments, for which reason it became necessary to provide that portion of assistance. However, the MOF refused to recognize this. In response, the Ministry of Education changed the respective ordinance to make the criterion for becoming a wealthy body "exceeding a fiscal capability index of 1.0 during the past three years." This was intended to restore consistency to the system and reduce the assistance to these three local governments.[87]

From the second half of the 1990s, there was a succession of large bankruptcies. School fees were not paid, for example, because a parent's company went bankrupt or they were middle- to senior-aged employees dismissed as part of restructuring. Applications were hence made to pay in installments or delay payment. In the end, the problem of an increasing number of students leaving schools emerged. As a result, universities began low-interest school-fee financing schemes.[88] For example, according to a 1999 survey conducted by the Japan Association of Private Universities and Colleges, 1.38 persons per school left a private senior high school for economic reasons, and 10 persons per school were still late in their payment as of the end of the fiscal year. Among these cases, there was one in which no contact was possible because the telephone had been disconnected due to the inability to pay for phone bills. In another case, a student tried to get a part-time job at a gas station to cover tuition, but it did not work out and the student had to leave school. Even if students had wanted to transfer to a public school, no such transfer system had been established, and this was also deemed to be a problem.[89]

Moreover, up until this time, private universities had demanded that tuition fees be paid before it was announced whether the student had passed the entrance examination to a national university, thereby preventing students from absconding to national universities if they were subsequently offered a place there.

However, in the economic recession, there was a growing motivation to go to the comparatively cheaper national university, and there was an increase in students who had been accepted by national universities leaving their private universities. For a while, the paid tuition fees were not refunded. However, opinions were raised that it was morally questionable to take tuition fees even though no classes were being taken. It was therefore thought that the Ministry of Education should provide some guidance on the issue. The public began to take a more critical view toward payment to universities.[90] Then, in 2003, while the Japanese economy was beginning to see deflationary trends, the only area in which there was a noticeable rising trend was that of education costs. Hence, the burden on the household budget further increased.[91]

These soaring education costs were occasionally mentioned in newspaper articles, but ultimately this was not treated as a "societal problem"; rather, it continued to be seen as inevitable, and as something that people needed to put up with. As will be elaborated in further detail in the next chapter, there are not many political points of contention regarding education in the broad sense. If such issues arise, the focus of attention tends to be from an ideological point of view; and consequently, the burden of education is very rarely raised as an issue during elections. The LDP, which was for a long time the ruling party, has naturally included education-related items in election manifestos. However, these have often been more regarded as matters of principle, such as emphasis being placed on moral education. Problems tied with public finance, such as dispensing with fees, have practically never been included. On the other hand, opposition parties such as the Socialist Party and the Communist Party have manifestos that advocate dispensing with fees for senior high schools and the enhancement of scholarships. However, either the financial resources have not been clearly enough articulated or many aspects seem to have lacked a grounding in reality. Moreover, because of their position as the opposition, they did not have the means to realize these policies.

Considering these points, it was hugely significant that the DPJ ran on a manifesto that included child allowance payments and dispensing with fees for senior high schools in the general election of 2009, took hold of the government, and put these policies into practice. In particular, upon entering the 2000s, as part of the "nothing-is-sacred structural reform" by the Koizumi administration and subsequent governments, the National Treasury contribution system for compulsory education was reformed. Although it was not abolished, the National Treasury's share was reduced from a half to a third. As a result of these circumstances, the education budget was in an increasingly difficult position. Against this backdrop, the slogan "from public works and construction to people" was put forward, and in the fiscal year 2010, there was suddenly the highest growth in the education budget for 30 years (see Chapter 5). Of course, there may still be people who point out that the budget is far from international standards, even with this increase. However, considering the historical background, it would appear to deserve a more affirmative appraisal from those involved in education. For example, the following statement was given by a DPJ Diet member during the deliberation of the Diet.

We have been receiving certain praise, such as for the ongoing reform to the education system and for our examination of the necessary reviews concerning how the system should be in the next fiscal year and onward, as well as for the revision to the act on standard teacher numbers to realize small class sizes, the dispensing with tuition fees for senior high schools, and the increases made to the education budget for the past two years.[92]

Moreover, a Diet member from the LDP party, which was the opposition at that time, questioned the purpose of raising the consumption tax rate, asking in particular whether there was a need to position as the main use of the tax not just general social security and welfare but also education.

If we think about things pragmatically, this constitutes reform of tax and social security by the Kan Cabinet. Based on the current discussion, I get the impression that the purpose of the consumption tax will be for social security. In order to properly secure the education budget, I think it is important to position education as one major objective in the argument for the consumption tax.[93]

However, looking at the current state of Japan overall, it would seem that appraisal of the DPJ administration has been remarkable low. This is partly because the manifesto was impossible to realize to begin with, but showpiece manifesto policies (sometimes including contradictory policies) were added, and these accumulated each time there was an election, due to the excessive prioritization of regime change. In particular, the problem of financial resources had been pointed out from the start, but this was not something that could be simply explained by the fact that tax revenues did not grow due to economic recession alone. To begin with, despite passionately calling out for a reduction in wastefulness, expenditure had increased under the DPJ administration. Initially, attention was given to the review and prioritization of this government program. As the original aim for such review was to formulate the budget with citizen participation and secure transparency of the process, securing financial resources was not its primary target from the outset (Nihon Saiken Inishiachibu, 2013: 23–24). For such reason, this method was initially met with applause from the people, also thanks to its novelty, but later encountered fierce opposition.

The 2010 House of Councilors Election ended in defeat for the DPJ, and thus began the government referred to as a "twisted Diet," in which the DPJ became a minority in the House of Councilors. However, the relationship between the election results and the actual number of votes was not at all simple. For both proportional representation and single-member constituency systems, the DPJ still obtained more votes than the LDP at that time. In the first place, the 2009 House of Representatives Election was a landslide victory for the DPJ, which made it difficult for them even to maintain the same level of seats. In any case, the subsequent defeat of the DPJ was brought about by the electoral system. They lost votes in the districts of regional areas in particular, resulting in the loss of many seats—despite winning a higher proportion of votes in urban areas, this did not lead to an increase in votes.

The biggest problem for the DPJ was that it was clear that much of their original manifesto would encounter problems with financial resources and would not be realized. They persisted in pulling out more "wish-list programs," which only lengthened the manifesto list. Nor did they have a solid party platform. The regime change became an objective in and of itself, and they were not clear about what must be done in this new direction for government; nor did they hold a unified opinion as a party (Nihon Saiken Inishiachibu, 2013: 248–251, 274–275). As for the people themselves, there may have been many who were simply annoyed with the LDP's long hold on power, voting with the awareness of bringing about a regime change at any cost. As will be explored further in Chapter 7, the showpiece policies put forward by the DPJ actually included some that cannot be said to have gained popular support. In particular, although the education policy was an important showpiece policy, the general public did not seem to accurately understand it.

The following chapters will examine how politics incorporates such voices of the people, or even preceding such stage, what they themselves thought about specific policy measures.

NOTES

[1] For example, this is known from questions raised by Shozaburo Araki (Chairman of the Teachers' Union Central Executive Committee), speaker at the House of Councilors' Committee on the Budget, on June 18, 1948, and by Toshikatsu Tanaka (Japanese Socialist Party) at the plenary session of the House of Councilors, on April 5, 1949. Note that, a little later, the morning edition of the *Asahi Shimbun* (Tokyo) on September 6, 1953, reported that there were still many cases of the provision of junior high school facilities being dependent on the borrowed premises of elementary schools, and considered whether this might be one of the biggest focal points in the budget of the fiscal year of 1954 for culture and education. The Ministry of Finance's view on building junior high schools was that this should proceed autonomously under the municipalities; by contrast, the Ministry of Education argued that this should be a national burden.

[2] Page 3 of the morning edition of *Asahi Shimbun* (Tokyo) May 27, 1951.

[3] Public finance demand estimates were carried out for each major administered program; moreover, for local governments for which the total amount of the finance demand amount exceeded public finance revenues, the insufficient amount was distributed to the local government from the national government's General Account. However, as there were no limitations on the purpose, in local areas with public finance struggles, there was absolutely no guarantee that this money would be allocated to educational expenditure (Tokuhisa, 2008: 228).

[4] Page 1 of the morning edition of *Asahi Shimbun* (Tokyo), December 23, 1951.

[5] Page 1 of the evening edition of *Asahi Shimbun* (Tokyo), April 3, 1952.

[6] Page 1 of the evening edition of *Asahi Shimbun* (Tokyo), February 4, 1954.

[7] The common name is "compulsory education standard law," while the formal name is the "law regarding standards for grade compilation and teacher number decisions for public compulsory education schools" (1958).

⁸ In other words, rather than putting educational necessity first, the following principle of appropriateness was adopted: the number of teachers decided should be the number deemed appropriate from both the educational perspective and the public finance perspective. The number of elementary school students peaked in 1958 and that of junior high school students in 1962. Using the rule of thumb of what level of compensation is possible so that the natural reduction of the number of teachers arises through the natural reduction of children, proposals of a stepped reduction in the standard number of people were made by the Ministry of Education to the Ministry of Finance and the local government agencies. This was agreed and the standard law was adopted. Such was the background to the law (Yotoriyama, 2012: 63).

⁹ Page 2 of the morning edition of *Asahi Shimbun* (Tokyo), January 24, 1948. Based on this report, the fees for government universities would be raised from 600 yen to 1,200 yen, government higher schools and colleges from 400 yen to 900 yen, and government old-system middle schools from 200 yen to 600 yen. Concerning private schools, humanities universities would be raised from 2,000 yen to 2,800 yen; science universities from 2,500 yen to 3,300 yen; senior high schools, technical colleges, and humanities' university preparatory courses from 1,600 yen to 2,800 yen; science university preparatory courses from 2,000 yen to 3,300 yen; and old-system middle schools from 1,200 yen to 2,000 yen. The Ministry of Finance had asserted that the tuition fees would increase threefold.

¹⁰ Page 1 editorial of the morning edition of *Asahi Shimbun* (Tokyo), June 4, 1948. In the end, the national universities, higher schools and colleges, and old-system middle schools settled at 1,800 yen, 1,200 yen, and 600 yen, respectively. In addition, the editorial expressed concerns over the students, comparatively privileged with respect to their academic advancement, demonstrating opposition through inappropriate means such as strikes. It argued that due to inflation, it was unreasonable to exempt only school costs, and that tuition fees equivalent to a monthly fee of 150 yen for university could not be considered unreasonable or expensive.

¹¹ Page 2 of the morning edition of the *Asahi Shimbun* (Tokyo), June 28, 1948.

¹² Page 2 of the morning edition of the *Asahi Shimbun* (Tokyo), February 28, 1949. It was reported also that entrance fees would double to become 600 yen for universities, 400 yen for higher and technical colleges and preparatory courses, and 200 yen for new senior high schools.

¹³ When we refer to scholarships in the Japanese context, it does not mean benefits. Traditionally, the Japanese scholarship system has consisted of mostly loan systems.

¹⁴ For example, Hidetoshi Tomabechi of the Democratic Liberal Party (which later became the Liberal Party, and in a conservative merger in 1955 with the Japan Democratic Party, the Liberal Democratic Party) asserted this in the House of Representatives Budget Committee Second Subcommittee on June 29, 1948.

¹⁵ Reply by Toshihiro Kennoki Secretary of the Ministry of Education in response to the question of Hidetoshi Tomabechi in Note 12.

¹⁶ Page 3 of the evening edition of *Asahi Shimbun* (Tokyo), January 12, 1955.

¹⁷ Page 2 of the evening edition of *Asahi Shimbun* (Tokyo), January 16, 1955.

¹⁸ Page 5 of the morning edition of *Asahi Shimbun* (Tokyo), January 21, 1955. Oouchi drew a comparison with the period before the war and compared the price of goods.

He asserted that, on the contrary, private university tuition fees were being kept comparatively low, and this was exacerbating the poorness of treatment concerning teacher compensation. On the other hand, however, he pointed out that the discontent at that time concerning tuition fees was a matter of disparity between national universities and private universities, at which they were comparatively high. This highlights the problem that the national budget was remarkably biased in favor of national universities. Moreover, considering that the beneficiaries of the Japan Scholarship Foundation scholarships were also favored in selection from among the national universities, the situation was pointed out as being extremely unfair.

[19] Page 10 of the morning edition of *Asahi Shimbun* (Tokyo), February 22, 1960.

[20] Page 1 of the morning edition of the *Asahi Shimbun* (Tokyo), December 14, 1962.

[21] Page 4 of the morning edition of the *Asahi Shimbun* (Tokyo), January 29, 1963. Incidentally, the textbooks for compulsory education are currently distributed for free, but this was not implemented directly after the war. Initially, in the fiscal year 1951, textbooks had been freely distributed for elementary grade-1 National Language and Arithmetic; however, due to public finance hardship, this was temporarily abandoned in the fiscal year 1953. Later, in the fiscal year 1963, the same free distribution resumed and gradually expanded to address the needs of all school grades. The current situation of free distribution of text books for all years of compulsory education was achieved from the fiscal year 1969 onward.

[22] The Ministry of Education sent a report in the name of the Chief of the Elementary and Secondary Education Bureau to each prefectural education committee on February 4, 1964, requesting all efforts to constrain the rise in the tuition fees of public secondary schools. At this time, there was a strong rising trend in the cost of goods, and as part of the economic policy to place constraints on rises in the price of goods, the government formulated a budget premised on not implementing hikes on public fees. As it was not possible to get residents to share the burden of a portion of facility construction expenditure due to the partial amendment of the Local Public Finance Act, there was an expectation to increase the share of expenses of the prefectural governments; hence, the motion to cover the increased share of the burden with tuition fees.

[23] Mothers passionate about the education of their children are nowadays referred to in jest as "*kyoiku mama* (education mama)." This phrase actually derives from the term "*kyoiku kajo mama*" (education-excessive mama), which was coined by Keiichi Shigematsu (Kobari, 2011).

[24] Page 11 of the morning edition of *Asahi Shimbun* (Tokyo), September 22, 1964.

[25] This dispute was settled through negotiations with management (the board of trustees) on February 5.

[26] Page 14 of the morning edition of *Asahi Shimbun* (Tokyo), January 29, 1965.

[27] Page 15 of the morning edition of *Asahi Shimbun* (Tokyo), November 29, 1966. The Association of Private Universities of Japan stated that a minimum of a 15% increase in tuition fees across-the-board was needed.

[28] Page 1 of the evening edition of *Asahi Shimbun* (Tokyo), February 20, 1967. The purpose of this rise in tuition fees was reportedly to rectify the disparity with private universities, rather than being a financial resources' measure.

[29] Page 15 of the morning edition of *Asahi Shimbun* (Tokyo), February 17, 1968.

30 "Tenseijingo" column on Page 1 and the editorial on Page 2 of the morning edition of *Asahi Shimbun* (Tokyo), February 18, 1967.

31 Page 15 of the morning edition of *Asahi Shimbun* (Tokyo), November 11, 1968.

32 Page 8 of the evening edition of *Asahi Shimbun* (Tokyo), February 11, 1969.

33 Page 14 of the morning edition of *Asahi Shimbun* (Tokyo), February 23, 1970.

34 However, in the metropolitan areas of Tokyo, Chukyo, and Kansai, the population increased, and due to this agglomeration, a situation of pressure on senior high school positions continued even into the 1970s. Many public senior high schools were established by the prefectural governments. While it was to be the local governments to establish the schools, based on the principle that the establisher takes the burden, in the budget of the fiscal year 1975, the Ministry of Education requested National Treasury assistance for the establishment of new high schools (page 3 of the morning edition of *Asahi Shimbun* (Tokyo) September 9, 1974).

35 The first reform was the Meiji promulgation of the school system, and the second reform was the post-war enforcement of the new-school system.

36 This refers to the Central Council for Education Report of June 1971.

37 Although it is called "tuition fees," the tuition fees of private schools are the compensation for educational services. In the case of national and other public universities, it had been understood that the user fee or service fee for use of facilities (i.e., service buildings) was something prescribed by the Minister of Education. This is the opinion expressed at that time by the Japan Association of National Universities. There is a position asserting that because the national universities are not private enterprises, the fee cannot be considered to be the compensation for services comprising the content of education. Hence, an argument was made that it was wrong to compare the tuition fees of national universities with those of private universities.

38 The above three questions and replies were from the 65th session of the House of Representatives' Standing Committee on Education No. 2 (February 17, 1971).

39 Page 2 of the morning edition of *Asahi Shimbun* (Tokyo), December 4, 1971.

40 Page 3 of the morning edition of *Asahi Shimbun* (Tokyo), December 8, 1971.

41 Page 7 of the evening edition of *Asahi Shimbun* (Tokyo), December 9, 1971.

42 Page 6 of the morning edition of *Asahi Shimbun* (Tokyo), December 17, 1971.

43 Page 2 of the morning edition of *Asahi Shimbun* (Tokyo), December 29, 1971.

44 Page 1 of the morning edition of *Asahi Shimbun* (Tokyo), January 10, 1972. At the same time, the Ministry of Home Affairs announced a policy to increase the tuition fees of public senior high schools by 1.5 to 2 times (up until then it had been an average of 800 yen per month). Incidentally, later, the formulation of the budget bill was delayed by unrest in the Diet. Consequently, the fee rise did not come into effect in that spring.

45 Page 3 of the morning edition of *Asahi Shimbun* (Tokyo), January 18, 1972.

46 Page 1 of the morning edition of *Asahi Shimbun* (Tokyo), January 25, 1972. The 106 universities corresponded to about 40% of all private universities at that time. Average tuition fees became 104 thousand yen (up by 13%), and the average initial year payment, including entrance fees, etc., became 255 thousand yen (up by 9%).

47 Page 3 of the morning edition of *Asahi Shimbun* (Tokyo), December 1, 1972. The disparity between national and private universities was described as follows in the article: "while private university students pay 10 times as much as national university students,

in terms of quantity, their education environment for study is but a quarter the level of that of national university students."

48 Page 3 of the morning edition of *Asahi Shimbun* (Tokyo), December 26, 1972.

49 Page 21 of the morning edition of *Asahi Shimbun* (Tokyo), April 7, 1973.

50 Page 2 of the morning edition of *Asahi Shimbun* (Tokyo), June 1, 1973. Up until then, under a 5-year plan from 1970, there was a grant system that provided up to 50% of ordinary costs that were included in full-time teacher salaries, but it was practically becoming useless due to the sharp rise in the cost of living.

51 Page 6 of the evening edition of *Asahi Shimbun* (Tokyo), February 12, 1974.

52 Page 1 of the evening edition of *Asahi Shimbun* (Tokyo), April 26, 1974.

53 Page 6 of the evening edition of *Asahi Shimbun* (Tokyo), January 27, 1975.

54 Page 6 of the evening edition of *Asahi Shimbun* (Tokyo), January 28, 1975.

55 However, due to the policy of "beneficiary pays," the tuition fees and entrance fees of private universities were raised, and because the Japanese economy had become wealthy, there was actually an increase in the stratum of people in society who could, even if unreasonably, shoulder the burden of school costs. As a result, the subsidies to private schools did not lead to a reduction in the share of the burden of students advancing to private universities (Suetomi, 2010: 77).

56 Page 2 of the morning edition of *Asahi Shimbun* (Tokyo), March 16, 1976. Tuition fees at national universities rose from 36,000 yen to 96,000 yen; and fees were increased at junior colleges, technical colleges, and high schools by 1.67 to 2.67 times.

57 Page 3 of the morning edition of *Asahi Shimbun* (Tokyo), June 6, 1976. See Note 18 of this chapter for more on this issue.

58 Page 2 of the morning edition of *Asahi Shimbun* (Tokyo), January 29, 1977.

59 Page 1 of the morning edition of *Asahi Shimbun* (Tokyo), August 4, 1977; and Page 1 of the morning edition of *Asahi Shimbun* (Tokyo), August 14, 1977.

60 According to page 22 of the morning edition of *Asahi Shimbun* (Tokyo), November 16, 1977, Shirayuri Gakuen Junior High School had the highest cost at 1.03 million yen, followed by Aoyama Gakuin Junior High School at 914 thousand yen. On page 22 of the morning edition of *Asahi Shimbun* (Tokyo), November 23, 1977, the same issue was raised for senior high schools, and it presented Toho Gakuen Music High School as having the highest cost at 1,473,200 yen, followed by Shirayuri Gakuen Senior High School at 1,049,800 yen, while Kaisei and Musashi were examples of high cost for academic high schools. After one year, the average would exceed 600,000 yen.

61 Page 1 of the morning edition of *Asahi Shimbun* (Tokyo), December 9, 1977.

62 Page 22 of the morning edition of *Asahi Shimbun* (Tokyo), March 14, 1978.

63 Page 22 of the morning edition of *Asahi Shimbun* (Tokyo), March 15, 1978. The article about the remote-island family that, unable to send money for schooling, moved to the city, was called "Education emigration."

64 Page 22 of the morning edition of *Asahi Shimbun* (Tokyo), March 19, 1978.

65 Page 15 of the morning edition of *Asahi Shimbun* (Tokyo), June 14, 1979. This class gap progressed through senior high school, maintaining the same degree, and then drastically widened at university.

66 Page 22 of the morning edition of *Asahi Shimbun* (Tokyo), April 23, 1982.

67 Page 23 of the morning edition of *Asahi Shimbun* (Tokyo), May 27, 1982.

[68] Page 1 of the morning edition of *Asahi Shimbun* (Tokyo), December 27, 1981.
[69] Page 2 of the morning edition of *Asahi Shimbun* (Tokyo), September 19, 1982.
[70] Page 1 of the morning edition of *Asahi Shimbun* (Tokyo), October 11, 1983. However, in the end, the annual amount settled at 252 thousand yen.
[71] Page 23 of the morning edition of *Asahi Shimbun* (Tokyo), December 24, 1983.
[72] Page 10 of the evening edition of *Asahi Shimbun* (Tokyo), January 4, 1985.
[73] Page 21 of the morning edition of *Asahi Shimbun* (Tokyo), February 7, 1985.
[74] Page 3 of the morning edition of *Asahi Shimbun* (Tokyo), November 6, 1985.
[75] Page 23 of the morning edition of *Asahi Shimbun* (Tokyo), December 13, 1985.
[76] Page 3 of the morning edition of *Asahi Shimbun* (Tokyo), July 15, 1986.
[77] Page 1 of the morning edition of *Asahi Shimbun* (Tokyo), December 16, 1986.
[78] Page 4 of the morning edition of *Asahi Shimbun* (Tokyo), December 24, 1986.
[79] Page 3 of the morning edition of *Asahi Shimbun* (Tokyo), June 19, 1987. Among the private universities, Tokyo University of Science first adopted the tuition fee partial exemption system targeting privately financed international students. At the time, the Japanese government had set forth a plan of "100,000 International Students for the Start of the 21st Century," but the escalating strength of the yen caused tuition fees to soar. Moreover, scholarship funds and accommodation provision was not keeping up with the required living expenses, and it was pointed out that this was particularly a large problem for privately financed international students (page 4 of the morning edition of *Asahi Shimbun* (Tokyo), March 29, 1987).
[80] Page 27 of the morning edition of *Asahi Shimbun* (Tokyo), December 25, 1989.
[81] Page 1 of the morning edition of *Asahi Shimbun* (Tokyo), December 22, 1987.
[82] Page 22 of the morning edition of *Asahi Shimbun* (Tokyo), December 24, 1995.
[83] Page 38 of the morning edition of *Asahi Shimbun* (Tokyo), October 23, 1998.
[84] The morning edition/Shizuoka page of *Asahi Shimbun*, October 26, 1998. Later, similar articles appeared in the Chiba and Saitama pages in the same year.
[85] The morning edition/Tochigi page of *Asahi Shimbun*, August 16, 1993.
[86] Page 3 of the morning edition of *Asahi Shimbun* (Tokyo), April 1, 1995.
[87] Page 26 of the morning edition of *Asahi Shimbun* (Tokyo), February 13, 1994.
[88] Page 15 of the evening edition of *Asahi Shimbun* (Tokyo), December 5, 1998.
[89] Page 39 of the morning edition of *Asahi Shimbun* (Tokyo), June 16, 1999.
[90] Page 33 of the morning edition of *Asahi Shimbun* (Tokyo), June 4, 2002.
[91] Page 8 of the morning edition of *Asahi Shimbun* (Tokyo), February 1, 2003.
[92] Statement by Masayoshi Nataniya (DPJ, Shin Ryokufukai Faction) at House of Councilors Standing Committee on Education and Science (October 27, 2012).
[93] Statement by Hirokazu Matsuno (LDP, Mushozoku no Kai) at House of Representatives Standing Committee on Education and Science (March 30, 2012). In response, the Minister of Education, Culture, Sports, Science and Technology, Yoshiaki Takagi replied, "With the declining birthrate and aging population advancing, in order to have a sustainable social security system, I think it is important that generations active in the workforce are healthy. Therefore, it doesn't stop at healthcare, pensions, and nursing care; rather, it also includes raising children and training people—and education is naturally one of the important themes with regard to this."

CHAPTER 7
Battleground Issues on Education Costs

1. Shifting of Education Cost Burden to Self-Responsibility

(1) Formation of Mistrust toward the Government

In a democratic society, policy cannot be executed without broad support from the people. However, as our lifestyles grow more affluent, and when a certain level of living is guaranteed, the things that people wish for from government gradually diversify. Moreover, since politicians try to secure support from the ordinary people, they tend to advocate fiscally unfeasible policies, if not going as far as delivering the big treats. In other words, populist policies become the battleground issues. In actuality, offering only populist policies will not suffice. According to Toshimitsu Shinkawa, politicians must adopt the following kinds of strategies in order to avoid becoming the target of criticism from the public (Shinkawa, 2004):

1) Limitation of agenda. Remove battleground issues that become the cause of criticism from the political agenda.
2) Reformulation of battleground issues. With respect to policies that would cause loss, provide some kind of positive significance and develop compensatory policy in place of loss-causing policy.
3) Lower visibility. Two points: first, do not clearly show who is deciding the policy; second, lower the policy effect by introducing it in stages rather than all at once in order to disperse the minus effect.
4) Find a scapegoat. Inflame the antipathy between groups that hold different interests and change where criticism is directed.
5) Form nonpartisan agreements. Form agreements with parties outside one's own political party and make it harder for criticism to be pointed only at one's own party.

Currently, Japan is in bad economic shape, and people's incomes are not growing. Amid this situation, income redistribution policies, in particular, easily prompt an extremely large backlash from those who do not receive any benefit but must share in the expense of the tax burden (especially the middle class), as this is perceived as a one-way outpouring of money from the government (Miyamoto, 2008: 45–46). Recently, even though the rate of people on livelihood protection is low, the media repeatedly cover the issue of welfare fraud, and this strengthens criticism toward the issue. For example, in a representative's question addressed by Hirohiko Nakamura (LDP, Sunrise Party of Japan, Mushozoku no Kai) in the plenary session of the House of Councilors, he mentioned the following: that the issue of livelihood protection was an urgent one; that the number of welfare recipients was now in excess of 2 million people, the highest number on record; that the initial budget for the fiscal year 2012 had swollen to 3.7 trillion yen; that improper receipt of medical treatment aid was increasing, with particularly deplorable cases in Osaka City; that the city's public finances were being crippled by livelihood protection; and that the poverty business was rampant.[1] Although a policy of increasing the consumption tax was decided by the DPJ Noda administration, the public's aversion to increasing taxes is still strong. Under these circumstances, politicians find it difficult to push ahead with cost incurring policies that would easily receive the people's support. Although the "fiscal laxity" of wasteful public works of the LDP's years of government had been criticized, the "fiscal laxity" in relation to education, welfare, and social security that was given comparative emphasis by the DPJ Government was also criticized (due to its weak packaging and explanation in terms of financial resources and regulations). Moreover, this criticism, far from incurring a public backlash, seems to have to some degree rung a sympathetic chord among the people.

As mentioned in Chapter 3, there are two models of social security, the targetism model, which extremely narrows down the recipient targets, and opposite to this, the universalism model, which attempts to provide services to all members of society. Japan's livelihood protection system is a typical example of the former. This is a service whereby benefits are given only to the people who pass a review called means testing, which verifies whether they are entitled to benefits. Needless to say, in the targetism model, money that has been provided by the middle and higher income classes' tax-burden is transferred to the lower income classes. As the middle and higher income classes do not derive benefit from this, they develop a critical view toward the lower income classes. Doubts are constantly raised as to whether people are really eligible for benefits and whether the means testing is being conducted fairly. On the other hand, free elementary education is a benefit that anyone can enjoy. Specifically, people pay this burden a little at a time, and then children at the eligible aged can all receive the benefit. Fundamentally, the time arrives when all adults have received this benefit in the past. By placing such universalism at the center of policy, the suspicions directed at different people become weaker and it becomes possible to promote solidarity in society (Ide, 2012: 255–260). Of course, with universalism, its fundamental principle is to not select which persons receive merits, which also leads to an increased share of the burden for everyone. The merit of universalism, however, is that even though members of society must share in the burden, they do it acceptingly as they can receive this service without review, if necessary.

It is obvious if one thinks about it, but the perceived tax pain is not decided simply by the absolute heaviness (or size) of the share of the tax burden. More than the actual paying of taxes, the thing that the tax payer is more concerned with is the receiving of some kind of benefit from paying these taxes. Hence, an important issue is whether the tax payer feels they are receiving these benefits. In fact, in northern Europe, a region known for its large tax burden, the perceived tax pain is not that high. But in Japan, the perceived tax pain exceeds the average of developed countries (Ide, 2013: 7–9). When one gives logical consideration to this matter, one can easily imagine how an extremely difficult situation arises.

The strength of this perceived tax pain is because of the lack of perceived benefit. Thus, the resistance to raising taxes strengthens, and there is even an increase in those who think that this kind of government is just taking taxes for nothing. In this way, people lose trust in the government (see Chapter 4). As the government does not have sufficient financial resources, it becomes difficult to enhance services for the residents (and meet their demands). Accordingly, the residents take an increasingly critical view toward the government, and this develops a pervasive mood that raising taxes is outrageous. If the public finance deficit is expanded, it becomes unavoidable to put the scanty tax revenues into fiscal rehabilitation. When this happens, the taxes that are paid are mostly not returned to the residents' actual livelihoods. In particular, the tax-paying middle classes call out more loudly to "reduce the excesses." They direct their criticism to the recipients of services paid to the low income class, and this leads to the raising of misgivings about the fraudulent receipt of benefits and to resentment that, although they are not paying a share of the tax burden, they are unilaterally receiving benefits. This in turn strengthens calls to make review stricter, which means that, in order for the government to appease these voices, even more expenditure must be injected into paying for monitoring. These services for the residents gradually become squeezed, and this gives rise to an "intolerant" society that monitors each other using scanty resources (Ide, 2013).

(2) Discontent toward Welfare Recipients

As mentioned by Anthony Giddens, welfare-state policies have brought about a weakening of the oppositional axis dividing the haves and the have-nots. The problem is, however, that oppositional viewpoints have emerged with respect to procuring the funds required to execute these welfare policies. Increasingly, voters no longer have allegiance to a particular political party, and as this trend strengthens, political parties enthusiastically try to attract these swinging voters. The progressive tax system, which had previously attracted broad support, also gradually begins meeting resistance. Moreover, as the people of the New Right say, the bureaucratic organizations of the welfare state become inflexible and inefficient while wastefulness can be seen everywhere. As a result, the government gives the impression that they are out of touch with people's needs. On the other hand, despite concentrating their interest on economic variables (issues of poverty and affluence), the socialists have a tendency not to consider other battleground issues, including emotions, morality, and cultural issues. In contrast to this, the conservatives endeavor to strike a common chord with people by compensating for emotions, morals, and cultural issues by protecting traditions (Giddens, 1994, trans. 2002: 100–104).

To begin with, the welfare state was not something won by the working class through revolution. Nor was it introduced by the bourgeoisie to placate the working class. It was born out of necessity to deal with mass unemployment at a time when there were many right-wing governments throughout Europe. Moreover, it becomes necessary to bring together the economy and the society in times of war, and this also increases the function and role of the state.

When there is an established welfare system, people looking to work will be actively incorporated into the labor market. In other words, the people's industriousness is manifested in the form of labor. Moreover, attempts to actively give these people the role of worker inside society are included inside the plan referred to as the welfare state. Furthermore, the welfare state was always a nation state embodying the wishes of the authorities to promote national solidarity. The process of constructing a welfare system was inseparable from that of constructing a state. Hence, when discussing the welfare state, it is impossible to avoid the concept of the nation state. Moreover, the welfare program is one kind of social insurance, which makes it one kind of risk management. The nation state can be considered to be the structural origins of the welfare state. In particular, through the war experience, the people of a nation state share the risk of uncertainty, and this facilitates solidarity and group efforts (or industriousness). Hence, the past development of the welfare state has a history in which steady growth in emphasis of this industriousness cannot be ignored (Giddens, 1994, trans. 2002: 172–177).

In Japan, among the social policy and the social welfare, there are elements that are historically inseparable from war-time structures (for example, Tomie, 2007). Putting aside these elements, let us narrow down the focus of debate to the construction of the postwar welfare state system.

It is sometimes pointed out that Japan does not have the type of social democracy that is referred to when looking at northern Europe, such as the type embodied by the Labour Party of the U.K. (Miyamoto, 2008: 90–94). Actually, the debate surrounding welfare policy in Japan has not been characterized by ideologically opposed positions (for example, the existence of the option of whether or not the state has responsibility for welfare). Instead, real ideological opposition has been limited to discussions about defense, diplomacy, and historical recognition, and a stronger motivation for the LDP has been to use welfare policy (not entirely successfully) as a policy to appease the left and win the hearts of the masses. On the left, the Japan Socialist Party (JSP) and the Japanese Communist Party (JCP) of course took the ideological stance of placing importance on welfare. Accordingly, in Japan, there have practically been no political parties outspokenly opposing or calling for the reduction of welfare policies. In particular, from the 1960s, there were resident movements concerning pollution problems and a corresponding strengthening of citizen awareness. This steadily gave rise to reformist local governments, particularly in urban areas. The spectacle of a reformist political party gathering support from the masses by implementing so-called welfare policies was a threat to the LDP (Shinkawa, 2005: 73–84; Takegawa, 2007: 123–125). Against this backdrop and that of unprecedented high economic growth, the history of postwar Japan was defined by a dramatic improvement in people's living standards and the blurring of any ostensible differences in social stratification (classes).

However, even if they were considered to be insufficient, expansion of the welfare measures naturally led to an increase in government expenditure. The issuance of Japan's long-term government bonds in the postwar era really began to rise in 1965. According to Masaru Mabuchi, the later increase in fiscal deficits can be summarized as follows. In 1965, the year following the Olympics, tax revenues considerably dropped due to a slowing of economic growth. As a result, when performing the revised budget, the decision was made to issue deficit-covering government bonds to cover for this shortfall in tax revenue. When following fiscal equilibrium, because the size of expenditure is fundamentally decided by tax revenues, requests that are not relevant to this are not recorded. However, this means that issuing deficit-covering government bonds creates the vulnerability of not being able to limit fiscal expenditure. The MOF, fearful that there was no way of applying the brakes to fiscal expenditure, set limits on the use of government bonds (construction government bonds). It further made sure that the government bonds were absorbed on the market and that there was no re-issuance underwritten by the Bank of Japan. However, the target of the construction government bonds was ambiguously defined, and in the end, their function as a supplementation for expenditure was maintained. In other words, setting limits on the use of government bonds did not really serve the function of putting the brakes on expenditure.

Finally, when the economy shifted from high to stable economic growth, the government strengthened its efforts to cover the lagging development of social capital by more actively directing public finance expenditure into public works. As large-scale development cannot be completed in a short timeframe, once a project had been started, long-term and constant expenses were generated. Moreover, as the LDP held government for a long period, we saw the emergence of the "tribe Diet members," who maintained close relationships with specific interest groups; and they further spurred the government on a path of aggressive fiscal expenditure. The percentage of expenses falling under the category of "natural appropriation increase on a committed basis" rose, and due to the loss of fiscal elasticity, the public finance authorities no longer had effective mechanisms of control. This is referred to as fiscal rigidity. To break free from this rigidity, the MOF attempted such measures as adopting the unified budget principle.[2] However, these measures did not last. As the economic conditions once again entered an upturn, the MOF's sense of crisis also faded.

Furthermore, the MOF at the time adopted a technique referred to as budget revival. As part of the budget revival negotiations it was carrying out with various ministries, it gave out funds, bit by bit, by entering them into the budget under the names of various jurisdictional arms of the MOF. Consequently, the total budgetary amount was unchanged even after the budget revival negotiations. However, the MOF disclosed what funds were available for these budget revival negotiations in advance, thereby making the process of budget compilation more effective. Nevertheless, as there was room for negotiation for these disclosed fiscal resources, this also meant that there was room for LDP intervention in the process of budget compilation.

As soon as the Kakuei Tanaka Cabinet was instated, they pursued an active fiscal policy under their Plan for Remodeling the Japanese Archipelago, but they gradually lost popularity due to events such as the first oil shock and the remarkable rise in land prices. Meanwhile, the reformist parties such as the Japan Socialist Party and the Japanese Communist Party continued to build their popularity in the urban areas. And the route of aggressive fiscal spending was, for the most part, transferred from public works to social welfare without much change. Compounding this issue, Tanaka pushed through 2 trillion yen in tax reductions in the 1974 budget in an attempt to gain more popularity with the people. The fiscal debt became decisive, and this was the basis for fiscal curtailment and a course of fiscal rehabilitation without increasing taxes starting from the late 1970s (Mabuchi, 1994).

In a public opinion poll by Jiji Press in 1982, there was a growing interest in public finance among the people, and support for "fiscal rehabilitation without increasing taxes" had increased. When asked how to address the revenue shortfall, 37.1% supported spending cuts, while only 2.5% advocated a tax increase. Putting the supporters of increasing taxes together with those advocating both temporary expenditure cuts and the issuance of debt-covering government bonds, they made up 14.7%, while the percentage of respondents resolutely opposed to increased taxes was as high as 52.9%. Among the respondents, there were 51.1% that, while advocating reductions in expenditure for the defense budget and Official Development Assistance (ODA), which the government had removed from the ceiling, thought that the government should maintain social security and the education expenditure to which it had applied the ceiling (Kato, 1997: 154). In other words, the people did not want any new burdens. As social security was insufficient and education costs were soaring, however, there seemed to be an assertion that social security and education could be covered if the funds were redirected from the defense budget or the ODA.

As mentioned in Chapter 5, Japan's public finance and its policy emphasis on public works cannot be discussed without mentioning fiscal investment and loans. While keeping the tax burden low, the government promoted a fiscal policy of consumer spending and savings, making these savings the resource for public works' investment. These means were used not only to advance the maintenance of social capital but also to maintain a constant level of progress in local area development. The striking disparities that had once existed between regions were no longer as big an issue. Of course, the relative economic disparities still remained. Considering that even food was a problem directly after the war, however, in only a few decades, everyone owned the basic lineup of electrical appliances and led an ordinary life, and one could feel a real sense of economic affluence. On the other hand, people were derided as economic animals, and death by overwork was a common societal problem. Lifestyles that gave priority to work (or the company) became established as matter of fact among Japanese.

There were undeniably positive aspects that were brought about (such as improvement of the standard of living, economic development, and so forth). However, as mentioned in Chapter 1 the problems of differences emerging in Japanese society, which had propensities for homogenous and group behavior, and expectations of the same remunerative treatment were not related to "inequality of opportunity" but rather to "individual effort" and "personal drive." Therefore, the problem of inequality of traditional social hierarchy and classes was removed from society. Also removed was the consciousness that the existence of economic disparity was unfair. This even led people to propose that it was necessary to have new analytical frameworks and problem establishment concerning inequality in an "affluent" society (Hara and Seiyama, 1999). Social stratification theories now have wide circulation. But as seen with the bashing of livelihood protection and similar concerns, while society reaches out to the socially vulnerable with one hand, there is also a welling up in society of discourse advocating that it is up to each person to look after themselves; that such persons are lazy or selfish; or that what comes to them is what they have brought upon themselves. For the middle class who carry the tax burden, their lifestyles are not necessarily pleasant, and their discontent is directed at the vulnerable who are the welfare recipients.

(3) Expectations of Individual Burdens by Parents
As has been seen in Chapter 6, the private burden of education costs rapidly increased in Japan. While the grievances over the pain of such burden were often heard, rarely would this lead to calls for a social solution to be provided. Outside the arena of theories, the reality for the parents is that the burden of education costs is a natural matter of course, and the scale and awareness of "it is the parents' responsibility" has been deeply established (Suetomi, 2010: 106–107).

This has actually been backed up by research. According to Kazuhisa Furuta,[3] relatively speaking, it is common in Japan for people to think that parents would naturally be expected to bear the cost of education (with more than 60% of respondents thinking it natural to pay the full amount). Careful examination of this mindset vis-à-vis the burden of education costs shows that the wealthy class, who believe in impartially providing opportunities to enter university, have a strong tendency to think that it is natural to bear the full costs. However, for society as a whole, the mindset concerning this education cost burden does not correlate with specific academic histories, types of employment, or other such strata variables (Furuta, 2007).

The Japanese households are in the predicament of individually making do while giving priority to education costs. The situation may not be so bad while the children are small, but once entering higher education, the household burden suddenly increases. Understanding this situation, child-rearing households will naturally attempt to accumulate savings. However, the time when it is perhaps feasible to save is during the period of the child's compulsory education. Yet, as that is a time when the parents' incomes are inadequate, there is a limit to the amounts that can be saved. Moreover, in recent years, the Japanese employment system has broken down, and it is no longer possible to expect income to rise with age. Under these circumstances, it is obvious that the birth rate will decrease. Moreover, because of the declining number of children, we see a structure of pouring money even more resolutely into education costs (Yano, 1996).

With public services, there is a benefit versus cost relationship. Concerning the benefit, there is the question of whether the recipient of this benefit is only the individual or whether the society also benefits, and based on this, whether the cost burden should be considered a private one or if there are grounds for receiving funds from tax revenues. Moreover, Yano (2013) calculated the percentage share of social revenue and that of fiscal revenue to show that public finance expenditure in universities is an efficient public investment. Nevertheless, the popularization of university brought into question a deeply rooted issue in ordinary Japanese society, namely, doubts concerning the social benefit of university education. In particular, according to Yano's research, about 70% to 80% held the opinion that it should be the individual's or the family's burden. Moreover, the distribution of opinion showed no significant correlations with any particular social strata. In fact, postwar higher education in Japan has relied on private schools, and this system has been supported by family budgets that have prioritized education. It is probably due to these circumstances that this mindset toward education has come to be considered as matter of fact. Moreover, the government has positioned university education very low in its order of priorities. This issue is really not about the choice of whether it should be the household budget or the government that bears the entire burden; rather, it is ultimately about establishing a realistic mindset that is accepting of an appropriate balance between the two (Yano, 2013).

In Japan, where there is a low awareness of the social benefit provided by education, only the private investment side is emphasized. If one's view on education is to emphasize equal treatment of students at school, and almost oversensitively to make demands on the selection methods for entrance examinations, etc., such as that they must be based on equity, then ultimately one's view will also regard the responsibility for academic performance to lie with the individual. The unsuccessful person must be content with reflecting in hindsight that his or her own efforts were not enough, while the successful person can consider the result to be that of his or her efforts. What is lacking here, however, is the perspective that asks whether it was a fortunate learning environment (whether there were significant differences in the actual learning environment between people), and that acknowledges that there are various social support mechanisms at play here that are not in plain view. It is not unnatural to think that education is deeply established in society and raises the people's intellectual level, which in turn has some kind of overall positive effect on society. However, this is not something that can be easily measured, and the reality of the situation can be difficult to grasp. Consequently, the current situation arises in which only households burdened with education costs call for a reduction of the burden, while other people lose interest in the issue of education. This would then likely become reflected in the view (incidentally, one based on individualism) that under the currently difficult fiscal situation, "if there is such financial leeway in public expenditure to spend on education, then I want it diverted to my own post-retirement social security," (Hamanaka, 2013: 228–232).

The remaining two chapters, including this one, focus on opinions and perceptions of the government, the state, and policies implemented by the government. Under the current system of indirect democracy, the most common method of realizing the policies one would wish for is the act of voting. Moreover, the bodies that present these policy options are the political parties. Let us look back at how the political parties have been involved, or not been involved, in the issue of education costs, and how the people have reacted to these policies.

2. Campaign Pledges and Manifestos

(1) The Start of the Manifesto Election

During elections, the voters cast one vote for a political party or candidate that is likely to implement the policies that they favor; and by doing so, they entrust this wish to that candidate. If the candidate wins many votes, this means that the people with the same opinion have the majority. Moreover, the policies that are implemented will be policies that have received a certain amount of support from society. Hence, the campaign pledges presented to the voters before the election have considerable significance: they are the source of the relationship of trust between the voter and the candidate.

In the past, however, the campaign pledges in Japan were generally aimed at pleasing everybody. The slogans were many, but the actual substance was weak. Therefore, as pointed out by Ichiro Miyake, voters in Japan did not decide individually based on campaign pledges. Instead, it is said that voter behaviors could be explained by networks of special interest (depending on participation in groups related to specific industries, for example, or the existence of acquaintances related to such networks), or by conservative or reformist ideology. It is not practical for a voter to be informed of the issues concerning each individual policy. In particular, in elections where the battleground issues are difficult to see, it is sometimes necessary to pay a cost to obtain the information that forms the basis for deciding whom to vote for. Moreover, during the Cold War era, only the differences on ideological standpoints were clear. Hence, when it came to the details of individual policies, it was probably easier to anticipate how the policy would turn out based on the ideology behind it. Therefore, the ideology formed the substance of the material provided as information on the differences between the political parties (Miyake, 1989: 147–148).

However, after the collapse of the Cold War system, the differences in these ideologies became less clear, and the power of the conventional left, in particular, weakened significantly. Nonetheless, differences of class or social strata proved to be insufficient as explanatory power. According to Hiroshi Hirano, arguments targeting age and vocation (in a sense not directly linked to class or social stratification) were variables that have an impact on voter behavior even today, but arguments based on income had hardly any explanatory power (Hirano, 2007: 15–30, 85–103).

However, the electoral system of the single-seat constituency with proportional representation was introduced for the House of Representatives, and this generated a real feeling of regime change. If the ideological differences were unclear, voters would have to decide for whom to vote by different factors not dependent on left-right ideology. What the DPJ presented for voters to see here was their "Manifesto."

In the U.K., which was where the manifesto originated, a "manifesto" normally does not contain the "numerical targets, achievement deadlines, or specific financial resources" of a specific policy, which have become the norm in recent years.

In Japan, as a result of the introduction of the single-seat constituency system, the role as a delegate of the people became clearer in the sense that political parties reflected the opinions of the voters. Consequently, the method of winning the voters' selection by proposing concrete policies was given great importance and adopted. This is despite the fact that a manifesto in its place of origin, the U.K., refers to the ideological guidelines of a political party. In Japan, this is not what was considered to be a manifesto; rather, it was the concrete policy itself that came to be called the manifesto. Not only that, but as the political parties regarded the manifesto as a mandate from the voters, they became bound to the content of their manifesto; and when they were unable to deliver what was written in the manifesto, they were criticized for "breaching the manifesto." While the ideological differences by political party were unclear, the political parties had to be selected by the single-seat constituency system. Moreover, the increasing number of unaffiliated voters led to the promotion of a kind of election that presupposed the importance of this Japanese version of the manifesto (Nakakita, 2012).[4]

(2) Historical Transitions of Battleground Issues in Elections

To a certain degree, the battleground issues and the voters' concerns for the election were of course reflected in not only the Japanese version of the manifesto that came to function in this way but also in the conventional campaign pledges that the political parties had always made. However, among all of this, what kind of attention was given to education? With the high cost of education having been such a talking point up until then, surely it must have become an issue of debate in the election.

According to the data of public opinion polls conducted by The Association for Promoting Fair Elections after the national elections from 1972 to 2000, the various concerns raised as battleground issues of the elections from the viewpoints of voters were those closely connected with daily life and the economy, such as "cost of living and the economy," "welfare and nursing care," "the tax system," and "economic recession." There was an impression that the issues of "cleaning up politics, morals, and reform" were common issues covered by the mass media; but, in fact, focus was only given to these issues when political turmoil or corruption scandals surfaced. Although the issues of "education and culture" and "agriculture" were stably selected, on average, the percentage given to these was a little over 10 %, rising to 20% in 2000, against a backdrop of discourses of lax education and increasing brutality of juvenile crimes. However, the issue of defense and that of the constitution, which are strongly reflected in the ideology of the political parties, did not rate that highly as battleground issues in the eyes of the voters (Taniguchi, 2005: 19–23).

This begs the question: just what were the battleground issues in the elections? Table 7-1 shows the characterizing traits of the elections of the House of Representatives in the post-war era, and the issues extracted by the author from a list of campaign pledges and manifestos of each political party featured in the *Asahi Shimbun*. In most cases, the method adopted for compiling the campaign pledges was as follows. The main items such as "diplomacy," "defense," and "cost of living," present at the time of the election, were selected; and the policies of each political party were organized according to these items. The battleground issues were considered basically to be those items that were the topics that had become battleground issues during the election; and these were the issues selected. Moreover, although the LDP, which was the ruling party, hardly ever referred to education in the election, education was touched on by opposition parties such as the JSP and the JCP. With respect to this point, the author made the slightly arbitrary judgment that the policies of the ruling party had a tendency to be realized, and that these reasonably had an impact on later policy. Therefore, when an issue was not largely discussed by the ruling party, it was not deemed to have been an active battleground issue in the election.

Looking at these issues, for some time after the war, there was a strong tendency for the battleground issues to clearly represent those of ideological differences between the political parties related to diplomacy and defense, such as the Treaty of Mutual Cooperation and Security between the United States and Japan, the Self-Defense Forces, and defense expenditure. However, these issues gradually became lower in order of priority. In particular, after the conclusion of the Cold War, the issues that were given higher priority were the consumption tax, public finance reform, the economy, and social security issues. The issues in which the voters shared a concern were those intricately connected to daily life, such as the cost of living, the economy, and the tax system. Accordingly, it was these issues that were actively treated as the battleground issues in most elections.

There have been many elections where education was never raised as a battleground issue. Even when battleground issues on education were raised, these were not necessarily given high priority. Moreover, when there were battleground issues on education, they were often not centered on issues of public finance, but rather on issues of ideology. The election for the House of Representatives in 2003 was a rare occasion at which the revision on the Basic Act on Education was discussed and the field of education was given priority as a battleground issue of the election. At this time, the Koizumi administration had followed a course of "nothing-is-sacred structural reform." The issue of the National Treasury's share of the expense of compulsory education had become a topic of debate, but this debate did not have the image of being a broad discussion among the people (aside from people

Table 7-1 Post-War House of Representatives Elections and Contested Issues

Election Name	Date Held	Election Highlights	Main Contested Issues (based on *Asahi Shimbun*)	Contested Issues on Education
22nd Diet	Apr. 10, 1946	Final election under Empire of Japan Constitution. First post-war election as universal suffrage election. Shidehara Cabinet.	Inflation, food, Emperor System, industrial reconstruction, unemployment measures, land problems	None
23rd Diet	Apr. 25, 1947	Yoshida Cabinet. Multiple-seat constituency.	Inflation, food, state control of economy and industry	None
24th Diet	Jan. 23, 1949	First general election under Constitution of Japan. Yoshida Cabinet "Collusion Dissolution."	Inflation, company reorganization, administrative reorganization, industrial revival	None
25th Diet	Oct. 1, 1952	Yoshida Cabinet "Surprise Dissolution." Election of committee members directly after introduction of public election system for education committee.	Rice prices, rearmament, tax reduction, tax deduction, unemployment measures, small and medium enterprise measures.	Support of 6-3 System, National Treasury's share of expenses of compulsory education system, scholarship system
26th Diet	Apr. 19, 1953	Yoshida Cabinet "Bakayaro Dissolution."	State control of industry, rearmament (National Security Force), strike regulation, rice price, tax reduction, emergency measures for demand economy, small and medium enterprise measures.	None
27th Diet	Feb. 27, 1955	Hatayama Cabinet "Voice of Heaven Dissolution."	Tax reduction, housing, rice (staple food), Self-Defense Forces, unemployment measures, trade with China/USSR	None
28th Diet	May 22, 1958	Kishi Cabinet "Discussion Dissolution." First general election after Conservative Alliance. Post-war record for highest voter turnout.	Security Treaty System, Self-Defense Forces, nuclear issue, diplomacy with the USSR and China, new economic 5-year plan, small and medium size enterprise measures, national pension, constitutional amendment	Moral education (time in school curriculum), teacher work performance evaluation, elimination of overcrowded classes.
29th Diet	Nov. 20, 1960	Ikeda Cabinet "Security Treaty Dissolution." Election following split of JSP and Democratic Sociality Party (DSP). Election following enactment of Security Treaty. Assassination of Inejiro Asanuma, Chairman of JSP just before the election.	Security Treaty system (established by the time of the election), nuclear armament and Self-Defense Forces, diplomacy with China/USSR, "Income Doubling Plan (economic growth)," trade liberalization, prevention of utilities' rates rise, tax reduction or tax increase to wealthy, contribution-type national pension.	Basic Act on Education, moral education, teacher work performance evaluation
30th Diet	Nov. 21, 1963	Ikeda Cabinet "Mood Dissolution" or "Doubling Income Dissolution."	Rise in consumer prices, diplomatic disputes such as Japan and Korea, and nuclear submarine port call.	Free compulsory education, making senior high school compulsory, university administrative freedom from government.
31st Diet	Jan. 29, 1967	Sato Cabinet "Black Mist Dissolution." New Komeito (NK) obtained seats for the first time in a House of Representative election.	Cleaning up politics, diplomacy with China, Security Treaty, defense issue, issuance of government bonds	None

Battleground Issues on Education Costs

Election Name	Date Held	Election Highlights	Main Contested Issues (based on *Asahi Shimbun*)	Contested Issues on Education
32nd Diet	Dec. 27, 1969	Sato Cabinet. LDP and friendly independents obtained 300 seats. JSP lost badly. NK and JCP strongly improved. Trend toward multiple parties in cities.	Security Treaty and return of Okinawa, rising cost of living, tax reductions, rice production	Measures to calm university conflicts
33rd Diet	Dec. 10, 1972	Tanaka Cabinet.	Plan for Remodeling the Japanese Archipelago, constraining cost of living, social welfare issues (pension, free medical care for elderly, etc.)	None
34th Diet	Dec. 5, 1976	Miki Cabinet. Election called due to expiration of term of office for existing members of the House of Representatives. Lockheed Scandal.	Inquiry into Lockheed, clean up politics, electoral system, stabilize cost of living, Security Treaty, diplomacy with China	Elimination of knowledge-skewed education, everyone advancing to senior high school, assistance for private schools
35th Diet	Oct. 7, 1979	Ohira Cabinet "Tax Increase Dissolution."	"Tax increase" including administrative reform and introduction of general consumption tax, inflation and energy policies, fixing political corruption, welfare and public burden, diplomacy with USSR	Enhancement of local national universities, establishment of open university, entrance examination reform such as universal examination for university admission
36th Diet	Jun. 22, 1980	Ohira Cabinet "Accidental Dissolution," Prime Minister Ohira dies during the period of election campaign. LDP recovers seats.	Cost of living (inflation) measures, welfare and the public burden (realization of Japanese-style welfare society), energy policies, Security Treaty and defense, administrative reform, cleaning up politics	Limiting class sizes to 40, eliminating examination hell, providing more relaxed education
37th Diet	Dec. 18, 1983	Nakasone Cabinet "Tanaka Decision Dissolution." Former PM Tanaka found guilty in Lockheed Scandal, LDP majority was broken.	Treatment of former PM Tanaka, increase or reduce tax?, nuclear disarmament, defense budget interlocking with 1% GNP, MHW plan for 80% co-payment for the employee's health insurance, agricultural products liberalization	School system reform, enrichment of moral education, realization of 40 class limits (elimination of violence in schools)
38th Diet	Jul. 6, 1986	Nakasone Cabinet "Pretending to be Dead Dissolution." LDP gain 300 seats alone. JSP obtains less than 100 seats in big defeat.	Constitution, political ethics, administrative reform, tax reduction and introduction of large indirect tax, yen appreciation measures, diplomacy and defense, nuclear power, Japanese welfare society	Elimination of bullying, criticism of societal emphasis on education, emphasis on morals and individuality, entrance examination reform, reduction of education burden by assistance to public schools and scholarship system, promoting class sizes of 40 (35)
39th Diet	Jan. 24, 1990	Kaifu Cabinet "Consumption Tax Dissolution." LDP loses to JSP in the 1989 House of Councilors election. LDP lost seats. JSP gained seats, but other opposition parties lost seats. After Recruit Scandal.	Selection of administration between liberalism and coalition between JSP, NK, and DSP, consumption tax, political corruption, rice problem, military expansion, land measures	None

Election Name	Date Held	Election Highlights	Main Contested Issues (based on *Asahi Shimbun*)	Contested Issues on Education
40th Diet	Jul. 18, 1993	Miyazawa Cabinet "Lying Dissolution." Boom of new parties following LDP split. LDP became opposition for the first time. JSP also lost many seats.	Rice deregulation problem, income tax reduction, consumption tax	None
41st Diet	Oct. 20, 1996	Hashimoto Cabinet. First election by single-seat constituency. LDP and New Frontier Party (NFP) were largest two political parties. DPJ became third largest party. Downturn for Social Democratic Party (formerly SPJ).	5% consumption tax, administrative reform (ministerial reform), legal framework for war contingencies, becoming a permanent member of the U.N. Security Council, company group contributions, history recognition	None
42nd Diet	Jun. 25, 2000	Mori Cabinet "Divine Nation Dissolution."	Economic measures including public works investment, choice of social insurance method and tax method of pension	None
43rd Diet	Nov. 9, 2003	Koizumi Cabinet. After the Liberal Party and the DPJ formed a coalition, a sense of two-party politics between the LDP and the DPJ. Manifestos were released.	Revision of Basic Act on Education, free expressways	Revision of Basic Act on Education
44th Diet	Sep. 11, 2005	Koizumi Cabinet "Postal Business Dissolution." Overwhelming victory by LDP. DPJ failed to make pension a contested issue.	Privatization of Japan Post, economic and fiscal reform, reduction of public servants, pension, child allowance	None
45th Diet	Aug. 30, 2009	Aso Cabinet. Big loss by LDP. DPJ obtains 300 seats. Change of Government. The number of early votes was a record high.	Economic measures (employment measures), pension reform, income compensation for agricultural income, abolition of gasoline tax, free expressway, medical system for late-stage senior citizens	Child allowance, free senior high school, improved university scholarship system
46th Diet	Dec. 16, 2012	Noda Cabinet. Big loss by DPJ, power recovered by LDP and NK. Second Abe Government.	Economic growth strategy, TPP, energy policy such as the nuclear issue, reconstruction, consumption tax, social security, constitutional amendment	Education system reform, emphasis on academic fundamentals, school text books, university entrance examinations, action against bullying problem

in the field of education). Moreover, needless to say, the debate that was conducted over the revisions to the Basic Act on Education stressed ideologically based battleground issues.

In relation to issues directly concerning the public finance of education, education costs and tuition fees, and the establishment of the system for the National Treasury's share of expenses for compulsory education, as discussed in Chapter 6, became battleground issues in the 25th House of Representatives election, which was held soon after the war. At the time, fiscal resources were insufficient, and the strong advice of the MOF and the Local Government Agency was to put together a budget based on ordinary fiscal resources. Moreover, because the establishment of the 6-3 System had been widely supported among the public, the conservative forces also found it difficult to back a proposal that would make cuts to the education budget related to compulsory education. However, aside from the reformists, the ruling LDP, even when raising the issue of education as a battleground issue, practically made no proposals related to mitigating the household's burden of education costs. In the 1970s, the issue of providing subsidies to private schools was raised; however, as already explained, priority was given to the "beneficiary-pays principle" due to the government's fiscal difficulties, and the tuition fees at national universities underwent fee rises to "appropriate prices." These policies did not lead to any easing of the household's education cost burden.

Considering this, the 45th election of the House of Representatives deserves special mention because the specific policy to reduce the education cost burden of households became a battleground issue. The child rearing support policies of the DPJ centered on the child allowance marked a switch in policy from the stance that child rearing was a private responsibility of the parents to one emphasizing society's responsibility: namely, rearing the children who later financially support the social security of senior citizens should be carried out under societal and public responsibility. In particular, child allowance came as a set, together with the removal of income-based means testing and the abolishment of the spousal deduction system. The reason for this was to establish child allowance based on universal principles. A very significant element of this policy's intention is to signify that child rearing is a societal responsibility. It was pointed out that the spousal deduction system had been an impediment to the economic autonomy of women, and it was also necessary from the viewpoint of promoting the gender equality agenda. By introducing the inclusion of fertility treatment in health insurance, childbirth payment, child allowance, dispensing of fees for senior high schools, and enhancement of scholarships, balance was restored to the welfare policies that were skewed toward senior citizens. It was a package that provided social support for children's growth and independence. From this perspective, the policy signified an important policy shift and was therefore not simply a case of "fiscal laxity."

However, there were not a large number of members of parliament within the DPJ Government that understood the architecture of these policies, the important foundational principles of which were not shared among the members of parliament. Furthermore, because the budget was a strain on fiscal resources, when the issues of the policy were raised, attention was only given to the monetary ones.

Consequently, the opportunity to explain and consider the foundational principles of the policy was lost. The relevant ministers (Education, Culture, Sports, Science and Technology; Health, Labour and Welfare; Measures Against the Declining Birthrate; Gender Equality) were frequently changed about. Moreover, shortfalls and deficiencies in the overall system were pointed out, such as the illegal receipt of benefits from foreigners residing in Japan and parents receiving payments when they were not actually living with their children. More than anything else, the expectations and the demands of the people had not been high regarding child allowance from the beginning of the DPJ Government.[5] Therefore, it was necessary to properly explain the foundational principles of the policy. However, as there were many problems inside the party, opportunities to do so were lost. Consequently, these initiatives by the DPJ lost the support of the public (Nihon Saiken Inishiachibu, 2013: 162–180).

In the 2009 election for the House of Representatives, when the LDP lost and the DPJ Government was born, there seem to have been relatively high expectations for the new government. However, the reason for the change of government was not based on policies. Rather, it was because the vote gathering system that had favored the LDP had collapsed; it was also because the voters had abandoned the LDP. On the other hand, as a result of the 46th election for the House of Representatives in late 2012, the DPJ collapsed and a new coalition government between the LDP and New Komeito was born. The strong element behind this, however, was not active support for the LDP, but instead a loss of trust in the DPJ from voters because of its various failed policies and inability to deliver on the promises contained in its "manifesto." However, the overwhelming victory of the LDP can be said to have been brought about by the single-seat constituency system—an electoral system that produces many "dead votes." Let us examine this mechanism in the next section.

(3) Election Results and Popular Will in Post-war Japan

Figure 7-1 shows the transition of the percentage of votes received by the political parties that had fielded candidates in the elections for the House of Representatives since the Conservative Alliance of 1955 (with the establishment of the LDP). Figure 7-2 shows the actual proportion of seats obtained in the House of Representatives. As long as a proportional representation system was not adopted, an unevenness between the percentage of votes received and the actual number of seats obtained would continue. Until the 40th election for the House of Representatives in 1993, a multiple-seat constituency electoral system was in effect. Hence, strong candidates, regardless of the size of their political party, gained a reasonable chance of being elected. Even under this situation, we can see that the LDP had been gaining a greater number of seats than the actual percentage of votes received.

Figure 7-3 shows the percentage of votes received by proportional representation since the elections for the House of Representatives adopted a single-seat constituency proportional representation system. Figure 7-4 shows the percentage of the actual number of seats obtained in the elections for the House of Representatives under the single-seat constituency system. Under this system,

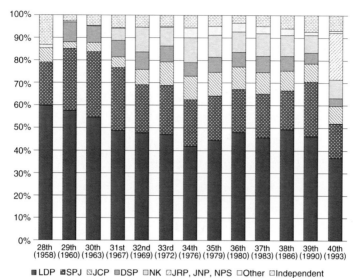

Figure 7-1 House of Representatives Election: Percentage of Votes Received (Multiple-Seat Constituency Era)

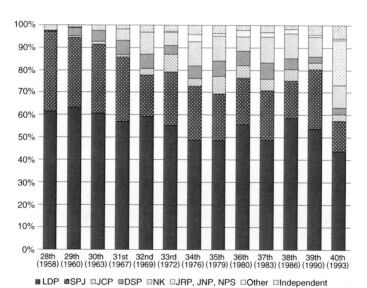

Figure 7-2 House of Representatives Election: Percentage of Seats Received (Multiple-Seat Constituency Era)
Source: Ministry of Internal Affairs and Communications (MIC)
Notes: SPJ=Social Democratic Party of Japan, DSP=Democratic Socialist Party, NK=(New) Komeito, JRP=Japan Renewal Party, JNP=Japan New Party, NPS=New Party Sakigake

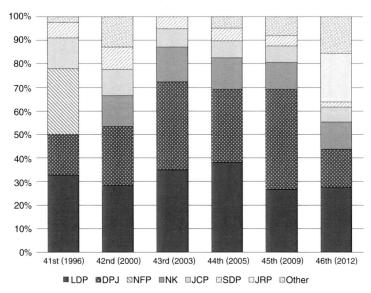

Figure 7-3 House of Representatives Election: Proportional Representative Percentage of Votes Received

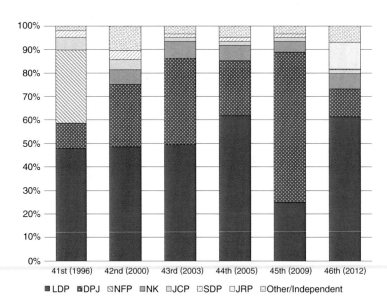

Figure 7-4 House of Representatives Election: Proportional Representative Percentage of Total Seats Received

Source: Ministry of Internal Affairs and Communications (MIC)
Notes: NFP=New Frontier Party, JRP=Japan Restoration Party

even when the difference between candidates is slight, only the candidate with the majority of votes (even if by one vote) will be elected and the number of "dead votes" increases. This can result in a large disparity between the proportion of votes received and the proportion of seats obtained.

To illustrate this, from the inception of the single-seat constituency system, based on the number of votes received, we can observe that the LDP did not even then have an absolute majority. For example, in the 2005 election for the House of Representatives, on account of the Japan Post reforms by the Koizumi administration, despite obtaining an overwhelming victory, this can be credited to the electoral system. The absolute percentage of votes received did not even reach above 40%. Moreover, in the 2012 election, when the DPJ went back into opposition and the LDP reclaimed government, although ultimately gaining the same percentage of seats as it had in 2005, in terms of the percentage of the number of votes received, it was below 30%, which was not so different from the number of votes obtained in the 2009 election that had ended with its crushing defeat. A large proportion of the reduction in the number of votes received did not go to the DPJ but to the other political parties, such as the Japan Restoration Party and Your Party. Although it might be asserted that this is simply the nature of the single-seat constituency system, in the interests of reflecting popular will, the reality of the large discrepancy between the actual votes received and the seats obtained must also be recognized among the voters.

In the case of the multiple-seat constituency system, as it was difficult for drastic fluctuation in the number of votes received to occur, there was no change in government. Both the ruling party and the opposition parties had become content in their respective positions, allowing for a mutual tendency to neglect to deepen and improve the quality of debate. Moreover, as the multiple-seat constituency system and the proportional representation system make it difficult for a particular party to obtain an absolute majority, it is easy for the foundation of government to become unstable due to the need to form coalition governments in order to rule. Furthermore, under a multiple-seat constituency system, the same party is forced to field multiple candidates. As this causes competition that is different in nature from that caused by differences in policy, it has been pointed out that this could lead to improper behavior or corruption.

However, it is often possible to predict the overall level of electoral shift beforehand, based on reports from the mass media, for example. According to a theory called "the spiral of silence" by Elizabeth Noelle-Neumann of Germany, if one recognizes one's view (or stance) to be in the minority, fearing isolation from the surrounding people, one restrains from voicing one's opinions in the public sphere. If this occurs, then the people who recognize that their views are in the minority will not publicly voice their opinions in society, and gradually only a unitary opinion will be observed in society as a whole. As a result, the dominant opinion will gain increased authority and the people not holding such opinions will be driven underground.

There is a strong streak of conformity in Japanese society, and apart from a section of people holding strong opinions (i.e., opponents), there seems to be a risk of opinions easily flowing in accordance with this kind of atmosphere. In an electoral system resulting in a clear distinction between winners and losers, such as the single-seat constituency system, if such result can be predicted in advance (specifically, in the case where the side with opinions closest to one's own will clearly lose), rational voters may avoid going to vote for a candidate and party that they know will lose regardless of their vote. Of course, voters who think this way are not necessarily large in number, and there may probably be a certain number of them who silently exercise their voting rights with the understanding that the means by which to express one's opinion in a democratic society is by voting. However, the problem that arises is that by commanding a number of seats in parliament that reflects popular will in a rather exaggerated form, the possibility of a discrepancy developing between the government and public opinion increases. And if such a discrepancy exists, then the people's mistrust toward the government and the parliamentary system may deepen. This can be said to call into question the foundation of indirect democracy.

3. The People's Verdict on the Education Policies Put Forward by the DPJ

(1) Data and Variables Used

Now, let us specifically examine people's attitudes on education costs, considering the trends of policy and political party support in the post-war era. This chapter uses data from the 2010 edition of Japanese General Social Surveys (JGSS),[6] because this survey contains questions that ask whether the respondent approved or disapproved of the individual key policies put forward by the DPJ at that time. These are valuable data providing a reliable measurement of nationwide popular will at the time.

Broadly speaking, these data can be used to conduct an examination from two perspectives. The first is the question of how far people think the government's responsibility should extend with respect to education, social security, and welfare, and what they consider the relationship between this burden and the tax burden to be. On this point, let us first examine the question, "Who do you think should be responsible for the following (individuals and families or national and local governments)? Choose a number from 1 to 5 for each." The following four items were listed: A) Guaranteeing the livelihood (living costs) of the elderly, B) Medical and nursing care of the elderly, C) Education of children, and D) Raising and taking care of children. The respondents were asked to select a number from 1 to 5, with values close to 1 (i.e., lower values) indicating the responsibility of individuals/families and values close to 5 (i.e. higher values) indicating the responsibility of national and local governments. Then, in a question on public burden, there was the following question: "Statement A and Statement B address the issue of public welfare and the public burden. Which statement is closer to your opinion? Please choose a number from 1 to 4. Statements A and B were as follows: "A: Even if taxes have to be increased, public services such as welfare should be improved" and "B: Even if public services such as welfare have to be weakened, the tax burden should be made lighter." The respondents selected a number from 1 to 4, with 1 being "Close to B" and 4 being "Close to A."

Next, let us examine the question asking whether respondents approved or disapproved of the policies put forward by the DPJ. The following seven policies were listed: A) Providing child allowance until graduation from junior high school, B) Making education at public senior high school practically free/providing a corresponding amount of subsidies to private senior high school students, C) Elimination of highway tolls, D) Reducing CO^2 emission by 25% by 2020 in comparison to the level of CO^2 emission in 1990, E) Increasing minimum wages, F) The same wages for everybody working on the same task in a company (regardless of sex, age, and employment contract), and G) Abolishing tax deduction for spouses. Four numbers were offered as choices indicating approval or disapproval and one number was provided for respondents to reply "Don't know." This book compiles the five results of A, B, E, F, and G, which are considered to be relevant to education and social security.

An examination of the kinds of variables used for these opinions will be provided later. For the time being, let us consider that the respondents to fall into the following categories: Sex (dummy variable of 1 when female.); Age (dummy variable of age 10, with the standard variable being age 20); Academic History (four dummy variables were created: Graduated from junior high school, Graduated from senior high school, Graduated from 2-year college or college of technology,[7] Graduated from university or graduate school, with Graduated from junior high school being made the standard variable); Adult Employment (using categories [8] that are standardly employed for international comparison), for which seven categories were created: Professionals and general managers, Office administration, [employed] Sales, Self-employed and Agriculture and Fisheries, Skilled work, Semi- and un-skilled work, and Unemployed, with office administration being taken as the standard variable; Household Income (for which seven categories were created: under 2.5 million, 2.5–3.5 million, 3.5–4.5 million, 4.5–6.5 million, 6.5–10.0 million, over 10.0 million, No answer, and Don't know, with under 2.5 million being taken as the standard variable). Marital Status (dummy variable with "Married" taken as 1; Widowed or Separated taken as 0), Children under the age of 20 (dummy variable of 1 in the case of there being such children).

(2) Balance between Public Service and the Public Burden

First, looking at the question of whether to choose social welfare even if this meant raising taxes, about 70% of the overall respondents selected options on the side of "A: Even if the taxes have to be increased, public services such as welfare should be improved." The respondents who wished for a small government and thought that taxes should be reduced even if it meant lowering services were thus limited to 30%. The responses tended to cluster in the middle numbers of "Somewhat close to ...," and strongly held opinions were few. Concerning the opinions that were clearly in agreement with the statements, those on improving public services and welfare drew about 20% of the responses, while the proponents of small government were less than 10%, at 6%. If this is analyzed according to the political party being supported, then by only considering the party platform, one can imagine conservative and small-government being oriented for the LDP, and a strengthening of welfare being backed by the supporters of the DPJ and JCP (although there are also segments where this cannot be taken to be the case). However, it is not possible to state any such clear results on this basis. Certainly, the will for a small government is comparatively stronger among the LDP and New Komeito supporters (including "somewhat close to ...," but this is about 38% and about 35%, respectively. On the other hand, for the DPJ and JCP, this is about 27% and about 29%, respectively. In the case of respondents who did not support a political party, this is about 30%. Considering that the total sample size exceeded 2,400 people, the question of whether this degree of difference in percentage can be considered to be significant is not clear-cut. In short, opinions concerning the issue of the public burden and that of public services cannot be said to be clearly reflected in their choice of support for political parties.

Figure 7-5 shows the distribution of responses concerning the responsibility of national and local governments and that of individuals and families for the four fields. Looking at this distribution, a tendency of support can be clearly observed for the field of welfare for the elderly as well as the fields of raising and taking care of children and education. Although there are many respondents who feel overwhelmingly that there is considerable national and local government responsibility with respect to welfare for the elderly, this is not the case for the raising and taking care of children and for education, as reflected by a substantial rise in the number respondents regarding these fields as the responsibility of individuals and families. This supports the commentary of 1-(3) of this chapter.

Moreover, as we observed when examining Table 4-1 of Chapter 4, when the relationship between the sense of burden and the question of whether responsibility lies with the government or the family is examined using the Goodman and

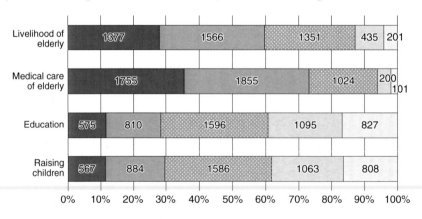

Figure 7-5 Does the Responsibility Lie with Governments or Individuals and Families? (From JGSS 2010)

Kruskal tau (τ), the value is very close to 0 for all of the four fields, as expected; and there are many people whose opinion that even if the taxes have to be increased, public services such as welfare should be improved does not concur with their awareness of the responsibility of the national and local governments. When this was examined by the respondents' academic history, the higher the level of education gained by the respondent, the greater the expected responsibility of the national and local governments (and the more popular the view that increasing tax was necessary).

When the level of education gained was low, there was no clear relationship between the issues. Although the absolute value of τ was low, with respect to education and the raising and taking care of children, τ had a negative value for low levels of education; and while believing that the national and local government's responsibility was strong, many of these respondents thought the tax burden should be reduced even if it meant reducing public services.[9]

Lastly, Table 7-2 shows the results of ordered logit estimation where the respective awareness items are taken as dependent variables. It shows that the larger the value of the dependent variable, the larger the preference for bigger government (the tendency toward tolerance for tax increases along with the belief that public services should be enhanced or that the responsibility of the national and local governments should be increased). Therefore, if the coefficient is a positive explanatory variable, this signifies a predilection for bigger government, and if negative, it signifies a preference for smaller government.

Concerning the respondents' views on education, there was a surprisingly large effect by age. However, as age rose (vis-à-vis age 20s) so did the inclination to recognize provision of education as the government's role. Looking at the different ages, from the age of being fresh out of school onward, the longer the time after the respondents' school days, the greater the awareness they had of the national and local governments' responsibility with respect to education. However, using only the results of a cross-sectional survey, it is not possible to determine whether this trend is due to the elapsing of years (i.e., the age effect) or whether it is due to differences in generational awareness (i.e., the cohort effect).

Moreover, although the variable of unemployed had a negative significance (with a greater inclination toward the responsibility of the individual and families), this is thought to reflect the presence of stay-at-home wives.[10] Another aspect worthy of mention when compared with other fields is the significant effect of whether or not the respondent has children. As this coefficient is positive, it means that among the respondents with children, there was an increased inclination to state that it was the national and local government responsibility. Moreover, for the fields of education, and raising and taking care of children, there was a strong tendency toward individual and family responsibility among the blue-collar and the self-employed strata.

With respect to welfare for the elderly, the opinion that it is the responsibility of individuals and families becomes more evident the higher the level of education attained. However, such tendency cannot be observed for education and raising and taking care of children. When it comes to selecting the "responsibility of

Table 7-2 Ordered Logit Regression Estimation on Whether It's the "Governments' Responsibility"

	Livelihood of elderly		Medical care of elderly		Education		Raising children		Increase taxes, enhance welfare	
	Coef.	S.E	Coef.	S.E	Coef.	S.E	Coef.	S.E	Coef.	S.E
Women	-.052	.056	-.008	.057	-.027	.056	-.133	.056 *	-.212	.083 *
30s	.043	.112	.109	.114	.240	.112 *	.121	.110	.010	.168
40s	.370	.114 ***	.446	.115 ***	.352	.113 **	.059	.112	.235	.168
50s	.194	.111 +	.313	.113 **	.399	.111 ***	.109	.110	.250	.168
60s	-.004	.115	.266	.117 *	.487	.115 ***	.134	.114	.090	.174
70s	-.062	.127	-.077	.129	.535	.127 ***	.053	.126	-.097	.197
80s	-.307	.161 +	-.361	.164 *	.246	.160	-.129	.158	-.052	.246
Grad. senior high	-.187	.084 *	-.170	.086 *	-.137	.083 +	-.037	.083	.230	.125 +
Grad. 2-year/tech college	-.186	.105 +	-.139	.107	-.237	.104 *	-.174	.105 +	.407	.158 *
Grad. university/graduate school	-.302	.100 **	-.252	.102 *	-.111	.099	-.035	.099	.656	.151 ***
Unemployed	-.066	.086	-.067	.087	-.220	.085 **	-.130	.084	-.012	.128
Professional/management	.041	.100	-.074	.102	.098	.100	.088	.100	.134	.148
Sales	-.040	.110	-.073	.112	-.086	.109	-.064	.109	-.161	.158
Self-employed/agriculture	-.236	.123 +	-.229	.125 +	-.521	.122 ***	-.306	.122 *	-.325	.184 +
Skilled worker	-.028	.126	-.052	.128	-.443	.125 ***	-.326	.123 **	-.556	.181 **
Semi-skilled/unskilled	.064	.099	.058	.102	-.224	.098 *	-.208	.098 *	-.367	.148 *
Household income > 2.5 mil. yen	-.230	.112 *	-.222	.115 +	-.254	.112	-.218	.112 +	-.068	.167
Household income > 3.5 mil. yen	-.035	.118	-.135	.121	.013	.118	.002	.118	.141	.178
Household income > 4.5 mil. yen	-.299	.105 **	-.169	.108	-.076	.105	-.038	.106	-.033	.156
Household income > 6.5 mil. yen	-.201	.109 +	-.162	.111	-.170	.109	-.097	.109	-.091	.163
Household income > 10 mil. yen	-.386	.132 ***	-.294	.133 *	-.242	.131 +	-.125	.130	-.072	.197
Household income undisclosed	-.117	.093	-.143	.096	-.088	.093	-.068	.093	-.015	.139
Married	.055	.068	.124	.069 +	-.070	.068	.010	.069	.011	.105
Children < age 20	-.102	.081	-.065	.082	.322	.080 ***	.136	.080 +	.159	.117
Threshold 1	-3.496	.169	-4.005	.185	-1.635	.155	-1.816	.155	-2.511	.244
Threshold 2	-2.244	.159	-2.868	.166	-.463	.153	-.671	.153	-.589	.235
Threshold 3	-.718	.155	-1.127	.158	.928	.154	.690	.153	1.725	.237
Threshold 4	.635	.155	.488	.157	2.024	.157	1.862	.156	-	-
N	4910		4915		4883		4888		2426	
-2 Log Likelihood	13889.494		12423.425		15034.822		15123.155		5653.935	

+p < .10 *p < .05 **p < .01 ***p < .001

individuals and families," it is important to exercise caution in judgement over whether the respondents are responding with the supposition that there is a monetary significance. With responsibility lying with individuals and families, if the respondents' line of thinking is that the education policy for children is decided by the parents, then there is no reason for the national or local governments to interfere. If this is the case, then it would be misleading to interpret these results just by looking at the aspect of education public finance.

Nevertheless, with respect to welfare for the elderly, as there is not a strong tendency for the elderly themselves, who are recipients of the government services, to support the principle that it is the responsibility of the national and local governments, there does not seem to be any reason to believe that it is the people who stand to benefit the most at the time to hold such view. Moreover, no matter what one's age, post-retirement livelihood is a risk from which one cannot escape.

On the other hand, the people affected by education and the raising and taking care of children are those with children of a young age or of school-going age. Once this time has passed, there are few merits that can be felt from an individual perspective. Therefore, the fields of education and raising and taking care of children are those that are prone to causing opposition of interests, depending on the presence of children.

(3) Concerning Support for the DPJ Policies

Next, let us examine the awareness of the policies related to education and social security that were advanced by the DPJ.

Figure 7-6 simply shows a distribution of approval and disapproval for each field. If we suppose this to be a distribution of opinion toward education and raising and taking care of children, like Figure 7-5, then more than a majority is in support of child allowance and the dispensing of fees for senior high schools,

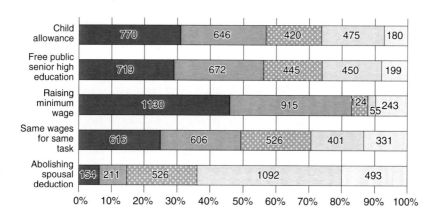

Figure 7-6 Support on DPJ Policies (JGSS 2010)

which could be considered surprising. However, the rate of agreement is less than 60% and there is large opposition as well. In particular, the fiscal resources for these policies were supposed to be realized from the abolition of spousal tax deduction. The ideology of the DPJ Government that considered the education and raising and taking care of children through the creation of a gender equal society was not necessarily widely accepted, and there was an overwhelmingly large amount of opposition to the abolition of the spousal tax deduction (probably because it was understood as effectively increasing the burden).

Moreover, when one looks at the evaluation of these policies according to the political party supported by the respondent there is a particularly large difference in support of the child allowance, depending on which political party is supported. Although those disagreeing with the policy are limited to 20% among the DPJ supporters, close to half of the respondents who support the LDP or other political parties are opposed to the policy. The distribution among New Komeito supporters is similar to the case of LDP supporters: among JCP supporters, opposition to the policy is up by around 40%, which is surprisingly close to the LDP supporters. A similar tendency is exhibited for the dispensing of fees for public senior high schools, although this is not as clear as for child allowance. Close to half of the LDP supporters were opposed, but this opposition was around 30% for DPJ and New Komeito supporters. When comparing awareness concerning education and the raising of children between the supporters of various parties, the relationship of the distribution of DPJ supporters and New Komeito supporters was actually closer than between supporters of the LDP and New Komeito, which formed the coalition government in 2014.

On the other hand, issues concerning wages and the abolition of the spousal tax deduction system did not produce as clear a difference in awareness based on which political party was supported. Nonetheless, with respect to the principle of having the same wages for everybody working on the same task in a company, while opposition to this policy exceeded 40% only among LDP supporters, opposition was at 30% among JCP supporters. One can therefore see a hint of an emergence of difference of ideology and stance between the political parties.

To take a further look at this comparison of awareness, an ordered logit model was likewise estimated for awareness of where the responsibility lies (with governments or families). Table 7-3 shows this result (with respondents answering "Don't know" excluded from the analysis).

Looking at the results, although the existence of children is a decisive factor is a correlation with marital status. Although it is omitted from the table, if one overlaps this analysis with the results of the analysis by sex, interesting findings can be identified. The negative result among the unemployed reflects opposition among women (stay-at-home wives; the result is not significant when limited to males). Moreover, the effect of employment variables is influenced by the male sample. On the other hand, there is a lot of opposition (compared with the lowest income group) among the comparatively low household income of 2.5–3.5 million yen. Meanwhile, when limiting analysis to the male sample, there is a positive significance among household incomes of above 10 million yen, where there is a

Table 7–3 Estimated Ordered Logit Regression for Support on DPJ Government Policies

	Child allowance		Free senior high		Raising minimum wage		Same wages for same task		Abolishing spousal deduction	
	Coef.	S.E	Coef.	S.E	Coef.	S.E	Coef.	S.E	Coef.	S.E
Women	-.233	.084 **	-.153	.084 +	.125	.091	.181	.084 *	.259	.097 **
30's	.059	.170	-.024	.171	-.046	.183	.313	.173 +	.244	.201
40's	-.943	.170 ***	-.642	.171 ***	.000	.183	.473	.172 **	.114	.201
50's	-.819	.169 ***	-.745	.170 ***	.175	.183	.821	.173 ***	.235	.196
60's	-.545	.175 **	-.571	.177 **	-.140	.190	.709	.180 ***	.089	.208
70's	-.505	.196 *	-.523	.198 **	-.062	.216	.800	.202 ***	-.052	.235
80's	-.069	.256	-.372	.263	-.216	.286	.866	.274 **	.178	.315
Grad. senior high	-.271	.125 *	-.152	.127	-.008	.139	.017	.132	.020	.152
Grad. 2-year/tech college	-.407	.155 **	-.208	.157	-.116	.173	.013	.163	.096	.186
Grad. university/graduate school	-.588	.148 ***	-.423	.150 **	-.428	.165 *	-.123	.156	.253	.175
Unemployed	-.007	.125	-.142	.126	.046	.137	.024	.128	-.483	.142 **
Professional/management	.079	.147	-.092	.146	.212	.158	-.022	.147	-.218	.162
Sales	.059	.157	-.131	.155	.063	.169	.057	.158	-.342	.177 +
Self-employed/agriculture	.274	.196	-.035	.194	-.502	.205 *	-.252	.191	-.394	.213 +
Skilled worker	-.001	.180	-.184	.179	.061	.197	-.189	.180	-.190	.194
Semi-skilled/unskilled	-.060	.147	-.076	.149	.058	.160	-.092	.149	-.376	.169 *
Household income > 2.5 mil. yen	-.011	.172	.077	.175	-.467	.189 *	-.170	.173	-.470	.209 *
Household income > 3.5 mil. yen	-.197	.179	-.108	.181	-.552	.198 **	.007	.185	-.321	.211
Household income > 4.5 mil. yen	-.073	.159	-.078	.160	-.479	.176 **	-.417	.163 *	-.157	.185
Household income > 6.5 mil. yen	-.477	.165 **	-.281	.167 +	-.814	.182 ***	-.420	.167 *	.092	.188
Household income > 10 mil. yen	-.636	.201 **	-.623	.201 **	-1.087	.222 ***	-.636	.205 **	.327	.225
Household income undisclosed	-.265	.143 +	-.172	.145	-.659	.160 ***	-.273	.147 +	-.229	.169
Married	.239	.105 *	.073	.106	.075	.116	-.059	.110	-.922	.126 ***
Children < age 20	1.107	.120 ***	1.353	.120 ***	.056	.128	-.052	.120	.092	.132
Threshold 1	-2.120	.241	-2.084	.243	-4.286	.292	-1.240	.246	-.585	.279
Threshold 2	-1.168	.238	-1.042	.240	-3.042	.270	-.006	.244	.778	.279
Threshold 3	.108	.236	.337	.239	-.584	.260	1.214	.245	1.802	.285
N	2303		2277		2216		2140		1976	
-2 Log Likelihood	5962.594		5865.896		4187.056		5785.537		4269.031	

+p < .10 *p < .05 **p < .01 ***p < .001

tendency toward supporting the abolition of the spousal tax deduction. This is probably because among the strata where the husband's income is not that high and wives work in a limited way (utilizing this spousal tax deduction), this merit would be lost if spousal tax deduction were to be abolished. However, if the household income is high, there is a high likelihood that the husband and the wife are already both working full-time and they are not receiving any benefit from spousal tax deduction.

From the aforementioned findings, we can conclude that, as mentioned earlier, the reason that the DPJ opted for increased support for child rearing was the party's stance of promoting and supporting the participation of women in society based on the premise that child rearing is a social act. Therefore, the abolition of spousal tax deduction had a strong correlation with the policy of supporting child rearing. However, as mentioned in Footnote 5 of this chapter, the facilities were with regard to views on child allowance and dispensing with senior high school fees, in both cases, support for these issues weakened in the higher level of education attained strata and the higher income strata. The relationship with age was also significant, with opposition becoming more prevalent as age increased. There was also a significantly high level of opposition among women. This point seems to contradict the aforementioned result showing a strengthening propensity with the increase in age of the respondents to consider responsibility for education to lie with the national and local governments. As the question's wording referred to responsibility for "education of children," it is possible that respondents did not necessarily interpret the national and local government responsibility in the context of public finance, instead envisioning it to actually relate to educational content. Moreover, perhaps the higher the respondents' educational level, the more likely it is that they would have understood the question to refer to the Japanese government's fiscal circumstances. It is therefore possible that their consideration represented more of a critical assessment of whether Japan in its current predicament had the fiscal leeway for that particular policy. Moreover, as the elderly respondents probably had concerns over the burden for their own pension and medical care, they could possibly have interpreted the policies on child allowance and dispensing with senior high school fees as simply pork-barreling, unless they had an adequate understanding of the policies. As these services were to be provided universally (i.e., to everyone) under the DPJ's plan, it is difficult to imagine that there would be intrinsic differences of opinion based on class or strata. However, the propensity for opposition based on the higher educational level and higher income class needs to be examined. Perhaps this is evidence that awareness of the policies had not adequately infiltrated society (i.e., had not been properly understood). Child allowance was abolished in the fiscal year 2011 because the budget for rebuilding in the wake of the earthquake disaster was inadequate. It was decided to accommodate for child allowance within the framework of the preexisting Child Allowance Act.[11] Moreover, income-based eligibility restrictions were also established for dispensing with fees for senior high schools.[12] As the ideology of universalism has collapsed, there is also the possibility that opposition among the middle to higher income strata will rise.

Views on issues related to wages, as one would expect, had a strong correlation with household income (for the minimum wage policy in particular, the correlation was especially clear; there was also a correlation with educational level for this policy). With regard to the same wages being paid to everybody working on the same task, the reason that the higher the age, the greater the opposition can perhaps be deemed as a reaction to the fact that the wages of elderly who are re-employed after retirement age are suppressed. Also, the high propensity to support the idea among women can be considered as a reflection of discontent over a large disparity in wages for the same work tasks based on employment status (regular employment or contractual employment).

Concerning the abolition of spousal tax deduction, opposition was overall large among women (reflecting a view that there are barriers to social advancement for women). However, as only married women benefit from this system, there is a correlation with marital status. Although it is omitted from the table, if one overlaps this analysis with the results of the analysis by sex, interesting findings can be identified. The negative result among the unemployed reflects opposition among women (stay-at-home wives; the result is not significant when limited to males). Moreover, the effect of employment variables is influenced by the male sample. On the other hand, there is a lot of opposition (compared with the lowest income group) among the comparatively low household income of 2.5–3.5 million yen. Meanwhile, , when limiting analysis to the male sample, there is a positive significance among household incomes of above 10 million yen, where there is a tendency toward supporting the abolition of the spousal tax deduction. This is probably because among the strata where the husband's income is not that high and wives work in a limited way (utilizing this spousal tax deduction), this merit would be lost if spousal tax deduction were to be abolished. However, if the household income is high, there is a high likelihood that the husband and the wife are already both working full-time and they are not receiving any benefit from spousal tax deduction.

From the aforementioned findings, we can conclude that, as mentioned earlier, the reason that the DPJ opted for increased support for child rearing was the party's stance of promoting and supporting the participation of women in society based on the premise that child rearing is a social act. Therefore, the abolition of spousal tax deduction had a strong correlation with the policy of supporting child rearing. However, as mentioned in Footnote 5 of this chapter, the facilities were not in place to cope with increased numbers of parents wanting to place their children in nursery schools. Due to the failure of sufficiently grasping these needs, it was not possible for any understanding of these policies to infiltrate society. Hence, widespread support of the policies could not be obtained. Consequently, the voters evaluated the policies based on their current (immediately apparent) interests and concerns, and could not effectively capitalize on the chance to implement a grand transformation to the conventional social security and welfare system. The next chapter aims to continue on from this point and deepen our understanding of changes in peoples' awareness.

NOTES

[1] "Diet Minutes" plenary session of the House of Councilors (January 30, 2012) 180–183.

[2] This represented a method of recording "reserves" in the initial budget beforehand for the anticipated amount of the revisions, based on the criticism that revising the budget

in the middle of a fiscal year invites the trend of an expanding fiscal deficit.

3 This is according to a "2003 Nationwide Survey on Work and Living." The survey was given to men and women throughout Japan aged 20 to 69 years. The valid sample was 1,154 respondents (with a response rate of 57.7%).

4 In other words, the function of the influential vote-gathering systems of the party members, the labor unions, and the various industry organizations weakened. The increase in non-affiliated voters also impacted the cohesiveness within each political party and "a market-competition style of democracy" (Nakakita, 2012), which generated a sense of unity among each political party which began to operate by means of the differences of specific policies (or manifesto).

5 With respect to this, the waiting lists for nursery schools in the urban areas became an issue, and there were consequently demands for greater efforts to expand nursery schools. The DPJ was no longer able to keep up with these demands in its responses.

6 The Japanese General Social Surveys (JGSS) are designed and carried out by the JGSS Research Center at Osaka University of Commerce (the Joint Usage/Research Center for Japanese General Social Surveys accredited by the Minister of Education, Culture, Sports, Science and Technology) in collaboration with the Institute of Social Science at the University of Tokyo. The microdata of "Japanese General Social Surveys JGSS-2010" (JGSS Research Center at Osaka University of Commerce) used in the analysis in this book were compiled and distributed by SSJ Data Archive, Information Center for Social Science Research on Japan, Institute of Social Science, the University of Tokyo.

7 This does not include so-called "vocational schools." If someone went from a senior high school to a vocational school, then this would be treated as having graduated from senior high school in this analysis.

8 These are based on the EGP class scheme proposed by Robert Erikson, John H. Goldthorpe, and Lucienne Portocarero. They are the most widely used in international comparative stratification research (Erikson et al., 1979).

9 Note, as supplementary information, that there is reference to the distribution of political support and education level. Looking at the tendency of political support by academic history, there is actually a clear trend. There are a comparatively larger number of supporters for the LDP among respondents whose highest level of education was junior high school or senior high school. The support for the DPJ was higher among the respondents who reached higher levels of education. Support for the New Komeito was similar to the LDP, in that there was a tendency for increased support the lower the level of education reached. No clear trends were observed for the JCP or other political parties. Although the number of respondents not supporting a political party was small for those whose highest academic level was junior high school (at less than half), there was not a clear tendency in the other academic levels, with about 60% of respondents not supporting a political party.

10 When this sample is limited to women, the unemployed variable is still significant; but when this sample is limited to men, the result is no longer significant.

11 This "Child Allowance" (*jidou teate*) can be interpreted as being equivalent to the new "Child Allowance" (*kodomo teate*) with income-based eligibility restrictions applied.

12 From the fiscal year 2013, dispensing with fees has come to be limited to households with an income of up to 9.1 million yen.

CHAPTER 8
Realization of Policies and Stance toward Political Parties

1. The Critical Gaze on "Bureaucracy"

(1) Parliamentary Cabinet System and Enforcement of Policy

One position consistently asserted throughout this book is that Japan's adoption of parliamentary democracy makes the government obliged to ensure that the people agree with (and support) the taking of taxes from them. From the citizen's perspective, any increased burden is met with displeasure, which makes it difficult to increase taxes. From the perspective of compiling the budget, attention is focused on working on its new parts. This implies, in other words, that the existing parts of the budget are assumed to be needed, that vested interests arise, and that these parts are not easy to whittle down. Such a structure makes the budget nonresponsive to large social reforms, while facilitating the formation of cozy relations within pockets of society and industry. In the eyes of ordinary people, this structure can appear to be actively resistant to change. Therein is the dilemma of a parliamentary democracy: while relying on the popular will for tax increases, it is difficult to reflect the popular will in the budget (Ide, 2011).

With respect to such parliamentary democracy, Arend Lijphart presents two models: the typical decision-by-majority democracy, like the Westminster model of the U.K.; and the typical consensus among a coexistence of multi-polar camps, like the consensus model of Switzerland. June Burnham and Robert Pyper organize the particular traits of the two models into nine specific points for each. The following summary presents those for the Westminster Model.

The first trait of the Westminster model is that the executive power is concentrated in a cabinet consisting of a single party with majority rule. The second is that, in principle, the relationship between the members of the government (cabinet) and the parliamentary assembly is in name only. In practice, however, the former has the dominating position.[1] Third, the structure of political power inside the parliament concentrates on one chamber, and when there are two chambers, the strong power is in the chamber with unilateral authority. Fourth, there is fundamentally a two-party system. Fifth, the type of societies that have a two-party system tend to be those with homogeneity in their industrial and social structure, as this limits the battleground issues to socioeconomic ones. Take, for example, a country where multiple opposing ethnic groups exist. There, it would be necessary to decide on a distribution of seats that takes into account these factors, and as that requires negotiation among heterogeneous groups, a consensus type of democracy is easier to adopt. The sixth point is related to the nature of government rule. Because elections are held based on simple battleground issues, the single-seat constituency system is adopted and elections operate by the voter selecting one or the other candidate based on the policies. Seventh, the system and structures are unitary. Eighth, sovereignty resides with the parliament, and there is no codified constitution to constrain the power of the parliamentary majority. Ninth, the members of parliament take on the responsibility as the representatives of the people, and referenda by the masses (direct democracy by the people's ballot vote) are treated negatively.

The type of public service that serves as a mechanism of government for the Westminster model is called the Whitehall model. This type of public service must be non-political and neutral. Generalists are hired, reared internally, and promoted based on successful outcomes. The accountability for the work of public servants resides not with the individual public servant but with the minister (hence, public servants have anonymity). On the flipside, because the public servants give necessary advice to the minister on the execution of policy and serve in an assisting role, their neutrality is essential. It is only their job to promptly carry out the decided policy. The system of command is unitary, the organizations are formed as field-specific ministries and agencies, and policy is implemented through mutual consensus (Burnham and Pyper, 2008, trans. 2010: 26–36).

In the U.K., this Whitehall model was quickly lost under the reforms of the Thatcher Government. For example, there was a process of delegating authority to local governments such as Scotland and Northern Ireland, and through membership in the EU, there was a process of specializing within individual policy fields. This splintered the vertical structures inside the country.

The mechanism of government in Japan is described in text books as a parliamentary cabinet system, but its nature is quite different from the same parliamentary cabinet system adopted by the U.K. According to Jun Iio, there is an often-heard criticism based on a misconception of the true nature of the parliamentary system, which misses the point of its existence: namely, the assertion that the Japanese parliamentary cabinet system rarely represents the popular will and might as well be a presidential (or similar) system that concentrates authority. Iio argues that with a parliamentary cabinet system, the cabinet and the prime minister derive their existence from an assembly that has been democratically elected, and that the relationship between the two is not fundamentally contradictory.

Therefore, the prime minister is elected from the representatives (members of parliament), who have received their credential to be there by an election. The prime minister forms the cabinet, and this cabinet runs the organizations of bureaucracy. Through these processes, the electorate prevents bureaucracy from becoming out of control; in other words, the parliamentary cabinet system possesses this aspect of control.

In the specific case of Japan, however, the LDP maintained power over a long period of time, during which there remained the customary practice of selecting a representative (prime minister) by the election of party chairmen, and it came to be common practice for the ministers to be selected by internal party logic based on "factional dynamics." Operating under this system, ministerial positions were not always filled by the most suitable candidates. It was not at all rare for there to be frequent cabinet reshuffles involving the replacement and switching of ministers, and it became common practice for ministers to act in accordance with bureaucratic will (as if they were a representative of the ministry of which they were in charge). Such behavior by ministers was not necessarily the logic of the prime minister or the cabinet as a whole. It became usual for ministers to allow the logic of their ministry to take precedence, and this made the cabinet prone to being often functionally ineffective. Iio calls this state of affairs the "bureaucratic cabinet system" (Iio, 2007: 21–25). The bureaucratic group that makes up this system includes the relationship with the external organizations in society that have ties to these ministries. As such, the bureaucratic cabinet system also reflects the will of these organizations in society. In this sense, the politicians (or cabinet) do not operate in a way that is entirely the will of the bureaucracy (i.e., the central ministries and agencies).

However, under these situations, even if the bureaucratic cabinet system reflects the will of specific industry organization, this does not necessarily mean that it reflects the broader popular will. Moreover, even the politicians and political parties of the cabinet do not put up a strong show of holding responsibility for the results of their decisions. Yet, criticism directed at the long period of LDP government rule concerns how the substance of politics does not reflect popular will, but it does not question the responsibility of the LDP government concerning the budgets they compiled. This is evidence of a lack of understanding about the concept of the parliamentary cabinet system and the correct way it should operate (Iio, 2007: 116).

However the changing of the electoral system for the House of Representatives from a multiple-seat to a single-seat constituency system not only subsequently led to the government changing hands to the DPJ, it also signified a large change in the status of prime minister and the requirements to become one. The strengthening of the cabinet functions that were enforced during the Hashimoto administration (involving the establishment of the Cabinet Office and the reaching of a consensus between the ministries by holding an authority one rank higher than each of the ministries) also served to strengthen the authority of the prime minister, and the significance of the conventional factions was also diluted. As a result, the choices of the prime minister no longer followed the internal logic of the LDP because it became impossible to ignore his popularity among ordinary citizens and trends of public opinion. Since becoming a single-seat constituency system, it has become decidedly more important for electoral candidates to receive official approval from the party (Takenaka, 2006). The Koizumi administration was formed by thoroughly making use of these changes.

Masaru Mabuchi adopts Bernard S. Silberman's idea of categorizing government organizations into specialization-oriented and organization-oriented bureaucratic systems. This type of categorization, which could be described as an ideal type by Weberians, is generally based on whether the succession rules for political leaders are stable or not. A typical example of the former is the U.S., and a typical example of the latter is Japan.

In the U.S., the term of office of the president is clearly decided, and the changeover of power is repeatedly carried out in accordance with fixed procedures. In countries such as the U.S., even if the political leaders change, the rules of succession are clearly prescribed, and there is little uncertainty even when there is a change of authority. On the other hand, even when the succession of political power is ineffective and an unruly situation like a coup d'état occurs, the bureaucracies holding the specialized functions must continue to govern effectively. Because the members of these bureaucratic organizations place importance on this specialty, if a changeover of authority occurs, the new government appoints effective personnel who will realize the government's policies in line with this specialty. Thus, there tends to be an exchange of personnel between the bureaucratic organizations and the private sector.

On the other hand, this kind of regime change has rarely occurred in Japan, and there is no way of telling when a prime minister or cabinet will be replaced. Moreover, the way this change will occur is dependent on the situation. In this way, the legitimacy of the political leader is jeopardized in countries with a high degree of uncertainty concerning the succession of leaders. Hence, bureaucratic systems with rigid organizations are formed to ensure stable governance. That is why the bureaucrats of such a country (while of course requiring a certain level of specialty for policy) must have unequivocal loyalty to the organization. In other words, the bureaucrat's primary function is to faithfully execute the policy that the government at that time wishes to implement. Because it is necessary to enhance the commitment of the members in such an organization, there need to be systems in place for promotion and salary raises in the government office organization itself. In this way, large replacements will not take place with a change of government (Mabuchi, 2010). Therefore, in the case of organization-oriented governmental bureaucracy, the organization of government offices can easily be constructed in a rigid fashion that is detached from popular will.

(2) Dysfunctions of Bureaucracy and Criticism Directed at Public Servants

The bureaucracy is a classic theme in the area of sociology that studies organizations. In the Japanese language, the kanji *kan* (官), of the word *kanryou* (官僚), originally carried the meaning of "the work of administering politics under the service of the monarch." The word *kanryou* (官僚) (official + colleague) meant a colleague of an official.

When *kanryou* (=bureaucrat) is used in its original sense, it refers to a "public servant of the state," and the meaning does not include the public servant of a local government[2] (Omori, 2006). It can often be observed that when the government offices of the central ministries are referred to as "Kasumigaseki," this normally implies that the people working there are being alluded to as bureaucrats in a critical and derisive tone.

However, as already mentioned in the Introduction and Chapter 3, it is not necessarily correct to criticize central government offices under the unitary understanding of them as "country" and "bureaucracy." In practice, there is a tangle of various interests among the different central government offices, and it is not rare for there even to be conflicts among the ministries and government offices (Imamura, 2006). Moreover, sociologically, a bureaucracy signifies nothing more than an organization that maintains complicated structures and forms that have been observed typically since modern times. Therefore, the word bureaucracy does not necessarily include the nuance of a government office organization. Actually, bureaucratic organizations refer to organizations that have been provided with the particular traits of a so-called bureaucracy, and these include schools, private-sector corporations, and NGOs. We all ordinarily use the word bureaucracy when offering criticism of an existing public servant system (in particular, the central government offices of "Kasumigaseki"). As a result, the word bureaucracy is naturally used with pejorative associations. However, the term itself only indicates the form of an organization in modern times, and so when it is used academically, it does not necessarily carry with it any negative connotations.

Since modern times have brought with them serious considerations about rationality of purpose, any complex, artificial organization formed with a specific purpose must inevitably be referred to as a bureaucratic organization. In modern society, there is an increase in the execution of complicated and difficult objectives, too large for any individual. In order that these objectives can be realized more rationally and efficiently, a process of sectionalism is carried out within organizations. It becomes necessary to more clearly define the allocation of roles, and the people who have been trained in areas of specialty must accomplish their respective duties. Accordingly, people are employed and assigned to roles based on their performance in bureaucratic organizations. That is why, in the administration of the state, various ministries and government offices of differing function and purpose stand side by side with one another. In sociological terms, however, adding to the critical opinion and interpretation of the bureaucratic organizations that we are familiar with, is the well-known discussion of Robert K. Merton's "dysfunction of bureaucracy" (Merton, 1957, trans. 1961: 179–207).

The term "to function" is used to mean to work well, serving a role in accordance with a purpose. In sociology, functional analysis refers to observing various organizations, rules, customs, and so forth, and analyzing how they act in society. Merton did not consider the term "function" to be necessarily restricted to a positive meaning. Instead, he used the term dysfunction to describe the performance of acts that have negative consequences, such as when an intrinsic purpose has been lost or smooth communication within society has been hindered due to the existence of a certain organization, rule, or custom, for example.

When a bureaucratic organization grows, that organization's autonomy will strengthen and it will actively work for its self-protection. This can occur for not only the organization itself but also for smaller units such as bureaus and departments in charge within the organization. Moreover, because of the ongoing process of functional differentiation inside the organization, the bureau in charge becomes thoroughly knowledgeable on its specialty but ignorant about all other circumstances. In other words, although an organization that has undergone functional differentiation to achieve large objectives is a bureaucratic organization, the people working there lose sight of the overall objectives and primarily only think about their own small bureau. Moreover, each of the ministries and bureaus may have relations with private-sector organizations in the associated market, and this steadily strengthens the territorial nature of their own organization. This is what is known as the negative side of the vertical administration system (Imamura, 2006: 84–88), and it can be interpreted as one kind of dysfunction of bureaucracy.

The criticism directed at public servants and officials has become very deeply rooted in modern-day Japan. Although it is hard to imagine amid the recent din of criticism directed at the bureaucrats and public servants, previously in Japan, there had been many affirmative evaluations of bureaucrats, such as assertions that "high economic growth was made possible in Japan because (even though the politicians were irresponsible) the bureaucrats were excellent (Nye et al. eds., 1997, trans. 2002: 321–340, article by Susan J. Pharr). This reversal of appraisal began from the recruitment scandal and developed further with the collapse of the asset bubble around 1990 and later. This begs the question of whether the quality of the bureaucrats and public servants did, in fact, sharply deteriorate through the 1990s and thereafter. It is difficult to demonstrate whether or not this was the case, as it cannot easily be determined what is meant by deterioration, and it is problematic that one must hence become subjective. Moreover, it further depends on one's way of thinking. For example, one quite plausible speculation is that the quality of young public servants has actually risen from the 1990s onward because of increased competition and a higher entrance bar due to the increase in young people wanting to become public servants and enjoy relatively better job security. Here, however, we are not concerned about measuring the quality of these public servants. Rather, our interest is why criticism of bureaucracy and public employees suddenly exploded from this time onward (Noguchi, 2011: 84–87).

Among the criticisms of "bureaucracy" in Japan, the major ones directed toward the government, such as that the bureaucratic functions are too inflated and should be reduced, cannot be considered to represent mainstream concerns. Of course, there are outspoken views on relaxing regulations and utilizing the power of the private sector. These are claims based on bureaucratic inflexibility (i.e., rigid rules) or illogical bureaucratic mechanisms. But the paradoxical side to such complaints is that even if these bureaucratic organizations had wandered from the intentions of the people or had characteristics that were irrational, unless we form different bureaucratic organizations to replace them, there is not much that can be done.

In other words, in order to correct the irrationality of a rigid bureaucratic system, the side opposing it would have to locate people with the specialty and place them rationally, draw up strategies, and institutionalize them. Ultimately, however, this institutionalizing creates nothing other than bureaucracy (Mabuchi, 2010: 36–38).

A more difficult criticism directed at the government services is that against the backdrop of the currently severe economic situation, many people look at the relatively stable positions of the public servants and comment, rather emotionally, "While the private sector is struggling, the public servants have it easy. They have it too easy." This is further exacerbated by politicians who would exploit these sentiments when canvassing votes. This is considered to be one factor behind the growing distrust toward the Japanese government. This sentiment along with the difficulty in increasing taxes are serious problems that are compounded when the voters' representatives, the politicians themselves, exploit these views.

Moreover, what gives rise to these criticisms is the system of government rule in Japan and the characteristics of organization-oriented bureaucratic systems (as described by Silberman), which is what this system is assumed to be, as mentioned at the start of this chapter. Of course, because the bureaucratic organization seems to move further away from the intentions and control of individuals as it gets bigger in size, it is important to adopt procedures of always checking and critically assessing it. However, in terms of the ordinary sentiment of the Japanese people, there do not seem to be very many of them who truly wish to see a small government. This is made clear from the analysis of the survey data in Chapter 7. The bulk of the concerns of voters lies with social security. Or putting it the other way around, the insufficiency of the Japanese social security system is the reason it attracts the people's attention. Moreover, just as there can be no discussion of welfare services if removed from the constructs of the state, we cannot contemplate putting a more substantial welfare system into operation without the existence of a certain number of public servants (i.e., a certain level of bureaucracy) (Noguchi, 2011).

(3) Affinity between Criticisms toward Bureaucracy and Neoliberalism

Bureaucratic organizations follow the path of rationalization to achieve smoother organizational operation. Following this path, the organization removes soft-hearted relationships between individuals and promotes formalism and anti-spiritualism. People perceive this behavior as cold and inhuman, calling it a "red-tape" response. But part of this is a necessary response in order to run the entire society. Moreover, when bureaucratic organizations, aiming to deliver efficient administration, proceed down the path of sectionalism, the resulting vertical structures can actually be a hindrance to efficient operations. The bureaucratic organizations that are meant to be operating rationally and efficiently can, in practice, become a symbol of irrationality and inefficiency. This can be interpreted as a dysfunction of bureaucracy.

Rationalization refers to the act of running operations based on a logic that can be explained in a way that even a third party can understand it using reason. Hence, this excludes logic that can only be understood by individuals with close relationships (e.g., harmonious affinity and unspoken understanding). It also decreases the possibility of there being charismatic people arbitrarily brandishing power by autocratic means. On the other hand, another result will be the rule of democracy, based on the bureaucratic mechanisms, adopting a decision-by-majority system as a means of persuading people. This will be perceived as impersonal, and although the threat of tyranny by individuals disappears, the tyranny by the majority takes its place. This is what Tocqueville, who was mentioned in Chapter 1, is referring to in "Democracy in America" (Tocqueville, 1888, trans.1987). One can expect that, in reaction to this absurd bureaucracy, a new charismatic personality will appear.

He or she, using powerful charisma, would argue that the "bureaucracy" is no good and that it is necessary to break away from this current state of bureaucratic rule. Such discourse would have strong appeal (Noguchi, 2011: 16–30). As the bureaucratic rule ordinarily necessitates dull, routine work, there will always be a latent desire for a reformer to someday come along to break everyone free of the situation. That is why the well-known British thinker and utilitarianism-oriented economist John Stuart Mill sounds a note of caution concerning the "dangers" of bureaucratic rule sometimes accepting strange proposals (Noguchi, 2011: 51–56).

Masahiro Noguchi is concerned that the "excessive" bashing of public servants and bureaucrats in Japan that has been becoming more prominent in recent years may inadvertently be shaking the very foundations of democracy. Because rule by bureaucracy is irrational and inefficient, slogans arise that advocate putting the "popular will" first and "acting" quickly. Efforts to realize these slogans lead directly to actions that have affinity with the "small government" of "neoliberalism," which calls for the slimming down of organizations.

One of the values at the foundation of democracy is an intrinsic respect for a diversity of opinions. In practice, this is something that needs to be paid for with the time and trouble of maintaining it (Morishima, 1977). Furthermore, a variety of opinions reflect a variety of viewpoints, but if each viewpoint were to be interpreted as a "vested interest," which can easily happen, things can soon get tied up in a crude debate that argues for just getting rid of it all. In such a scenario, the person striving to consider a variety of viewpoints is considered to be the villain caught up in vested interests and becomes an easy target for bashing, while the person criticizing the vested interest becomes the hero for making it easy to realize the popular will. Understanding this side of the argument is useful in understanding the bashing of public servants and bureaucrats in some local governments (although that is not to say that in some cases the bashing may not be justified, or that supposedly unavoidable wastefulness and inefficiency in operation does not still exist, despite past criticism).

However, as the organizations and systems maintaining modern society are inherently complicated, simplistic explanations should not be applied to their operation. Any attempts to make them easier to understand and explain in simpler terms would require some parts of the explanation to be arbitrarily removed, and such outcomes would be unreasonable. Because bureaucratic organization exists, so too do the rules created for the organization. In theory, all processing would be done in accordance with these rules, but political initiatives driven by anti-bureaucracy sentiment could result in parts of such processing being entrusted to the judgment of charismatic leaders. Such a leader would bear accountability for the policy decision. However, any arbitrary decisions deriving from the irrationality of a leader would lose the support of the people (as persisting in this way would be anti-democratic and it would simply represent an autocracy). The desire for politicians to avoid the criticism that they are autocratic easily invites the incentive to reduce the function of government and follow the policy of leaving it up to market mechanisms. By putting emphasis on market mechanisms, it is easy to follow a consistent logic and rigid policies (Noguchi, 2011: 94–117).

However, the idea that governments cannot do anything and that it should be left up to the market is an extreme view. If promoted to its end, this idea eventually negates the very existence of the government and the state. There is absolutely no possibility of such a view being accepted, and neoliberalists do not fully negate the existence of the state. What they do insist on is the transfer of public services to the private sector, the abolition of regulations, and the reduction in the role of the state. However, in order to protect private ownership, individual freedoms, and the freedom of corporate activities, there needs to be a strong authority that is capable of exercising state power if required. Accepting this point, the neoliberalists do not deny the role of the state and the government. When justifying their strong insistence on maintaining public order and upholding the self-defense force (or military), their logic is that they cannot establish anything without exercising state power (Harvey, 2005, trans. 2007: 34).

2. Reflection of Popular Will in Indirect Democracy

(1) Toward a Political Power Assertive on Burden Increase

Around the latter half of the 1970s, fiscal debt reached a crisis point in many Western countries. According to Habermas, this predicament had an effect on many government decisions concerning economic and social problems in the real society. However, due to the way that many countries and phenomena were complexly interconnected, there were no simple solutions. The people's expectations for social security and welfare were becoming higher, but governments could not deliver what was being requested without advanced economic growth. Due to the complex tangle of interests, if there is one person who benefits from the execution of a certain policy, it is not rare for there to be people who are hugely disadvantaged. Depending on the government, it can sometimes be very difficult to reach a consensus between the parties. Even if a half-finished policy were implemented, the effect would probably be diluted; and even if it performed well temporarily, the people among the complex tangle of interests disadvantaged by the policy would probably show stronger hostility toward the government. This becomes a situation in which the people perceive the government not to be answering their demands, and trust in the government is greatly diminished. More people begin to voice the complaint that "It's worthless paying taxes to such a government." Then, after diminished taxes, they complain, "This government pension system has gone bankrupt. I cannot trust this government." When more and more people believe the rhetoric, the government's actual ongoing survival becomes threatened (Noguchi, 2011: 70–74). If this increases the scale of the problems that the government must deal with, then the people witnessing these problems perceive a broader range of things to be the government's responsibility. The growth of this kind of public criticism can be observed even in the U.S., which aims for small government (Kettl, 2008, trans. 2011: 33–62).[3]

Once an administrative service is offered, rather than people becoming satisfied, it counterintuitively leads to a swelling of dissatisfaction. The explanation for this is not simply because once people receive a service, they become spoilt and no longer appreciate its worth. The actual reason for the dissatisfaction is because when a service is provided, this in itself creates a demand; and as that demand increases, the supply is perceived as being inadequate by the people wishing to receive the service. Say, for instance, that a policy providing assistance for school expenses to some people were implemented. When the recipients of this service appear in society, it is only natural for people not able to receive this service to want to be recipients as well. Thus, unless assistance for school expenses is provided to everybody, there will always be somebody dissatisfied about the service. But to fully remove this dissatisfaction, it would be necessary to commit considerable resources (Mabuchi, 2010).

If the people of Japan set a future course of public burden evasion, the only choice ultimately available would be to entrust the welfare and the education industries to market mechanisms. Japan's already high wages, however, would make it difficult for a service industry to offer low-priced services. Hence, it is doubtful that a service could be supplied to the market that is simple and affordable enough, even for middle-class people. That is a reason to be concerned about for the future. It is why the rational individual works hard at saving in preparation for the risks that lie ahead, and why economic activity wanes (Kenjo, 2004: 163).

If the government increased the public burden, however, it would accommodate increased demand for daycare (thereby increasing the workforce demand), promote women's entry into the workforce, and consumer buying power would rise. Thus, the needs of women wishing to juggle both career and family could be granted. In urban areas, in particular, dissatisfaction vis-à-vis daycare services, mainly for preschool age children, is known to be extreme. If a government made it a priority to invest capital in this area, it would surely contribute to reversing the declining birthrate (Kenjo, 2004: 184–193). If the current situation is allowed to continue, the population structure will become increasingly skewed, and the share of the public burden ultimately shouldered by the younger generation who have landed in this situation will weigh heavier and likely cause resentment toward such perceived unfairness.

One stream of opinion that cannot be ignored believes that the fiscal crisis facing the government justifies imposing income restrictions and some kind of exclusion measures. A clear line needs to be drawn here. Otherwise, ultimately after such policy effects fade, the end result will increase doubt among the people. Conversely, what is indispensable for the education, social security, and welfare policies that incur ordinary costs is support from the people of the middle class even under circumstances where stable tax revenue is secured. Thus, it is necessary to give adequate consideration to how to get the support of these people (Miyamoto, 2009: 100–102).

(2) Political Party Support and Voting Behavior

In order to realize policy, it is first necessary to gather supporters. This entails building a political party by gathering people with similar opinions on policy and having them sell these policy details to the public. Four political scientists from the University of Michigan in the U.S., Agnus Campbell, Philip E. Converse, Warren E. Miller, and Donald E. Stokes, shine a light on political support in their book *The American Voter*. In this book, they introduce the Michigan Model, which is now well known among political scientists. The key points of this model, as summarized by Ichiro Miyake, are the following: 1) most voters have a sense of attachment to a political party; 2) this sense of attachment is formed by socialization in the home; 3) even if leaders, policies, and general plans change, voters continue to hold a sense of attachment to the same party; 4) reasons for changing this sense of attachment are cases when the parents' sense of attachment to the political party was weak, those in which the reference group changed after becoming adult, or times in which there was large-scale social change; 5) the sense of attachment to a political party was accurately reflected by the psychological closeness and strength of sentiment to the party;[4] 6) if the sense of attachment to a political party was strong, the voter was more likely to vote for the political party; 7) the stronger the level of attachment, the more likely it was for the voter's orientation concerning the evaluation and recognition of political phenomena to be in agreement with the political party; 8) even if the voting behavior and the sense of attachment to a political party were not in agreement, this was temporary because of a specific battleground policy issue or the appeal of a candidate.

This sense of attachment to a political party has a more stable effect on voting behavior compared with attitudes on the candidates themselves or on individual policies. In Japan, the word political party attachment is not used very much. The term that is exclusively used is political party support. However, under a multi-party system in particular, political party support and support strength may not necessarily be in agreement. This is because support of a certain political party may not necessarily equate to the non-support of other political parties; and, according to a survey that used an actual sentiment thermometer,[5] close to 30% of respondents indicated a favorable evaluation of higher than 50 points for multiple political parties (Miyake, 1989: 100–114).[6]

Surveys of political party support that are measured by normal public opinion polls show no more than the distribution as it existed at the time of the survey. Even if the change in the rate of support is not that large, when focusing on individuals, there are a considerably large number of people who shift their party of support over a long time period.[7] Although the political support in Japan is more unstable than what is assumed by the aforementioned Michigan model, it is comparatively stable when compared with other political attitudes. Aside from the effect of political support based on parties representing industries, or the effect of political socialization later in life, the breadth of fundamental political support is associated with conservative or reformist ideologies. Moreover, according to an interpretation based on data at the time of the Cold War, the political party image more frequently comes from the ability to rule than from ideology or social groups. This is considered to be the factor decisively separating the LDP from the other opposition parties (Miyake, 1989: 126–127).

During elections, voters will end up voting for a political party or a candidate. The underlying significance of this in a parliamentary democracy is that the political parties that ultimately win seats have the decisive power to sway politics. However, it is often said that the stereotypical image of the ideology of the political party does not necessarily match the policies that political parties actually put forward. In Japan, the layer of safe political party support is not necessarily composed of a majority of the people. There are many people, in fact, who change whom they vote for depending on the election. Probably the best way to accurately understand political party support and voting behavior is to study in detail this relationship between voting behavior and voter mindset. This is why it will not suffice to use a questionnaire survey that is collected at a single point in time. Instead, it is necessary to verify the changes and trends in mindset and voting behavior among individuals using panel data that follow the same individual.

3. Relationship between Political Party Support and Attitudes on Policies

(1) Changes in Voting Behavior among Individuals

The data used here stem from the "Japanese Life Course Panel Surveys"[8] conducted from 2007 by the Institute of Social Science, Tokyo University. The sources of these data are men and women from all over Japan aged 20–40. As of 2014, the project is ongoing, and a follow-up survey wave is to be conducted once a year.

Included in this panel survey are data on voting behavior for the last four national elections (the 21st House of Councilors election of July 2007, the 45th House of Representatives election of August 2009, the 22nd House of Councilors election of July 2010, and the 46th House of Representatives election of December 2012). In the analysis, the data of the second, fourth, fifth, and seventh waves are used, which includes these voting results.

Table 8-1 follows the change in voting behavior based on the voting behavior of 2,587 people over four elections. Among these results, the most numerous sample is that of 216 people (8.3%) who did not vote in any of the four elections. After that, there were 153 people (5.9%) who voted LDP in all four elections, 148 people (5.7%) who voted DPJ in the first three elections but for another political party in 2012, 121 people (4.7%) who voted DPJ in all four elections, 77 people (3.0%) who voted DPJ in the first three elections but for the LDP in 2012, 67 people (2.6%) who voted for the DPJ in the first three elections but did not vote in 2012, 50 people (1.9%) who voted for New Komeito in all four elections, and 42 people (1.6%) who voted for the JCP in all four elections. Note that of the 434 people (16.7%) who voted DPJ in the first three elections, 313 actually voted for a party other than the DPJ in 2012. That means more than 70% of the people who voted DPJ in the first three elections voted for another party in 2012.

Looking at Table 8-1, although there certainly appear to be many people who voted for the same parties in the preceding and subsequent elections, there are also a significant number of people who did not. For example, the people who voted for the LDP in the House of Councilors election of 2007 swung considerably to

Table 8-1 Change of Voted Political Party from Panel Study (Change by Individuals)
Comparison of votes of 21st House of Councilors election(2007) and 45th House of Representatives election (2009)

	LDP	DPJ	NK	JCP/SDP	Other	No vote	Forgot
LDP	285	201	11	3	15	53	22
DPJ	91	728	4	28	48	46	28
NK	9	23	96	2	3	9	4
JCP/SDP	7	27	0	78	5	5	9
Other	11	11	0	0	21	3	3
No vote	66	192	4	13	11	370	64
Forgot	43	134	15	15	13	61	86

Comparison of votes of 45th House of Representatives election(2009) and 22nd House of Councilors election (2010)

	LDP	DPJ	NK	JCP/SDP	Other	No vote	Forgot
LDP	363	38	10	3	48	26	29
DPJ	106	802	16	25	121	125	116
NK	4	3	100	0	4	5	7
JCP/SDP	7	19	1	77	11	7	15
Other	11	9	2	0	73	8	8
No vote	44	33	9	6	18	372	57
Forgot	19	20	1	3	18	41	111

Comparison of votes of 22nd House of Councilors election (2010) and 46th House of Representatives election (2012)

	LDP	DPJ	NK	JCP/SDP	Other	No vote	Forgot
LDP	407	25	10	8	102	98	25
DPJ	238	233	15	40	352	216	50
NK	14	5	97	2	10	20	3
JCP/SDP	14	7	0	91	15	19	6
Other	70	23	1	11	195	40	18
No vote	75	21	5	9	89	514	30
Forgot	60	26	16	21	79	123	102

Source: Japanese Life Course Panel Survey (JLPS) by the Institute of Social Sciences, The University of Tokyo
Notes: LDP=Liberal Democratic Party, DPJ=Democratic Party of Japan
NK=New Komeito, JCP=Japan Communist Party, SDP=Social Democratic Party

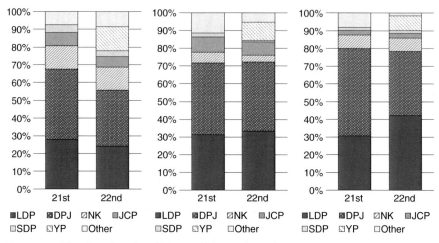

Figure 8-1 Trends in Results of House of Councilors Elections
Source: MIC
Notes: YP=Your Party

the DPJ; however, notably at the same time, there were a considerable number of cases of people not having voted in the previous election deciding to vote for the DPJ in 2009. From this, we can well understand that there were enormous expectations for regime change in 2009.

Looking at a comparison of 2010 with 2009, while there were not many people who swung from the LDP to the DPJ, a good number of people swung from the DPJ to the LDP. As a whole, however, there were many people who continued to vote for the the DPJ. In this election, the DPJ's vote ratio and seat ratio fell compared not only with the previous House of Representatives election but also with the House of Councilors election of 2007. Despite the air of defeat surrounding the DPJ, which was suffering ongoing party turmoil characterized by the Hatoyama administration's collapse over the relocation of the Futemma Base, in terms of the actual vote ratio, this was still higher for the DPJ than the LDP. Ultimately, however, due to the nature of the electoral system, the number of LDP seats increased (Figure 8-1). In the panel survey's sample, which is limited to a proportion of the younger generations, and not therefore representative of all of the voters, there were 554 proportional representation LDP voters and 924 proportional representation DPJ voters, showing that there were overwhelmingly more DPJ voters. It should be pointed out that among the people who voted DPJ in the previous House of Representatives election but swung on this election, compared with those who swung to voting LDP, there were quite a number of them that swung to vote for another party (e.g., Your Party) or chose not to vote at all.

We see a completely changed situation, however, when we look at the House of Representatives election of 2010 and the House of Councilors election of 2012. Among the people who voted for the DPJ in 2010, those who voted for DPJ in 2012 were not the majority; the overwhelming majority had swung to one of the other parties (e.g., the Japan Restoration Party, Your Party, or the LDP).

There were also many people who did not vote. The number of people who did not vote in both the previous 2010 election and this 2012 election, moreover, exceeded 500, which was close to 15% of this cross table sample. Although it is not possible to verify the voting behavior for the elections prior to this, by looking at this cross table alone, we can tell that there are a certain number of people who were not exercising their vote, either because they were disillusioned with politics or because they had lost interest. Moreover, as we can also see in Figure 7-3, the LDP recovered a large number of seats in this election (winning more than 60% of all seats), but their vote ratio did not reach 30% of proportional representation. The table shows that the LDP voters were certainly the largest number (878 people). However, this number does not differ much from the other 842 people who voted, and the LDP only gained 37% of the entire vote. Moreover, including the people who chose not to or forgot to vote, the LDP received just over 25% of voter confidence.

Two particular characteristics of the people who voted DPJ in both 2009 and 2012 are that 1) significantly more of them were born between 1966–1975 (rather than between 1976–1986); and 2) significantly less of them worked in sales, were farmers/self-employed, or were blue-collar workers (in contrast to office work). In other words, this means that the non-white-collar strata in the younger group had a propensity not to vote for the DPJ.

(2) Political Party Favorability Rating and Political Attitude
According to Yukio Maeda, who analyzed these panel data, the choice of the supported political party (not the political party voted for in the election) has stability to some extent: there are many people who change from supporting a particular party to not supporting any party at all, but there are not many people who switch allegiances from one party to another or repeatedly change the supported party. Among the women, there were many who were unwaveringly independent from any party, or who were politically apathetic, while among the people supporting a political party, there were many men. The more the number of LDP supporters, DPJ supporters, and unwaveringly independent people increased, the higher the level of education. However except for the small number of women's support for the DPJ, the overall relationships between social attributes and political party support are vague. In terms of individual mindset and political policies, for the gap mindset (i.e., that it is necessary for the prosperity of Japan that the income gap is big) and for the marriage mindset (i.e., generally speaking, a married person is happier than a person who is not married), there is a connection with LDP support and unwaveringly independent people; and for both cases, the more the person agreed with the statement, the stronger the tendency for that person to be an LDP supporter. In general, opinions on defense policy are clearly divided between LDP supporters and DPJ supporters, and there are no welfare-related grounds causing a division between the two. For defense and welfare, the views of LDP and DPJ supporters clearly differ from those of New Komeito and the JCP. Among the people without a clearly supported political party, there were those who were

repulsed by political parties and others with no feeling of opposition against political parties; and there was a strong general tendency among the former to vote LDP in 2005 and for the latter to vote DPJ in 2009 (Maeda, 2013).

Although people can only choose one "supported political party," as previously mentioned, an individual may give a high favorability rating to a political party even if it is not their first choice. Under such circumstances, it is conceivable that the individual could decide to change which political party to vote for. In this survey, there are questions that use the sentiment thermometer. Because the subjects were asked for their favorability ratings of the five parties (LDP, DPJ, New Komeito, JCP, and SDP) over the course of four surveys, we will here look at the changes in these. Moreover, it is pertinent to investigate whether this change was influenced by individual environmental (or attributable) factors and whether it relates to a change in mindset toward the policies.

However, the mindset on education policy, the policy directly relevant to this book, is not included in the survey. Instead, we will therefore use these data to analyze items of mindset related to various attitudes on politics and policy. We examine here whether there is some kind of relationship between changes in mindset and changes in political party favorability ratings. A question concerning mindset asked, "Do you agree or disagree with the following opinions? For each opinion, please mark a circle to indicate your degree of agreement/disagreement." The opinions stated on the survey were: A) Japan's military defense capabilities should be strengthened; B) The Treaty of Mutual Cooperation and Security between the United States and Japan should be strengthened; C) It is the responsibility of the government to narrow the income gap between people with a high income and people with a low income; D) Public works projects are important for securing local employment; E) Even when the budget must be tough, social welfare such as pensions and healthcare for the elderly should be enriched as much as possible; and F) Apart from the elderly and people with mental or physical disabilities, all people must live without counting on social welfare. Each opinion had five levels from agree to disagree.

For this analysis, however, "Agree" and "Somewhat agree" were collated and given the score of 1, while "Disagree" and "Somewhat disagree" were collated and given the score of –1. "Neither agree nor disagree" was given the score of 0. The answer "Don't know" was also an option, and this was also given the score of 0 for the sake of convenience.

First, let us look at the trend of the favorability ratings of the political parties. Table 8-2 lists the results. As already stated, using only the data from 2007, 2009, and 2012 ensures that the targeted data belong to surveys with data of national-election voting behavior. Even these can only be treated as a rough trend. The favorability rating for the LDP was at its lowest in 2010 directly after the change of government. Thereafter, it began to improve, reaching over 50 in 2013. The favorability rating of the DPJ, on the other hand, follows a downward course. There are not any significant changes in the favorability rating of the New Komeito, the JCP, and the SDP, with each lower than the LDP and the DPJ. New Komeito and the JCP show an increase in the standard deviation compared with the other parties.

This shows that the preferences (or scores) among the individuals are more dispersed for these parties.

Next, Table 8-3 shows the trend of scores for attitudes on policies and political opinions. The values range between 1 and -1, with positive scores indicating agreement. The movement that stands out over this period is a sharp increase in agreement for the strengthening of Japan's military defense and support for the Security Treaty, perhaps reflecting, in particular, the deteriorating relationship with

Table 8-2 Changes in Political Party Favorablity Rating (max score = 100)

		2008	2010	2011	2013
LDP	Ave.	42.65	40.48	44.67	52.05
	Std. Dev.	20.62	20.29	20.45	20.81
DPJ	Ave.	47.37	44.45	37.60	34.38
	Std.Dev.	18.73	20.87	21.40	20.72
NK	Ave.	33.28	30.95	31.88	32.62
	Std.Dev.	22.61	22.75	22.89	22.82
JCP	Ave.	33.50	33.78	32.97	32.32
	Std.Dev.	21.43	21.39	21.76	21.62
SPJ	Ave.	33.98	33.55	32.99	30.71
	Std.Dev.	20.24	20.48	20.60	20.92
N		3785	3070	4071	3675

Source: JLPS

Table 8-3 Changes in Score of Political Attitudes

		2008	2010	2011	2013
A) Strengthen defence	Ave.	.132	.096	.301	.389
	Std. Dev.	.738	.714	.682	.674
B) Maintain Security Treaty	Ave.	−.017	.034	.193	.290
	Std. Dev.	.661	.651	.628	.621
C) Narrow income gap	Ave.	.350	.293	.275	.276
	Std. Dev.	.677	.698	.675	.664
D) Secure employment through public works	Ave.	.370	.439	.454	.448
	Std. Dev.	.688	.686	.670	.667
E) Enhance welfare	Ave.	.663	.625	.561	.467
	Std. Dev.	.571	.590	.639	.674
F) Not entitled to welfare	Ave.	−.003	.066	.146	.279
	Std. Dev.	.774	.773	.753	.732
N		3895	3127	4226	3736

Source: JLPS

neighboring countries. In addition, the opinion that welfare should be enhanced remained dominant, but the score considerably decreased; in contrast, the opposite opinion toward welfare increased. It is not possible to evaluate the vote ratio of the House of Representatives election of 2012 as entirely representing a return to the LDP. A new conservative, third force in the political arena emerged in the shape of the Japan Restoration Party and Your Party, and both these parties advocate small government. We can expect the change in orientation to these political parties to be reflective of the trend of political opinions.

(3) Analysis of Panel Data

In Chapter 7, JGSS data were used to analyze the relationship between social attributes and political attitudes. As JGSS represent cross-sectional data (as data obtained from one survey), even if some relationship between mindset and social attributes were to be detected, the most rigorous assertion that can be made is that there is some kind of relationship in the distribution. For example, it is not possible to determine whether it is because people originally had that social status that they tend to hold these attitudes, or whether people tend to assume these attitudes by acquiring such social status. In other words, when there is a relationship between independent variables and dependent variables, it either means that dependent-variable change is brought about by independent-variable change, or it just means that the person with independent-variable characteristics also tends to have specific dependent-variable ones, and that independent-variable changes do not necessarily lead to dependent-variables change. Unless panel data are viewed, then it is not possible to distinguish which is the case. In order to perform this rigorous classification, it is essential to perform panel data analysis.[9]

Although there are several methods that can be used for panel data analysis, we will examine changes in the favorability ratings of political parties using the hybrid model that is advocated by Paul D. Allison (Allison, 2009).

The explanatory variables used here are sex (the dummy variable of woman = 1), birth cohort (the dummy variable assumes 1 if the birth year is within the range of 1966–75, with the standard category assigned to birth year within the range of 1976–86), educational background (three categories of junior/senior high school graduate, two-year/technical college graduate, university/graduate school graduate), occupation (as in Chapter 7, occupational classification is based on the Erikson-Goldthorpe-Portocarero typology), household income, marital status, and dummy variable showing the time of survey (2008 is made the standard variable, and 2010, 2011, and 2013 are included as dummy variables). Among these variables, sex, birth cohort, and educational background are those that do not change in the individual within the observation period. The other variables may change within the observation period. Concerning the other variables that may change, except the survey time dummies, models were cast for both the average score among the individuals and the score showing the difference from the average among the individuals and the score for each time period. This represents the hybrid model. For the calculation, random effect estimation was conducted for the analysis of the panel data.

The explanation of exact details of the analysis is provided in Allison (2009) and Nakazawa (2012). One thing that should be mentioned, however, is that the coefficients that are constant variables show a relationship between the individual characteristics that were originally possessed by the respondent and his or her favorability ratings towards political parties, which is the dependent variable (in other words, it changes between individuals). Allison does not proactively provide interpretation for a coefficient of the average among the individuals for the variables that may change. One thing that should be mentioned, however, is that the coefficient shows the difference between the individuals with average scores for political attitude as the dependent variable when the average among the individual has risen by 1. On the other hand, the coefficient of the variable that took the differences between the average among the individuals and the score of each time point among the individuals shows the amount of change of the political attitude as the dependent variable when there is a change of one explanatory variable for an individual. This coefficient matches the coefficient of the fixed effect model in the econometric model in the case that data have no loss (balanced panel data). In other words, when you want to see "the favorability rating of the political party of a person who has had a certain thought from the start" you should look at the coefficient of the average for the individual, and when you want to see "how favorability rating for a political party changes among a person who comes to hold certain thoughts" then you should look at the average coefficient for an individual.

Table 8-4 lists the analysis results. The occupation and household income were removed from the list as they had no significant effect on the favorability ratings of political parties, and they were unnecessarily complicated. The dummy variable coefficients at the time of the survey were also removed from the results because they only indicated the changes of the favorability ratings of the political parties from 2008, and the general trends can be evaluated from Table 8-2.

Looking at the differences among individuals, New Komeito and the SDP had low scores among people with high academic records. The reason for this was not clear, but at least on distribution, compared with junior/senior-high school graduates, New Komeito received low scores of 2.897 points among two-year/technical college graduates and 5.635 points among university/graduate school graduates. The SDP received a low score of 1.546 points for university/graduate school graduates. In contrast to this, women tended to give significantly higher points to New Komeito, the JCP, and the SDP.

First, let us take a look at the coefficient of the average for the individual. The LDP average for the individual is positively significant by defense capacity, security treaty, and public works project, while the income gap cancellation is significantly negative. In other words, originally the person with an affirmative opinion gives the Liberal Democratic Party a high score with respect to the three former issues and has an affirmative opinion of the latter one, giving the Liberal Democratic Party a low score. The coefficient of the average for the individual reflects the difference in ideology between political parties to some extent. People with an affirmative stance toward military defense and the Security Treaty tend to give high points to the LDP, and they also rate the DPJ highly (although not as much as

Table 8-4 Result of Panel Data Hybrid Model Analysis

	LDP		DPJ		NK		JCP		SDP	
	Coef.	S.E.	Coef.	S.E.	Coef.	S.E.	Coef.	S.E.	Coef.	S.E.
Female	.094	.579	.439	.578	3.665	.703 ***	3.887	.654 ***	5.474	.598 ***
Born 1966–1975	.607	.547	.814	.545	.001	.664	-.977	.616	-1.765	.564 **
2-year/tech college	.389	.655	.534	.653	-2.897	.795 ***	.234	.739	-.631	.676
University/graduate school	.974	.690	.995	.689	-5.624	.839 ***	-1.083	.779	-1.546	.713 *
Ave. in individual										
Married	.037	.643	-.439	.578 ***	2.104	.779 **	.038	.724	.799	.663
Strengthen Defence	1.710	.550 **	.814	.545 ***	-5.989	.663 ***	-4.271	.618 ***	-6.955	.566 ***
Maintain Security Treaty	8.114	.644 ***	.534	.653 +	5.606	.777 ***	-2.277	.724 **	-.271	.664
Government should reduce income gap	-5.160	.501 ***	.995	.689	-1.334	.606 *	2.583	.564 ***	1.272	.516 **
Local employment by public works	6.372	.510 ***	-1.113	.510 *	5.873	.616 ***	.407	.573	1.573	.525 **
Improve elderly healthcare regardless of fiscal state	-.844	.574	2.739	.573 ***	1.256	.693 +	1.522	.645 *	3.004	.591 ***
No entitlement to welfare	.509	.447	-.753	.447 +	-1.319	.539 *	-.630	.502	-.519	.461
Change in individual										
Married	-1.280	.798	1.511	.874 +	-1.039	.763	-.633	.794	-.990	.783
Strengthen Defence	1.612	.325 ***	-.189	.356	.237	.311	-1.026	.324 **	-1.011	.319 **
Maintain Security Treaty	1.989	.330 ***	-.745	.362 *	.548	.316 +	-.209	.329	-.605	.324 +
Government should reduce income gap	-.709	.306 *	.243	.335	.163	.292	.220	.304	.335	.300
Local employment by public works	1.290	.307 ***	-1.297	.337 ***	.082	.294	-.104	.306	-.498	.301 +
Improve elderly healthcare regardless of fiscal state	-.654	.326 *	1.165	.357 **	.233	.313	.375	.325	1.112	.320 **
No entitlement to welfare	.463	.250 +	-.292	.274	-.134	.240	-.545	.249 *	-.224	.245
N of observations	12617		12629		12587		12583		12560	
N of persons	4055		4057		4049		4048		4047	
R^2 (within)	.122		.135		.007		.006		.017	
R^2 (between)	.145		.056		.099		.065		.113	
R^2 (overall)	.150		.088		.081		.056		.096	

+$p < .10$ *$p < .05$ **$p < .01$ ***$p < .001$

Note: Other explanatory variables considered were employment and household income (both ave. in individual and change in individual).

the LDP). In the case of the Security Treaty, however, the DPJ is significant at the 10% level, and the coefficient is also small. This may reflect the party's stance on the U.S. base problem in Okinawa. Among the people supporting New Komeito, which is in coalition with the LDP, they are negative about strengthening military defense, although they are affirmative about the Security Treaty. The JCP and SDP supporters are also negative with regard to strengthening military defense, but in the SDP, the negative degree is weak and not significant concerning the Security Treaty.

The LDP/New Komeito stance and the JCP/SDP stance are in opposition to each other on the issue of the income gap, but the positive coefficient of the DPJ is not significant. On the issue of public works projects, opinion was significantly negative among the DPJ supporters but significantly positive among the LDP and New Komeito supporters. The support base for the SDP, which was in coalition with the DPJ when they formed the government, tended to be affirmative about securing employment through public works projects. On the issue of the enhancement of welfare, the divide in opinion takes the shape of the LDP on one side and the other parties on the other.

When looking at change within the individual, in other words, the coefficient becomes significant for the LDP, as it did for the average for the individual. This means that there is a relationship whereby the favorability rating for the LDP tends to be higher among people with affirmative opinions on defense, the Security Treaty, and public works, and lower among people with affirmative opinions on eliminating the income gap and enhancing welfare. Those among the DPJ supporters originally with affirmative opinions on the Security Treaty (at the 10% level), had the tendency to give a high favorability rating, although rising only by 0.534 points, but when there was a change in the individual toward having an affirmative opinion on the Security Treaty, we can see the favorability rating for the DPJ lowering by 0.745 points. Looking at New Komeito, the influence on the favorability rating from changes in opinion was practically nonexistent. The favorability rating can mostly be explained by the differences in ideology and orientation held from the start. The same can be said for the JCP, in that the proportion that is explained by difference in orientation from the start is large. Concerning the opinion that "people in society should subsist without counting on welfare," it is held from the start, although there was not a significant effect for the favorability rating itself. If we connect the favorability rating to an affirmative opinion, we can understand the favorability rating toward the political party to be low. As for the SDP, the average for the individual was positively significant for public works projects, but for the change in the individual, it was significantly negative (at the 10% level); and considering the people who held an affirmative view on securing employment through public works projects, we can see that their favorability rating toward the political party lowered.

The table does not show the effect of change on the favorability rating toward a political party for changes in occupation or income because there was very little. However, with respect to occupation, it is worth mentioning that those people among New Komeito, JCP, and SDP that were originally blue collar tended to provide a high score for the favorability rating. However, among the people supporting the LDP and DPJ, there were no significant relationships with occupation and income.

What we refer to as "political party support" refers to choosing a specific political party. But there are an overwhelmingly large number of people in Japan who select "no supported party." Therefore, the political party favorability rating based on the sentiment thermometer studied here has a different index concept, and the results that can be observed do not necessarily match the aforementioned survey of Maeda (2013). Generally, people who subscribe to a political party do so with strong conviction, and this type of people in particular would need some kind of strong impetus to make them switch their support to a different political party. Favorability rating, on the other hand is considered to be a concept with a much higher likelihood of fluctuation. However, if a favorability rating changes toward a political party, especially in Japan, where there are many people with no supported political party (i.e., a large swinging voter base), this can be expected to directly influence voting behavior in an election.[10]

(4) What Should Be Done to Reflect the Popular Will?

Excluding some political parties, there are cases where political parties have labor unions and industry associations that serve as vote gathering mechanisms. However, the organizational power of these associations is weakening, and it is becoming more difficult for a situation in which people with particular attributes support a certain political party to occur. This is because voting behavior can easily be swayed by images and media coverage before an election; and due to the single-seat constituency, the end result tends to be an exaggeration of voter sentiment. In prior research on this, there seem to have been many findings that Japanese attitudes toward welfare are not directly connected to political party support or voter behavior. When we look at panel surveys of the younger population base, it seems that welfare has been actively made a battleground issue, and we see a splitting of opinion.

There was a large drop in the DPJ support ratio in the election of 2012, but the battleground issues of the two major parties of the LDP and SPJ, under what is referred to as the 55-year system, were concentrated in the ideological arena of the constitution, the Security Treaty, and the Self-Defense Force. The oppositional structures of the two parties became institutionalized, and the function of elections for the selection of policy was not fully realized. Moreover, this ideological divide was not necessarily relevant to the lifestyle concerns of the people as a whole. That is why issues such as the economy, welfare, and education (even though these are considered important by the people and raised as topics of debate) did not surface as serious battleground issues in the election. However, after the collapse of the Cold War, the ideological divide that existed up until then lost its relevance. Issues such as taxes and social security were brought to the foreground. Yet, although the differences between Japan's political parties had been clear in the ideological arena with regard to issues such as the constitution, the Security Treaty, and the Self-Defense Force, there had never been any clear divide between the political parties in their debates centered specifically on the allocation of resources for education and social security. The political parties advocating socialist principles were opposed to increasing taxes, and positions like this probably made it hard to communicate party intention to the voters due to the entanglement of political party ideology and assertions at the time of the elections. The points of difference concerning education policy between the political parties centered on such issues as the content of education and the National Flag and National Anthem, while concerns of equalization of educational opportunities and tuition fees did not become battleground issues. If equalization of education opportunities and the lightening of the tuition fee burden were raised as election slogans, there would have been no guarantee that the policies would be supported (it would also have been difficult to wage an election campaign using a slogan that negated these policies). Therefore, from the standpoint of the LDP, which had a long hold on power, the party's true feeling was probably not to consider or mention public burdens in the public finance arena.

The election of 2009 was different from past elections in that issues related to education and public finance, such as child allowance and dispensing with fees for public senior high schools, became battleground issues. Moreover, as mentioned in Chapter 7, fiscal resources were planned so that the policies came in a set with the abolition of spousal tax reduction, as well as with the idea to realize gender equality in society and to raise children as an entire society. With respect to this point, it was very significant that the battleground issues relating to education, public finance, and social security were presented in this election. However, the political party's intention was not very well communicated. The mood among voters in this election was not to vote on social security and education as battleground issues but rather to implement regime change. It would be more accurate to say that the novelty for a DPJ government was preferred due to the lack of confidence in the LDP Government. With respect to education, the DPJ Government certainly fulfilled some of the election promises, but with respect to the payment of the child allowance, it encountered fiscal resource problems and was unable to achieve the policy aims.

When putting forward policy to enhance public services for Japan, which is plagued by fiscal issues, it is necessary to consider the deeper issue of public burden. In future, if any policies get put forward that do not thoroughly explain the fiscal resources, this will be taken as a further act of irresponsibility. However, the LDP and New Komeito returned in a coalition government, child allowance was abolished, and means testing was applied to dispensing with senior high school fees. This has established new divisions between the stances of the political parties. This need not be understood negatively as a failure of policy; instead these divisions should be actively appealed to as battleground issues that show differences of stance between the political parties. Up until now in Japan, it has been problematic that no political party has proposed policies that responsibly and properly address the relationship between the public burden and the public services provided. From its inception, the DPJ has been a motley crew. Inside the party, there are people with ideologies more conservative and nationalistic than the LDP, and it is certainly not the case that there are no members advocating the principle of small government. Although schisms occurred at the end of the term of government, this should be understood as a good chance to make political assertions and reorganize the party.

With the arrival of the aging society, if we are to suppose that the social security system in Japan will be one that follows a pay-as-you-go plan, then just as people talk about the intergenerational divide, we can expect generational interests to cause intergenerational conflict. There is debate on whether there actually is an intergenerational divide, but the formation of public sentiment is based on whether or not something exists, as well as whether or not there are many people who believe it exists. Hence, public sentiment will form regardless of whether or not the gap actually exists. The questions about the tax system, such as whether income tax will remain at the center, as it has until now, whether consumption tax will come to be considered as the basic tax, or whether taxes will be raised, are largely dependent on the social design that the voter envisages. Moreover, the question of what to do with the tax system in the future is not unrelated to the discussion of the intergenerational gap. With a tax system centered on income tax, the burden of the working generation will be the central revenue. However, with consumption tax, the tax system is more broadly spread out. Consumption tax is discussed as if it were only a regressive tax. However, the regressive characteristics are only highlighted when considering the public burden side. Tax should be evaluated based on what it is used for in total. If public services were to be provided universally, making consumption tax the basic tax is the only option. Getting the public to understand that point was the means by which consumption tax became the basic tax in northern Europe.

Elderly people have a higher share of the vote while the younger people have a lower share of the vote. However, all people will become elderly people if they survive long enough. As this means that it is easier for votes supporting welfare for the elderly to be collected, it is natural that the policies of political parties tend to be aware of issues concerning the elderly (Miyake, 1989: 94–95). The impact of a policy for education (as far as such policy is thought to be limited to child-rearing households) will be limited. It is therefore necessary, particularly for modern-day Japan, to appeal to society broadly about the publicness and public benefit of education when considering the problem of the public burden of education cost.

Among the people, there are many who understand that Japan has fiscal problems. Therefore, unless sold persuasively, even all-round policies for social security, welfare, and education will not receive widespread support. As mentioned in Chapter 7, it has been unfortunate for the Japanese people that although there has been a strong public opinion that it is necessary to enhance welfare and public services even if this means higher taxes, there has not been any political party able to realize these policies. The political parties should be presenting clear policies to the people related to public services as provided by a public burden; and based on these policies, they should be giving voters the actual option to either select a small government or enhanced public services, even at the cost of an increased public burden. Political parties should not be presenting irresponsible policies that reduce the individual burden for welfare and education, while claiming that there is no need to increase the public burden. History has already shown that these proposals do not broaden support.

Looking at the results presented in this chapter, there appear to be some clear differences among the political parties with regard to their political stances on government size and public services. However, it is also a contradiction that the LDP and New Komeito have formed a coalition as they represent stances and supporter bases quite far apart on the issue of welfare. The people should be offered easy-to-understand options based on policy stance and not on bringing stability to the political situation.

Supplementary Commentary

As the following digresses from the central theme of this book, I at first hesitated to include it, but as it further presents a valuable opportunity to do so, I wish to simply mention it here. One of the extremely perturbing observations of the results of this panel survey analysis was an increasing trend of support for strengthening the defense capacity and the Security Treaty system, which can be referred to as a clear tendency for nationalism and conservatism (Table 8-3). It seems obvious that the background to this is the deteriorating relationship with neighboring countries, including China and South Korea.

As of February 2014, the second Abe administration is gathering considerable support, and the support of the DPJ is very low. It now seems strange to refer to the LDP and DPJ as the two major parties. It has been stated in this book that the results of the House of Representatives election of 2012 did not necessarily suggest that there was active support for the LDP. However, it would be on shaky grounds to go so far as to assert that the second Abe administration is losing the support of the people. Currently, there is a high support rate for the cabinet and the situation is still very fluid. Although there may be big changes in the future, the situation is different from the first Abe administration in that it is quite noticeable that the level of critical appraisal in the media has reduced compared with before.

One of the points that can be observed from the panel data analysis of Table 8-4 is that although people who were nationalistic from the start tended to evaluate the LDP highly, people who thought that the military defense capability should be reinforced and those who supported the Security Treaty tended also to evaluate the LDP highly. It would appear that this is not unrelated to the high level of support that the LDP is currently receiving. Although the DPJ Government was characterized, in particular, by numerous policy failures, its reputation was also decisively damaged by its perceived "cowardly" posture surrounding issues of territory and historical recognition and an inability to come up with effective solutions.

It was the LDP Government that originally left the territorial problem unresolved. The responsibility of the LDP Government of that time should also, therefore, be brought into question, rather than pushing all of the responsibility onto the DPJ. In addition, there is a considerable problem with the strong sentiment of nationalism in China and South Korea and the news covering it; and one cannot deny that it is not only Japanese conservatism that is the problem. However, as there is profit to be had for the party and politicians in the form of gaining seats in parliament, if the LDP, which is recovering its political power, is acquiring support from nationalist hardliners, it is possible that the brakes will not be applied to this movement. Opinions on nationalist historical recognition differ considerably among the political parties, but there is no great difference in interest between the political parties on the issue of territory (although this is not entirely the case). Currently, the opposition parties are facing the dilemma that if they make a strong assertion externally to gather support, they will lose the people critical of strong nationalism, but if they do not make strong assertions, they will not be able to gain support. This kind of dilemma is, in fact, a serious problem for those who would take a stance on enhancing public services such as education, as discussed in this book. As mentioned throughout, public services cannot be thought to exist outside of the state, which means that it is impossible to ignore the control of the people by the authority of the state. It is necessary to capture personal income for taxes that make up fiscal resources, and this necessitates control of personal information by the power of the state. Therefore, trust in the government is essential for the welfare state. On the basis of the past actions of Japanese governments and the behavior of politicians, it may be hard to ask the people to hold such trust. In the first place, this kind of confidence is not generated by unilateral orders and compulsion. Using the power of force will just destroy the confidence at its core. Yet, as will be further discussed in the Epilogue, the people who are choosing such politicians are none other than the people of Japan. Of course the general will of the people may not match the intentions of the government, but since Japan professes to be a democratic society, the Japanese government should, to a certain degree, reflect the will of the people. Therefore, we must consider that the people of Japan need to shoulder more responsibility for the results of acts performed by the Japanese government than before the war. Although this may reflect some of my own personal fears, I cannot help but consider these concerns.

NOTE

[1] The presidential system is in total contrast to this.

[2] When referring to public servants in Japanese, rather than using kanji *kan* (官), the kanji *kou* (公) [public] is used for local governments. The police departments are an example of this. The top-level police personnel who receive their salaries from the National Treasury are formally called *keisatsukan* (警察官) [police officials], while the personnel of the local police department are formally called *chihoukeisatsushokuinn* (地方警察職員) [local police employees] (Omori, 2006: 14–15).

[3] Because the opinion favoring small government is strong in the United States, policies to increase public servants can easily meet with resistance from public opinion. However, as maintaining a certain level of staff is necessary to meet the citizens' needs, it becomes necessary to outsource some work to private companies. Therefore, the decision not to increase public servants does not decrease expenditure; rather, the management strategies for the government (system of orders and directives) become more complicated

(Kettl, 2008, trans. 2011: 47–48).

4   In the case of the U.S., because it is a two-party system, there is a sense that belonging to a political party is a one-dimensional measurement with the Republican Party and Democratic Party at two ends of the line, and no supported party in the center. The strength of the sense of belonging is shown on the same line.

5   A picture of a thermometer calibrated from 0 to 100 degrees (or points) is drawn on the questionnaire. The respondents mark the level of favorable sentiment that they have toward the party, with 100 points being the maximum.

6   The political party receiving the highest points on the sentiment thermometer was more likely to be the supported political party.

7   According to Ichiro Miyake, in the period from the election of the House of Councilors of June 1983 and that of the House of Representatives in December 1983, LDP support rose by 5%, "no supported party" rose by 4%, and support for the other parties changed by only about 1–2%. However, looking at the individual data, 80% of the most stable voter support was for the LDP. The New Liberal Club lost one-third of its supporters a half-year later, while only one-quarter of the "no supported party" respondents consistently indicated no supported party (Miyake, 1989: 116–17).

8   This study received Grants-in-Aid for Scientific Research (S) (18103003, 22223005). Donations were received from Grants-in-Aid for Scientific Research and OUTSOURCING Inc. to conduct The University of Tokyo Institute of Social Science's panel survey, and permission was granted from the Research Planning Committee of the Japanese Life Course Panel Surveys.

9   Although not mentioned in this book, because it would require a specialized discussion, the author has given separate consideration to the significance of panel data analysis. Please refer to this if interested (Nakazawa, 2012). A simple view of the hybrid model used in this chapter is also discussed here.

10   Another point to add regarding the correlation of favorability rating toward a political party based on this sentiment thermometer is that there is no correlation between the LDP and the DPJ/JCP/SDP through each wave. A high correlation coefficient of around 0.7 existed between the JCP and SDP for each wave. The LDP and New Komeito are joined in coalition, and although a correlation coefficient close to 0.4 existed in 2008, this is tending to drop. In the 2013 survey, it was 0.26. Moreover, although a correlation hardly existed between the DPJ and New Komeito at the start, in the 2013 survey, it exceeded 0.28, and correlation between them and the LDP was rising. The correlation between the DPJ and JCP and the correlation between the DPJ and LDP was trending from 0.3 to a high range of 0.4, and the relationship with the favorability rating toward the SDP in particular was strengthening.

EPILOGUE
The Responsibility to Publicly Support Education

1. Tolerating "Failure"

(1) Legacy of the DPJ Government

> A report from the pollster Geoffrey Garin in spring 1990 gives us an account that, if not a metaphor, nevertheless has representative significance: "When we bring up the cost of the savings and loans bailout [the need to repay hundreds of billions of dollars in federally insured accounts in failed savings and loan institutions], we often hear people say, 'Why do the taxpayers have to come up with the money? Why can't the government?'" This anecdote discloses a basic line of tension in our thinking, a deep misunderstanding of democracy—as though government could operate without taxpayers!
> (Bellah et al., 1991, trans. 2000: 114).

For Japanese, there is a familiar ring to the above commentary. Is the system of indirect democracy that we adopted really effectively functioning under any kind of premise? This book presents arguments centered on the public burden of education expenditure. Ultimately, however, it is underpinned by the very question of what democracy is.

A slogan was put forward when the DPJ executed the change of regime: "Politics Take Command." The background for this slogan can be understood as the discrepancy between the popular will and the intentions of Kasumigaseki (the central bureaucracy), wherein bureaucratic actions were diverging from popular will that was based on self-interest, leading to the goal of creating a system that directly reflects popular will. The intention was to break out of the system of control that had been constructed over a long period of time in Japan by the LDP governments and the central bureaucracy, as discussed in Chapter 8. Considering the ideas and constructs of indirect democratic rule, this in itself is not strange.

However, the DPJ had not adequately established a mechanism for decision-making. Consequently, the resulting system was one of decision making by individualistic personalities. Human rivalry led to opposition of the originally developed policies, representatives were reselected several times, and instead of working toward reconciliation, rivalry only intensified. Moreover, as the DPJ rapidly grew powerful, assuming power soon after it was founded, the majority of its members of parliament had only experienced one or two elections. Meanwhile, most of the members of parliament who had experienced three or more elections received some kind of role during the term of government, while those who had only experienced one or two elections did not receive any role. As a result, there was a very large disparity between the members who played central roles in the party and the those with very few election wins under their belt who were popular amongst the electorate (Nihon Saiken Inishiachibu, 2013: 212–226). As a proportion of the members of parliament were relying on bureaucratic criticism for its centripetal force, there was a revolt from the bureaucrats that made it impossible to effectively make use of their specialist knowledge. It must be said that in terms of organization and leadership, they had not really matured enough to be chanting the slogan "Politics Take Command." Meanwhile, from the voters' point of view, the reason why the change of regime occurred was because the voters wanted a change of government more than anything else. The actual mindset behind this desire was anger, resignation, and a pessimistic outlook. Careful examination of the issue of disputed territories with neighboring countries and that of nuclear power after the earthquake disaster show that these did not simply occur due to contemporaneous factors during the DPJ's reign. Hence, while the DPJ did make mistakes in their initial responses, we can understand that the actual issues themselves were either neglected or had continued on from the LDP government. It is unlikely that if the LDP had remained in power, they would by now have effectively dealt with these currently existing issues.

What is the lesson to be learned here? Perhaps people thought: "The DPJ Government has had a terrible string of failures—enough is enough, I have had my fill. If the government can deliver stable growth, it will be fine."

Economic issues are certainly directly linked to the people's daily lives. The DPJ government was unable to deliver big results. Moreover, by repeatedly breaking various promises, they were guilty of deeply betraying the trust of the people who believed in the "manifesto" and the "promises." However, in the House of Representatives election of 2012, although the LDP enjoyed a sweeping win, a large part of this victory was caused by the single-seat constituency electoral system. In terms of the actual votes, there was not much difference in number with that which had previously represented a big electoral loss (Chapter 7). On that point, the question of whether the LDP now truly receives support is an entirely different matter. Many of the people are hoping to get out of a long-continuing recession, and perhaps because they have given the highest priority to this matter, they tolerate the current government in general, despite its heavy-handed ways. The current situation in which there is no clear opponent to the government poses a very big problem for Japan. The DPJ was defeated, and their level of exposure in the mass media has significantly dropped. The parties that are attracting the media's attention now are, much rather, the "Japan Restoration Party (JRP)" and "Your Party (YP)," both of which have a strong conservative streak, similar to the LDP. Among the people, there merely seems to be a growing mindset that: "I have had enough of unstable government." There is also a sentiment that it would have been better if the regime change had never happened.

More than 30 years ago now, the U.K., which had once boasted great prosperity, was suffering a serious economic malaise that earned it the nickname of "the sick man of Europe." The prominent economist Michio Morishima, who was studying at university in the U.K. at the time, concluded that once the U.K. became a developed country with a decent standard of living, it maintained a democracy under which the people gave strictly fair examination and effected change of government even if it meant paying the cost of making a slight sacrifice of economic growth (Morishima, 1977: 50–55). The changing of government improves the mutual policies and the ability for these to be implemented. But there are sacrifices and costs that must be made for these changes to take place. Today's Japanese are being tested as to whether they have enough tolerance to handle this. It will be interesting to know how the change in regime by the DPJ will be viewed far into the future.

(2) Filling in the Gaps in Society

The societies that we live in each have their own peculiar history and culture. No-one lives in an ideal type of capitalist society or socialist (or communist) society. Many communist states failed because they ignored their unique histories and cultures and tried to construct a society that was too loyal to the ideal (and hence idealistic), or their viewpoint was too overbearing in perceiving society as something that could be fully controlled. The same also applies to capitalism. Movements that aim to bring the principles of profit and efficiency to all arenas of social life ignore its unique history and culture, causing a backlash from the people, whereby the situation can become unreasonable (Morishima, 1988: 136).

If neoliberalism, which advocates the principles of profit and efficiency, became more entrenched in society and competition were encouraged, then the functions of society would be reduced. An actual reduction of government functions would be fine if the people and the local organizations made up for the shortfall, but it would also create competition among organizations in the private sector, and links with the community and families would no longer be maintained in the same way as before. This would cause the advancement of individualism, leading to the growth of fragmentation in society. When a society fragments and loses its sense of unity in this way, it becomes necessary to have some kind of means of restraining it. Conservative thought can take on the role of filling this void, and that is why neoliberalism and conservatism fit easily together. For example, at first glance, we can see contradictions in talk that combines global competition, patriotism, and family. However, many of the conservatives among the neoliberalists will explicate such points. In practice, the thought of establishing policy measures aimed at strengthening the link between patriotism and family—or in other words, controlling phenomena related to the inner aspects of individuals—is dangerous, and the idea that this could happen is problematic (Miyamoto, 2009: 11–15). While Japan continues to lag behind other countries in social security, the traditional family is collapsing, and the private sector does not have the leeway to make up for it. In this situation, it is easy to produce an incentive to fill in for something for which the government is not expected to play a role, through the indoctrination of conservative moral ideologies. The arena of education may increasingly become a place where the transmission of such ideologies can be expected. However, could such activities of indoctrination be successfully implemented? If we look back to Japan just after the war, the social security and welfare system were weak and people came to rely on savings, knowing that it was not possible to rely on the government. It can even be said that the government actively promoted this. It became customary for people to put part of their income into savings as a provision for future education costs, housing costs, and life after retirement. However, after the collapse of the asset bubble, personal incomes did not rise, and households could no longer afford to save. Nevertheless, people feel uneasy about the government's social security system, and they know they will have to pay for the education costs for their children. If it is understood that public assistance will be meagre, people will work to protect their livelihood and even invest a little money in savings. If such a state were to continue, it would only be natural for trust in the government to fade. Therefore, it would be completely illogical to implement ideological principles such as teaching patriotism through such means as education.

Public-spiritedness and willingness to help out in society are not softhearted ideologies. Rather they encourage fundamental consideration of the problems of social mechanisms. It is not practical for us to survive on our own, and we live in a society that is a web of organizations, structures, and systems. Moreover, the overall society is formed by people fulfilling their roles as individuals. The public burden is one of the mechanisms of maintaining such a society. Therefore, tax is not something that is plundered in a one-sided way. On the contrary, if an adequate social security system is constructed for education and life after retirement, uneasiness toward the future decreases and it no longer becomes necessary to encourage people to be overly frugal with their savings. However, in order to construct such a system, everyone must shoulder some part of the burden.

In Japan, as a grounds against increasing the consumption tax, it is argued that if the tax is increased when the economy is in recession, people will be less inclined to consume, which would further negatively impact the economy. This was the underlying reason behind the Reagan Administration's tax reduction policy in the U.S., based on a theory of the Laffer curve, advocated by Arthur Laffer. In simple terms, if the tax rate were 100%, all income would be taken as tax by the government and this would take away people's incentive to work. If the tax rate were 0%, then the government's revenue would be zero. Therefore, the tax rate that yields the maximum tax revenues for the government should theoretically exist somewhere between 0 and 100%. When a tax rate is higher than the tax rate that yields maximum tax revenues, the incentive to work drops because the tax rate is too high and the overall tax revenue falls. Therefore, lowering the tax rate increases people's incentive to work, increases people's incomes, and tax revenues accordingly increase. Based on this reasoning, if the tax rate were lowered to the level thought to maximize total tax revenues, it would result in reduced fiscal deficit, and savings and investments would increase. The economy would therefore be stimulated. However, there is an insufficient amount of actual scientific data to support the existence of the Laffer curve (Shindo, 1994). Nevertheless, we still hear the argument that reduction of wastefulness is needed before raising taxes. The reality of this argument is that tax payers have a lack of trust in the government. The European countries, most notably the northern European countries that are described as welfare states, have been early in implementing an indirect tax system. Meanwhile Japan has met with much resistance to the consumption tax, which was finally introduced in 1989. The tax system has various defects, and problems have also been pointed out with respect to income tax, for example, such as the "9 : 6 : 4" problem. When problems are pointed out with the capture rate, it creates a tremendous distrust toward the tax burden.

When debating tax systems, one must also include discussion on how public services are provided. When there is a fiscal crisis, there is strong pressure to provide services that are narrowed down to specific targets as a measure of somehow turning the meagre fiscal resources into services. However, there is no guarantee that this will be realized as an efficient fiscal operation. According to Taro Miyamoto, the credibility of the government of a welfare state tends to be higher when there is provision of universal services to all citizens. When a service is based on targetism, it naturally means that selective criteria (such as income-based restrictions) must be imposed. This also requires the cost of monitoring to ensure that the services are running in accordance with the criteria; and when making such judgement, there is room for administrative discretion, which awakens all kinds of suspicions about the running of the system in the perception of the community (Miyamoto, 2009: 18–22).

People's attitudes and customs can form over many years, and it is difficult and even sometimes impossible to suddenly try to change them. One wonders if sufficiently investing in time and effort from now on and building a new structure that supports the entire society will perhaps result in a shortcut to a better system.

(3) Reconsidering the Structures of Democracy
When discussing the problem of tax, for some reason the mass media talks solely about the "burden." For example, we see only simple conversations that assert that an increased consumption tax rate equals a reduced income. Yet, we should be thinking of the raising of the tax rate not just in terms of increased burden but also as part of a total picture that includes what the money is spent on and the benefits that can be received from this. Of course, in today's Japan, where the fiscal debt has become enormous, even if the tax rate were increased, it is possible that these funds would be put toward rehabilitating the public finances, and the taxpayers

would be unable to experience any observable merits. Moreover, the reality of the size of government debt has brought about various evaluations among economists as to whether this is an urgent problem that could produce some kind of economic crisis. At any rate, the current situation cannot be left unattended. In fact, if the government really did neglect this problem, Japan would end up being forced to spend all tax revenues on fiscal rehabilitation.

If politicians speak about enhancing public services, then they must speak about them as part of the total picture that includes the necessary burden. It is up to the voters to make decisions on such informed basis. The voters should consider that it is not possible for any public service to be enhanced without increasing the tax burden.

The state and the government maintain enormous power, and this needs to be constantly checked. This power is not there to unilaterally control people in a way that completely diverges from the popular will. People seem to hold one of two images of the state and government: one is of a government holding power that monitors and oppresses people, namely, as the other party that should be resisted; and the second is of a government with transcendence-like power that people should unilaterally follow. With the issue of the tax burden as well, an image tends to be painted in which there is a government that has diverged from the people and is haphazardly practicing wastefulness. The mass media also enjoys playing up this issue. But in reality, compared to their counterparts in other countries around the world, public servants working for government agencies in Japan cannot be considered to be abnormally insincere, propagators of injustice, or even just lazy. All members of an organization cannot be expected to be perfect human beings. By watching the news, however, one gets the impression that public servants should be perfect and flawless. If we demand that public servants be perfect and flawless, then they will surely fail to meet our expectations. However, what is it that has led to this loss of trust in public services?

Intolerance has many detrimental consequences. Certainly wastefulness and unlawfulness should be avoided. In particular, public servants belong to government institutions and wield social power, and so it is perhaps necessary to make sure that there are checking functions, such as the mass media, that are constantly at work. The public employee might be included as part of a cause that is looked down on. Of course, the salaries of public employees are paid from taxes, and it is well understood that any wrongdoings by them should not be tolerated. If we consider their mistakes in terms of how frequently they occur, the incidence rate is probably not that high. That clearly identified mistakes are rare serves as evidence that the system is functioning. But often, some of these mistakes are suddenly made into a problem of the entire system, leading to the demand that a system needs to be built that strengthens supervision. Often people jump to such heavy-handed solutions before giving rational consideration of how to avoid these problems under the current system. There need to be more prudent decisions that consider whether the proposed solution would serve as a deterrent, whether it would mean a greater cost in terms of time, mind, and money, or whether it would cause the loss of the very human relationships that allow these structures to operate smoothly in organizations, thereby causing dysfunction.

Also, if we consider the basis and the grounds of a government's existence, we should not be allowed to weaken our support for it because it is not making a profit or because of wastefulness. It is easy to call something wasteful, but it is not as easy to actually determine if it is wasteful or not (Ihori, 2008). This is because the government pays a cost to ensure the continuation of matters that can never be measured in terms of efficiency and economic rationality alone. For example, there are fields that can be easily linked to productivity and economic profit, and there are fields where this is not possible. But how dry would a human society be if it only contained the former kind? In a sense, it is the existence of aspects which cannot be measured only economically, such as culture, arts, and sports that add the humanness to humankind. If we were to replace all of this with economic ideas, and call anything that does not yield numerical achievements wasteful, then we would be left with nothing but a cramped and intolerant society. Do we really want to aspire to such a society?

What is the purpose of a government, anyway? What kind of ideas are the structures of the democratic system and the indirect democratic system built on? What is the purpose of the tax burden? If society heads in such a direction, I think it is time for us to reassess the situation.

2. Education and Publicness: the Public Burden of Education

The analysis of this book reveals that there is a low recognition of publicness in education among the people of Japan. Thus, paying as much as possible for one's children becomes a natural part of parental affection, and educational achievements are considered to be of private benefit, having been obtained through individual effort. As higher education becomes more expensive, the private burden becomes heavier, and it is easy to regard the results and benefits obtained from higher education as private also. This is one of the problems concerning the burden of education costs in Japan.

Moreover, another problem is that there are few contexts in Japanese society where the public benefit of education is felt. There are many people who share in not knowing what function school education serves, and these people probably do not feel very strongly that education must be maintained by investing public expenditure in it, which does reflect poorly on the people involved in education (including the author). Hence, this leads the author to the simple conclusion that there must be more effort put into advocating the public significance of education from a social perspective and gaining greater understanding from society at large.

Since the 1990s, while the declining birthrate has advanced, the percentage of students going on to higher education has risen. Now only 20% of senior high school graduates enter the workplace upon graduating. There are many people with a conventional image of university who think there are too many people going on to university. However, if we compare the number of students who actually graduate from a higher education institution internationally, it is about 50%, which is lower than the OECD average (about 60%). The three stage theory, which was advocated by educational sociologist Martin Trow as a developmental theory for higher education, is well known. When the rate of students going on to higher education is below 15%, this is called the elite stage. Then, 15–50% is called the mass stage, and when the rate exceeds 50%, it becomes the universal stage. The social function of higher education institutions is said to change depending on the stage of this development.

There are already more than 700 universities with 4-year degree programs in Japan. In practical terms, it is simply not possible for them all to be research-focused universities. Moreover, when half of the same-age generation advances to higher education institutions, the graduates cannot be described as a social elite. As a practical issue of concern, it is unavoidable that educational content will change to suit the needs and level of the students. Moreover, the universities of Japan must push forward to some extent with functional differentiation to suit the students who have enrolled. In other words, as in the case of senior high schools in the past, when the rate of advancement to high education rises, the role that a society expects a school to fulfill will also change. The senior high schools must also functionally be specialized based on the schools that students wish to advance to, including some degree of vocational education as a specialization. Among such students, there may be those who have advanced through school without learning the compulsory curriculum. Therefore, if the provided education aims to equip these students with solid knowledge and skills, then this type of senior high school can step into a new social position, and it may gain societal trust. The policy to make senior high school free reflects the current situation in society, where it is becoming socially necessary to increase the rate of students advancing to higher education and for students on a practical career path to graduate from senior high schools.

Universities do not necessarily need to fit the conventional image of an advanced research institution that rears elites. Of course, the need for these universities still remains. Actually, these universities are competitive at a global level, and in this context, society still expects results. Yet, there are still many people who begrudge public support for these universities. The higher education institutions that are able to compete at such a level, however, are extremely limited. Therefore, it is necessary to consider that there are other aspects of social contributions from universities. By understanding the social significance of the existence of universities, it may be possible to reassess the public burden.

At the same time, insufficient preschool education in Japan also needs to be given attention. It is common knowledge among sociologists that one's social class and the environment in which one is raised still have an impact on academic results and level of education. It is questionable, however, whether this is recognized among the general public. It is thought that the effects of the environment in which one is raised can be mitigated by taking steps at an early stage of childhood. For this to happen, it is necessary to propagate throughout society a sense of values and common understandings of the unfairness of a society in which one's class background can directly affect one's academic grades and whether one advances to higher education.

Finally, if the idea that society should make the cost of education a public burden becomes widely accepted, then it is possible that this will bring about change through voting behavior. As the first step toward this, it is important to explain the social significance of education and allow the demands and voices advocating this to be raised.

References

Aghion, Philippe, Yann Algan, Pierre Cahuc, and Andrei Shleifer. 2010. "Regulation and Distrust," *The Quarterly Journal of Economics*, 125(3): 1015–1049.
Aghion, Philippe, Yann Algan, Pierre Cahuc. 2011. "Civil Society and the State: The Interplay between Cooperation and Minimum Wage Regulation," *Journal of European Economic Association*, 9(1): 3–42.
Akutsu, Yōichi. 2008. "Fukushikokka ni Okeru Shakai-Shijō to Jun-Shijō (Social Market and Quasi-Market in Welfare States), *Kikan-Shakai-Hoshō Kenkyū (Quarterly of Social Security Research)*, 44(1): 82–93.
Algan, Yann. and Pierre Cahuc. 2010. "Inherited Trust and Growth," *American Economic Review*, 100(5): 2060–2092.
Algan, Yann, Pierre Cahuc, and Andrei Shleifer. 2013. "Teaching Practices and Social Capital," *American Economic Journal: Applied Economics*, 5(3): 189–210.
Allison, Paul D. 2009. *Fixed Effects Regression Models*, Thousand Oaks: Sage.
Allmendinger, Jutta. and Stephan Leibfried. 2003. "Education and the Welfare State: the Four Words of Competence Production," *Journal of European Social Policy*, 13(1): 63–81.
Amable, Bruno. 2003. *The Diversity of Modern Capitalism*, Oxford: Oxford University Press.(Japanese Translation by Toshio Yamada et al. 2005. *Itsutsu no Shihon-shugi: Gurōbarizumu Jidai ni Okeru Shakai Keizai Shisutemu no Tayōsei*, Tokyo: Fujiwara Shoten)
Amano, Ikuo. 2006. *Kyōiku to Sembatsu no Shakai-shi (Social History of Education and Screening)*, Tokyo: Chikuma-shobo.
Amano, Chieko. 2007. *Kodomo to Gakko no Seiki: 18-Seiki Furansu no Shakai-Bunka-shi (A Century of Children and Schools: The Socio-cultural History of France in the Eighteenth Century)*, Tokyo: Iwanami-shoten.
Amou, Masatsugu. 2013. "Nihon no Yosan Seido ni Okeru Shīring no Igi: Zaisei Akaji to Seikan Kankei (The Significance of the Ceiling in the Japanese Government System: The Financial Deficit and the Relationship between Politics and Bureaucrats)," in Eisaku Ide ed. *Kiki to Saiken no Hikaku Zaisei-shi (Comparative History of Finance under the Crisis and Reconstruction)*, Kyoto: Minerva Shobo, 160–181.
Annetts, Jason, Alex Law, Wallace McNeish, and Gerry Mooney. 2009. *Understanding Social Welfare Movements*, Bristol: Policy Press.
Aoki, Makahiko. 2008. *Hikaku Seido Bunseki Josetsu (An Introduction to Comparative Institutional Analysis)*, Tokyo: Kodansha.
Aoki, Osamu, ed. 2003. *Gendai Nihon no Mienai Hinkon: Seikatsu Hogo Jukyū Boshi Setai no Genjitsu (Invisible Poverty in Contemporary Japan: Realities of Single-Mother Households Receiving Public Assistance)*, Tokyo: Akashi-Shoten.

Aoki, Osamu, and Hiroshi Sugimura, eds. 2007. *Gendai no Hinkon to Fubyōdō: Nihon, Amerika no Genjitsu to Han-Hinkon Senryaku (Poverty and Inequality Today: Realities and Anti-Poverty Strategies in Japan and the United States)*, Tokyo: Akashi-Shoten.

Aoki, Osamu. 2010. *Gendai Nihon no Hinkon-kan: 'Mienai Hinkon' wo Kashika-suru (People's Views on Poverty in Contemporary Japan: Visualizing "Invisible Poverty")*, Tokyo: Akashi-Shoten.

Aso, Makoto, Akira Harada, and Takashi Miyajima. 1978. *Durukemu: Dōtoku Kyōiku-ron Nyūmon (Durkheim: An Introduction to Moral Education)*, Tokyo: Yuhikaku.

Beck, Ulrich. 1986. *Risikogesellschaft: Auf dem Weg in eine andere Moderne*, Frankfurt am Main: Suhrkamp Verlag.(English Translation by Mark Ritter, 1992, *Risk Society: Towards a New Modernity*, London: Sage, Japanese Translation by Ren Azuma, and Midori Ito. 1998. *Kiken Shakai: Atarashii Kindai e no Michi*, Tokyo: Hosei University Press.)

—— 1997. *Was ist Globalisierung?: Irrtümer des Globalismus – Antworten auf Globalisierung*, Frankfurt am Main: Suhrkamp Verlag.(English Translation by Patrick Camiller. 2000. *What is Globalization?* Cambridge: Polity press, Japanese Translation by Toshiaki Kimae et al. 2005. *Gurōbaru-ka no Shakaigaku Gurōbarizumu no Gobyū, Gurōbaru-ka e no Ōtō*, Tokyo: Kokubunsha)

Bellah, Robert N. 1957. *Tokugawa Religion: The Values of Pre-Industrial Japan*, Free Press. (Japanese Translation by Akira Ikeda. 1996. *Tokugawa Jidai no Shūkyo*, Tokyo: Iwanami-shoten)

Bellah, Robert N., Richard Madsen, William M. Sullivan, Ann Swidler, and Steven M. Tipton. 1985. *Habits of the Heart: Individualism and Commitment in American Life*. University of California Press. (Japanese Translation by Susumu Shimazono and Keishi Nakamura, 1991, *Kokoro no Shūkan: Amerika Kojin-Shugi no Yukue*, Tokyo: Misuzu-shobo)

—— 1991. *The Good Society*. Alfred A. Knopf, Inc.(Japanese Translation by Keishi Nakamura. 2000. *Yoi Shakai: Dōtoku-teki Ekorojī no Seidoron*, Tokyo: Misuzu-shobo)

Blekesaune, Morten. and Jill Quadagno. 2003. "Public Attitudes toward Welfare State Policies: A Comparative Analysis of 24 Nations," *European Sociological Review*, 19(5): 415–427.

Breen, Richard, Ruud Luijkx, Walter Müller, and Reinhard Pollak. 2009. "Nonpersistent Inequality in Educational Attainment: Evidence from Eight European Countries," *American Journal of Sociology*, 114(5): 1475–1521.

Brinton, Mary C. 2008. *Lost in Transition: Youth, Education, and Work in Postindustrial Japan*, Tokyo: NTT Publishing.

Brooks, Clem. and Jeff Manza. 2006. "Social Policy Responsiveness in Developed Democracies," *American Sociological Review*, 71: 474–494.

Buchanan, James M. and Richard E. Wagner. 1977. *Democracy in Deficit: The Political Legacy of Lord Keynes*, New York: Academic Press.(Japanese Translation by Minoru Fukasawa and Takeshi Kikuchi. 1979. *Akaji Zaisei no Seiji Keizai-gaku*, Tokyo: Bunshin-do)

Burnham, June. and Robert Pyper. 2008. *Britain's Modernized Civil Service*. Macmillan.(Japanese Translation by Hiroaki Inatsugu et al. 2010. *Igirisu no Gyōsei Kaikaku: Gendai-ka suru Kōmu*, Kyoto: Minerva Shobo)

Castles, Francis G. 1989. "Explaining Public Education Expenditure in OECD Nations," *European Journal of Political Research*, 17: 431–448.

Chew, Kenneth S. Y. 1990. "Is There a Parent Gap in Pocketbook Politics?" *Journal of Marriage and Family*, 52(3): 723–734.

—— 1992. "The Demographic Erosion of Political Support for Public Education: A Suburban Case Study," *Sociology of Education*, 65: 280–292.

Coleman, James S. 1968. "The Concept of Equality of Educational Opportunity," *Harvard Educational Review*, 38(1): 7–22.

Dewey, John. 1916. *Democracy and Education: An Introduction to the Philosophy of Education*, New York: Macmillan. (Japanese Translation by Yasuo Matsuno, 1975, *Minshu-shugi to Kyoiku*, 2 vols, Tokyo: Iwanami-shoten)

DiMaggio, Paul J. and Walter W. Powell. 1983. "The Iron Cage Revisited: Institutional Isomorphism and Collective Rationality in Organizational Fields," *American Sociological Review*, 48(2): 147–160.

Durkheim, Émile. 1893. *De la Division du Travail*. (English Translation by W.D. Halls with an introduction by Lewis A. Coser, 1997, *The Division of Labor in Society*, New York: Free Press, Japanese Translation by Gentaro Ii, 1989, *Shakai Bungyō-ron*, Tokyo: Kodansha)

—— 1922. *Éducation et Sociologie*.(English Translation by Sherwood D, Fox, 1956. *Education and Sociology*, New York: Free Press, Japanese Translation by Kōken Sasaki. 1976. *Kyoiku to Shakaigaku*, Tokyo: Seishin-shobo)

—— 1938. *L'Evolution Pégagogique en France,* 2 vols.(English Translation by Peter Collins, 1985, *The Evolution of Educational Thought: Lectures on the Formation and Development of Secondary Education in France*, London: Routledge & Kegan Paul, Japanese Translation by Tōichiro Koseki, 1966, *Furansu Kyōiku Shisō-shi*, 2 vols., Ōtsu: Kohrosha)

Edlund, Jonas. 2006. "Trust in the Capability of the Welfare State and General Welfare State Support: Sweden 1997–2002," *Acta Sociologica*, 49(4): 395–417.

Erikson, Robert, John H. Goldthorpe, and Lucienne Portocarero. 1979. "International Class Mobility in Three Western European Societies: England, France and Sweden," *British Journal of Sociology*, 30(4): 415–441.

Esping-Andersen, Gøsta. 1990. *The Three Worlds of Welfare Capitalism*, Oxford: Polity Press. (Japanese Translation by Norio Okazawa et al. 2001, *Fukushi Shihon-shugi no Mittsu no Sekai: Hikaku Fukushikokka no Riron to Dōtai*, Kyoto: Minerva Shobo)

—— 1997. "Hybrid or Unique?: The Japanese Welfare State between Europe and America," *Journal of European Social Policy*, 7(3): 179–189.

Fukuda, Kan'ichi. 1970. *Kindai no Seiji Shisō: Sono Genjitsu-teki, Riron-teki Shozentei (Modern Political Ideas: Practical and Theoretical Assumptions)*, Tokyo: Iwanami-shoten.

Fujimura, Masashi. 1995. *Maiyā Kyōiku Shakaigaku no Kenkyū (A Study of John Meyer's Sociology of Education)*, Tokyo: Kazama-Shobo.

Fujita, Hidenori. 2003. "Giji Shijō-teki-na Kyōiku Seido Kōsō no Tokuchō to Mondai-ten (Quasi-market Models of Education System: Their Features and Problems)," *Kyoiku-Shakaigaku Kenkyū (The Journal of Educational Sociology)*, 72: 73–94.

Furuta, Kazuhisa. 2006. "Shōgakukin Seisaku to Daigaku Kyōiku Kikai no Dōkō (Student Aid Policy and the Opportunity of Higher Education)," *Kyōikugaku Kenkyū (The Japanse Journal of Educational Research)*, 73(3): 1–11.

―――― 2007. "Kyōikuhi Shishutsu no Dōki Kōzō no Kaimei ni Mukete (The Structure of Motives for Educational Expenditures: Decision Tree Analysis of Attitudes towards Education)," *Kyōiku Shakaigaku Kenkyū (The Journal of Educational Sociology)*, 80: 207–225.

Galbraith, John Kenneth. 1998. *The Affluent Society: Fortieth Anniversary Edition*, Boston: Houghton Mifflin Company. (Japanese Translation by Tetsutaro Suzuki. 2006. *Yutakana Shakai*, Tokyo: Iwanami-shoten)

Giddens, Anthony. 1985. *The Nation-State and Violence*, Cambridge: Polity Press. (Japanese Translation by Kiyobumi Matsuo and Masatoshi Obata. 1999. *Kokumin Kokka to Bōryoku*, Tokyo: Jiritsu shobo)

―――― 1994. *Beyond Left and Right: The Future of Radical Politics*, Cambridge: Polity Press. (Japanese Translation by Kiyobumi Matsuo and Ryusuke Tatematsu, 2002, *Saha Uha wo Koete: Radikaru-na Seiji no Mirai-zō*, Tokyo: Jiritsu-shobo)

Glennerster, Howard. 2003. *Understanding the Finance of Welfare: What Welfare Costs and How to Pay for It*, Bristol: Policy Press.

Glennerster, Howard, and John Hills eds. 2003. *The State of Welfare: The Economics of Social Spending: Second Edition*, Oxford: Oxford University Press.

Habermas, Jürgen. 1973. *Legitimationsprobleme im Spätkapitalismus*, Suhrkamp Verlag.(English Translation by Thomas McCarthy. 1976. Legitimation Crisis, Heinemann Education, Japanese Translation by Sadao Hosoya, 1979, *Banki Shihon-shugi ni Okeru Seitō-ka no Sō-mondai*, Tokyo: Iwanami-shoten)

Hamanaka, Junko. 2013. *Kenshō, Gakureki no Kōyō (An Investigation of the Function of Educational Credentials)*, Tokyo: Keiso-shobo.

Hara, Junsuke and Kazuo Seiyama. 1999. *Shakai Kaisō: Yutakasa no Naka no Fubyōdō (Social Stratification: Inequality in An Affluent Society)*, Tokyo: University of Tokyo Press.

Harvey, David. 2005. *A Brief History of Neoliberalism*, Oxford: Oxford University Press. (Japanese Translation by Osamu Watanabe et al. 2007, *Shin-Jiyūshugi: Sono Rekishi-teki Tenkai to Genzai*, Tokyo: Sakuhin-sha)

Hashimoto, Nobuya. 2013. "Kingendai Sekai ni Okeru Kokka, Shakai, Kyōiku: Fukushikokka to Kyōiku to-iu Kanten kara (Nation, Society, and Education in the Modern and Contemporary World: The Welfare State and Pedagogical Perspectives)," in Teruyuki Hirota, Nobuyuki Hashimoto, and Makoto Iwashita, eds. *Fukushikokka to Kyōiku: Hikaku Kyōiku Shakai-shi no Aratana Tenkai ni Mukete (The Welfare State and Education: Towards the Development of a Comparative Social History of Education)*, Kyoto: Showa-do, 3–76.

Heidenheimer, Arnold J. 1981. "Education and Social Security Entitlements in Europe and America," Flora, Peter. and Arnold J. Heidenheimer eds. 1981.

The Development of Welfare States in Europe and America, New Brunswick, NJ: Transaction Publishers, 269–304.

Higuchi, Yoshio, and Zaimushō Zaimu Sōgō Seisaku Kenkyū-jo (Ministry of Finance, Policy Research Institute), eds. 2006. *Shōshi-ka to Nihon no Keizai Shakai (Declining Birth Rate and Economic Society in Japan)*, Tokyo: Nippon Hyoron-sha.

Hiraishi, Naoaki. 1997. *Nihon Seiji Shisō-shi: Kinsei wo Chūshin ni (Political Ideas in Japan: Focusing on Modern History)*, Tokyo: Foundation for the Promotion of The Open University of Japan.

Hirano, Hiroshi. 2007. *Hen'yō suru Nihon no Shakai to Tōhyō Kōdō (Changes in the Voting Behavior of Japanese Society)*, Tokyo: Bokutaku-sha.

Hirao, Ryoji. 2002. "Seikatsu Hogo Seido (Public Assistance System)," in Hiroyuki Hayashi and Yoshiyuki Yasui eds. *Shakai Fukushi no Kiso Riron (Basic Theory of Social Welfare)*, Kyoto: Minerva-shobō, 98–117.

Hirota, Teruyuki. 2004. *Shikō no Furontia: Kyōiku (The Frontier of Thought: Education)*, Tokyo: Iwanami-shoten.

―― 2009. *Hyūmanitīzu: Kyōiku-gaku (Humanities: Pedagogy)*, Tokyo: Iwanami-shoten.

―― 2013. "Fukushikokka to Kyōiku no Kankei wo Dō Kangaeru-ka (How do we Think about the Relationship between the Welfare State and Education)," in Teruyuki Hirota, Nobuyuki Hashimoto, and Makoto Iwashita, eds. *Fukushikokka to Kyōiku: Hikaku Kyōiku Shakai-shi no Aratana Tenkai ni Mukete (The Welfare State and Education: Towards the Development of a Comparative Social History of Education)*, Kyoto: Showa-do, 230–248.

Hokenmaier, Karl G. 1998. "Social Security vs. Educational Opportunity in Advanced Industrial Societies: Is There a Trade-Off?," *American Journal of Political Science*, 42(2): 709–711.

Hori, Katsuhiro. 2009. *Shakai-Hoshō: Shakai Fukushi no Genri, Hō, Seisaku (Social Security: Principles, Laws, and Policies in Social Welfare)*, Kyoto: Minerva-shobo.

Ibuka, Yuji. 2004. *Kindai Nihon Kyōiku-hi Seisaku-shi: Gimu Kyōiku Kokko Futan Seisaku no Tenkai (History of Expenditure on Education in Modern Japan: Development of the National Treasury's Share of Expenses for the Compulsory Education System)*, Tokyo: Keiso-shobo.

Ichikawa, Shogo. 2000. *Kōtō Kyōiku no Hembō to Zaisei (Changes and Finance in Japan's Higher Education)*, Machida: Tamagawa University Press.

Ide, Eisaku. 2011. "Fukushikokka Zaisei no Kihon Rinen to Kōsō (Basic Principle and Design of Finances in Welfare States)," in Jun'ichi Saito, Taro Miyamoto, and Yasushi Kondo, eds. *Shakaihoshō to Fukushikokka no Yukue (The Future of Social Security and Welfare States)*, Kyoto: Nakanishiya Publishing.

―― 2012. *Zaisei Akaji no Engen: Kan'yō-na Shakai no Jōken wo Kangaeru (The Origin of Government Debt: Thinking about the Conditions of Tolerant Societies)*, Tokyo: Yuhikaku.

―― 2013. *Nihon Zaisei: Tenkan no Shishin (Finance in Japan: Precepts of Conversion)*, Tokyo: Iwanami-shoten.

Ihori, Toshihiro. 2008. *Saishutsu no Muda no Kenkyū (A Study of Waste in*

Governmental Expenditure), Tokyo: Nikkei Publishing.

Iio, Jun. 2007. *Nihon no Tōchi Kōzō: Kanryō Naikaku-sei kara Giin Naikaku-sei e (The Governance System in Japan: From a Bureaucratic Cabinet System to a Parliamentary Cabinet System)*, Tokyo: Chuokoron-shinsha.

Imamura, Tsunao. 2006. *Kanchō Sekushonarizumu (Bureaucratic Struggles in the Central Government)*, Tokyo: University of Tokyo Press.

Inoki, Takenori. 2012. *Keizai-gaku ni Nani-ga Dekiru-ka: Bummei Shakai no Seido-teki Wakugumi (What Can Economics Do? Institutional Frameworks in Civilized Societies)*, Tokyo: Chuokoron -shinsha.

Ishi, Hiromitsu. 2009. *Shōhi-zei no Seiji Keizai-gaku: Zeisei to Seiji no Hazama de (Political Economics of Sales Tax: Between the Tax System and Politics)*, Tokyo: Nihon Keizai Shimbun Publishing.

Ishii, Takuji. 2012. "Kyōiku ni Okeru Kōhi, Shihi Gainen: Sono Nihon-teki Tokushitsu (Concepts of Public and Private Spending in Education)," in Yotoriyama, Yosuke, and Fukushikokka Kōsō Kenkyūkai (Research Society of the Welfare State Plan), eds. *Kō-kyōiku no Mushō-sei wo Jitsugen-suru: Kyōiku Zaisei Hō no Saikōchiku (Realizing Free Education: Reconstruction of the Educational Financial Act)*, Tokyo: Ōtsuki-shoten, 339–377.

Iversen, Torben. and John D. Stephens. 2008. "Partisan Politics, the Welfare State, and Three Worlds of Human Capital Formation," *Comparative Political Studies*, 41: 600–637.

Iwashita, Makoto. 2013. "Shin-Jiyū Shugi Jidai no Kyōiku Shakai-shi no Arikata wo Kangaeru (Thinking about the History of an Educational Society in the Age of Neoliberalism)," in Teruyuki Hirota, Nobuyuki Hashimoto, and Makoto Iwashita, eds. *Fukushikokka to Kyōiku: Hikaku Kyōiku Shakai-shi no Aratana Tenkai ni Mukete (The Welfare State and Education: Towards the Development of a Comparative Social History of Education)*, Kyoto: Showa-do, 301–320.

Iwata, Masami. 2007. *Gendai no Hinkon: Wākingu Pua, Hōmuresu, Seikatsu Hogo (Contemporary Poverty: Working Poor, Homeless, and Public Assistance)*, Tokyo: Chikuma-shobo.

Jæger, Mads Meier. 2009. "United But Divided: Welfare Regimes and the Level and Variance in Public Support for Redistribution," *European Sociological Review*, 25(6) 723–737.

Jinno, Naohiko. 2002. *Zaisei-gaku (Public Finance)*, Tokyo: Yuhikaku.

—— 2007. *Kyōiku Saisei no Jōken: Keizaigaku-teki Kōsatsu (Conditions of Reconstructing Education: Economic Consideration)*, Tokyo: Iwanami-shoten.

—— 2013. *Zeikin: Jōshiki no Uso (Tax: Misunderstood Common Sense)*, Tokyo: Bungei-shunju.

Kameyama, Toshiaki. 2007. "Shitizunshippu to Shakai-teki Haijo (Citizenship and Social Exclusion)," in Hiroyuki Fukuhara, ed. *Shakai-teki Haijo/Hosetsu to Shakai Seisaku (Social Exclusion/Inclusion and Social Policy)*, Kyoto: Horitsu Bunka-sha, 74–100.

Kaneko, Motoshisa. 1987. "Juekisha Futan-shugi to Ikuei-shugi: Kokuritsu Daigaku Jugyōryō no Shisō-shi ('Levy on Beneficiery' or 'Promotion of Merit': An Ideological History of Tuition Policies for National Universities)," *Daigaku*

Ronshu: Research in Higher Education Issue, 17: 67–88.
Kaneko, Terumoto. 1967. *Meiji Zenki Kyōiku Gyōsei-shi Kenkyu (The History of the Educational Administration in the Preceding Term of Meiji)*, Tokyo: Kazama-shobo.
Kariya, Takehiko. 1994. "Nōryoku-shugi to Sabetsu tono Sōgū: Nōryoku-shugi-teki Sabetsu Kyōiku-kan no Shakai-teki Kōsei to Sengo Kyōiku (Meritocracy Encountering Discrimination: The Social Condition of Meritocratic Education as Discrimination in Postwar Japan)," in Hisato Morita et al. eds. *Kyōiku-gaku Nempō 3: Kyōiku no Naka no Seiji (Annual Review of Pedagogy 3: Politics in Education)*, Tokyo: Seori-shobo, 233–265.
—— 1995. *Taishū Kyōiku Shakai no Yukue (Direction of Mass Education in Society)*, Tokyo: Chuokoron-shinsha.
—— 1998. "Kyōiku, Kikai to Kaisō: Byōdō-shugi no Aironī (Education, Opportunity and Social Stratification: The Irony of Egalitarianism)," in Yutaka Saeki et al. eds. *Gendai no Kyōiku Kiki to Kaikaku 9: Kyōiku no Seiji Keizai-gaku (Contemporary Education, Crisis, and Reform 9: Political Economics in Education)*, Tokyo: Iwanami-shoten, 83–107.
—— 2004. *Kyōiku no Seiki: Manabi Oshieru Shisō (A Century of Education: Thinking about Learning and Teaching)*, Tokyo: Kobun-do.
—— 2009. *Kyōiku to Byōdō: Taishū Kyōiku Shakai wa Ikani Seisei Shitaka (Education and Equality: How the Mass Education Society Appeared)*, Tokyo: Chuokoron-shinsha.
Kariya, Takehiko. and James E. Rosenbaum. 1995. "Institutional Linkages between Education and Work as Quasi-Internal Labor Market," *Research in Social Stratification and Mobility*, 14: 101–136.
Kato, Junko. 1997. *Zeisei Kaikaku to Kanryō-sei (Bureaucrats, Politicians, and Tax Reform)*, Tokyo: University of Tokyo Press.
Katz, Michael B. 1975. *Class, Bureaucracy, and Schools: The Illusion of Educational Change in America: Expanded edition*, Praeger (Japanese Translation by Hidenori Fujita et al. 1989. *Kaikyū, Kanryō-sei to Gakkō: Amerika Kyōiku Shakai-shi Nyūmon*, Tokyo: Yushin-do Kobun-sha).
Kenjo, Yoshikazu. 2001. *Saibunpai Seisaku no Seiji Keizai-gaku: Nihon no Shakai Hoshō to Iryō (The Political Economics of Redistribution Policy: Social Security and Medicine in Japan)*, Tokyo: Keio University Press.
—— 2004. *Nenkin Kaikaku to Sekkyoku-teki Shakai Hoshō Seisaku: Saibunpai Seisaku no Seiji Keizai-gaku II (Reform of the Pension System and Positive Social Security Policy: The Political Economics of Redistribution Policy II)*, Tokyo: Keio University Press.
Kerckhoff, Alan C. 2001. "Education and Social Stratification Process in Comparative Perspective," *Sociology of Education*, Extra Issue: 3–18.
Kettl, Donald F. 2008. *The Next Government of the United States: Why Our Institutions Fail Us and How to Fix Them*. New York: W. W. Norton & Company Inc. (Japanese Translation by Hiroaki Inatsugu et al. 2011. *Naze Seifu wa Ugokenai-noka: Amerika no Shippai to Jisedai Seifu no Kōsō*, Tokyo: Keiso-shobo)
Kikkawa, Toru. 2006. Gakureki to Kakusa, Fubyōdō: Seijuku Suru Nihon-gata

Gakureki Shakai (Education and Social Inequality: Contemporary Educational Credentialism in Japan), Tokyo: University of Tokyo Press.
——— 2009. *Gakureki Bundan Shakai (A Society Divided by Educational Attainment)*, Tokyo: Chikuma-shobo.
Kim, Pil Ho. 2004. "Political Preferences and Attitudes towards the Welfare State: Cross-National Comparison of Germany, Sweden, the U.S. and Japan," *Comparative Sociology*, 3(3–4): 321–351.
Kobari, Makoto. 2011. "Kōdo Seichō-ki ni Okeru Kazoku to Kazoku no Okonau Kyōiku: Taishū Shakai ni Okeru Kazoku no Kakusa to Kodomo no Kyōiku no Fubyōdō (A Sociological Study on Families and Home Education in the High Economic Growth Period of Japan: Inequality of the Family and Childhood in the Mass Society)", *Doshisha Joshi Daigaku Gakujutsu Kenkyu Nempo (Doshisha Women's College Annual Reports of Studies)*, 62: 71–81.
Kobayashi, Masayuki. 2009. Daigaku Shingaku no Kikai: Kintō-ka Seisaku no Kenshō (Opportunity for Higher Education in Japan: An Evaluation of Policies), Tokyo: University of Tokyo Press.
Koçer, Rüya Gökhan, and Herman G. van de Werfhorst. 2012. "Does Education Affect Opinions on Economic Inequality?: A Joint Mean and Dispersion Analysis," *Acta Sociologica*, 55(3): 251–272.
Kondo, Hiroyuki. 2001a. "Kaisō Shakai no Hen'yō to Kyōiku (Education in Changing Stratification System)," *Kyōiku-gaku Kenkyū (The Japanese Journal of Educational Studies)*, (68): 351–359.
——— 2001b. "Kōdo Seichō-ki Ikō no Daigaku Shingaku Kikai: Katei no Keizai Jōtai kara Mita Sūsei (Opportunity of Higher Education after the High Growth Periods : Trends by Quintile Income Group of Households)," *Osaka Daigaku Kyōiku-gaku Nempō (Annals of Educational Studies: Osaka University)*, 6: 1–12.
——— 2002. "Gakureki-shugi to Kaisō Ryūdōsei (Educational Credentialism and Fluidity in Social Stratification)," in Junsuke Hara, ed. *Ryūdō-ka to Shakai Kakusa (Fluidization and Social Disparity)*, Kyoto: Minerva-shobo, 59–87.
Kondo, Hiroyuki, and Kazuhisa Furuta. 2009. "Kyōiku Tassei no Shakai-Keizai-teki Kakusa: Sūsei to Mekanizumu no Bunseki (Socioeconomic Differences in Educational Attainment: Trends and Mechanisms), *Shakaigaku Hyōron (The Japanese Journal of Sociology)*, 59(4): 682–698.
——— 2011. "Kyōiku Tassei ni Okeru Kaisō-sa no Chōki-teki Sūsei (The Longitudinal Trend in the Effects of Educational Attainment on Social Stratification)," in Hiroshi Ishida et al., eds. *Gendai no Kaisō Shakai 2: Kaisō to Idō no Kōzō (Social Stratification in Contemporary Society 2: The Structure of Inequality and Mobility)*, Tokyo: University of Tokyo Press, 89–105.
Korpi, Walter. and Joakim Palme. 1998. "The Paradox of Redistribution and Strategies of Equality: Welfare State Institutions, Inequality, and Poverty in the Western Countries," *American Sociological Review*, 63: 661–687.
Kreft, Ita, and Jan de Leeuw. 1998. *Introducing Multilevel Modeling*, London: Sage. (Japanese Translation by Takayoshi Onodera et al., 2006. *Kiso-kara Manabu Maruchi Reberu Moderu*, Kyoto: Nakanishiya Publishing).
Kurosaki, Isao. 1999. *Kyoiku-Gyōsei-gaku (Educational Administration Research)*,

Tokyo: Iwanami-shoten.
Labaree, David F. 1997. "Public Goods, Private Goods: The American Struggle over Educational Goals," *American Educational Research Journal*, 34(1): 39–81.
Lewis, Gail ed. 1998. *Forming Nation, Framing Welfare*, London and New York: Routledge.
Mabuchi, Masaru. 1994. *Ōkurashō Tōsei no Seiji Keizai-gaku (The Political Economics of Control by the Ministry of Finance)*, Tokyo: Chuokoron-shinsha.
—— 2010, *Kanryō (Bureaucrats)*, Tokyo: University of Tokyo Press.
Maeda, Yukio. 2013. "Seitō Shiji no Hendō: 2007nen kara 2012nen made (Changes in Political Party Support from 2007 to 2012)," Distributed Paper in the Symposium on Panel Data Analysis in 2013 at the Institute of Social Sciences of the University of Tokyo.
Maekawa, Kihei. 2002. "Mombushō no Seisaku Keisei Katei (The Policy Formulation Process in the Ministry of Education)," in Hideaki Shiroyama and Sukehiro Hosono, eds. *Zoku Chūō Shōchō no Seisaku Keisei Katei: Sono Jizoku to Hen'yō (The Policy Formulation Process of the Central Government: Maintenance and Changes)*, Hachioji: Chuo University Press, 167–208.
Maruyama, Fumihiro. 1998. "Kōtō Kyōiku Hiyō no Kakei Futan (A Household's Burden of Higher Education Cost)," *Sugiyama Jogakuen Daigaku Kenkyū Ronshū: Shakai-kagaku-hen (Journal of Sugiyama Jogakuen University, Social Sciences)*, 29: 197–208.
—— 2009. *Daigaku no Zaisei to Keiei (University Finance and Management)*, Tokyo: Toshin-do.
Matsuda, Shigeki. 2013. *Shōshika-ron: Naze Mada Kekkon, Shussan Shiyasui Kuni ni Naranai-noka (Declining Fertility Society: Why does Japan's Society Prevent Marriage and Childbirth?)*, Tokyo: Keiso-shobo.
Matsui, Ichimaro. 2008. *Igirisu Kokumin Kyōiku ni Kakawaru Kokka Kan'yo no Kōzō (British Government Involvement in National Education)*, Sendai: Tohoku University Press.
Merton, Robert K. 1957. *Social Theory and Social Structure: Toward the Codification of Theory and Research: Revised Version*, New York: Free Press. (Japanese Translation by Togo Mori et al. 1961. *Shakai Riron to Shakai Kōzō*, Tokyo: Misuzu-shobo).
Meyer, John W. and Brian Rowan. 1977. "Institutionalized Organizations: Formal Structure as Myth and Ceremony," *American Journal of Sociology*, 83(2): 340–363.
Meyer, John W., Francisco O. Ramirez, and Yasemin Nuhoğlu Soysal. 1992. "World Expansion of Mass Education, 1870–1980," *Sociology of Education*, 65(2): 128–149.
Miki, Yoshikazu. 2012. *Nihon no Zeikin (Tax System in Japan)*, Tokyo: Iwanami-shoten.
Miyadera, Akio. 2006. *Kyōiku no Bumpai-ron: Kōsei-na Nōryoku Kaihatsu towa Nani-ka (Distribution of Education: Equity in the Development of Potentialities)*, Tokyo: Keiso-shobo.
Miyake, Ichiro. 1989. *Tōhyō Kōdō (Voting Behavior)*, Tokyo: University of Tokyo

Press.

Miyamoto, Taro. 2008. *Fukushi Seiji: Nihon no Seikatsu Hoshō to Demokurashī (The Politics of Welfare: Democracy, Employment and Welfare in Japan)*, Tokyo: Yuhikaku.

—— 2009. *Seikatsu Hoshō: Haijo Shinai Shakai e (Security in Daily Life: Toward a Society that does not Exclude the Weak)*, Tokyo: Iwanami-shoten.

—— 2013. *Shakai-teki Hōsetsu no Seiji-gaku: Jiritsu to Shōnin wo Meguru Seiji Taikō (Politics in Social Inclusion: Political Conflict between Independence and Approval)*, Kyoto: Minerva-shobo.

Morgan, Kimberly J. and Monica Prasad. 2009. "The Origins of Tax Systems: A French-American Comparison," *American Journal of Sociology*, 114(5): 1350–1394.

Mori, Shigeo. 1993. *Modan no Ansutansu: Kyōiku no Arukeorojī (Instances of Modernity: Archaeology in Education)*, Tanashi: Harvest-sha.

Morinobu, Shigeki. 2010. *Nihon no Zeisei (The Tax System of Japan: What Is the Issue?)*, Tokyo: Iwanami-shoten.

Morishima, Michio. 1977. *Igirisu to Nihon: Sono Kyōiku to Keizai (The United Kingdom and Japan: Education and Economy)*, Tokyo: Iwanami-shoten.

—— 1988. *Sacchā Jidai no Igirisu: Sono Seiji, Keizai, Kyōiku (The United Kingdom under the Thatcher Administration: Its Government, Economy, and Education)*, Tokyo: Iwanami-shoten.

Morotomi, Toru. 2013. *Watashitachi wa Naze Zeikin wo Osameru-noka: Sozei no Keizai Shisō-shi (Why do we Pay Tax? The History of Economic Ideas Regarding Taxation)*, Tokyo: Shincho-sha.

Musgrave, Richard A. 1959. *The Theory of Public Finance: A Study in Public Economy*, New York and London: McGraw-Hill Book Company. (Japanese Translation by Kazuo Kinoshita et al. 1960. *Zaisei Riron:* Vol. 1 to 3, Tokyo: Yuhikaku)

Nagao, Tomiji. 1978. *Seiyō Kyōiku-shi (The History of Education in Western Societies)*, Tokyo: University of Tokyo Press.

Nakabayashi, Mieko. 2004. "Zaisei Kaikaku niOkeru Kokumin Ishiki no Yakuwari (The Role of People's Attitudes in Fiscal Reform)," in Masahiko Aoki and Kotaro Tsuru, eds. *Nihon no Zaisei Kaikaku: Kuni no Katachi wo Dō Kaeru-ka (Fiscal Reform of Japan: Redesigning the Framework of the State)*, Tokyo: Toyo-Keizai-shimpo-sha, 569–602.

Nakakita, Koji. 2012. *Genzai Nihon no Seitō Demokurashī (Political Party Democracy in Contemporary Japan)*, Tokyo: Iwanami-shoten.

Nakamura, Kengo. 2007. "Shakai Riron kara Mita Haijo: Furansu ni-okeru Giron wo Chūshin ni (The Concept of Exclusion from the Viewpoint of Social Theory: Focusing on the Discussion in France)," in Hiroyuki Fukuhara, ed. *Shakai-teki Haijo/Hosetsu to Shakai Seisaku (Social Exclusion/Inclusion and Social Policy)*, Kyoto: Horitsu Bunka-sha, 40–73.

Nakazawa, Wataru. 2012. "Naze Paneru Dēta wo Bunseki-suru noga Hitsuyō-nanoka: Paneru Dēta Bunseki no Tokusei no Shōkai (Why We Need Analyze Panel Data? Introduction of the Characteristics of Panel Data Analysis), *Riron to*

Hōhō (Sociological Theory and Methods), 27(1): 23–40.
Naruse, Tatsuo. 2001. *Kokumin Futan no Hanashi (The Story of National Burden)*, Tokyo: Jichitai-kenkyu-sha.
Nihei, Norihiro. 2009. "Shitizunshippu/Kyōiku no Yokubō wo Kumikaeru: Kakusan-suru Kyōiku to Kūdō-ka suru Shakai-ken (Recombination of the Relationship between Citizenship and Education: Diffusion of the Role of Education and the Hollowing of Social Rights)," in Teruyuki Hirota, ed. *Jiyū eno Toi 5: Kyōiku, Semegiau Oshieru, Manabu, Sodateru (Questions about Freedom Volume 5, Education: Contest over Teaching, Learning, and Breeding)*, Tokyo: Iwanami-shoten.
Nihon Saiken Inishiachibu (Rebuild Japan Initiative Foundation). 2013. Minnshu-tō Seiken Shippai no Kenshō: Nihon Seiji wa Nani wo Ikasu-ka (The Verification of the Failure of the Democratic Party in Japan's Administration: What can be done to Account for These Experiences?), Tokyo: Chuokoron-shinsha.
Noguchi, Masahiro. 2011. *Kanryō-sei Hihan no Ronri to Shinri: Demokurashi no Tomo to Teki (The Logic and Psychology of the Critics of Bureaucracy: Interests for Democracy)*, Tokyo: Chuokoron-shinsha.
Nukaga, Misako. 2003. "Tabunka Kyōiku ni Okeru Kōsei-na Kyōiku Hōhō Saikō: Nichibei Kyōiku Jissen no Esunogurafi (Reconsidering Equity Pedagogy in Multicultural Education: Ethnography of Teaching in Japan and the United States)," *Kyoiku Shakaigaku Kenkyū (The Journal of Educational Sociology)*, 73: 65–83.
Nye, Joseph S., Philip D. Zelikow, and David C. King, eds. 1997. Why People Don't Trust Government, Cambridge, MA: Harvard University Press. (Japanese Translation by Emi Shimamoto, 2002, *Naze Seifu wa Shinrai Sarenai-noka*, Tokyo: Eichi Publishing)
OECD. 2012. *Education at a Glance 2012: OECD Indicators*, Paris: OECD Publishing.
—— 2013. *Government at a Glance 2013: OECD Indicators*, Paris: OECD Publishing.
Offe, Claus. 1987. *Anthology of the Works by Claus Offe*. (Japanese Translation by Masami Jufuku. 1988. *Kōki Shihon-sei Shakai Shisutemu: Shihon-sei Minshu-sei no Sho-seido*, Tokyo: Hosei University Press.)
Ogawa, Masahito. 2010. *Kyōiku Kaikaku no Yukue: Kuni kara Chihō e (The Direction of Educational Reform: From Central to Local Government)*, Tokyo: Chikuma-shobo.
Ogawa, Toshio, and Masanori Takahashi, eds. 2001. *Kyōiku Fukushi-ron Nyūmon (An Introduction to Education Welfare Theory)*, Tokyo: Koseikan.
Omoda, Sonoe. 2013. *Shakai Keiyaku-ron: Hobbuzu, Hyūmu, Rusō, Rōruzu (Theory of the Social Contract: Hobbes, Hume, Rousseau, Rawls)*, Tokyo: Chikuma-shobo.
Omori, Wataru. 2006. *Kan no Shisutemu (Continuity and Transformation in the Japanese Bureaucracy: the "Kan" System)*, Tokyo: University of Tokyo Press.
Oshima, Michiyoshi, and Ide Eisaku. 2006. *Chūō Ginkō no Zaisei Shakaigaku: Gendai Kokka no Zaisei Akaji to Chūō Ginkō (The Economic Sociology of the*

Central Bank: Financial Deficit and the Central Bank in Modern Nations), Tokyo: Chisen-shokan.

Ota, Naoko. 1990. "Igirisu ni-okeru Kyōsei Shūgaku Seido no Seiritsu to Sono Igi (The Establishment of the Compulsory Education System in the United Kingdom and its Significance)," in Masana Maki, ed. *Kōkyōiku Seido no Shiteki Keisei (History of the Establishment of the Public Educational System)*, Matsudo: Azusa Publishing, 124–149.

―― 1992. *Igirisu Kyōiku Gyōsei Seido Seiritsu-shi: Pātonāshippu Genri no Tanjō (The History of English Educational Administration: the Emergence of the Principle of "Partnership")*, Tokyo: University of Tokyo Press.

Ozawa, Hiroaki. 2012. "Gakushū-hi ni Okeru Shihi Futan no Genjō (The Current Situation of the Private Burden on Education)," in Yotoriyama, Yosuke, and Fukushikokka Kōsō Kenkyūkai (Research Society of the Welfare State Plan), eds. *Kō-kyōiku no Mushō-sei wo Jitsugen-suru: Kyōiku Zaisei Hō no Saikōchiku (Realizing Free Education: Reconstruction of the Educational Financial Act)*, Tokyo: Ōtsuki-shoten: 378–415.

Pampel, Fred C. and John B. Williamson. 1988. "Welfare Spending in Advanced Industrial Democracies, 1950–1980," *American Journal of Sociology*, 93(6): 1424–1456.

Pechar, Hans. and Lesley Andres. 2011. "Higher-Education Policies and Welfare Regimes: International Comparative Perspectives," *Higher Education Policy*, 24: 25–52.

Pedriana, Nicholas. 1999. "The Historical Foundations of Affirmative Action 1961–1971," *Research in Social Stratification and Mobility*, 17: 3–32.

Pempel, T.J. 1978. *Patterns of Japanese Policymaking: Experiences from Higher Education*, Boulder: Westview Press. (Japanese Translation by Koichi Hashimoto. 2004. *Nihon no Kōtō Kyōiku Seisaku: Kettei no Mekanizumu*, Machida: Tamagawa University Press.)

Peter, Tracey, Jason D. Edgerton, and Lance W. Roberts. 2010. "Welfare Regimes and Educational Inequality: A Cross-National Exploration," *International Studies in Sociology of Education*, 20(3): 241–264.

Pilichowski, Elsa. and Edouard Turkisch. 2008. "Employment in Government in the Perspective of the Production Costs of Goods and Services in the Public Domain," *OECD Working Papers on Public Governance*, No.8, Paris: OECD Publishing.

Preston, Samuel H. 1984. "Children and the Elderly: Divergent Paths for America's Dependents," *Demography*, 21(4): 435–457.

Ramirez, Francisco O. and John Boli. 1987. "The Political Construction of Mass Schooling: European Origins and Worldwide Institutionalization," *Sociology of Education*, 60(1): 2–17.

Raudenbush, Stephen W. and Anthony S. Bryk. 2002. *Hierarchical Linear Models: Applications and Data Analysis Methods: Second Edition*, Thousand Oakes: Sage.

Rosenberry, Sara A. 1982. "Social Insurance, Distributive Criteria, and the Welfare Backlash: A Comparative Analysis," *British Journal of Political Science*, 12(4): 421–447.

Saito, Jun. 2010. *Jimin-tō Chōki Seiken no Seiji Keizai-gaku: Rieki Yūdō Seiji no Jiko Mujun (The Political Economy of the LDP Regime)*, Tokyo: Keiso-shobo.
Sandel Michael J. 2009. *Justice: What's the Right Things to Do?*, New York: Farrar Straus & Giroux. (Japanese Translation by Shinobu Onizawa, 2010, *Korekara-no Seigi no Hanashi wo Shiyō: Ima wo Ikinobiru-tameno Tetsugaku*, Tokyo: Hayakawa Publishing)
Sato, Yoshimichi, and Fumiaki Ojima eds. 2011. Gendai no Kaisō Kōzō 1: Kakusa to Tayōsei (*Social Stratification in Contemporary Society 1: Disparity and Diversity*), Tokyo: University of Tokyo Press.
Shindo, Eiichi. 1994. *Amerika: Tasogare no Teikoku (The United States: The Twilight Empire)*, Tokyo: Iwanami-shoten
Shavit, Yossi. and Hans-Peter Blossfeld eds. 1993. *Persistent Inequality: Changing Educational Attainment in Thirteen Countries*, Boulder: Westview Press.
Shiga, Sakura. 2013. *Takkusu Heibun: Nigeteiku Zeikin (Tax Haven: Escaping Tax)*, Tokyo: Iwanami-shoten.
Shinkawa, Toshimitsu. 2004. "Nihon no Nenkin Kaikaku Seiji: Hinan Kaihi no Seikō to Genkai (Politics of Pension Reform in Japan: Successes and Limitations in Avoidance of Criticism)," in Toshimitsu Shinkawa and Giuliano Bonoli, eds. *Nenkin Kaikaku no Hikaku Seiji-gaku: Keiro Izon-sei to Hinan Kaihi (Comparative Political Science of Pension Reform: Path Dependency and Avoidance of Criticism)*, Kyoto: Minerva-shobo, 299–333.
―――― 2005. *Nihon-gata Fukushi Rejīu no Hatten to Hen'yo (Development and Changes in the Japanese Welfare Regime)*, Kyoto: Minerva-shobo.
Sonoda, Hidehiro. 1993. *Seiyō-ka no Kōzō: Kurofune, Bushi, Kokka (Structure of Westernization: Black Ships, Samurai, and Nation)*, Kyoto: Shibunkaku Publishing.
Stiglitz, Joseph E. 2000. *Economics of the Public Sector*, New York: W. W. Norton & Company. (Japanese Translation by Shirō Yabushita. 2003. *Kōkyō-Keizai-gaku*, Tokyo: Toyō-keizai-shimpo-sha.)
Stoddard, Christiana. 2009. "Why did Education Become Publicly Funded? Evidence from the Nineteenth-Century Growth of Public Primary Schooling in the United States," *The Journal of Economic History*, 69(1): 172–201.
Suetomi, Kaori. 2010. *Kyōiku-hi no Seiji Keizai-gaku (Structural Analysis of Educational Expenses in Japan)*, Tokyo: Keiso-shobo.
Svallfors, Stefan. 1997. "Worlds of Welfare and Attitudes to Redistribution: A Comparison of Eight Western Nations," *European Sociological Review*, 13(3): 283–304.
Takechi, Hideyuki. 2000. "Fukushi Seisaku to Seifu Soshiki (Welfare Policy and Government Organizations)," in Takashi Mieno and Kōichi Hiraoka, eds. *Fukushi Seisaku no Riron to Jissai: Fikushi Shakai-gaku Kenkyū Nyūmon (Theory and Practice of Welfare Policy: An Introduction to Welfare Sociology)*, Tokyo: Toshindo, 35–60.
Takegawa, Shogo. 1999. *Shakai Seisaku no Naka no Gendai: Fukushi Kokka to Fukushi Shakai (Welfare State and Welfare Society: Challenges for Social Policy)*, Tokyo: University of Tokyo Press.

―――― 2007. *Rentai to Shōnin: Gurōbaru-ka to Kojin-ka no Naka no Fukushi Kokka (Solidarity and Recognition: The Welfare State in Globalization and Individualization)*, Tokyo: University of Tokyo Press.

Takenaka, Harukata. 2006. *Shushō Shihai: Nihon Seiji no Henbō (Control by the Prime Minister: Change in Japanese Politics)*, Tokyo: Chuokoron-shinsha.

Tanaka, Hideaki. 2013. *Nihon no Zaisei: Saiken no Michisuji to Yosan Seido (Finance in Japan: The Route for Reconstruction and the Government Budget System)*, Tokyo: Chuokoron-shinsha.

Tanaka, Satoshi. 2005. *Jinkaku Keisei Gainen no Tanjō: Kindai Amerika no Kyōiku Gainen-shi (The Conception of Character Formation: Critical History of An Educational Idea in Modern America)*, Tokyo: Toshin-do.

Tani, Satomi. 2006. *Amerika no Daigaku: Gabanansu kara Kyōiku Genba made (Universities in the United States: From Governance to Practice)*, Kyoto: Minerva-shobo.

Taniguchi, Naoko. 2005. *Gendai Nihon no Tōhyō Kōdō (Voting Behavior in Contemporary Japan)*, Tokyo: Keio University Press.

Taylor, Charles. 2004. *Modern Social Imaginaries*, Durham: Duke University Press. (Japanese Translation by Naritoshi Ueno. 2011. *Kindai: Sōzō-sareta Shakai no Keifu*, Tokyo: Iwanami-shoten)

Taylor-Gooby, Peter, Hartley Dean, Moira Munro, and Gillan Parker. 1999. "Risk and the Welfare State," *British Journal of Sociology*, 50(2): 177–194.

Tayor-Gooby, Peter, Charlotte Hastie, and Catherine Bromley. 2003. "Querulous Citizens: Welfare Knowledge and the Limits to Welfare Reform," *Social Policy & Administration*, 37(1): 1–20.

Taylor-Gooby, Peter. 2004. "New Risks and Social Change," Peter Taylor-Gooby ed. *New Risks, New Welfare: The Transformation of the European Welfare State*, Oxford: Oxford University Press, 1–28.

Tepe, Markus. and Pieter Vanhuysse. 2010. "Elderly Bias, New Social Risks, and Social Spending: Change and Timing in Eight Programmes across Four Worlds of Welfare, 1980–2003," *Journal of European Social Policy*, 20(3): 217–234.

Thane, Pat. 1996. *Foundations of Welfare State: 2nd edition*, London and New York: Longman. (Japanese Translation by Kazuko Fukaya et al. 2000, *Igirisu Fukushi Kokka no Shakai-shi: Keizai, Shakai, Seiji, Bunka-teki Haikei*, Kyoto: Minerva Shobo)

Tocqueville, Alexis de. 1888. *De la Démocratie en Amérique.*(Japanese Translation by Gentaro Ii. 1987. *America no Minshu Seiji*, Vol.1 to 3, Tokyo: Kodansha)

Tokuhisa, Kyoko. 2008. *Nihon-gata Kyōiku Shisutemu no Tanjō (The Establishment of A Post-war Education System in Japan)*, Tokyo: Bokutaku-sha.

Tomie. Naoko. 2007. *Kyūhin no Naka no Nihon Kindai: Seizon no Gimu (The Poverty-Relief System in Modern Japan: Duties of Life)*, Kyoto: Minerva-shobo.

Tönnies, Ferdinand. 1887. *Gemeinschaft und Gesellschaft: Grundbegriffe der reinen Soziologie*. (Japanese Translation by Juichi Suginohara, 1957, *Gemainshafuto to Gezerushafuto: Junsui Shakaigaku no Kihon Rinen:* Vol.1 and 2, Tokyo: Iwanami-shoten)

Tsujimoto, Masashi. 1990. *Kindai Kyōiku Shisō-shi no Kenkyū: Nihon ni-okeru*

Kō-Kyōiku Shisō no Genryū (A History of the Idea of Modern Educational: Origins of the Conception of Public Education in Japan), Kyoto: Shibunkaku Publishing.
Turner, Ralph H. 1960. "Sponsored and Contest Mobility and the School System," *American Sociological Review*, 25(6): 855–867.
Ueda, Shoichi. 2003. *Shuseibun Bunseki (Principal Component Analysis)*, Tokyo: Asakura-shoten.
Uno, Shigeki. 2007. *Tokubiru: Byōdō to Fubyōdō no Riron-ka (Tocqueville: Thinking about Equality and Inequality)*, Tokyo: Kodansha.
Uzuhashi, Takafumi. 1997. *Gendai Fukushi Kokka no Kokusai Hikaku: Nihon Moderu no Ichizuke to Tenbō (International Comparison of Contemporary Welfare States: The Location and Foresight of the Japanese Model)*, Tokyo: Nihon Hyoron-sha.
Wada, Kōhei. 2006. "Jinkō-gaku kara Mita Waga-kuni no Shōshika (Declining Fertility Rate in Japan from the Viewpoint of Demography)," in Yoshio Higuchi and Zaimushō Zaimu Sōgō Seisaku Kenkyū-jo (Ministry of Finance, Policy Research Institute), eds. 2006. *Shōshi-ka to Nihon no Keizai Shakai (The Declining Birth Rate and Economic Society in Japan)*, Tokyo: Nihon Hyoron-sha, 25–47.
Watanabe, Yasushi. 2010. *Amerikan Demokurashī no Gyakusetsu (The Paradox of American Democracy)*, Tokyo: Iwanami-shoten.
Weber, Max. 1956. *Wirtschaft und Gesellschaft, Grundriss der verstehenden Soziologie, vierte, neu herausgegebene Auflage, besorgt von Johannes Winckelmann*, Kapitel IX. Soziologie der Herrschaft. (Japanese Translation by Terushiro Sera, 1960, *M. Weber Keizai to Shakai, Shihai no Shakaigaku Vol1*, Tokyo: Sobunsha)
Wilensky, Harold, L. 1975. *The Welfare State and Equality: Structural and Ideological Roots of Public Expenditures*, Berkeley: University of California Press. (Japanese Translation by Yoshihiro Shimodaira, 1984, *Fukushi Kokka to Byōdō: Kōkyō Shishutsu no Kōzō-teki, Ideorogī-teki Kigen*, Tokyo: Bokutaku-sha)
Yamagishi, Toshio. 1999. *Anshin Shakai kara Shinrai Shakai e: Nihon-gata Shisutemu no Yukue (From A Secure Society to A Trust Society: The Direction of the Japanese System)*, Tokyo: Chuokoron-shinsha.
Yamaguchi, Kazuo. 2009. *Wāku Raifu Baransu: Jisshō to Seisaku Teigen (Work Life Balance)*, Tokyo: Nihon Keizai Shimbun Publishing.
Yanagi, Haruo. 2005. *Gakkyū no Rekishi-gaku: Jimei-shi Sareta Kūkan wo Utagau (A History of the Classroom: Doubting Axiomatic Space)*, Tokyo: Kodansha.
Yano, Masakazu. 1996. *Kōtō Kyōiku no Keizai Bunseki to Seisaku (Analyses of Economics and Policies regarding Higher Education in Japan)*, Machida: Tamagawa University Press.
—— 2001. *Kyōiku Shakai no Sekkei (The Design for A Learning Society)*, Tokyo: University of Tokyo Press.
—— 2013. "Hiyō Futan no Misuterī: Fukakai na Ikutsu-ka no Kotogara (The Mystery of the Economic Burden of Education: Several Unresolved Issues)," in Teruyuki Hirota et al., eds. *Daigaku to Kosuto: Dare ga Do Sasaeru-noka (Universities and their Costs: Who Supports Universities and How)*, Tokyo: Iwanami-shoten, 169–193.

Yotoriyama, Yosuke. 2012. "Kyōiku Jōken Seibi Kijun Rippō Naki Kyōiku Zaisei Iten Hōsei: Seiritsu, Tenkai, Soshite Shukushō to Saihen (Transfer of the Educational Budget System without Legislation regarding the Maintenance of Standard Educational Conditions: Establishment, Development, Reduction, and Reorganization)" in Yotoriyama, Yosuke, and Fukushikokka Kōsō Kenkyūkai (Research Society of Welfare State Plan), eds. *Kō-kyōiku no Mushō-sei wo Jitsugen-suru: Kyōiku Zaisei Hō no Saikōchiku (Realizing Free Education: Reconstruction of the Educational Financial Act)*, Tokyo: Ōtsuki-shoten, 30–128.

Yotoriyama, Yosuke, and Fukushikokka Kōsō Kenkyūkai (Research Society of Welfare State Plan), eds. 2012. *Kō-kyōiku no Mushō-sei wo Jitsugen-suru: Kyōiku Zaisei Hō no Saikōchiku (Realizing Free Education: Reconstruction of the Educational Financial Act)*, Tokyo: Ōtsuki-shoten.

Yumoto, Kenji, and Yoshihiro Sato. 2010. *Suwēden Paradokkusu: Kō-Fukushi Kō-Kyōsōryoku Keizai no Shinjitsu (Sweden Paradox)*, Tokyo: Nihon Keizai Shimbun Publishing.

Yumoto, Masashi. 2008. *Nihon no Zaisei: Nani ga Mondai-ka (Finance in Japan: What is the Issue?)*, Tokyo: Iwanami-shoten.

Index

A
Act on Promotion and Subsidies to Private Schools 170
affirmative action 37, 45
Aghion, Philippe 102, 124
Akutsu, Yōichi 66
Algan and Cahuc 103
Algan, Yann 102
All-Campus Joint Struggle Committee 161
Allison, Paul D. 232
Allmendinger, Jutta 69
alternative school 50–51
Amable, Bruno 85–86, 93
Amano, Ikuo 32
Andres, Lesley 70
anti-tax and anti-welfare movements 105
Aoki, Osamu 72
Araki, Shozaburo 178
Ariès, Philippe 24
aristocracy 26–27
attitude toward government responsibilities 120, 122

B
Basic Act on Education 153, 195, 196, 198–199
Basic School Survey 43
Beck, Ulrich 71, 83
Bell, Andrew 57
Bellah, Robert N. 30–31, 67, 243
beneficiary pays 182
beneficiary-pays principle 162–163, 199
Beveridge, William 69
Bismarck, Otto von 65
Blair, Tony 84
Blekesaune, Morten 107
Breen 5
Brooks, Clem 124
Brownlee, W. Elliot 144
Bryk, Anthony S. 118
Buchanan, James M. 129–130
budget compilation 135–136
burden of education cost 191
bureaucracy 25, 53–54, 66, 215, 217–222, 243
bureaucratic cabinet system 217
bureaucratic organization 187
bureaucratization 14, 55
Burnham, June 215–216

C
Cahuc, Pierre 102
campaign pledges 193
Campbell, Agnus 225
ceiling 136
Central Council for Education 168, 181
charter school 50–51
Chew, Kenneth S. Y. 100, 124
child allowance 198–199, 209, 212, 214
Child Allowance Act 212
Child Learning Cost Survey 139–140
Child Welfare Law 77
Christian Sunday school 24
Civil Information and Education Section (CIE) 155
Coleman, James 31–32
complement 94
Confucianism 58–59
conservative regime 70–71, 79, 92, 104, 123
consumption tax 145, 186, 195
contest mobility 33
Converse, Philip E. 225

D
de-commodification 73, 81
Democracy in America 222
Dewey, John 26, 43
DiMaggio, Paul J. 62
Disabled Persons Welfare Law 77
division of labor 14, 25
Domori, Yoshio 159
Durkheim, Émile 24–26
dysfunction 220

E
Edgerton, Jason D. 123
Edlund, Jonas 105
EGP class scheme 214
Elizabeth Noelle-Neumann 203
entrance examination 36
Erikson, Robert 214
Esping-Andersen, Gøsta 70, 79, 92, 104, 107
establishment 30
externality 42, 48–49

F
finance deficit 136
first Abe administration 239
fiscal crisis 129, 131, 224, 247
fiscal deficit 131, 172, 214, 247
fiscal equilibrium 189
fiscal rehabilitation without increasing taxes 190
Fiscal System Council Interim Report 163
Ford system 25
Foucault, Michel 65
Free Tuition Fees at Public High Schools and High School Tuition Support Fund Program 140, 143
Friedman, Milton 50
from cradle to grave 65
Fujimura, Masashi 62
Fujita, Hidenori 50–51
Fukuda, Kan'ichi 53
Fulton Report 66
Furuta, Kazuhisa 4–5, 191

G
Galbraith, John Kenneth 51–52
General Headquarters (GHQ) 155–156
Giddens, Anthony 53–54, 187–188
Gini coefficient 75
Goldsheid, Rudolf 144
Goldthorpe, John H. 214
Goodman and Kruskal tau 206
Goodman and Kruskal's gamma coefficients 109–110
government responsibility 206–207, 212

H
Habermas, Jürgen 130–131, 223
Hashimoto administration 217
Hatoyama administration 6, 228
Head Start Program 143
Heidenheimer, Arnold J. 70
Hirano, Hiroshi 193–194
Hirota, Teruyuki 34
Hobson, John M. 144
Hokenmaier, Karl G. 70
Hori, Katsuhiro 16
Horio, Teruhisa 40

I
Ichikawa, Shogo 166
Ide, Eisaku 146, 186–187, 215
Iio, Jun 216–217

Ikeda, Hayato 77, 147
inclusion 84
individualism 30
Industrial Revolution 25
industrialization 97
inequality of opportunity 191
institutional isomorphism 61
International Social Survey Programme (ISSP) 8, 17, 107–108, 110
iron law of oligarchy 45
Ishida, Baigan 59
Ishii, Takuji 74
Ito, Hirobumi 63
Iversen, Torben 103
Iwakura, Tomomi 60

J
Jæger, Mads Meier 104
Japan Association of National Universities 181
Japan Association of Private Universities and Colleges 166, 174–175
Japan National Railways 79
Japan Scholarship Foundation 4, 158, 173, 180
Japan Student Services Organization 4
Japan Teachers' Union 137, 157
Japan Student Services Organization (JASSO) 4, 17
Japanese General Social Surveys (JGSS) 204, 214, 232
Japanese Life Course Panel Surveys 226
Japanese scholarship system 179
Japanese-style welfare system 75
Jecht, Horst 144
Jefferson, Thomas 30, 44
Jinno, Naohiko 144, 149
Johnson, Lyndon B. 143

K
Kakuta, Kokichi 155
Kan Cabinet 177
Kaneko, Terumoto 60
kanryou 218–219
Kariya, Takehiko 33, 36–37, 39, 123, 153–154, 157–158
Katz, Michael B. 55
Kay-Shuttleworth, James P. 57
Kenjo, Yoshikazu 16, 105–106, 131, 224
Kennoki, Toshihiro 179
Kerckhoff, Alan C. 123

Kikkawa, Toru 4
Kim, Pil Ho 104
kindergartens 143
Koçer, Rüya Gökhan 122–123
kodomo teate 214
Koizumi administration 138, 176, 195, 203, 218
Kondo, Hiroyuki 5, 34–36, 74
Kōno, Yōhei 163
Korpi, Walter 82
Kreft, Ita 118
Kurosaki, Isao 40
kyoiku mama (education mama) 180

L
Labaree, David F. 27, 32
Laffer curve 246–247
Lancaster, Joseph 57
late capitalism 131
Le Grand, Julian 66
Leibfried, Stephen 69
liberal regime 70–71, 79, 92, 104, 123
liberalism 29
Lijphart, Arend 215
Livelihood Protection Law 77
Local Public Finance Act 180
Local Public Finance Committee 156
Local Public Finance Equalization Distribution System 155
Lockheed Scandal 169
Lowe, Robert 57–58

M
Mabuchi, Masaru 189–190, 218, 221, 224
Maeda, Yukio 229–230, 236
Maekawa, Kihei 151
magnet school 51
manifesto 176–178, 193–194, 214
Mann, Horace 29
Manza, Jeff 124
Marshall, Thomas H. 69
Maruyama, Fumihiro 9
mass education society 153
Matsui, Ichimaro 56
Matsuno, Hirokazu 183
mechanical solidarity 25
Medicare 31
Merton, Robert K. 219
methodical socialization 26
Meyer, John W. 61–62, 85
Michels, Robert 45

Michigan Model 225
Mill, John Stuart 222
Miller, Warren E. 225
Minobe, Ryokichi 94
Mitsukuri, Rinsho 60
Miyake, Ichiro 193, 225–226, 238, 241
Miyamoto, Taro 73, 75, 77, 79, 82, 85, 94, 101, 186, 188, 225, 246–247
modern society 25–26
modern state 53–54
modernization 14, 21, 24, 97
monitorial system 56
Morgan, Kimberly J. 81
Mori, Arinori 67
Morinobu, Shigeki 1–2, 145
Morishima, Michio 222, 245
multiple-seat constituency electoral system 200
multiple-seat constituency system 203
Munakata, Seiya 40
Murayama, Matsuo 164
Musgrave, Richard A. 47, 144

N
Nadao, Hirokichi 159–160
Nagao, Tomiji 56
Nakamura, Hirohiko 186
Nakamura, Kengo 84, 94
Nakamura, Tekisai 59
Naruse, Tetsuo 17
national burden 10–13, 17, 23
National Survey on Education Costs 172
National Treasury 138, 155, 166, 168, 175–176, 195–196, 199
National Treasury Subsidization System 167
National Treasury's Contribution System for Compulsory Education 156
Neo-Confucianism 58–60, 67
neoliberalism 64, 97, 222, 245
new capitalism 30
New Right 187
newcomers 38
Noda administration 186
Noguchi, Masahiro 220–224
Northcote and Trevelyan Report 54
nothing-is-sacred structural reform 176
Nukaga, Misako 38

O
Offe, Claus 130–131
Ogawa, Masahito 137–138

Ogawa, Toshio 72
Ogyu, Sorai 67
Oka, Nobuemon 154
Oouchi, Hyoe 159, 179
Ordinance for Enforcement of the School Education Act 153
organic solidarity 25
Ota, Naoko 57–58, 67

P
Palme, Joakim 82
panel data 232–233
Pechar, Hans 70
Peter, Tracey 123
political party support 225
populism 30
"pork barreling" style of politics 147
Portocarero, Lucienne 214
Powell, Walter W. 62
Prasad, Monica 81
pre-primary education 143
Preston, Samuel H. 100
Principal Component Analysis (PCA) 86
Private School Promotion Survey Committee 167
privatization 41
Programme for International Student Assessment (PISA) 123
progressive income tax 81
progressive tax 151
progressive tax system 145
Progressivism 30
proportional representation system 200
public economics 47–48
public finance 133–135
public finance deficit 147
public spending on education 6–7, 13, 15–17, 23, 43, 73–74, 90, 93, 99–100, 111, 121, 124
Pyper, Robert 215–216

Q
Quadagno, Jill 107
quasi-market reform 50

R
Rai, Shunsui 59
Ramirez, Francisco O. 61
rationalization 221
Raudenbush, Stephen W. 118
Rawls, John 44

Reagan, Ronald W. 30, 78, 246
redistribution 29
redistribution policy 99, 104, 121, 131, 186
regressive consumption tax 81
regulatory state 98
replacement level fertility 1
responsibility of the individual and families 207
revenu minimum d'insertion (RMI) 84
Roberts, Lance W. 123
role of government 8, 108
Roosevelt, Franklin D. 30
Rosenberry, Sara A. 105

S
Saito, Jun 147–148, 152
Sakata, Michita 164
Schaffle, Albert E. F. 63
school choice 41
school choice system 50
second Abe administration 239
Second Provisional Commission for Administrative Reform 172
sectionalism 221
selectivism 81–82, 106
Sen, Amartya 37
Shiga, Sakura 151
Shigematsu, Keiichi 160, 180
Shinkawa, Toshimitsu 105, 185, 189
Silberman, Bernard S. 218, 221
single-seat constituency system 137, 194, 200, 218
Skocpol, Theda 144
small government 222
social democratic regime 70–71, 92, 104, 123
social exclusion 83–84
Social Expenditure Database (SOCX) 86
Social Stratification and Social Mobility Survey (SSM Survey) 5, 35, 44
sociology of public finance 144
Sonoda, Hidehiro 60
spiral of silence 203
sponsored mobility 33
spousal deduction system 199
spousal tax deduction 210–211, 213
SSJ Data Archive 214
standard law world 157
Stein, Lorenz von 63
Stephens, John D. 103
Stiglitz, Joseph E. 48
Stoddard, Christiana 93

Stokes, Donald E. 225
student loans 17
Suetomi, Kaori 73–74, 168–169, 182, 191
Survey on Local Educational Expenditures 139
Survey on Student Life 74
Suzuki, Zenko 172
Svallfors, Stefan 107, 125

T
Takagi, Yoshiaki 183
Takechi, Hideyuki 50
Takegawa, Shogo 29, 52, 70, 78, 97–98, 132, 189
Tamamatsu, Misao 60
Tanaka, Hideaki 132, 135, 146, 151
Tanaka, Kakuei 77, 190
Tanaka, Toshikatsu 178
targetism 81
tax burden 149, 187, 190
tax haven 1
tax reduction 147
tax revenue procurement capability 131
tax revolt 99
Taylor, Charles 52–53
Taylor-Gooby, Peter 2, 82–83, 99
Thane, Pat 93
Thatcher, Margaret 78, 97
Tocqueville, Alexis de 26–27, 44, 222
Tokuhisa, Kyoko 155–156, 178
Tomabechi, Hidetoshi 179
Tönnies, Ferdinand 43
Touraine, Alain 94
Trow, Martin 250
trust in the government 100–102, 187
Tsujimoto, Masashi 58–60
Tsuru, Kotaro 124
Turner, Ralph H. 33
types of capitalist systems 86

U
Uchida, Masao 60
universalism 81, 187

V
value-added tax 81
van de Werfhorst, Herman G. 122–123
vocational education 70
voucher system 50

W
Wagner, Adolf H. G. 63
Wagner, Richard E. 129–130
War on Poverty 143
Ward, Lester F. 33
Weber, Max 24–25, 54, 61, 144
welfare regime 107
welfare state 29, 188
welfare-state liberalism 30
Westminster model 215
Whitehall model 216
Wilensky, Harold L. 42, 71, 97, 124

Y
Yamaga, Sokou 58
Yamagishi, Toshio 103
Yanagi, Haruo 56–57, 66
Yano, Harumichi 60
Yano, Masakazu 8, 13, 42, 45, 169, 192

Z
Zenkyoto 161